A VERY DANGEROUS WOMAN

A VERY DANGEROUS WOMAN

THE LIVES, LOVES AND LIES OF RUSSIA'S MOST SEDUCTIVE SPY

DEBORAH McDONALD
AND
JEREMY DRONFIELD

ONEWORLD

A Oneworld Book

First published in North America, Great Britain and Australia
by Oneworld Publications 2015

ISBN 978-1-78074-7088
ISBN 978-1-78074-7095 (eBook)

Text design and typeset by Hewer text UK Ltd, Edinburgh
Printed and bound in Great Britain by TJ International Ltd, Padstow, Cornwall

Oneworld Publications
10 Bloomsbury Street
London WC1B 3SR
England

Stay up to date with the latest books,
special offers, and exclusive content from
Oneworld with our monthly newsletter

Sign up on our website
www.oneworld-publications.com

Visit www.mourabudberg.com for more information
about Moura and news about *A Very Dangerous Woman*.

Contents

Part 1:
Flouting All Conventions:
1916–1918

Part 2:
Love and Survival:
1918–1919

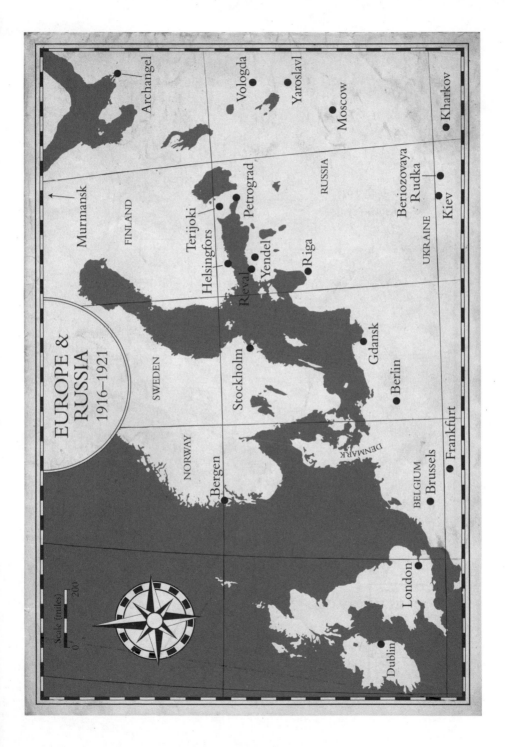

Descendants of Ignatiy Zakrevsky

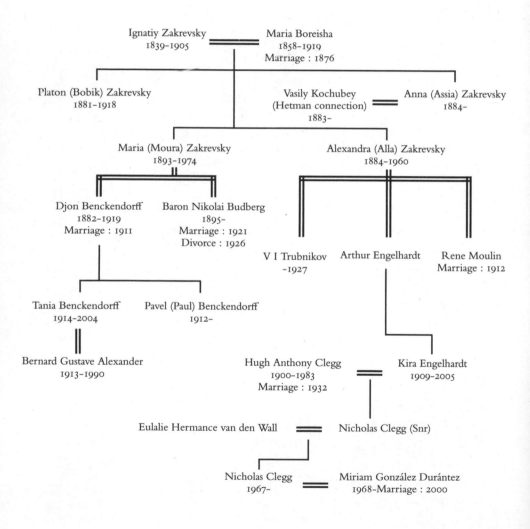

Illustration Credits

With kind thanks to Georgi Särekanno the keeper of the Jäneda Museum, to David King, to the Hoover Institution Library, to Peter Lofts, to Allan Warren, and also to the Manuscripts and Special Collections section of the University of Nottingham for granting permission to use their illustrations of Meriel in her nursing uniform and Moura in the snow. Thanks also to Dimitri Collingridge for the use of the photograph of Moura, to the Hoover Institution Archives, Stanford University for allowing us to reproduce the photograph of Yakov Peters and to Getty Images, the National Portrait Gallery, the Rare Book and Manuscript Library at the University of Illinois and the Library of Congress for all allowing us to reproduce images.

1 © Deborah McDonald.
2 Wikimedia Commons. Thanks to U A Lora.
3 © Tania Alexander.
4 © Buchanan Collection, Manuscripts and Special Collections, University of Nottingham. BU B 8/1/43/4.
5 Wikimedia Commons. Thanks to fireramsey.
6 © Georgi Särekanno, private collection.
7 RN Museum © Trustees of the Royal Navy Submarine Museum
8 R N Museum © Trustees of the Royal Navy Submarine Museum
9 © Buchanan Collection, Manuscripts and Special Collections, University of Nottingham.BU B 8/1/56/2.
10 © Georgi Särekanno, curator of the Jäneda Museum, and by kind permission of Enno Must.
11 Wikimedia Commons. RIA Novosti archive, image 6464/RIA Novosti/CC-BY-SA
12 Robert H. B. Lockhart Papers, Box 9, Folder 12, Hoover

Institution Archives. Courtesy of Hoover Institution Library & Archives, Stanford University.

13 © David King Collection.

14 Robert H. B. Lockhart Papers, Box 10, Folder 17, Hoover Institution Archive. Courtesy of Hoover Institution Library & Archives, Stanford University.

15 © National Portrait Gallery.

16 By kind permission of Dimitri Collingridge

17 ©Tania Alexander

18 © Georgi Särekanno, Jäneda Museum.

19 Robert H B Lockhart Papers, Box 9, Folder 20, Hoover Institution Archives. Courtesy of Hoover Institution Library & Archives, Stanford University.

20 Courtesy of the Rare Book & Manuscript Library, University of Illinois at Urbana-Champaign.

21 © Tania Alexander.

22 © David King Collection.

23 © National Portrait Gallery, London.

24 © Getty Images.

25 © Peter Lofts collection RM004.

26 © Courtesy of the Library of Congress.

27 Wikimedia Commons. With thanks to Allan Warren.

Preface

Moura Budberg was a mystery to everyone who knew her. Even her closest friends and her children never quite figured her out.

London in the 1950s wasn't short of remarkable characters, but few men or women had the magnetic charm or the air of danger and mystery that surrounded Baroness Budberg. Conducting her soirées in her dark, slightly shabby flat in Kensington, she managed to attract the exotic blooms of the literary and political crop. Graham Greene, Laurence Olivier, Tom Driberg, Guy Burgess, Bertrand Russell, Hamish Hamilton, David Lean, E. M. Forster, Lady Diana Cooper, Enid Bagnold, Peter Ustinov – all came at various times to Moura's salon to drink gin and vodka and be enchanted.

Officially, Moura lived off her earnings as a translator of books and plays, as a script consultant and editor for Alexander Korda, and occasionally from donations charmed out of her rich friends. Moura was renowned for having been the mistress of both Maxim Gorky and H. G. Wells, who were besotted with her, and the lover of many other men. Physically she wasn't a prepossessing lady – ageing and overweight, deeply lined, with a large nose badly broken in childhood, wrecked from head to foot by her appetites for food, vodka and cigars. Baroness Budberg was a walking ruin – the harrowed shell of a being who had once possessed beauty, litheness and unsurpassed attraction.

Her charisma still compelled attention and devotion, even in her ruined state. H. G. Wells, whose offers of marriage she turned down repeatedly, said of her, 'I have rarely seen her in any room with other women in which she was not plainly – not merely in my eyes but to many others – the most attractive and interesting presence.'[1]

There were always rumours about her. She had been a spy, a betrayer, a double or even triple agent, in the service of MI6, MI5, the KGB . . . nobody could tell for sure, but everybody had his or her own opinion on the matter. She knew simply *everybody* who was anybody, and liked to convey that she knew everything about them as well. People who entered the sprawling social web the Baroness spun around herself were warned by the older acquaintances to watch their step and their tongues – Moura knew all, saw all, and had powerful, dangerous connections. But hardly anyone, enveloped in one of her bear hugs and subjected to her charm, could resist her.

Baroness Budberg – or the version she presented to the world – was a figure made partly out of fables and lies. Some of them (and not necessarily the most flattering ones) were her own inventions, concocted or stolen from the lives of others and added to the living mythology of Moura Budberg. She had spied for the Germans in the First World War; had spied for and against the British and the Russians; had worked as an agent for the fearsome Bolshevik secret police during the Red Terror of the Revolution; was the mistress of the British agent who plotted to bring down Lenin; had been the trusted agent of Stalin; and she might even have committed murder.

If there were any grains or shards of truth scattered in the folds of myth, nobody cared to discern what they might be, or separate them from the lies. Each man and woman who knew the Baroness – family member, friend, acquaintance or enemy – liked to imagine that he or she had put a finger on what made her tick, or knew concealed truths about her. Few of them, in fact, knew more than a fragment about her.

What they most wanted to know was the truth about her earliest adventures – her love affair with the British diplomat and secret agent Robert Bruce Lockhart in revolutionary Russia, and her involvement in his plot to bring down the Bolshevik government.

Almost all her friends wished that she would write her memoirs. The writer and peace campaigner Peter Ritchie Calder felt 'a deep affection for her, and I've always thought what a marvellous book could be written about her'.[2] He wasn't the only one. Publishers Alfred A. Knopf and Hamish Hamilton tried to arrange for her to produce an autobiography, and although she took and spent the advance, not a word was written. She had begun a memoir decades earlier, but nobody ever saw it, and it was burned – along with most of her other papers – shortly before she died in 1974.

After her death, several attempts were made to write a biography, but most came to nothing for lack of source material.

In 1979, five years after the Baroness had gone to her grave, biographer Andrew Boyle attempted to write her life. His book *Climate of Treason* – which caused Anthony Blunt to be exposed as a Soviet spy – had topped the bestseller lists, and he turned his attention to the woman who, coincidentally, had tried to tip off MI5 about Blunt decades earlier. He found her a much deeper mystery than any Cambridge spy, and almost as well defended by her circle of close friends. The exchanges of letters between Boyle and the members of Moura's circle show a curtain quickly being drawn down around her as soon as her family realised what he was up to.

Boyle got as far as sketching out an outline, in which he noted that 'a virtue must be made of explaining the tentative nature of the material'[3] relating to her early life. But the biography was never written – the writer who had penetrated the mystery of the last Cambridge spy couldn't catch a sure enough hold on Moura Budberg to bring her to life.

One biographer succeeded where Andrew Boyle failed. Nina Berberova was a Russian novelist who had the priceless advantage of having known Moura during her early years in exile, from around 1921 to 1933. Other than that, Moura's life was almost as mysterious to Berberova as it was to any other person. As a highly spirited writer of fiction, she wasn't deterred, and where her source material failed, she didn't hesitate to invent – not only decorative details but vital facts.

Since then, more material has come to light. Aside from the large archives of letters to Gorky, Wells and Lockhart, more recently the file kept on her by MI5 from 1920 to 1951 has been released. Added to facts uncovered by Andrew Boyle and tied to new research into the historical background of the 'Lockhart Plot', it has become possible to piece together the whole story of her life, and uncover some surprising and quite startling facts.

What Moura did in her life, what she was reputed to have done, and what she claimed to have done are difficult to tell apart. Sometimes it's impossible to tell them apart. It is tempting to take a cynical view of Moura's untruths – that she aggrandised herself or simply couldn't distinguish fact from fiction. But what she was really doing was creating an artistic truth for herself. She did it all her life, but it was only in the course of her intimacy with Maxim Gorky, when she delved deeply into the mind of a literary creator, that she herself began to understand what she was doing. Trying to sum up what Gorky did in the process of converting life experience into fiction, she commented that 'Artistic truth is more convincing than the empiric brand, the truth of a dry fact.'[4]

There was her life and motive encapsulated. She wasn't a magpie – she didn't steal experiences because of their attractive gleam, or embellish her own in order to seem more interesting. Where Gorky created literary art out of people's lives, Moura tried to create an artistically 'true' life for herself out of them, even as she was living it.

And her stealing and invention weren't wholesale – just a little touch here and there. Her life, quite by chance, had a dramatic structure normally found only in novels; she was aware of the fact, and ensured that in her letters and her utterances at the time, and in her recollections afterwards, the right words were said and the right attitudes struck at the dramatically appropriate junctures. Whether it was a courageous farewell in the gloom of a night-time rail station, a vow to love unto death or a noble valediction on a mountain crag, she played her part to the full. That it was embellished and charged deliberately with drama did not make any of it less real, either for her or for the people who acted in the play of her life.

The contributions that have gone into the making of this life story are too numerous to list in full. If it hadn't been for the late Andrew Boyle's work in gathering the tales of her friends while they were still living, this book would not have been possible. Neither could it have been done without the memoir written by Moura's daughter Tania, *An Estonian Childhood*.

Others who have helped this book on its way, and who have earned our thanks, include:

Archivists who have provided copies of documents and letters relating to Moura Budberg's life: Arcadia Falcone of the Harry Ransom Center, University of Texas; David K. Frasier of the Lilly Library, University of Indiana; Carol Leadenham, Sean McIntyre and Nicholas Siekierski of the Hoover Institution archives, University of Stanford; Dennis J. Sears,

Rare Books and Manuscripts Library, University of Illinois; and the staff of the House of Lords archives, Westminster.

Enno Must, Director of Jäneda Mõis, and Georgi Särekanno, Head of Jäneda Museum, kindly gave Deborah an hour of their time to show her round the manor in which Moura lived in Estonia and which now contains a museum devoted to her and the Benckendorff family.

Biographers and historians who have shared their expertise and information: Andrea Lynn, for her help and for sharing information about Moura's life and her relationship with H. G. Wells; John Puckett for creating an invaluable translation of the report by Yakov Peters on the Lockhart Case; Professor Barry P. Scherr of Dartmouth College, University of Chicago, for providing notes on the Gorky/Budberg correspondence held in Russian archives and for information on their relationship; Caroline Schmitz for translating the German correspondence between Paul Scheffer and Moura; Miranda Carter and Nigel West for information and advice.

Heartfelt thanks to those friends and acquaintances of Moura Budberg who shared their memories and thoughts about her in conversation with Deborah: Lord Weidenfeld; Michael Korda; Nathalie Brooke (née Benckendorff); and Jamie Bruce Lockhart, who also gave permission to use letters from Robert Bruce Lockhart's archived documents. Thanks also to Simon Calder and family for allowing us to use the epigraph written by his late grandfather, Peter Ritchie Calder.

Finally, profoundest thanks to our agent, Andrew Lownie, for first seeing the potential of this story and for bringing us together to write it; and to Fiona Slater, Rosalind Porter and everyone at Oneworld for believing in the book and letting it see the light.

Deborah McDonald
Jeremy Dronfield
January 2015

Note on dates and place names

The Julian ('Old Style' or OS) calendar was used in imperial Russia until it was replaced by the Gregorian ('New Style' or NS) calendar after the Revolution. As a Catholic invention, the Gregorian calendar was resisted by Orthodox countries until very late. Eastern Orthodox Churches still use the Julian system for their ecclesiastical calendars.

The Julian calendar was thirteen days behind the Gregorian. Thus, the 'October Revolution' actually took place in NS November, and in pre-revolutionary Russia Christmas took place when it was January in the rest of Europe. In the narrative that follows, to avoid such anomalies, OS Julian dates will be given when dealing with Russian events prior to the official change (which occurred on 31 January 1918), and NS Gregorian after.

Shifting national borders and changes in rulership have caused several of the places featured in this story to change their names. Because of its Germanic tone, the name of St Petersburg was changed to Petrograd on the outbreak of war in 1914; following the Revolution, in 1924 it became Leningrad, before finally reverting to St Petersburg in 1991. The port city of Reval in Estonia became Tallinn in 1920. The Estonian village now called Jäneda, where Moura spent summers and Christmases at her husband's country seat, was then known (at least to anglophone writers) as Yendel.

In this book, the names used are those that were current during the time in which the story is set. Similarly, Ukraine is referred to as *the* Ukraine. One exception is the people of Latvia, who were referred to by anglophones as *Letts* or *Lettish*; this has been avoided for the sake of clarity.

Prologue

London, 1970

Baroness Moura Budberg, moving as quietly and as gracefully as her age and arthritis allowed, entered the Russian Orthodox church in Kensington. Passing between the red marble pillars, her footsteps masked by the chanting of the choir, she paused before the icon of Christ, and lit a candle, that she might be forgiven her sins.

Of these she had many – more than a single lifetime's worth, sins of all shades from the blackest transgressions to the most scarlet.

She was in her late seventies, yet Moura's Slavonic cheekbones and feline eyes still hinted at the allure that had captivated men in her younger days. Aristocrats and diplomats, secret agents and intellectuals, prime ministers and princes, all had fallen under her manipulative spell. And yet, for all her sins, the only one for which she had really suffered was no sin at all – that of falling in love. The one man she had truly loved with all her heart had slipped out of her grasp. Now, long decades after the passion of their youth – a wild and dangerous affair sparked amidst the flames of the Revolution – she had come here today, to this church of exiles, to mourn his death.

Moura had ruthlessly lied her way through life: survival was what mattered, at any cost. She had used her sex and her powerful mind to manipulate men, had spied and betrayed, and suffered in her turn. She could safely say she had led a colourful life, despite not having shared it with the man she loved.

The choir chanted its haunting Russian melody, and incense filled the air. The gleaming gold leaf of the icons and the elaborate murals, the white vaulting and gilded dome above the altar were all in stark contrast to Moura herself: her dress, like her mood, was black and all-enveloping. She had felt the need to fortify herself with a few gins and a cigar before coming here. Other than the priest and choir she was the only person present: this was her own private memorial service. She was here to thank Christ for the life of Robert Bruce Lockhart, agent, writer and adventurer, her lost lover. At last, now he was dead, Moura had him to herself.

How different life might have been if he hadn't betrayed and forsaken her – her dear Locky, her Baby-Boy. They could have been together all their lives, and there would not now be such a bitter twist of despair in her mourning for him. She recalled the night they were seized by the Cheka; the thunderous hammering on the door, the terrifying ride to the Lubyanka. He, the conspirator, the plotting assassin, expected execution. The gunshots of the firing squads echoed through the building as the Red Terror began to spread through the streets of Moscow. Alone in his room, hour by hour he expected them to come for him. Moura alone knew the full truth about why he was spared – the degrading sacrifice she had made in return for his life.

And she recalled the time before Lockhart – so gay and easy it seemed now, a mere prelude before the Revolution, when every summer was a lazy idyll and every winter a snowy wonderland . . .

PART I

Flouting All Conventions: 1916–1918

A Russian of the Russians, she had a lofty disregard for all the pettiness of life and a courage which was proof against all cowardice . . . Into my life something had entered which was stronger than any other tie, stronger than life itself. From then onwards she was never to leave . . . until we were parted by the armed force of the Bolsheviks.

Robert Bruce Lockhart, *Memoirs of a British Agent*, 1932

I

The Eve of Revolution

December 1916

The week before Christmas, Yendel, Estonia

A sleigh sped along the arrow-straight driveway of the Yendel estate, bells jingling, the horses' cantering hoofbeats muffled on the packed snow. It flickered through the shadows cast by the naked boughs of the beeches lining the drive, raced by the frozen lake and past acres of glittering parkland, heading towards the house.

Seated in the sleigh, swathed in furs, were two women, with three small children gathered to them like fragile parcels. The younger woman gazed out at the icy world with a serene complacency in her feline eyes. The other woman – middle-aged and handsome – kept her attention on the children, fearful of their falling out of the speeding, open sledge. The journey from the village railway station had been a short one, and straight, but Margaret Wilson was not a woman to take unnecessary risks with her charges. Their mother, seated beside her, was another matter. Madame Moura loved her children, but was happy to let their nanny take the burden of care. And possessing a courage that was close to recklessness, she didn't think of danger. Life had yet to teach her the lessons of protection and survival. (Her poor father had never learned those lessons; he had put his high principles before self-preservation, and suffered for it.)

The house came into view. The sleigh reduced speed, the high hiss of the runners fading. It was a house that could not fail to be noticed, especially in this season. The manor at Yendel was known, with dull country literalness, as the Red House; its ruddy brick bulk, four-square and bracketed by fairy-tale turrets, stood out lividly in the snowy land-scape, surrounded by hoar-frosted shrubberies and the white needles of the silver birches that skirted the lake.

Moura's thoughts were on the lively events of the past few days and the coming pleasures of Christmas. There would be dinners and fireside singing, lively company and sleigh-rides . . . and more. Moura anticipated a season of delights. Her husband, who was away at the war, might not be present for much of the holiday, but Moura could easily stand that. If only his mother would stay away too, that would be ideal. But it was their house – one of the many seats of the grand Benckendorff family, into which Moura had rather hastily married when she was little more than a girl.

The sledge drew to a halt amidst a cloud of condensing horse-breath. The doors of the manor swung open, and the servants came forward to take the luggage. Moura unwrapped herself from the fur rugs, lifted the youngest of the children – baby Tania – and stepped down onto the snow.

There had been snow on the ground on the day Moura was born, nearly twenty-five years earlier and many hundreds of miles away. In March 1892 she came into the world,[1] fourth and dearest child of Ignatiy Platonovich Zakrevsky, member of the landed gentry and high-ranking lawyer in the service of the Tsar.

She was born on the Zakrevsky family estate at Beriozovaya Rudka, in the Poltava region of the Ukraine. It was a beautiful house – a grand edifice built in the style of a classical villa, with columns, arches and portico, but with a Slavonic flavour: little onion cupolas and the exterior stuccoed and painted in the imperial Russian style, salmon pink trimmed with white.[2] An exquisite place to be born, but not such a good place for a wild spirit to grow up.

Ignatiy Zakrevsky and his wife had three children already – a boy called Platon (known as 'Bobik') and twin girls, Alexandra (Alla) and Anna (known as 'Assia'). The newborn was christened Maria Ignatievna Zakrevskaya.[3] The name Maria was from her mother, but the girl soon became known to everyone as 'Moura'. She was the darling of the family. Her father especially doted on her, 'the favourite toy of his middle age and he spoilt her unashamedly'.[4] When he had visitors, he would stand her on a table to recite poems. She relished attention and applause; indeed she demanded it, and could grow incensed on the rare occasions when she didn't get it.[5] Her charisma and intelligence ensured that she was able to hold the attention of all who met her.

Beyond the elegant house and park, Beriozovaya Rudka was a rustic, dull place for such a child to grow up. The Zakrevsky estate encompassed thousands of acres of forest and farmland, much of it given over to sugar beet, which was processed in the estate's own factory. But though his wealth came from the land, Ignatiy Zakrevsky was no farmer. His energies were devoted to justice – criminal justice through his place in the court system, and social justice through his campaigning and charitable acts. Much of his work was done in St Petersburg, and Moura was happiest during the seasons when the family lived at their apartment there.

There was a meeting of temperaments between father and daughter – both were liberal in thought, and inclined to be impulsive and imprudent. Ignatiy Zakrevsky was chief prosecutor for the Imperial Senate, the highest judicial body in Russia. But his radical political views – including his campaign to introduce jury trials into the judicial system – went against the conservatism of Tsar Nicholas II, and he eventually lost his post. The final misdeed was his active support for Émile Zola in the Dreyfus affair. In 1899 he was forced to resign from the Senate.

It was a time when radical and conservative tendencies were coming ever more into conflict. Peasants and workers were suffering abysmal privations. In the year of Moura's birth, almost half a million people in the Poltava region died from cholera and typhus, weakened by malnutrition. A series of savagely cold winters had caused famine, and what little spare food there was had been earmarked by the state for export. At the same time, the Tsar took his land taxes from the impoverished farms. So desperate did the peasants become that they resorted to eating 'famine bread' made of rye husks mixed with goosefoot weeds, moss and tree bark or whatever else came to hand.[6] Ignatiy Zakrevsky urged the government not to be complacent, warning that their failure to introduce social and judicial reforms would lead to an uprising sooner or later.

He was right, but he didn't live to see it. In early 1905, during a trip to Egypt with his twin daughters Alla and Assia, Ignatiy Zakrevsky suffered a heart attack and died. His widow, with children to support and a family estate to maintain, was left with an inheritance far smaller than it ought to have been, Ignatiy's final eccentric act having been to leave a portion of his fortune to the Freemasons.

St Petersburg was too expensive, so Madame Zakrevskaya took Moura, twelve years old and with her exuberant personality starting to reach full bloom, to live permanently at Beriozovaya Rudka. It was the beginning of a bleak period in Moura's life: she had lost her beloved father, and was now doomed to years of dismal country life. It had a baneful effect on her and helped guide her into making a regrettable decision.

The hard snow creaked under Moura's heels as she stepped out of the sleigh. While the male servants collected the luggage, she took a moment to look around her and gaze up at the house.

Yendel's Red House was darker and less elegant than Beriozovaya Rudka, resembling a tumescent hunting lodge more than a manor house, but Moura was happy here, in a way she had rarely been in her childhood home. What mattered most to Moura was life and people and fun – not places. At Yendel she was the mistress of the house, and could surround herself with her choice of company. Estonia was also closer to Petrograd (as the capital was now called). Just an overnight train journey and a short jaunt in a sleigh, compared to the long, exhausting haul to the far end of beyond that she recalled from her childhood journeys to the Ukraine.

Petrograd in 1916 was not a stable place to be, so an extended holiday at Yendel was doubly good. The common people were restive. Their lot had not changed in the past quarter-century – other than for the worse. The effects of poverty and repression were ever-present, and the Patriotic War[7] against the German and Austro-Hungarian empires, already into its third year, was draining Russia's manpower and its wealth. The military hospitals were full, and the bread shops were empty.

The political frictions went to the very top of the imperial tree. Just a few days ago, on 16 December, Moura had attended the infamous ball given by Prince Felix Yusupov at the Moika Palace,[8] where hundreds of Petrograd's finest dined and danced in the ballroom while Rasputin was being put to death in the cellars below. Regarded by the elite as a baneful influence on the Tsar and Tsarina, he had been lured to the palace at midnight, fed poisoned cake and wine, and then subjected to an ordeal of abattoir violence at the hands of his murderers, who seemed unable to make him die. Eventually it was done. Meanwhile, the ball danced on. The imperial family mourned the loss of their counsellor, and the outraged Tsarina lusted for revenge.

Insurrection was in the air, but hardly anyone – least of all Moura – believed that it would blow up in revolution. It was just more of the same turmoil that had been part of Russian life for centuries. From time to time it flared up, but always died down again. Moura's liberal sympathies lay with the people, but not so much that she would worry herself over them. She may have been somewhat like her father, but she was not him.

With little Tania in her arms, she turned to watch the other two children being shepherded from the sledge by their nanny: four-year-old Pavel had to be extricated from the rugs, but Kira, the eldest, stepped out gracefully. Aged nine, Kira was older than her mother's marriage, and her parentage was uncertain: not her paternity but her maternity. The little girl was a part of the complicated tangle of life that Moura was already building up around her.

With her father dead and the family's wealth reduced, Moura had not been sent away to school like her elder siblings. Her entire life between the ages of twelve and seventeen was bounded by the family estate and the bleak Ukrainian Steppe that surrounded it, a flatland that seemed to go on forever, relieved only by trees and the occasional dome of a church.

She was educated by tutors and governesses, but her closest companion was her nursemaid, 'Micky', who had been with the family since before Moura's birth. Micky's real name was Margaret Wilson, and she was a woman of character – young, beautiful, strong-willed and utterly devoted to her charges. She was also a woman with a past that had made her life in her home country untenable.

Born in Liverpool in 1864, Margaret had married young, to an Irishman who stayed with her long enough to give her a son and then went off to take part in one of the frequent uprisings that broke out in Ireland in the 1880s – the so-called Land War – and was killed there. Margaret, a spirited, unconventional girl, became mistress to a British cavalry officer, Colonel Thomas Gonne, who had served in Ireland and was old enough to be her father. In July 1886 she gave birth to a daughter, Eileen. As if there were some pattern at work, a few months later Colonel Gonne died of typhoid fever, and Margaret was again left alone with a child – this one shamefully illegitimate.[9] Her life from that time on must have been intolerable, but eventually help came from a surprising source.

In 1892 Ignatiy Zakrevsky was visiting England on business. He came into the company of British people who were like himself – wealthy, upper class and politically radical. Among them was Maud Gonne, actress, supporter of Irish nationalism and mistress of the poet W. B. Yeats. She was also the daughter of the late Colonel Thomas Gonne, which made her the half-sister of Margaret's little daughter Eileen, who was now six years old. Maud had been helping Margaret support Eileen since her birth (in the teeth of opposition from her uncle, the late Colonel's brother).[10]

Ignatiy Zakrevsky took an interest in young Margaret, and an arrangement was agreed. Zakrevsky – a man whose charitable impulses often outweighed his good sense – would take Margaret with him back to Russia, where she would teach English to his twin daughters, Alla and Assia. Meanwhile, Eileen would be taken care of by Maud.[11]

When Ignatiy Zakrevsky returned to Russia with Margaret, it was intended that she be employed for twelve months and that her duties would consist simply of teaching English to the twins. But she was soon drawn into the heart of the family, and the original plan was forgotten. Margaret ended up spending the rest of her long life with the family.[12] Having had little education, Margaret was no teacher, and aside from English, the Zakrevsky children were taught other subjects by tutors.

Moura was born within weeks of Margaret's arrival, and she became nursemaid to the infant, and later her companion, friend and a kind of surrogate mother. All the Zakrevsky children adored her. While the parents knew Margaret formally as 'Wilson', the children called her 'Ducky', which later evolved into 'Micky'. The name stuck, and she was Micky for ever after. Regarding herself as part of the family, she never took a wage; instead, she simply had to mention anything she needed, and it would be provided. Her tastes were simple and her needs few.

Micky had a great influence on the children – especially Moura. Never learning to speak Russian properly, she made the children (and the rest of the family) speak English. The result, it was said, was that Moura grew up speaking better English than Russian, and spoke her native language with an English accent.

Confined to Beriozovaya Rudka during her early teens, Moura was frustrated by the isolation and dullness of the place, and gradually began to exhibit the waywardness and sensualism that would mark the whole of her adult life. Had Micky been her real mother rather than just a surrogate, one might have said that the trait was inherited.[13]

But Moura had gifts that Micky had not – prodigious gifts that were uniquely hers. And she had strong desires to go with them. Her need to be at the centre of a fascinating social whirl became more intense as she approached womanhood, and her talent for getting and holding people's attention grew and grew. She could charm, delight and seduce. Her glittering, sly eyes would fix themselves on a person, and she would make whoever she talked to feel, in that moment, as if they were the most important person in the world to her. And as she matured physically, she discovered the power of her sexual attractiveness. She became a dangerous young woman; a danger not least to herself. A contemporary said of her:

> Her face radiating peace and calm, and her large, wide-set eyes sparkling with life ... her bright quick mind, her profound ability to understand her interlocutor after hearing only half a word, and her reply, which would flash across her face before she spoke ... gave her an aura of warmth and rarity ... Her lightly pencilled eyes were always eloquent, saying exactly what people wanted to hear: something serious or funny, sad or smart, soft and cozy. Her body was straight and strong; her figure was elegant

But at the same time:

> There was something cruel in her face, which was a little too broad, with her high cheekbones and wide-set eyes, but she had an unbelievably endearing, feline smile.[14]

Few could resist her, and not many wanted to.

The first man she was said to have bedded – or the first whose name is known – was Arthur Engelhardt. The circumstances were confused, entangled with myth and rumour. Engelhardt appeared on the scene in 1908, when Moura was sixteen. At around this period a baby girl also appeared, named Kira. It was alleged later that Kira was Moura's child by Engelhardt, but there was good reason to believe that she was the child of Moura's elder sister Alla, who also had a relationship with

Engelhardt. An unusual situation, in which the paternity of a child was known, but its maternity was in doubt.

Whatever the truth of Kira's parentage, it was Alla who married Engelhardt, and Kira was recorded as their daughter.[15] It was a doomed marriage, and Alla's life would be dogged by strife and drug addiction.

Meanwhile, Moura put the Engelhardt affair behind her, and finally escaped the social wasteland of the Ukraine in 1909. Her other elder sister, Alla's twin Assia, was married to a diplomat and living in Berlin, one of the most exciting cities in Europe for wealthy socialites. Assia was a typically wayward Zakrevskaya girl, her marriage having begun with an affair and an elopement. She invited Moura to come and stay with her. 'Bring your smartest clothes,' she wrote, 'as there will be plenty of parties, Court balls and other functions to go to.'[16] How could Moura resist? She packed her dresses, said farewell to Micky, and – aglow with excitement – set off for Germany.

It was just as Assia had promised: a life of society, sparkle and intense experience. It was also the beginning of a new epoch in Moura's life. In Berlin she was introduced to a friend of her brother Bobik, who was also in the diplomatic service. Assia thought this man – a young nobleman who was ten years older than Moura – would be a good escort for the seventeen-year-old. Moura thought so too.

Djon Alexandrovich von Benckendorff came from a branch of a large Estonian aristocratic family. Along with the other Baltic provinces, Estonia was part of the Russian Empire, and there were several Benckendorffs in the imperial Russian diplomatic service. Djon had been groomed to be part of the next generation, and was already well on his way, having recently inherited his father's large estate at Yendel. On top of his other advantages, Djon was an intelligent young man, coming almost top of his year at the Imperial Lycée in St Petersburg.

Moura set her sights on him. She had the aristocratic connections, the bearing and personality to attract a conventional, conservative member of the nobility such as Djon. He probably failed to realise that she was not at all conventional, had a mind of her own, and was thoroughly independent in spirit. When he met her, she turned the full power of her charisma on him, and he soon came under her spell. Their courtship began.

She was never in love with him, but his wealth and position appealed to her, and her mother considered him a suitable match. With such a

man Moura would want for nothing, and have a wonderful social life.
Mixing with the aristocracy at parties night after night suited her, and
she quickly decided that as long as she lived she was never going to be
'ordinary'.

At a Court ball at the Sanssouci Palace – the flamboyant Rococo
marvel at Potsdam belonging to the German royal family – Moura and
Assia were presented to Tsar Nicholas, who was visiting as a guest of his
second cousin, Kaiser Wilhelm. It was a ball comparable to the ones
given by the Tsar himself at the Winter Palace in St Petersburg, which
were renowned for being unbelievably lavish, with as many as three
thousand aristocratic guests flaunting their wealth, dressed in colourful
uniforms and magnificent gowns, sparkling with jewels and decorations.
At the Sanssouci ball the Zakrevskaya girls, 'in their beautiful Court
dresses, with gold studded trains and traditional Russian head-dress
studded with pearls', made such an impression that the Crown Prince
was heard to exclaim, 'Quelle noblesse!'[17]

This was the kind of intense, giddy society that Moura had been
craving since childhood. She agreed to marry Djon, and the wedding
took place on 24 October 1911. Moura was finally liberated, and would
never have to return to life in the stultifying atmosphere of Beriozovaya
Rudka and the cloying clutches of her mother.

For the next three years the couple lived in Berlin, where Djon had
a rising position at the Russian Embassy. Djon adored his bride, and
Moura's magnetic charm must have made him believe that the feeling
was returned. It wasn't, but neither was there any ill feeling – not yet,
anyway. Moura's status rose, and she became a focus of attention within
the Embassy and Berlin's wider diplomatic circles. She spent days out at
the races, and weekends away at house parties.

Their life was not confined to Berlin. Djon had a luxurious apartment in St Petersburg, where they would stay when he was given leave.
There were great balls at the royal palaces; the Tsar and Tsarina opened
these evenings by dancing a formal polonaise, and at midnight the
dancing would stop for a huge sit-down supper.[18] Many years later,
Moura recalled one of these events:

Inside it was suffocating, what with all the candles and the flowers and
the fires, everybody wore pads under their armpits to soak up the per-
spiration, and outside it was twenty or thirty degrees below zero, one

arrived in sleighs bundled up in furs, and shawls and robes, and there were bonfires in the palace courtyard so that the grooms and coachmen could warm themselves up while they waited. It was all very beautiful, and I remember the poor Tzar staring down my bodice when I curtsied, and the look the Empress gave him! So silly when you consider she was already spending her afternoons with Rasputin.[19]

For just over a year the couple lived the carefree life of young aristocrats without responsibilities. Then the children began to appear. The first was Pavel, born on 29 August 1913. With the wealth of the Benckendorffs at their disposal, they were barely inconvenienced by the baby. Micky was summoned from Beriozovaya Rudka, and continued her work caring for the second generation of children.

With her came Kira. Alla's marriage to Arthur Engelhardt had been an unhappy one, and they had divorced in 1912. Alla, erratic and drug-addicted, had been unable to care for Kira; the little girl was sent back to Beriozovaya Rudka. Thus, when Micky came to take up her role as nurse to Moura's new child, Kira came with her and joined the nursery of the Benckendorffs. She was treated as one of the family, further obscuring the truth about her parentage.

Moura had everything – wealth, an august husband who adored her, a place in the high society of two of the most cosmopolitan cities in Europe, and the first of her beloved children. It couldn't last. The young couple's lavish lifestyle was curtailed by the coming of war in 1914. Germany and Russia joined the conflict on opposing sides, and Russia's diplomats were withdrawn from Berlin.

Shortly after the outbreak of war, Djon joined the Russian army, and became a staff officer at the headquarters of the Northwest Front, and spent long periods away from home.

Moura had lost the society of Berlin, but she still had the imperial glamour of St Petersburg – or Petrograd as the Russians now patriotically called it, eschewing the old Germanic form. For more intimate socialising, she could retreat during the holiday seasons to the country estate at Yendel. She had Micky to take care of the children – now including baby Tania, born in 1915 – and little changed in her social life. All that was really different was the absence of Djon, and that was an absence Moura could easily bear.

★   ★   ★

Micky was having difficulty getting Pavel out of the sledge. He had lost the toy soldier he'd insisted on carrying in his little hand all the way from Petrograd, and wouldn't get out until it was found. *Another absent soldier*, Moura thought. Just like the boy's father; but this one's absence seemed to be more regretted. Setting Tania down, Moura joined in the search, turning over rugs and feeling in the cracks between the seats. Eventually the errant soldier – a hussar with a sword – was discovered; he had retreated to the floor and concealed himself among a tangle of furs. Pavel snatched the soldier from Moura's hand and held him up triumphantly to be admired by Micky.

The nurse smiled – a little tightly, Moura thought. Was Micky also reminded of a real-life soldier – her dead lover, the cavalry colonel? From time to time letters postmarked in Ireland would arrive for Micky; everyone knew that they came from Eileen, her daughter. She was a grown woman now, and had made Micky a grandmother. Whenever one of her letters came, Micky would be irritable and out of sorts for the rest of the day.[20] But she always brightened up afterwards. Nothing could keep Micky's spirits down for long.

Moura turned back towards the house, squaring her shoulders in anticipation. There was a lot to do. The kitchen staff to shake up after their months on hiatus; parties to plan; guests to invite; outings and jaunts to conceive. She would certainly invite her friends from the British Embassy. Moura, with her anglophone upbringing, had a special affection for the British. And then there were her friends from the war hospital, where she had been serving as a nursing volunteer. And a whole host of relatives and society friends.

The Benckendorffs would be represented by Djon's brother Paul and his wife, and probably by Djon himself for a while, but hopefully not by his mother, and especially not the other female relatives. The Benckendorff aunts were like a private not-so-secret police, noting every fault in Moura's character and behaviour; and they never shrank from giving an opinion. Even Micky, who was fond of Djon, learned to loathe the Benckendorff aunts. In the troubled years that were approaching, she would be forced to spend her energy protecting the children from their influence and Moura's reputation from their wagging tongues.

Some might say that Moura's reputation was beyond protecting – already she had become a legend in Petrograd, and not just for her social brilliance. Intriguing, titillating rumours were forever springing up and circulating, attributing all manner of nefarious activities to her, including the remarkable claim that she was a German spy.[21] How much was the product of overheated imaginations and how large a kernel of truth the stories might have (if any) was impossible to discern, and so people tended to believe what they wanted to about Madame Moura von Benckendorff. And so it would always be.

Oblivious, and thinking only of the Christmas festivities to come, Moura lifted Tania in her arms and skipped lightly up the steps and through the arched doorway into the warm hallway; in her wake came Micky, Pavel and Kira, followed by the servants bearing the last items of luggage.

The doors swung closed behind them, shutting out the cold and sealing in the joy of the season.

2

Choosing Sides

December 1916–October 1917

30 December 1916

Sir George Buchanan, British Ambassador to Russia, stood at one of the tall windows in the huge reception room in the Alexander Palace. Outside he could see Tsar Nicholas taking his daily walk in the snow-covered gardens, accompanied by his retinue.[1]

The palaces of Petrograd were magnificent, but those of Tsarskoye Selo,* the imperial family's country retreat, a dozen miles from the city, were of a separate order of splendour. On one side of the park stood the Catherine Palace, a vast glory in ice-white and sky-blue stucco, rank upon rank, row after row of pillars and lofty windows, bordered in ornate mouldings lavished with gold leaf, and surmounted by a huge pinnacle of golden domes. On the adjacent side was the Alexander Palace, the smaller fondant-and-cream marvel where the family actually lived in relatively understated opulence.

Sir George had travelled down that day from Petrograd, having requested an audience with the Tsar to talk over the political situation in Russia. For an ambassador, he took an uncommon interest in the internal affairs of the country, and enjoyed an unusually close friendship with the Tsar. Sir George Buchanan was described by one of his junior consuls as 'a frail-looking man with a tired, sad expression' whose monocle, refined features and silver hair 'gave him something of the appearance of a stage-diplomat', but who possessed 'a wonderful power of inspiring loyalty'.[2] Sir George was deeply worried. He believed that the Tsar and Tsarina had little conception of just how divided and unhappy their empire was, nor how tenuous their own position. Their

---

* Tsar's Village.

own ministers were misleading them, and the government was riddled with agents working for German interests. The gossip in Petrograd now was not of whether the imperial couple would end up being assassinated, but which of them might go first.[3]

For a man with Sir George's insight, the evidence of unrest was profoundly worrying. Violent insurrection was lurking around the corner. He was concerned about his own family, and was considering sending his daughter Meriel to stay with her Russian friend, Moura von Benckendorff, at her country estate in Estonia. Yendel was close enough to the capital to be easily accessible, but far enough to be out of danger if the sparks hit the powder keg in Petrograd.

Meriel and Madame Moura did voluntary nursing together at the city's war hospital. They were well acquainted through Moura's diplomatic connections, which had brought her into the sphere of the British Embassy. The young lady had apparently been brought up by an English-speaking nanny and had an affection for things British. Many of the younger male attachés had been very taken by her charms, as had the British naval officers whose ships berthed at Reval,* the Estonian port.[4] Her husband's relations held posts throughout the imperial government and diplomatic service. Indeed, the sad news had reached Russia this very day that Count Alexander von Benckendorff, Russia's Ambassador to Great Britain, had died in London. His brother Paul was Grand Chamberlain; both were favourites of the imperial family, and the news was bound to have upset the Tsar.[5]

The family were already in a state of shock following the murder of Rasputin (the Tsarina was grief-stricken, but some said the Tsar was relieved to be rid of him). They had confined themselves here, taking comfort in trivial entertainments and denying to themselves that there was any real unrest among their people. Sir George had attempted to warn His Majesty some weeks ago that Rasputin was regarded as a poisonous influence, and that there was talk of a plot against his life, but the Tsar had declined to listen.[6] Would he listen to reason now?

At last, His Majesty Tsar Nicholas II, Emperor and Autocrat of All the Russias, returned from his walk in the gardens, and Sir George was summoned into his presence. As soon as he entered the room, he guessed that his mission was futile. Whenever the Tsar wished to talk seriously

---

* Now called Tallinn.

with Sir George, he welcomed him in his study, where they would sit and smoke. But today the Ambassador was ushered into the formal audience chamber, and found the Tsar standing in state. That meant he was willing to hear Sir George as Ambassador of Great Britain, not in the role of friend and counsellor on all political matters. He had guessed what the visit portended, and didn't wish to hear.

Sir George tried nonetheless. Using every reserve of charm and persuasion, he turned the conversation to Russian politics, and tried to convince the Tsar to appoint a new president of the council who would be approved by the Duma, Russia's parliament, and heal the rift between the ruler and his own state. Reminding His Majesty of his warning about Rasputin, Sir George described the unrest that was rife throughout the government, the Duma and the entire country. The Tsar said he knew perfectly well that there was talk of insurrection, but that it would be a mistake to take it too seriously.

Making one last effort, Sir George abandoned reason and tried an appeal to emotion, citing his long devotion to the Tsar. 'If I were to see a friend,' he said, 'walking through a wood on a dark night along a path which I knew ended in a precipice, would it not be my duty, sir, to warn him of his danger? And is it not equally my duty to warn Your Majesty of the abyss that lies ahead of you?'[7]

Tsar Nicholas was moved, and when they parted, he took the Ambassador's hand and pressed it warmly. 'I thank you, Sir George,' he said.

But as time passed, it became evident that nothing would change. About a week after the meeting at Tsarskoye Selo, Sir George was told by a Russian political friend that there would be a revolution before Easter. But he needn't be alarmed – the revolution would come from within the political elite, would be temporary and would merely force the Tsar to accept a proper constitution. Such a revolution would forestall any danger of a revolution among the workers and peasants, which would be an altogether more violent and dreadful affair.[8]

This was somewhat reassuring. Nonetheless, when his daughter Meriel was invited to visit Moura von Benckendorff at Yendel, Sir George encouraged her to go.

Sunday 26 February 1917

Strange how the most life-altering journey might begin with the lightest
of steps: with careless laughter and gay farewells, and not a trace of foreboding of the nightmare that is to come.

Moura parted the heavy bedroom curtain and looked out into the
evening dark, moving close to the glass to see through the lamplit reflection of her own glittering eyes. The snow lay heavy and silent across the
landscape, glowing eerily under a rising Estonian winter moon. The
stars were out, and tonight the wolves would be running in the forests.
Moura shivered. It was a good night for a journey, a good night for
change.

She hummed happily – the haunting gypsy melody she had sung for
her spellbound guests the evening before, sitting on the hearth rug, the
crackling fire reflecting in her golden eyes . . .

Her breath hazed the glass, obscuring the view. A good night for a
journey indeed: time to shake the sleepy country snows of Yendel from
her heels and get back to the city. The long-extended Christmas holiday
was over at last, and the day appointed for the journey back to Petrograd
had arrived. She needed the city as she needed breath. Any city would
do at a pinch – they were all lively in their various ways – but Petrograd
was life itself, the beating heart of empire, and people were its blood.
Even with the troubles that had scoured it – the anti-war feelings, the
workers' soviets* stirring trouble, the shortages and protests and strikes
– it was still the breath of life to Moura, and she loved to feel its pulse.

She thought about the ball at the Moika Palace, and the death of
Rasputin. Moura was smart enough to know that the bitter retribution
of the Tsarina would stir up the masses still further, but was not timid
enough to fear the consequences herself. Pah – let the wolves run! She
could run faster.

She didn't know – nobody at Yendel knew – that the patter of their
feet and the rank gust of their breath had already begun sweeping
through the city.

The maid snapped shut the clasps on the last valise, and Moura came
out of her dream, turning away from the window. The maid bobbed a

---

* *soviet*: an elected council.

curtsey, slid the valise off the dresser and went out of the door. The trunk had already been taken down by a footman. There was a faint jingle of bells outside. Moura glanced out; the sledges were being brought round to the drive, the horses stamping their feet on the packed snow. They were as eager to depart as she was.

Moura took a last look at herself in the mirror, adjusted her fur hat, and followed her luggage downstairs.

Convivial chatter and the laughter of children filled Yendel's hall that evening. After a hurried dinner, the small house party − consisting of Moura's children and her two closest friends − had gathered in the entrance hall while the sleighs were made ready, taking one last lingering taste of the manor's warmth and comfort before venturing out into the cold. The two young women lounged in the comfortable chairs by the fire, chatting. There was Meriel Buchanan, daughter of the British Ambassador − she had a long, rather mournful face, but her rosebud mouth broke into a smile at the sight of Moura descending the stairs. The other young lady was Miriam Artsimovich − American-born, despite her name. They were the last and dearest of the holiday guests, lingering on to the very last gasp of the holiday. Both were dressed for the cold.

'My daaahlings,' Moura pronounced theatrically as she made her entrance. Despite speaking English better than Russian, she enjoyed investing it with a heavy Slavonic cadence.

While the women rose as if royalty had made an appearance, the children gathered round her. Pavel, son of his father, and Tania, daughter of her mother − and of course Kira, of uncertain parentage. Moura stooped to kiss her little darlings, while Micky stepped in to impose some order. She was one of the few people whom Moura loved and utterly trusted.

Standing aside, Moura posed to show off her exquisite fur-trimmed travelling outfit to her friends. It was duly admired, and while they waited for the coachman's summons, the three of them fell into breathless conversation − as excited as the children were about the impending night-journey.

Their talk was all of society gossip, the journey ahead, and of the war. All three women worked as volunteer nurses at the hospital of St George, where rumours circulated among the soldiers about the special sort of care given to wounded officers by the lady Moura.[9] But there were *always* rumours about her of one kind or another. There were always people credulous enough to believe, and Moura herself took delight in encouraging them.

Entirely absent from their conversation was any mention of the latest events in Petrograd. The news of the storm that had begun to break the previous day had not yet reached Estonia; the papers had merely reported shops being looted, and that there were strikes in the factories. It sounded much the same as in the weeks prior to the holiday, and they were so accustomed to it that it had not cast a pall on their conviviality.

When the time came, the travelling party – three ladies, three children, Micky, and Moura's maid – went out into the freezing dark and squeezed into the open sleigh, wrapping themselves in rugs and furs. While the women fussed and chattered, the house servants waited, freezing obediently in the arched loom of light from the great hall door, waiting to bow their farewells.

'Feet *inside* the sledge, little Pavel!' Moura swept the boy onto her lap. 'The wolves will bite them!'

'There are wolves?' the little boy asked.

'Always there are wolves,' said Moura. 'And on a night like this they long to feast on the feet of careless little children! But – we shall outrun them! Away!'

The coachman shook the reins, and the sledge leaped forward with a shivering jingle of bells, its runners hissing and the horses' hoofbeats thumping gently, muffled by the snow.

It was a short but searingly cold journey to the local village station at Aegviidu, where they had booked a compartment aboard the Petrograd train. The night glowed; the sky was clear and dotted with stars, and a rising moon shone on the still, silent expanses of snow.[10] They drove on down the road that ran straight from the house, past the frozen lakes, and twisted through the woods beyond. The quiet of the sleigh's passage in the icy shades of the woods filled the women with eerie shivers of exhilaration. Here and there, woodsmen's cottages loomed up, with lights glowing yellow in their windows, filling Meriel's head with thoughts of fairy-tale witches.

Aegviidu station was a lopsided timber-faced building with grand pretensions, standing alone on the flat space between the village road and the open rail tracks. Its waiting room was full of soldiers and unwashed, sheepskin-clad peasants. Fortunately, the genteel young women didn't have to endure the company for long before they heard the chuff and whistle of the incoming train.

Every carriage was already packed to bursting with passengers who had boarded at Reval. Even the corridors were full. The three ladies were once more spared the impertinent proximity of the grimy peasantry. The Benckendorff name, together with Meriel's diplomatic connections, had earned them a private carriage, arranged through the head of the district police. This would be the last time their position would afford them such special treatment.[11] Locking the door, the women arranged themselves for the night's journey, settling into accustomed comfort while out in the corridors the proletariat snored propped up on stools or stretched out on the floor.

At eight o'clock the next morning, the train steamed into the Baltic station in Petrograd, and the travelling party got their first real intimation of trouble.[12] The palatial halls of the station felt strangely eerie and perturbed, although it was difficult to say exactly how or why. William, Sir George Buchanan's chasseur and butler, was there to meet them with the embassy motor car.[13] Accompanying him – rather surprisingly – was Brigadier General Knox, the military attaché, splendid but alarming in full uniform, his face grave.[14]

Moura asked what the matter was, and he turned his severe eyes and glum moustache towards her. There had been riots in the town, he told her, and strikes.

'*Pff* – there are always riots,' said Moura; 'every day, strikes.'

'Indeed, madam, but they are somewhat worse of late. Vehicles are forbidden to travel without a pass.'

Moura's cheeks paled a little, but she was still unconvinced that such an air of gloom could be justified. While William grumpily wrestled the heaps of luggage onto a handcart, the ladies followed the General through the echoing halls of the grand station. The embassy motor car was waiting for them. The women looked at the car, at the children, and at each other. How could they possibly fit everyone in? Meriel suggested that they order a cab for the servants and the luggage. General Knox's long face lengthened, and he shook his head. There were no cabs; the *izvozchiki** were on strike.

---

* *izvozchik*: sleigh or carriage driver for hire.

'Can't the servants go in a tram?' Moura suggested. 'Then we can take the luggage with us.'

General Knox suppressed an impatient sigh. He had been up since six, and still had a lot to do that day; the British military staff were on high alert.[15] 'There are no trams,' he said. He was carefully avoiding telling them the whole truth about what had been going on in the city in the past two days. The last thing he needed was a clutch of hysterical females on his hands. 'They are on strike,' he repeated. '*Everyone* is on strike. We shall have to get everything into the motor somehow.'[16]

By this time, the other travellers from the train were congregating in the snow outside the station, growing restive and irritable as they wondered how on earth they were going to get home. One man had managed to find a small sledge; he piled his luggage on it and set off down the street while the remaining crowd began to pick arguments with the station's helpless porters.

Moura and her friends, the three little children, General Knox, Micky, Moura's maid and all their combined luggage were squeezed into the car, and it set off, followed by a host of envious gazes. On the General's instructions, William took a roundabout route, avoiding the major thoroughfares of the Nevsky and Morskaya. They wound their way into the Admiralteysky district, seat of the Russian government, where Moura had her apartment and where the grand British Embassy stood on the riverside between the Winter Palace and the Summer Garden.[17]

Moura's complacent calm was gradually eroded as the car drove through the snow-swept city. They passed an abandoned tram with its windows all broken, and a soldier wielding a rifle stopped them to check their permit. He found everything in order and they were allowed to carry on through deserted, desolate streets which had been bustling with people last time Moura was here, with rushing yellow trams and sledges. Everywhere was silent, foreboding, anticipating trouble.[18] Shops were boarded up. The few people who were about kept their heads down and hurried along as if fearing attack. Here and there were checkpoints manned by groups of soldiers and armed police, who eyed the car with intense suspicion as it passed, but made no move to stop it. Moura shivered, feeling the brooding malevolence, and unconsciously drew her children closer. There was more to this than just strikes and riots. There was death here.

General Knox's cautious route brought them by St Isaac's Cathedral and out on the fashionable English Quay. As the motor made its solitary way beside the frozen Neva river, the passengers sensed an air of silent dread; it surrounded the Winter Palace and the Petropavlovskaya* fortress on the island opposite – the old citadel of St Petersburg, with its imperial flag hanging forlornly in the gloomy air. The bridges over the river were empty. It was as if the city were cowering before a wolf, waiting for it to pounce.

Moura and the children were dropped off at her apartment. The car continued on to the Embassy, where Meriel was met by her anxious parents. Sir George, regretting that she had come back from Yendel so soon, forbade her to go out of doors again.[19]

The three young ladies had got safely home, and not a moment too soon.

Later that same morning, the swollen storm clouds finally burst: the silent streets were flooded with crowds of rioters and protesters, shouting and chanting, accompanied by the clatter of hoofs and the rattle of gunshots. The Tsar's soldiers had thrown in their lot with the workers; they came raging out of their barracks, and battle was joined on the streets of Petrograd, soldiers and revolutionaries fighting against the Cossacks and the police.

It was the culmination of acts of violence that had been going on sporadically for days. The people's patience had been bitten down to the quick. The peasants and workers had at last reached the point where they would take no more of the disorganisation and injustice that led to empty shops and empty bellies for the poor, and unstinting luxury for the rich. The continual flood of soldiers returning from the terrible conditions in the trenches, only to half-starve on their arrival home in Russia, had added to the unrest.

While Moura and her guests were frolicking in the snows at Yendel and relaxing in the fire-lit comfort of the manor, in Petrograd there had been blood on the streets. The authorities had put up posters forbidding demonstrations. The people ignored them. And then, on Sunday 26 February, the government put a burning match to the powder train. While the young ladies at Yendel lunched and anticipated their

---

* Peter and Paul.

homeward journey, demonstrators who had gathered in the suburbs of
Petrograd were converging on the government district. There were military strongpoints at every major junction, patrols of soldiers and armed
police everywhere. As the demonstrators marched along the Nevsky
Prospekt, the main thoroughfare leading into the heart of the city, the
first shootings occurred. The incidents were sporadic: nervous, inexperienced troops led by fearful, angry officers shot at and wounded dozens
of people. The demonstrators scattered, and some began to hurl brick-
bats back at the soldiers. In Znamenskaya Square, the violence reached
a bloody peak when a regiment opened fire and killed fifty people.[20]

With those shots, Russia propelled itself down a road from which
there was no return. For Moura, and for every Russian, the world was
about to change.

Buildings were barricaded; the Palace of Justice was set on fire and
any place housing the police became a target for the crowd's rage. They
stormed the prisons and set the prisoners free. By Monday morning,
when Moura and her friends arrived, holiday-fresh and lighthearted, an
uneasy lull had fallen over the city – a shocked pause and intake of
breath – before the violence exploded again with ever greater ferocity.
In the battles that broke out that day, an infantry regiment fought the
Cossacks and the police in defence of the rebellious citizens; only a few
days before, the situation had been reversed, Cossacks fighting against
the police, while the army killed the people. Nobody knew whose side
anybody was on: district by district and regiment by regiment, the sympathies of the officers and men swayed this way and that; nobody had
any fixed allegiance – nobody, that is, except the starving workers and
the ruling aristocrats. Their sides had been chosen for them by birth and
circumstance.

Among the aristocrats there was at least one exception. While the
February Revolution unfolded in the streets outside her apartment, the
sounds of gunfire and yelling mobs echoing off the grand façades,
Madame Moura von Benckendorff watched with alert eyes and knew
one thing: whichever side won the fight for Mother Russia, that would
be the side she would attach herself to. Others might suffer and perish,
but Moura would survive.

She had no inkling yet how heavy a toll her choice, when she eventually made it, would exact from her.

For the upper classes, the foreign expatriates and diplomats, the change was slow to affect them. Despite the unrest and the killing of so many civilians in the Nevsky on Bloody Sunday, that same afternoon the English ladies came as usual to their regular sewing party at the Embassy. Not put off by a bit of shooting, they braved the ugly streets on foot, past soldiers and burning buildings. In the ballroom of the Embassy, trestle tables were set up and loaded with bales of flannel, lint, cotton wool, scissors and sewing machines. The ladies made them up into packages for sending to the ambulance trains going to the front, or to the military hospital.

Everything else shut down for the duration of the storm. Shops and restaurants ceased trading, newspaper offices were closed, and red flags could be seen everywhere. Supporters of the Revolution pinned red ribbons to their clothes. Soon, everyone was wearing them: to do otherwise was to court trouble. The revolutionaries demanded the overthrow of the government and the Tsar, the institution of a republic, and the end of the so-called Patriotic War. The proletariat rallied to the cause, and gradually formed a concerted revolutionary movement. The workers' soviets were becoming a potent political force. The violence subsided and the negotiations began; when the Duma reconvened, the soviets were formally invited to elect representatives.

On 2 March, the keystone in the old structure of government fell: Tsar Nicholas II, who had continued to reside at Tsarskoye Selo throughout the crisis, abdicated. He had seemed little concerned about the fighting in the capital. With two of his daughters worryingly ill with measles, he hardly noticed what was going on in the outside world. He was informed that there had been virtually no organised resistance to the uprising: even his own Imperial Guards had defected. Realising that defeat was inevitable, the Tsar gave up his throne.

With the abdication a void opened up at the heart of Russia – a void which even the peasants and the soviets believed had to be filled by a traditional kind of leader. Supporters of the Revolution called for a new republic – but a republic that had a 'strong Tsar' at the head of it. The title had come adrift from its imperial moorings, and seemed to have turned into a myth of heroic sovereignty: the people envisaged an elected ruler, embodying the will and character of Russia and its people.[21]

Such a man was standing by. The void left by the abdication drew into itself the one man who had the position, the charisma and the will to take on the role of inspirational figurehead. Moura noticed him too.

Alexander Kerensky came out of the soviets, but he was not a worker. He was a lawyer, a fervent socialist, a spellbinding orator and an ambitious politician. He was also vain, eccentric and a renowned philanderer. He was born in 1881, in the same provincial city as Lenin (their fathers were acquainted). Despite him being a decade younger, Kerensky's career advanced quicker. While Lenin was still ideologically locked inside the furnace of red-hot, uncompromising Bolshevism (and physically stranded in Switzerland), Alexander Kerensky was the coming man of the new revolutionary age.

His rise was rapid. As vice-chairman of the Petrograd Soviet, Kerensky was invited to join the new Provisional Government – the first of a succession of unstable coalitions that would rule Russia during the optimistic springtime and stormy summer that followed the first revolution. As the coalitions struggled to retain their grip, Kerensky rose from Minister of Justice (in which office he abolished capital punishment and restored civil order) to Minister of War. By the summer he had gained the premiership and taken up residence in the Winter Palace.

In appearance he cut an unprepossessing figure, with prim, pallid features, his hair austerely cropped and bristled; as Minister of War, he took to wearing the uniform of a common soldier (albeit exquisitely cut). But in him was a fire. A British vice-consul who saw him speak at the Bolshoi Theatre in Moscow (a popular venue for revolutionary speeches) witnessed his overpowering oratory: even the wealthy were hypnotised by his 'gospel of suffering' in a speech that lasted two hours and called for self-sacrifice and support for the troops at the front and for the poor workers:

He raised his eyes to the balcony boxes, while with fierce staccato sentences he lashed himself into a passion . . .

As he finished his peroration, he sank back exhausted into the arms of his aide-de-camp. In the limelight his face had the pallor of death. Soldiers assisted him off the stage, while in a frenzy of hysteria the whole audience rose and cheered itself hoarse . . . A millionaire's wife threw her pearl necklace on to the stage. Every woman present followed her example, and a hail of jewellery descended from every tier of the huge house. In the box next to me, General Wogak, a man who had served the Tsar all his life and who hated the revolution as a pest, wept like a child.[22]

History has forgotten the precise circumstances that brought Moura into contact with Kerensky. Perhaps it was through his wife Olga, who was a nursing volunteer in the war hospital. Or it might have been at the British Embassy, where Moura had many friends, and where Kerensky was frequently a guest of Sir George Buchanan. Whatever the circumstances, as the balance of power shifted, Moura eyed her chances, and made her move. While the nation draped the mantle of a Russian Bonaparte around Kerensky's shoulders, and while her husband Djon was still away at the war, Moura turned the irresistible force of her personality upon the new premier, and became his lover.

It was discreetly done, and only the most inveterate society gossips got wind of it, unlike Kerensky's other dalliance at the time, his wife's cousin Lilya, who lived openly with him in the Winter Palace.[23] Kerensky loved Moura, but there was good reason for discretion on both sides: he suspected that she was working for British intelligence.[24] He may have had good reason.

In Petrograd in 1917 there existed a small group of Russians who were sympathetic to Germany. Some were merely fond of German things, but others supported Germany in the war. All were regarded as potential traitors. Brought together by German secret service agents, they gathered to discuss their politics in the salon of a sympathetic lady known only as 'Madame B'. This woman, it would seem, was none other than Moura Benckendorff. She spoke German fluently, knew many Germans from her years in Berlin, and had a penchant for societies and politics (she and Djon were active in a similar Anglo-Russian society).

But what neither the German agents nor the pro-German Russians knew was that Madame B was working for Kerensky's counter-espionage department, and was reporting secretly on her guests' discussions and activities. Naturally enough, but perhaps not entirely to Kerensky's liking, British intelligence took an interest in Madame B, and one of their agents – Captain George Hill – attended one of her salons. Hill was well acquainted with Moura, and later became a good friend, as well as an associate in espionage work.[25] Here, perhaps, is t explanation for the persistent rumours that Moura was a German spy, and the reason that her acquaintances in the British intelligence and diplomatic services seem never to have taken those rumours seriously. They knew she was double-crossing the Germans.

In Kerensky's eyes, Moura's fondness for her British friends must have hinted at a double or triple purpose in her affair. Seduced and spied upon, Kerensky didn't seem to mind. This was Moura's great talent, a gift she would perfect through constant practice: the ability to play one side against the other, and gain advantage for herself; to commit treachery and make the betrayed love and forgive her. For Moura, the wages of sin was survival.

But she hadn't yet perfected either her arts or her wits, and wasn't aware of the miscalculation she had made. As Kerensky's oratory went on, while Moura looked to her own survival and her own pleasure, the war continued, and so did the shortages. Peace had returned to the streets of Petrograd, but contentment hadn't. Kerensky's charisma was a currency that would yield ever thinner returns as 1917 progressed. In the meantime, Moura lived on the interest.

Her social circle remained as active as ever, with dinner parties and evenings at the opera and theatre, where productions went on playing to packed houses of the rich while the poor continued to starve. Along with other women of her class – the wise ones, at least – she had modified her appearance. Fine dresses with exquisite millinery and accessories were out; in came plainer couture, or even proletarian drab and headscarves – at least while in the city. To be a wealthy aristocrat might still be acceptable (just about), but to look like one in public was not.

One thing that didn't change was the annual social cycle: late in the summer Moura and the children left Petrograd and set out for Yendel once more.

A burst of shrieking laughter drifted in through the open window – male and female voices suddenly raised in scandalised hilarity somewhere below. Moura glanced out to see what the fuss was about. It wasn't right that there should be entertainment going on without her at the centre of it.

Yendel had changed since she last looked through this window. The estate had gone through its seasonal transformation. The frozen acres had melted into expanses of rolling field and meadow, hazy under the summer sun; ice sheets had become placid lakes, and the chilling forests were now shady, fragrant pine-woods.

And yet, no matter what the seasons did, Yendel no longer had quite the same old ease. To the west, the war front crept ever closer as the Germans forced the Russians back, and in the port of Reval there was unrest among the Russian sailors, who had caught the bug of Bolshevism and were trying to spread it to their British allies.

Unable to see where the laughter was coming from, Moura wrapped her peignoir about herself and went down to investigate. She found most of her guests sitting on the terrace, surrounded by the detritus of a late breakfast – the women in déshabillé, the men in shirt sleeves, some still in pyjamas and dressing gowns. Yendel was never a place to stand on formality: not while Moura presided over it.

They all looked up when she appeared. There was Captain Francis Cromie, the British submarine commander, whose flotilla was harboured at Reval and whose heart harboured a particular dedication to Moura. He was a handsome man, with a square jaw and soulful eyes, and a brave sailor – the scourge of German shipping in the Baltic – but Moura managed to resist him. Meriel Buchanan was there, of course, along with Miriam and the aptly named Baroness Fairy Schilling, a pretty, racy young thing. Also visiting was Edward Cunard, of the shipping family, who held a post as secretary at the British Embassy. Finally, there was young Denis Garstin, a cavalry subaltern who worked in the British Propaganda Mission. He was a budding writer, and had been brought into propaganda by his friend Hugh Walpole.[26] Denis was a bright, lively, optimistic fellow, despite being a veteran of the battles of Loos and Ypres. An idealist, he was excited by the Revolution; he believed it had been caused by the war and was 'the greatest thing in the history of our times':

> The Revolution has raised the level of the war and of our ideals, and restrained all tendency to imperialism, so that the ideals we began to fight for, and forgot, have become our declared peace terms – universal democracy.[27]

Moura was fond of Denis, and called him 'Garstino' because of his literary pretensions. Cromie was simply 'Crow'.

Last night they had all picnicked by the light of a huge bonfire in the woods and sat watching the sparks fly upwards into the dark canopy.[28] Now they were ready for more fun. Meriel had suggested bathing in the lake. Edward had protested that he and Denis had no bathing costumes: they could hardly swim naked, could they? *Yes!* insisted the party unanimously, causing the hilarity and indignant protests that had drawn Moura from her bed. The young men's modesty was preserved by Baroness Schilling, who found them suitable costumes. 'Our virtue is safe!' said Denis. 'What a good Fairy!'

While youth disported itself in the glittering lake, Moura noticed her mother-in-law, also drawn by the sounds of laughter and rumours of indecency, patrolling nearby, looking for evidence of scandalous behaviour. As dowager, she had her own small house on the estate, on the far edge of the lake. (The house took its name from the lake: Kallijärv.) She had a low opinion of her son's disreputable wife – a harlot indulging herself in naked fornication while poor Djon was away at the war. Discovering that the guests were neither naked nor fornicating, the old lady went away disappointed.

The days of summer 1917 – the last golden summer of the old imperial age – were dwindling. Soon it would be time to return to Petrograd. Even for Moura the city had lost some of its attraction. Making the most of Yendel, they relished every drop of pleasure. As well as midnight picnics and morning swims, there were rides on a *liniaker*, a precarious cart with a single plank seat on which one sat with arms around the waist of the person in front; Denis was tickled by Fairy's hysterical wails at the jolting ride, which startled the poor horse into going even faster. They spent nights in Reval, the sleepy little port city, with its golden-domed cathedral and ancient streets of crooked houses, all huddled around the fortified naval port. Signs of war and revolutionary fervour were present even in this quaint corner. There was fervour of another kind too, if Denis Garstin was to be believed – he teased Cromie about his infatuation with Moura, sitting aboard his submarine, all duty forgotten, sighing over his unrequited Russian love.

It was all in stark contrast to the strife they had left behind in Petrograd, and the bitter conflict on the German front. One by one, the guests went back to their regular lives. Before he left, 'Garstino' set down some doggerel verses about his time at Yendel, concluding:

Oh God. And I must take a train
And go to Petrograd again,
And while I deal out propaganda
My nicer thoughts will all meander
Back, back to Yendel, oh to be
In Yendel for eternity.[29]

It was an idyll that couldn't last. One year later, the optimistic Denis Garstin would be dead, killed in action on the north Russian shore. The lovelorn Francis Cromie would also be in his grave, cut down in a savage gunfight while defending the British Embassy from Bolshevik raiders.

When summer faded to autumn, Moura returned to Petrograd. Kerensky's grip on power was becoming more tenuous with each passing day. The coming man of the new era had turned out to be merely a man for a passing season; throughout the summer months there had been sporadic Bolshevik uprisings, increasingly frequent and ever more violent.

Kerensky took strong measures against his enemies, but it was too late: many of his former supporters had gone over to the Bolsheviks, who had become a cohesive force under the inspirational guidance of Lenin and Trotsky. Revolutionaries were arrested, their newspapers were suppressed, but Kerensky had lost control of the situation. People were starving, they were sick of the war that he had insisted on continuing; they were no longer charmed by his oratory or his charisma.

The soviets had become militarised, and on 25 October they struck. Bridges and key points throughout Petrograd were seized, and the Winter Palace, where Kerensky had set up his office and his home, came under attack. Kerensky went into hiding, from which he tried to muster an armed resistance to the Bolshevik forces. His known associates in Petrograd began to be arrested, and those who escaped were hunted down.[30]

Moura was not among them – her discretion had spared her that. But it was clear that she had made the wrong choice. The wolves were running again, and Russia's second great revolution had unseated the mount she had chosen to run with.

Nothing would ever be the same again.

3

Red Winter

December 1917–January 1918

Two Christmases came that year, and neither was a happy one.

A horse-drawn cab drove through the Admiralteysky district, heading towards the Palace Quay. The *izvozchik* kept his malnourished horse to as fast a pace as it could manage; it wasn't safe to be on the streets at any time, let alone after dark, but a fare was a fare. Horses and drivers were starving for want of trade, and like every other soul in this blighted city who looked like they might have a few roubles on them, *izvozchiki* were prey to the robbers and murderers that roamed everywhere. At the bridges and street corners, little groups of soldiers sat warming themselves around braziers, but they did little to keep order. The mob was the law.[1]

Inside the cab, Moura looked out at the familiar streets. How many times she had passed through them in cars, carriages and cabs, or strolled gaily in the summer along the avenues, in the shadow of the Winter Palace and the dome of St Isaac's. All secure within the great apparatus of the imperium; the web of aristocracy, ringed around by splendour and military might. She had never thought it could all come to this – a shabby cab rattling through haunted streets. The golden pinnacles were still there, and the Palladian buildings gleaming under the night sky, but the life was gone.

Sitting beside Moura, lost in his unhappy thoughts, was Djon, her husband home from the war, probably for good this time. The Bolsheviks had agreed a ceasefire with the Germans in November, and negotiated a temporary armistice to be maintained until January 1918. In the meantime, peace talks were under way at Brest-Litovsk in Poland.* Already

---

* Now part of Belarus.

there was discord among the Bolsheviks. Their leader, Lenin, wanted a quick end to the war, to hasten the consolidation of the Revolution, but the majority of the Central Committee, including Trotsky, People's Commissar for Foreign Affairs, were pressing for a plan to renew the fighting, engage the sympathies of the German proletariat, and spread revolution throughout western Europe.[2]

Djon's patriotic heart was breaking, torn three ways by the war and the Revolution. He had ties to Germany through his diplomatic past, as well as through the long and cosmopolitan ancestry of the Benckendorffs, but he had been a true Russian all his life, utterly loyal to the Tsar. At the same time, he fretted for the future of his native Estonia, caught between the two great powers. Would it continue under the Bolsheviks, or be ceded to Germany, or would it achieve its independence?

For Moura, the main effect of the armistice was to force her to be in Djon's company far more than was comfortable. Filled with angst, shorn of the advantages of his rank, his position and his opulent lifestyle, he was daily becoming a less and less congenial spouse. There was friction, tension, frequent arguments.

Petrograd looked bleak now, not like the magical city it had once seemed. A place of confinement. There was no excitement here any more, only fear, and no chance of seeking fun and fulfilment elsewhere. There would be no more Christmases at Yendel for Moura and her friends. It had become dangerous there. Just a few weeks ago, with the family still in residence, the estate had come under attack.[3]

It was a terrifying experience. In the wake of the October Revolution, the fierce spirit of Bolshevism had run here and there throughout the Russian Empire, resisted in some places, catching hold in many more. One of the places it caught fire with a vengeance was Estonia. Armed gangs roamed the countryside, looting and terrorising. At Yendel, a band of peasants – those people who had been little more to the Benckendorffs than a faceless labour force and a malodorous, sheepskin-clad presence in the railway stations – came to the manor house seeking blood and booty. Moura, terrified for the lives of her children, gathered them to her, and with the mob marching up the drive, fled the house.

On that occasion, the peasants didn't attack the house itself. They stopped at the estate farm, whose imposing stable blocks, barns and piggeries straddled one branch of the roadway. There they set abou stealing the horses and cows and vandalising anything they couldn't take. Moura and the children hid in the gardens for five hours, freezing, listening to the shrieking of the pigs as they were slaughtered in their sties.

The idyll of Yendel was gone forever.

Fear was everywhere. There was anarchy in the countryside and crime on the city streets. But real terror came now from the state. Common Russians had always had reason to fear their government, but this was different. This time it was the bourgeoisie who had most cause for dread. With the country in a state of civil war, the Bolsheviks organised their state with astonishing speed, taking over the existing bureaucracy and purging its upper ranks of untrustworthy individuals. The Red Army, composed of the old regiments, likewise purged of unsympathetic officers, was almost instantly fit to take on and beat the scattered White monarchist forces. By early December the Bolsheviks had a political security police mobilised. Its full name was the All-Russian Extraordinary Commission for Combating Counter-revolution and Sabotage. It immediately became known by the shorter name 'Cheka',* and its officers known as Chekists, names which soon became bywords for terror.

The same decree that created the Cheka also brought in a requirement for all wealthy citizens to be registered.[4] The dispossession of the ruling and landed classes was beginning. The foresighted among them began hiding their treasures. Most, though, still failed to see the full enormity of the downfall that was coming to them. For the time being, they still enjoyed what little remnants of pleasure and dignity they could salvage. They braved the streets to shop, paying stupendous prices for everything, and often getting robbed within minutes of making any purchase.[5] They even ventured out at night to visit one another for dinner parties, their loyal servants scraping together what dishes they could from the meagre supplies, and stoically put up with the almost constant electricity failures.

Moura and Djon's cab turned onto the Palace Quay. Lights could be seen shining in the windows of the British Embassy – the electricity was working tonight; a happy omen, perhaps. Sir George Buchanan was giving a Christmas reception for the hundred or so staff and attachés of the Embassy, as well as for a select group of close Russian friends who

---

* Contraction of *chrezvychaynaya komissiya*, 'extraordinary commission'.

had not yet fled the country. Moura and Djon von Benckendorff were among them.

It was a poignantly British affair, marking Christmas on the day it would fall in Britain – which was 12 December here. This was Sir George's way of bidding farewell to the country that had been his beloved second home for the past seven years. It had been a triumph, being given the Petrograd posting,[6] but now it looked like it could be the death of him. He had always appeared frail, but now he was really unwell – 'hopelessly worn out', Denis Garstin thought.[7] The stress of being thrust into the impossibly difficult position of having to represent the British government to the hostile Bolsheviks had driven him to a physical breakdown a couple of weeks ago, and he had applied for home leave. He was a broken man, whose mind no longer functioned properly.[8] But he continued his work in the meantime and did his duty as host.

Most of Moura's close friends were there – Miriam Artsimovich and her fiancé, Bobby Yonin. Francis Cromie was present, despite being on alert over his submarine flotilla, still based at Reval (but not for much longer). Denis Garstin was there – 'Garstino', still busy in the propaganda office and still bright and cheerful despite the Bolsheviks having knocked flat a good deal of his enthusiasm for the socialist cause. And of course there was Meriel. She was distraught, knowing very well that when her father took up his leave in the New Year, they would be leaving Russia for good, and she was holding back her tears.[9]

It was a strange evening, and a melancholy party, despite the concert and variety entertainment that had been laid on. The electricity held out, and the chandeliers blazed all night. There was a sit-down supper consisting of dishes miraculously conjured from virtually nothing by Sir George's Italian cook, supplemented by tins of bully beef. There was dancing, lively conversation and laughter among the guests, who were determined to enjoy themselves, but the constant atmosphere of tension pervaded everything; all the attachés had loaded pistols in their pockets, and there were rifles and boxes of cartridges hidden in the chancery offices. Mobs had looted the Winter Palace again earlier that month, and there were fears that any social gathering could turn into a bloody siege in an instant. Meriel would recall later that 'for the moment we tried to forget the ever-present lurking danger, the sadness of approaching good-byes, the desolation and want hidden behind the heavy red brocade curtains'.[10]

When the evening drew towards its close, the British officers sang

'God Save the King'. The Russians were deeply moved; one man turned to Meriel with tears in his eyes. 'You don't know what it means to hear your men sing that,' he said, 'while we Russians have no emperor and no country left.'[11] When the song was over, Bobby Yonin sat at the piano, and the room filled with the slow, insistent opening chords of '*Bozhe, Tsarya khrani*',* the Russian national anthem. A hush fell. Meriel glanced across at Moura and her husband. Djon's face was drawn with such anguish, Meriel's self-control gave way at last, and she cried.[12]

Christmas Day

In England it was January now, but in Russia it was the 25th of December, the day appointed for the British departure from Petrograd.

There had been a fresh fall of snow in the night, and the embassy motor cars made heavy going of the short drive to the Finland station in the pre-dawn light. To Meriel's eyes, depressed and grief-stricken, the station looked grubby and bleak. This was the place where Lenin had famously arrived when he returned from his exile in Switzerland to begin fomenting the great revolution. From here the trains ran to the north, into Finland. The British were going home by the overland route which avoided the dangerous German-infested waters of the Baltic.

Just a handful were leaving today – the Buchanans, the heads of the military and naval missions, General Knox and Admiral Stanley, and a few of their attachés – and the Embassy would continue to exist, after a fashion, but without an ambassador. There was an atmosphere of defeat, a hauling-down of the flag.

A group of the Buchanans' friends came to see them off, including Denis Garstin, Francis Cromie and other members of the British missions who were staying behind. William the chasseur, who had driven the motor, was also remaining at the Embassy to manage its domestic staff. When Miss Buchanan gave him her hand, he couldn't speak for emotion. Only three Russian friends had come – Moura was one, along with Miriam and Bobby. Most Russians were too scared to venture out on the streets or be seen publicly in company with the British Ambassador.[13] Passing by the scowling Red Guard sentries at the station entrance, Sir George and Meriel both wondered if they would make it safely to Finland.

---

* God Save the Tsar.

Commissar for Foreign Affairs Leon Trotsky, with whom Sir George had suffered an extremely uneasy relationship during the past few months, had refused to reserve accommodation for them on the train. Sir George donated two bottles of his best Napoleon brandy to the station master, and sleeping berths were duly provided. Some things never changed, and the preciousness of brandy to a Russian was one of them.

For Moura, the departure of her friends marked the end of an era. Her upbringing by Micky had given her a powerful affinity with the British; she was at ease with the language and strongly attached to her British friends. When she embraced Meriel, both their faces were wet with tears, and Meriel didn't trust herself to speak. It was bitterly hard for Moura to see her mother country throwing away its cordial relationship with Britain, entering into a dark period of mistrust and hostility.

There would no longer be an ambassador in Petrograd, but the Embassy would be kept in place, managed by Francis Lindley, counsellor under Sir George since 1915 and now chargé d'affaires. The British government, unable to condone what it saw as the Bolsheviks' treason, was breaking off its official diplomatic links. However, it was maintaining a semi-official presence. A new man was coming out from London to be Britain's 'unofficial agent' in Russia, whose task it would be to conduct diplomacy with Trotsky and the Bolsheviks. He was a gifted young fellow who had been a consul in Moscow until last summer, when he'd been sent home by Sir George after a scandalous affair with a French Jew, Madame Vermelle.[14] Now, on the instructions of Prime Minister David Lloyd George, he was being sent back to Petrograd. His name was Lockhart.

Moura might have been conscious of an era coming to an end, but what she didn't know was that a new one – the most profoundly important of her life – was about to begin.

It took time for the new socialist era to arrive.

Through the winter, as the revolutionary year of 1917 gave way to the new Bolshevist year of 1918, the place of the aristocrats and the bourgeoisie remained in a state of limbo while the Bolsheviks focused on consolidating their grip on the country and arguing over what was to be done about Germany. The expropriation of lands had begun in the autumn, and most of the great country estates were now in the hands of the government, but private homes and personal wealth were still largely untouched. That would all change during the coming year.[15]

Moura Benckendorff, all but alone now in Petrograd, began reverting to her core instinct – self-preservation. With the departure of so many of her friends, Djon back in her life, and no influence in the government, Moura was at her lowest. Her marriage was all but dead. There were political differences between Djon and Moura, as well as emotional ones. The earnest, sentimentally patriotic Djon mourned the loss of the Tsar, who was now living under house arrest in Tobolsk, Siberia, with the rest of the former imperial family. Moura, though she regretted the passing of her luxurious lifestyle, knew, like her father had, that the old system was corrupt and had brought about its own fall. Like many of her generation, she was in favour of democratic socialism.

Moura and Djon argued frequently during those months after the Revolution, but how much of it was politics and how much was Moura's personal frustration and dissatisfaction with the dull confines of her new life was impossible to say.

Having been betrayed by Russia, Djon von Benckendorff took refuge in his mother country. Estonia was socialist, and Yendel was vulnerable to the roaming gangs, but it was no more dangerous than Petrograd now, and Djon had close family there. What was more, with the balance of the peace negotiations tilted heavily in Germany's favour, he hoped that Estonia might become independent, or at least be absorbed into monarchist Germany. Djon went to Yendel and settled down to make his life there.

Moura was torn. Her life was in Petrograd. Her elderly mother was here, still living in the Zakrevsky apartment and no longer healthy enough to travel. What remnants Moura had of a social life were here. She had retained a British connection – and some personal independence – by taking a position as an interpreter at the Embassy. (Whispers soon began, suggesting that there was more to her role there than translating; her reputation for espionage continued to cling to her. But nothing was ever known for certain.) Most important, her children were here.

As the new year began to unfold, Moura discovered an unexpected distraction from her troubles. At least, that was how it looked to begin with – a trifle, an entertaining diversion. She had no idea of the unfamiliar paths the diversion would lead to. Moura, who would do almost anything to survive, was on the brink of her most dangerous gamble, and an affair that would alter the course of her life. The woman for whom self-interest was paramount was about to discover self-sacrifice.

4

The British Agent

January–February 1918

17 January 1918

There was a dead horse frozen into the snow near the corner where the Palace Quay opened onto the Troitskiy Bridge. It looked like it had been there for days. Lockhart regarded it despondently as he was driven past under the loom of the street-lamps. The poor beast pulling the sleigh that had brought him and his companions from the Finland station looked as if it too was on the brink of collapse. It was the same everywhere – the horses bone-thin, the people depressed, and the snow piling up on the roadways so that even the sleighs had heavy going.[1]

Lockhart had been back in Russia less than a day and already he felt disheartened. This wasn't the Petrograd he had last seen in the summer, when Kerensky was still struggling to hold down the lid on the soviets. Lockhart had been acting consul-general in Moscow at the time, an unusually elevated post for a man who wasn't yet thirty. But then Robert Hamilton Bruce Lockhart was an unusual man.

He was an adventurer, in the Victorian mould, the kind who shaped the British Empire. A Scotsman born into an ancient lineage of Scotsmen, Lockhart claimed proudly that he had 'no drop of English blood' in his veins.[2] A man of daring, acute intelligence, charisma, skilled equally with a pen or a revolver, he had at least one debilitating weakness – women. He was capable of ruining himself over them. In his youth, a promising career in Malaya had been compromised by his involvement with the beautiful – and married – ward of a sultan. Forced to part from her, Lockhart wrote her pages of poems that ached with longing and regret.[3]

In 1912 he was given a post as a vice-consul in Moscow. He took to Russia with prodigious enthusiasm, bathing himself in its culture and gorgeous language. He was also drawn into the seedier nightlife of the capital. In 1914, on a rash impulse, he returned to England and married a young Australian woman called Jean Turner, and brought her back to Moscow to live with him. While she struggled to adapt, Lockhart continued with his career, becoming immersed in the diplomatic and intellectual life of Moscow and Petrograd. He grew close to Moscow's liberal elite, especially Mikhail Chelnokov, the Mayor of Moscow, who was a vital source of intelligence on the thinking of Russia's progressive politicians. He fed his literary cravings on Tolstoy, and on the company of living writers like Hugh Walpole (who later took up a post in the Embassy's propaganda section) and Maxim Gorky. Lockhart's career was moving upward; he gradually became a favourite of Sir George Buchanan, and his perceptive reports on Russian life and politics were noticed by both the Foreign Office and the intelligence service.[4]

As in Malaya, it was his taste for thrills and women that was his undoing. Having tried hard to curtail his disreputable socialising after his marriage, he was eventually sucked back into it. He was too fond of the night-restaurants where gypsy music played and the atmosphere was rich with sensual promise. Madame Vermelle wasn't his first sexual liaison, nor even his first with a married woman. But it was the first of his affairs to reach the ears of Sir George. In early September 1917, to forestall a scandal, the Ambassador regretfully sent young Lockhart home on 'sick leave'.[5]

Six weeks later, while Lockhart was dividing his time between writing reports on Russia's political situation for the Foreign Office and relaxing on his uncle's Highland estate, the October Revolution exploded.

The British government, appalled by the treasonous behaviour of the Russian lower orders, and dreading that Russia would withdraw from the war, didn't know what to do. Within the circles of the Foreign Office and the War Cabinet, the detailed and percipient reports written by Mr R. H. Bruce Lockhart attracted notice, and he was called upon to elaborate, and to give his opinion on future actions. Should His Britannic Majesty's Government maintain contact with the Bolsheviks? Criminal insurrectionists they might be, but they were now the *de facto* government of Russia. What was to be done?

During December 1917 Lockhart was dined, courted and interrogated by scores of politicians and diplomats. Then, on the last Friday before Christmas, he was summoned to 10 Downing Street.[6] He was accompanied by a gathering of experts on Russia, including intelligence officers Colonel H. F. Byrne and Colonel John Buchan.[7] They were taken to the Cabinet Room, where a meeting of the War Cabinet had just ended. Ministers were standing about, chatting. Prime Minister David Lloyd George, looking old and tired but still fizzing with energy, was standing by the window, arguing with Lord Curzon (whom he famously despised), and gesticulating with his pince-nez. When Lockhart was presented, the Prime Minister peered at him intently. 'Mr Lockhart? *The* Mr Lockhart?' Everyone in the room turned to stare. 'From the wisdom of your reports, I expected an elderly gentleman with a grey beard!' While Lockhart stood there feeling self-conscious and looking foolish, the PM patted him on the back. 'Pitt was prime minister when he was younger than you are,' he said, and invited the ex-consul to a chair.

The Welshman and the Scotsman, with no drop of English blood between them, sat down to business.

Lloyd George could see what most members of his Cabinet (many of whom sat in on the interview) could not. Great Britain must negotiate with the Bolsheviks. There were men present who resisted the idea in the strongest terms. The Bolsheviks were not to be trusted, they said. Lord Robert Cecil, the Under-Secretary of State for Foreign Affairs, was leader of a large and vocal faction who insisted that the Bolshevik Revolution was a German plot to knock Russia out of the war. Trotsky, it was rumoured, was in fact a German agent. Was he not at this moment with the Germans, negotiating an end to the war? Why, there was even said to be secret intelligence evidence *proving* that Trotsky was working for the German government.

The Prime Minister didn't believe it, and neither did Lockhart. Sweeping aside all opposition, Lloyd George rose to his feet and delivered his judgement. Russia was in chaos, he declared, and whatever else happened, it was essential that the British get in touch with Lenin and Trotsky. Such a mission would require tact, knowledge and understanding. 'Mr Lockhart,' he said, 'is obviously a man whose right place at this moment is in St Petersburg and not in London.'

And on that, he brought the meeting to an end.[8]

They had their man, but it took time, and many more meetings, to decide what his duties were to be. Lockhart could be given no official authority. The situation was far too delicate. Officially, the British government was diplomatically incommunicado with the Bolshevik government. Therefore Lockhart was to be Britain's 'unofficial agent' in Petrograd. He would be head of a mission, with a small staff under him, but he would have no powers, no authority. All he could do was attempt to talk to Lenin and Trotsky – to open up communication, in secret and entirely off the record. It was quite likely that they would refuse to recognise him or grant him the proper diplomatic privileges. On the face of it, Lockhart was being put in an impossible situation.

In the days before his departure, he met with another man in an impossible situation – Maxim Litvinov, the Bolshevik Ambassador to Great Britain. Litvinov was a bewildered man. He had been residing in exile in London at the time of the Revolution, and had been startled to hear of his ambassadorial appointment through the newspapers.[9] He was not officially recognised by Britain, had no staff and no proper embassy (surreally, the old Russian Embassy and Consulate were still carrying on as if the Revolution hadn't happened). Accordingly, his meeting with Lockhart was held over lunch in a Lyons' Corner House.[10]

The two men were joined by British intelligence expert Rex Leeper (who had been at the Downing Street meeting) and the Russian journalist Theodore Rothstein. A socialist radical, Rothstein hated British capitalism but feared German militarism more.[11] He had a lively, quixotic temperament, and helped the meeting run cordially. There, on the Lyons' luncheon table, Litvinov obligingly wrote Lockhart a letter of introduction to Trotsky: 'I know him personally,' he wrote, stretching the truth in his eagerness to oblige, 'as a thoroughly honest man who understands our position and sympathises with us.' In the same letter Litvinov pleaded with Trotsky for a bit of proper support for himself, and for his telegrams to be replied to; it was difficult to be a diplomat when even one's own government acted as if one didn't exist. The letter completed, the four men resumed their lunch. Studying the dessert menu, the Russian was delighted to see 'diplomat pudding' listed; he ordered it, only to be told that it was all gone. Litvinov shrugged philosophically. 'Not recognised even by Lyons,' he sighed.[12]

With the letter in his pocket, Lockhart journeyed up to Scotland to take ship for the first leg of his voyage. It was a new and rather exciting experience. His journey home from Russia in September had been modest and even a little ignominious; his return, with his new status and vitally important mission, was entirely different. He would be sailing for

Norway aboard a specially tasked Royal Navy cruiser with two destroyers as escort.

His wife Jean came to Queensferry to see him off. She had accompanied him to Russia once, but even had it been safe, she wouldn't do it a second time. Their relationship was not a happy one, and Lockhart felt guilty for having married her; whether one looked at it financially, romantically or morally, the poor woman had got a bad bargain.[13]

Just three companions – his mission team – were going with him aboard HMS *Yarmouth*. Captain William Hicks had been to Petrograd before as an adviser to the Russian army on poison gas. He was charming, a good linguist, and knew the people and politics of Russia. He also had a background in intelligence, attached to the staff of Colonel Byrne.[14] 'Hickie' would become Lockhart's closest companion in the trials of the coming months – 'a most loyal colleague and devoted friend'.[15] Also going with him were Moscow businessman Edward Birse as the mission's commercial expert, and Edward Phelan, a young civil servant from the Ministry of Labour. More staff would be seconded from the Embassy in Petrograd, but for now, these four men were the entirety of the British mission.

One member of the party was missing. Lockhart had been provided with an orderly to help manage his diplomatic ciphers, a huge Irish guardsman who was perpetually drunk and had offered to fight Lockhart in Princes Street for half a crown. He had disappeared somewhere between Edinburgh and Queensferry, and wasn't missed.

In a brilliant Scottish dawn, the *Yarmouth* weighed anchor and, with her two destroyers leading the way, began steaming slowly down the Forth estuary past the massed lines of the Royal Navy's battle fleet. Lockhart, recalling his childhood, imbued with the tales of Robert Louis Stevenson, felt a thrill at the onset of what promised to be a great adventure.

Had he known that it was an adventure that might be the death of him, he might have felt differently. But he would undoubtedly still have gone – he was that kind of man.

After a harrowing voyage through a mountainous North Sea, during which even veteran seamen were sick, the *Yarmouth* struggled up the fjord to Bergen in a snowstorm. There Lockhart was reunited briefly with Sir George Buchanan. It was just over a week since the former Ambassador and his party had left Petrograd, and they had been waiting some time for the *Yarmouth* to arrive and take them back to Britain. Sir George was pleased to see his former favourite, but he was tired and ill (ten months of revolution had aged him ten years, Lockhart reckoned) and the whole party were demoralised and dispirited.[16]

They were not the only refugees from Russia Lockhart encountered on his journey. As he and his three companions continued by land and sea through Norway, Sweden and Finland, more and more British expatriates were met making their way home, along with Russian aristocrats fleeing the Revolution. The hotels along the route were full to bursting.

The previously 'safe' route in and out of Russia, avoiding German forces, had itself become a war zone. The chaos of Russia was leaking into all its provinces and protectorates. Fighting between the Red and White forces of the Finns and the Russians was breaking out everywhere in the duchy of Finland. In Helsingfors* there was shooting in the streets. Lockhart and Hicks, having ventured out looking for accommodation for the night, found themselves caught up in a massacre – Red Russian sailors armed with machine guns were pursuing a fleeing mob, spraying the street with bullets. Lockhart and Hicks had to throw themselves onto the bloody snow among the corpses to avoid being cut down. Their British passports, together with Lockhart's letter from Litvinov, saved their lives when they were picked up and challenged, and bought them assistance from the local Red forces.

Even with official help the journey was tense and arduous. On the way from Helsingfors to Petrograd, a rail bridge had been half-destroyed, and the passengers were obliged to make their way across the precarious structure on foot, and board a second train on the far side.

By the time his party disembarked at Petrograd, Lockhart had lost some of his thirst for adventure. It wasn't the dangers that troubled him so much as the chaos and the air of doom and depression. He had always felt, long before the Revolution, that there was a cold greyness hiding behind the beautiful façade of Petrograd, even in summer – 'Beneath its lovely exterior,' he wrote, 'its heart was chill.'[17]

There was certainly a bitter cold here now. Lockhart looked gloomily at the dead horse in the bank of snow by the corner of the Troitskiy Bridge as the sledge slowed to a halt in front of the British Embassy. Petrograd had become a place of death.

---

* Now Helsinki.

His first visit had been in 1915, summoned by Sir George to report on the huge anti-German riots that had broken out in Moscow in June that year. He was acting consul-general at the time, and came to Petrograd with a mixture of excitement and trepidation, fearful of being held in some way responsible for the riots, but thrilled to be noticed by the Ambassador. In those days, few people had imagined that revolution could come to Russia. Lockhart had been one of the few. He saw the evidence everywhere, in the people's feelings about the Tsar, the Duma, and about the police who kept them in order. He reported to Sir George that there was widespread disgust at the Russian government, and the imperial family were growing ever more unpopular; a workers' uprising could not be ruled out.[18] By the middle of 1917 he had become a frequent visitor to the Embassy, trusted by Sir George and involved in diplomacy with Kerensky and his government. The mood had been different then, and many of the younger British men, filled with ideals about democracy and justice, believed that there was hope for the new Russia, rid of despotism, and soon to be rid of poverty and repression.

Just half a year on, and Russia was stained red with blood and Bolshevism, and everything looked very different. Lockhart, Captain Hicks, Birse and Phelan alighted from the sleigh, and while their luggage was fetched by the servants, they passed in through the rather modest-looking doorway in the grand façade, and mounted the imposing stairway that lay behind it.

For the time being, every department of Lockhart's life was dominated by diplomacy, including with his own side. Lockhart had feared that he might be resented by Francis Lindley, the chargé d'affaires who was nominally in charge now that there was no ambassador. But he was careful to consult Lindley about everything and treat him as if he were actually in charge. The embassy staff were divided into those who favoured recognising and doing business with the Bolsheviks, and those who were opposed – the 'recognitionists' and 'anti-recognitionists'. Lindley couldn't make up his mind which he was, and Whitehall had given him no official line to follow. None of that mattered much, of course, because neither Lindley nor any of his staff had any official contact with the Bolshevik government. That was Lockhart's job.

Trotsky was Lockhart's main concern, but the Commissar for Foreign Affairs was still away at Brest-Litovsk, failing to negotiate satisfactory peace terms with the Germans. Therefore Lockhart dealt initially with his stand-in, Georgy Chicherin, who suggested that with Russian–German relations going so badly, now would be a good time for Britain to extend a hand of friendship towards Russia. Always assuming, Chicherin added blandly, that Britain was willing to accept the great socialist International that was coming – the world revolution that would destroy the bourgeoisie for good.

The Bolsheviks had already decided on their diplomatic attitude to Britain, and lost no time publicising it, which made things exceptionally awkward for Lockhart. Having intended his mission to be discreet, off the record, and entirely secret, he was embarrassed to find himself being trumpeted in the Bolshevik press as Lloyd George's 'man of confidence'; he was said to be a politician of considerable influence at home, and wholly sympathetic to the Bolshevik cause. America's intelligence man in Russia (who had swallowed the preposterous fantasy that Trotsky was a German agent) reported to the US government that Lockhart was a dangerous revolutionary.[19]

This was pleasing to the Bolsheviks, but deeply uncomfortable for Lockhart. But at least it would have the advantage of obliging Lenin and Trotsky to meet him.

For the first week, Lockhart and his companions lodged with various members of the embassy staff. This wouldn't do, so he lost no time in taking an apartment; he found one in a grand mansion at 10 Palace Quay, just a hundred yards from the Embassy. It had a view of the river and the Petropavlovskaya fortress, and was large enough to serve as res-idence and headquarters of the Lockhart mission. The rent was peppercorn-cheap for such a lavish place; had he wished, he could have had a palace. Many of Petrograd's grand buildings stood empty, and their aristocratic owners were anxious to have them occupied and guarded against the mob.[20] The apartment also possessed a fine wine cellar, for which a good price was negotiated. And so the social life of the mission was catered for.

Its social and diplomatic lives were inseparable from each other. As he had done since his very earliest days in Russia, the British agent devoted his all to immersing himself in every source of knowledge. The British Embassy came equipped with a social network that extended beyond the British colony and into Russian society. Those members of the Russian ruling classes who had the courage to stay in Petrograd (or who had no option) were a valuable source of intelligence. They were able to give insights into the mind and mood of Russia, and a few even had some understanding of – and indeed an element of sympathy with – Bolshevism and its leaders.

One Sunday evening when Lockhart had been in Petrograd for just over a fortnight, Hicks brought a guest to dinner. A young Russian lady from a family of diplomats and aristocrats, she was very well known and popular among Petrograd's British community. Hicks had known her during his last period in Petrograd. Her name was Madame Maria von Benckendorff, though everybody knew her as Moura.

Robert Bruce Lockhart had always been susceptible to feminine charm, but Madame Benckendorff was something new and extraordinary in his experience. Recalling his first impression of her many years later, he was captivated all over again by the powerful allure she possessed. As with everyone else who knew her, the attraction for him was in her eyes, 'which in tranquillity looked like wells of melancholy and danced with merriment when she was amused'. To his mind her attractiveness surpassed that of all other Russian women of her era.[21]

For the present, though, Lockhart's mind was far too full with diplomacy and politics to take proper notice of Moura's physical attractions. The conversation over dinner that Sunday evening turned on Russia's peace negotiations with Germany.[22] Lockhart, having been struck by her looks, was impressed by Moura's intellect. As with the Moscow liberals – who had all been men – she knew the mood and temper of her country, and her opinion was hard currency to him.

Two days earlier, Lockhart had had his first meeting with Leon Trotsky. The People's Commissar for Foreign Affairs had just returned from Brest-Litovsk, where he had laid down a breathtaking and extremely rash challenge: since Germany would not moderate its territorial demands, no peace agreement could be reached. All discussion was over. And yet Russia would not be continuing the war; indeed, it would continue the process of demobilisation it had already begun. In other words, Russia was taking its ball and going home, and Germany could make up its own mind what to do about it. Trotsky was confident that the Germans would not dare go back on the offensive; their troops would lack the will. Both Germany and Austria-Hungary had recently been plagued by strikes, and Trotsky believed that the workers of the West were ripe for revolution. He assured the Central Committee accordingly, and in a speech to the Petrograd Soviet on the evening of 15 February,* he declared himself ninety per cent certain that Germany would not attack.[23]

Lockhart wasn't so sure; and neither was he wholly convinced by Trotsky's show of confidence. At that first meeting – which ran for two hours – he sensed that Trotsky was privately worried about the German reaction to his 'no peace, no war' declaration. For Lockhart, the man's anger at the way the Germans had humiliated him during the negotiations – flatly denying the Bolsheviks' terms and demanding great swathes of territory in return for peace – proved once and for all that Trotsky was not a German agent, no matter what some fools in Whitehall might think. He struck Lockhart as courageous, patriotic and enormously vain – 'a man who would willingly die fighting for Russia provided there was a big enough audience to see him do it'.[24]

But Trotsky's ire against the Germans was nothing compared to his anger against the British. In Lockhart's opinion, it had been a dreadful mistake to treat him as a criminal during his time in American exile. Kerensky had wanted him returned to Russia, but the British interned him in Canada first, stoking up his hostility and turning him away from the moderate Mensheviks and towards the Bolsheviks.[25] Sir George Buchanan had personally paid the price for this, forced to weather the storm of Trotsky's dislike. He had also contributed to it, by participating in the secret channelling of funds to the anti-Bolshevik Don Cossacks and communicating with their leader, Alexei Kaledin, a subterfuge which Trotsky learned about.[26] Buchanan had tried to resist implementing this policy (fearing violent reprisals against the British in Russia), but his hand had been forced by Whitehall. The fear and stress of the situation had contributed to his breakdown.

And now Lockhart was left with the result: a deeply suspicious and hostile Trotsky. In fact, he was less hostile than might have been expected – much of his anti-British talk was for public consumption.[27] Behind closed doors he was willing to put his feelings aside and do what was in Russia's interests – and for the time being that included talking to the British. But underneath, the anger was real, and would have repercussions as the spring and summer of 1918 unfolded. Clever as Lockhart

---

* Gregorian date. Russia had switched calendars on 31 January; the next day was 14 February.

was, taking on the combined cunning of Trotsky and Lenin might be a challenge too far.

For the time being, the question that blotted out all others was whether Russia would stay in the war – and if not, what sort of peace terms would be agreed. What would the Russian people do? What did they think? Lockhart was eager to hear any and all informed opinions on the subject, and so it dominated the conversation throughout that first dinner party with Hicks and Moura.

In the two days since Lockhart's meeting with Trotsky, there had been dramatic developments. On Saturday 16 February, the German government telegraphed the Russians that, in the absence of a peace agreement, hostilities would resume at noon on Monday. Lenin and Trotsky were shaken, but made no immediate move. Lenin – who had argued for peace all along – reminded Trotsky of their personal agreement whereby he must now accept Germany's peace terms. Trotsky brushed off the idea – he was still convinced that the Germans wouldn't actually attack.[28] Meanwhile, the news was kept absolutely secret from the Russian people; even the military weren't informed that they might have to start fighting again. On the Sunday evening – while Lockhart, Captain Hicks and Moura were discussing the very same subject – the Bolshevik Central Committee began a secret all-night debate.

By Monday morning there were already reports coming in of German military activity along the front line. Those who were wise enough to know what was going on were worried. Lockhart, who was now having daily meetings with Trotsky, noted in his diary that there was little hope of the Bolsheviks being able to resist the Germans. Russia might well be conquered, which would be a disaster for the Allies: 'Our number seems up,' he wrote. 'Trotsky says that even if Russia cannot resist she will indulge in partisan warfare to the best of her ability.'[29]

At noon on Monday, German forces began their attacks. The depleted Russian forces put up little resistance, and by the end of the week the German army had captured more ground than in the whole of the preceding three years.[30] Meanwhile, the terrified, confused Bolsheviks argued furiously among themselves. Lenin, fearing the destruction of Russia, the collapse of the Bolshevik regime, and the end of all hope for the Revolution, pushed for finding out what Germany's terms were and accepting them.

By Sunday 23 February the Germans had conquered most of the lands on Russia's western border, from the Ukraine to the Baltic. On that day they declared their terms: Russia must cede all the territory now in German hands. Moura was personally affected by the German offensive and by the peace terms – Estonia, the land of her husband, and of her beloved Yendel, was among the conquered territories.

That same evening, Moura again came to dinner at 10 Palace Quay, along with a group of friends. Her acquaintance with Mr Lockhart was becoming a constant. The British agent was deeply impressed by the young lady. Lockhart believed that Russian women were more courageous and 'superior in all respects' to their men. He admired Moura's mind and was affected by the magnetic charisma she possessed. She had languages – fluent English, French, Italian and German. 'She was not merely fascinating,' he would recall many years later; 'she was remarkably well read, highly intellectual, and wise beyond her years.' Lockhart was a man of his era, and couldn't resist adding that her wisdom was exceptional because 'unlike many clever women, she knew how to listen to the wisdom of men who had wisdom to dispense'.

But for Lockhart, as for so many others, she was more than all of this; the overriding impression of Moura, which followed her from her earliest youth to her oldest age, was simply expressed: 'Men adored her.'[31]

During those weeks of February and March 1918, while the world around them once more began bursting into flames, a bond started to grow between the British agent and the Russian lady. Moura had 'a lofty disregard for all the pettiness of life and a courage which was proof against all cowardice,' Lockhart observed. 'Her vitality . . . was immense and invigorated everyone with whom she came into contact.' The more he learned about her, the more he admired her. 'Where she loved, there was her world, and her philosophy of life had made her mistress of all the consequences. She was an aristocrat. She could have been a Communist. She could never have been a bourgeoise.' Their acquaintanceship began socially, and slowly, insensibly, became more intimate. 'During those first days,' he recalled, 'I was too busy, too preoccupied with my own importance, to give her more than a passing thought. I found her a woman of great attraction, whose conversation brightened my daily life.'[32]

She would become much more than that – infinitely more. For the time being, Lockhart and Moura made a little social heaven for themselves in the midst of the reigniting war and the gloom of the impoverished city.

5

'What Children We Were'

February–March 1918

The snow glowed a faint blue under the light of the waning moon.
All was still, not a soul about, just the silent light on the soft snow,
the star-dusted vault overhead, and the rare peace of the city at night.
Occasional gunshots could be heard in the distance, but otherwise it was
quiet.

Standing close, Moura and Lockhart looked back across the frozen
Neva at the lights glittering along the Palace Quay. The British Embassy
beside the Troitskiy Bridge, further along the Winter Palace. In between
stood the mansions where Lockhart had his flat and headquarters. The
lights were few, and in every shadow there was danger, but in their
memories they would recall moments like this as precious idylls.

It had become their practice, as the first weeks passed and the regular
dinner parties no longer provided enough of each other's company, to
take a sleigh and drive along the banks of the Neva.[1] They would go in
the evening, and head out across the bridges to the islands, where the city
sprawled out over the river delta – Vasilyevsky Island, where the university
and the stock exchange were, Krestovsky Island with its pleasure gardens
and yacht club, or the huge Petrogradsky Island, the city's original heart,
under whose shoulder nestled the Petropavlovskaya fortress.

All these places had been the playgrounds, institutions and residences
of the ruling classes for the past two hundred years, ever since Peter the
Great decided to build his port city here, on land wrested from the
Swedes. Hundreds of thousands of serfs had laid the roads, dug the
canals, laboured on the bridges and piled up the palaces and mansions,
and tens of thousands had died doing it. Now their descendants had
claimed it all back.

It could be dangerous to be out after dark. People with sense never went out alone, and they walked in the middle of the street to avoid alleys and doorways. Lockhart always carried a revolver in his pocket, with his hand constantly resting on its grip.[2] But these two young people had little regard for risk, Moura especially. Lockhart's ardent nature was getting the better of him, and he was capable of careering full-tilt to destruction for the sake of gratifying it. This woman fascinated and transfixed him.

Moura kept her thoughts and feelings to herself in those early weeks. Their sleigh-rides were moments of carelessness snatched from the political tide that was rising around them. But something was changing in her. She had never felt any particular devotion towards any man. Her fling with Engelhardt had meant little to her – the act of a stifled teenager yearning to escape. Kerensky had been a misjudged bid for survival. Djon she had married because he was a portal into the life of excitement and glamour she craved, but there had never been any depth of feeling; now she had reached a point where she felt contaminated by his touch. It was a relief when he fled to Estonia.

All the other handsome, dashing, attractive men who flocked around her had failed to snare her feelings. There were a few – Denis Garstin and Francis Cromie in particular – for whom she felt affection, but none inspired any romantic feeling, let alone love.

But this man, this Lockhart, with his rather prissy mouth and protruding ears, who described himself as 'broken-nosed, with a squat, stumpy figure and a ridiculous gait',[3] was different somehow. Certainly, he was a man who made no secret of his desire. On their pleasure drives, with their sleigh speeding along, Lockhart would take advantage of their close confinement to try to kiss her. She didn't respond; instead she sat, 'strangely thrilled, bewildered and a little frightened before the strange feeling that subconsciously I felt growing in me'.[4]

It would be some time before she put a name to that unaccustomed feeling. And if she ever managed to understand *why* she felt it, she never wrote it down or confided it to anyone. It was true that Lockhart had a presence that commanded attention – as she did herself – and a compelling gaze. He was a man one either loved or detested. One jealous rival called him a 'contemptible little bounder', while some in the Foreign Office regarded him as little better than a traitor.[5] But nobody could doubt his talents. From the very first he valued Moura for her knowledge and her intellect, which were both considerable. A later lover, who was inclined to be disdainful about the loose, 'Russian' manner of her thoughts, admitted that her mind was 'active, full and shrewdly penetrating' with 'streaks of extraordinary wisdom'. She could 'illuminate a question suddenly like a burst of sunshine on a wet February day'.[6]

For Lockhart, carrying the burden of Great Britain's relations with the vast power of Russia, illuminating wisdom was a commodity without price. He was a superbly confident young man, and inclined to trust his own wisdom, but he would take all the shrewd penetration he could get – especially when it came from a person with Moura's other attractions.

Perhaps that was what had woken the strange, dormant feeling that was stirring in her now, as she stood close beside Lockhart, gazing out over the moonlit snow-city. Until this moment Moura – as her friends and relations saw her – had stood for high society, fun, mystique: a hostess with magnetic charm, a singer of haunting gypsy melodies, a taunter of lovestruck men; nobody had taken her for a source of wisdom.

If she wasn't careful, if this feeling wasn't kept in check, sooner or later Lockhart would make another of his attempts to kiss her and she wouldn't resist. And who could tell where that might lead, what unknown feelings that might unlock?

Their conversations already sailed close to the brink of deeper intimacy. They joked about 'Bolshevik marriage'[7] – the dismantling of the institution of matrimony that the revolutionary feminists were calling for. None called more stridently than Alexandra Kollontai, the new People's Commissar for Social Welfare, who advocated a culture of sexual liberation, where women and men would be free to have lovers and friends as they chose, and thereby break down the bourgeois system which kept married women in servitude. Her ideas ran foul of Lenin – who was in some ways a staunch conservative – and weren't received well by working-class women.[8] But her free-love ideas titillated the liberal elite. To Lockhart and Moura, who were tip-toeing out to the very edge of bourgeois courtship like explorers on an ice floe, it was an exhilarating and amusing subject for conversation. But – at least as far as Moura was concerned – not for action.[9] For now there were little parties with their friends and sleigh-drives along the river and out to the islands, and the promise of something more, always a little out of reach.

'What children we were then,' Moura would recall, looking back on this magical time, 'what old, old people we are now.'[10] Just eight months had gone by when she wrote those words; eight months in which both their lives were transformed. If they hadn't had each other, they might never have survived; but then, if they hadn't had each other, they might never have been launched into the terrible, wonderful nightmare at all.

The German army, vast and unstoppable, was pushing the frontier eastward day by day. It was just a matter of time before they would be in Petrograd. The Russian army, depleted by Trotsky's demobilisation and his 'no peace, no war' policy, fell back towards their homeland. Many of them – the Latvians, Ukrainians and other men from the empire's outer nations – had already seen their homelands consumed by the advance. The Bolsheviks argued among themselves and tried frantically to negotiate, but the Germans were resolute – all conquered territories were to be ceded to Germany, and then there would be peace. No negotiations. And in the meantime they went on conquering more.

Lockhart's mission, less than a month old, looked like failing. His overriding purpose in Russia was to persuade the Bolsheviks to stay in the war. Sooner or later, the Central Committee would agree to swallow Germany's terms, and it would all be over. On Sunday 24 February he forced an emergency meeting with Trotsky, who was holed up in his office in the Smolny Institute, the former school 'for noble maidens' which had been requisitioned as the Bolshevik headquarters. Lockhart found it a bizarre place; the doors still bore the plaques denoting girls' dormitories, linen stores, classrooms – but the Bolsheviks had made it into a sty. Unwashed soldiers and workmen lounged everywhere, litter and cigarette butts were all over the floors.[11]

Trotsky – whose office was an island of order and cleanliness among the filth – was in a towering rage. Having demanded to know whether Lockhart had any message from London (he hadn't), Trotsky railed against the Allies, especially the British, for their intrigues in Russia, blaming them for the country's situation. The allegations that Trotsky was a German agent were still being bruited about by the diplomatic missions, together with the patently fabricated evidence. Lockhart winced inside; he had received a message from the Foreign Office that very day, in which the damned fool Lord Robert Cecil was still expressing these very suspicions. Trotsky had a pile of the incriminating documents on his desk, and he thrust them angrily at Lockhart, who was already painfully familiar with them – every Allied mission in Petrograd had seen copies. A few months later it would be proven that all the documents, which supposedly came from a variety of sources all over Europe, had all been concocted on a single typewriter. But still the anti-Bolshevik hotheads believed the claims.[12]

Lockhart tried to laugh the matter off, but Trotsky wasn't having it. 'Your Foreign Office does not deserve to win a war,' he fumed, sickened by Britain's vacillating policy on Russia. 'Your Lloyd George is like a man playing roulette and scattering chips on every number.'[13] Lockhart couldn't help but agree. In his opinion, Britain should either recognise the Bolsheviks and do business with them before they had a chance to make friends with Germany, or come out and make war on them in earnest. This constant indecision would just lead to disaster for Russia and for Europe.

The meeting ended with a promise. Although Russia would have to accept the Germans' terms, and the peace treaty would be signed, Trotsky believed the treaty would not be honoured. The Bolsheviks had no intention, he said, of letting bourgeois, monarchist Germany walk off with a third of Russia's territory. The peace, once signed, would not last long. It was a morsel of reassurance for the British.

But private promises would make little difference to the immediate course of events. To the outside world, it was clear that there would be peace between Germany and Russia. Therefore the time had come for the Allied governments to withdraw their embassies – or what was left of them – from Russia. The day fixed for departure was Thursday 28 February. Lockhart had the task of arranging exit visas for the British personnel. He went with an armful of passports to be stamped. Some of the military personnel were suspected by the revolutionary authorities of conducting covert anti-Bolshevik activities, and Lockhart had to invoke Trotsky's name (and some subterfuge) to get all the passports approved and stamped.

His own was not among them. Despite the pressure on him to accept that his mission was not only doomed but misguided, Lockhart wouldn't be leaving with the rest. Telegrams arrived from the Foreign Office warning him to abandon his cosy relationship with the Bolsheviks. His wife Jean wrote imploring him to change tack or his career would be ruined. People were vilifying him. Although Lloyd George had continued to support Lockhart in Cabinet and to press for recognition of the Bolsheviks,[14] he was losing ground to the consensus. Arthur Balfour, the Foreign Secretary, and his deputy Robert Cecil led the anti-Bolshevik party. General Knox, who was now advising the Cabinet on Russia, had called Lockhart's 'flirtation' with the Bolsheviks 'wrong and immoral'. Another officer with experience in Russia gave his view that Lockhart was 'a fool or a traitor' and ought to be hanged.[15]

And yet Lockhart had elected to stay, and believed he had good reasons for doing so. The peace treaty hadn't been signed yet, and he had faith in Trotsky's promise of a short-lived peace.[16]

What Lockhart had no way of knowing – although perhaps he should have guessed – was that the Bolsheviks were misleading him. Lloyd George wasn't the only one playing freely with his roulette chips. Lockhart was a valuable asset to Lenin and Trotsky, a man with powerful connections, and they were keen to make use of him. The other Allies had unofficial agents in Petrograd – such as the larger-than-life American Raymond Robins. An emotional, dramatic man and a good friend of Lockhart's, Robins was officially in Russia as head of the American Red Cross, but in fact was acting as the United States' unofficial agent. But neither he nor any other agent had been personally despatched by their countries' leaders. Lockhart was unique: a direct conduit to the British Prime Minister. Robins had no such access to President Woodrow Wilson. Therefore it was vital for Lenin and Trotsky that they maintain a good relationship with the British agent. He was their only hope of influencing the Allies directly. The Bolsheviks were anxious to prevent Japan intervening in Siberia, so Japan's allies must be reassured that Russia was not going to become friendly with Germany or remain out of the war permanently. And so they fed Lockhart promises that the war would resume sooner or later – promises which they could be sure would fly straight to Whitehall, Downing Street and the War Cabinet.[17]

Trotsky's opposition to making terms with Germany was genuine enough, but the real will of the Revolution lay ultimately with Lenin. The day after the embassies left Petrograd, Lockhart had his first meeting with the great leader, in his spartan office in the Smolny Institute.[18] At first sight he was inclined to be amused by Lenin's almost comical appearance – the bald, chubby-faced little fellow was 'more like a provincial grocer than a leader of men' – but he immediately recognised the power in him. Whereas Trotsky was 'all temperament', Lockhart found

Lenin coldly authoritative – he was 'impersonal and almost inhuman. His vanity was proof against all flattery.'[19] Trotsky was present at the meeting, and Lockhart was struck by his silent obeisance. Behind closed doors in Party meetings, Lenin was strongly in favour of a lasting peace with Germany – indeed, if it had been solely up to him, without the electoral power of the Central Committee to thwart him, he'd have had peace months ago – but for the time being he allowed Lockhart to believe that the peace – if signed – might not last. Indeed, Trotsky admitted, there was a genuine fear that the Germans, given Russia's weakness, might invade, or force the Bolsheviks out and install a bourgeois puppet government.

And so Lockhart went on believing that he was doing the right thing, and that his diplomatic mission wasn't dead.

Politics and diplomacy weren't the only reasons he wished to stay in Russia, possibly not even the principal ones; they were just the reasons he was willing to admit to publicly. Privately, there was a much more compelling reason to stay. Moura. His feelings about her were moving beyond mere fancy and romantic fascination, evolving into something that sleigh-rides and stolen kisses could not satisfy.

Moura was in her element during those days, as February gave way to March. She was as happy as she had ever been in her life. All dullness and drabness had receded, and even with all the uncertainty and privations of the Revolution, her life was burgeoning.

Despite the edicts being issued by the government, she still had Djon's huge apartment for herself and her children, without the uncongenial presence of Djon himself. And she still had Djon's money. If you were rich enough and had the right connections, there was still a semblance of the good life to be had in Petrograd.

And there was Lockhart. Moura was still struggling with her unfamiliar feelings about him, but the thrill she felt in his company was strong and irresistible. They dined in company at each other's apartments, and in their spare hours had their occasional sleigh-rides, but still Moura resisted his overtures and treated their friendship as a jest.

Her days were filled with her work at the British Embassy. Even though the diplomatic staff had departed at the end of February, the place wasn't shut down, and wasn't deserted. Aside from Lockhart, a handful of men – including some of her closest friends – had stayed.

Captain Francis Cromie was one. He had been serving as naval attaché for several months, and was now to be caretaker head of Britain's diplomatic remnant in Petrograd. He was also still responsible for the Royal Navy submarine flotilla in the Baltic. The command had been officially dissolved in January, when the Navy ceased collaborating with the Russian Admiralty,[20] but the subs were still there, and still at risk of falling into German hands. He had moved them from Reval to Helsingfors, where they were in the care of skeleton crews.

Like Lockhart, Cromie too had romantic reasons for staying, but more complicated ones. He was attached to Moura, but she was growing away from him, and he had begun to develop an amour with the beautiful Sophie Gagarin,[21] who lived in the British Embassy building with her relative, Princess Anna Saltikoff. The princess owned the building and leased it to the British government, and kept an apartment for herself in half of it.[22]

Also staying was Denis Garstin, with whom Moura now worked in the propaganda office as a translator. (Her friend Miriam had also taken a job alongside her as a clerk.) Moura adored her 'Garstino' with a sisterly affection, and the feeling was reciprocated. Garstino's position was becoming uncertain. The Bolsheviks were so profoundly suspicious of any hint of British subterfuge, propaganda was no longer practicable.

Garstin's chief, and Moura's employer, was an enigmatic, slippery fellow called Hugh Leech, a British businessman with a background in the oil industry. Leech was officially a commercial agent for British businesses in Russia. He ran the trading firm of Leech & Firebrace for that purpose, and the Embassy's propaganda office was officially just a sideline.[23] In fact, although few knew it at the time, Hugh Ansdell Farran Leech was deeply involved in covert activities. He was an agent of the Secret Intelligence Service – the SIS[24] – and throughout 1917 his firm had received tens of thousands of pounds in British government funding for his anti-Bolshevik propaganda activities. Since the Revolution he had been involved in further schemes to fund the anti-Bolshevik Don Cossacks and buy up controlling interests in Russian-based banks and businesses to prevent the Germans gaining influence.[25]

Moura also provided translation services to Commander Ernest Boyce, the head of the SIS Petrograd office.[26] Whether or not she knew that two of the men she worked for were agents of British intelligence 'she probably did; she was too smart not to notice what they did, and she'd already had contacts with SIS agent George Hill), Moura delighted in the atmosphere of intrigue that had begun to surround the old Embassy. Life – which had seemed so dismal and hopeless at the beginning of the year – was becoming exciting and fulfilling in every way.

She might have guessed that it couldn't last. On 2 March the German aeroplanes which had been making intermittent flights over Petrograd began dropping bombs. The next day, the Bolsheviks capitulated to the inevitable, and signed the treaty of Brest-Litovsk, accepting the German terms in full. On 8 March they announced the treaty's ratification to the public. Lenin was reviled as a Judas by the far left of the Party, but he weathered the storm and kept his position. Germany had conquered most of the western subject states of the old Russian Empire. With the signature of the treaty by the beaten Bolsheviks, Russia lost a third of its people and lands. Among them was Estonia, which became nominally independent under German protection.

So Djon von Benckendorff had got what he desired – peace, order and a semblance of freedom for Estonia with German monarchist patronage. The border between Estonia and Russia slammed shut. Moura was cut off from Yendel, and her children from their father.

Less than two weeks later, Moura underwent another parting. As a precaution against the risk of German invasion, the Bolsheviks had decided to move the capital to Moscow. Besides its strategic vulnerability, they found Petrograd too European, both in character and in proximity. The Asiatic style of Moscow suited the Bolsheviks better. That meant that Lockhart's little mission would have to abandon the apartment on Palace Quay and follow the seat of Bolshevism to the new capital, more than four hundred miles away.

All the time, the political situation – and Lockhart's task – grew ever more tense. Lloyd George continued to believe that communication with the Bolsheviks should be maintained. But the War Cabinet feared that Germany would take over Russia *in toto* and thereby gain a strategic position in the Pacific. That was unthinkable, so the Cabinet voted to notify Japan that if it wished to intervene against Russia in Siberia, such a move would be approved. The United States gave a similar approval.[27] Lockhart tried to persuade his government to offer the Bolsheviks support to fight a partisan war against Germany. Instead, it began laying plans to launch its own invasion of the northern Russian coast at Murmansk and Archangel – ostensibly as a move against German influence east of the Baltic. The Germans were still fighting, still snatching territory that had been ceded to them but which they hadn't yet occupied. There seemed every possibility that they might continue to advance beyond the agreed borders.

The British government also began to consider the possibility of using covert measures to bring down the Bolshevik regime. The stakes were rising, and the principal players – Moura and Lockhart included – were about to be drawn deeper than ever into the game.

For the time being, they acted as if all was well. The British mission's last week in Petrograd coincided with the festival of Maslenitsa – the traditional Russian Orthodox 'butter week' of indulgence before the onset of Great Lent. On Monday, Moura threw a small luncheon party in her apartment. The guests were her four remaining British friends.[28]

There was Francis Cromie, handsome and debonair as ever, the only one who would be staying on in Petrograd, to continue managing the British presence there. Cromie was finding it a financial strain living in Bolshevik Russia – a leg of mutton cost £2, and he complained to people back home that the 'conditions have to be lived under to be believed'.[29] But life was still easy if one were willing and able to spend a fortune, as Moura was.

Young Denis Garstin was another guest, as full of life and gaiety as always – the 'prince of good fellows' as one of his commanding officers had called him.[30] He had been hand-picked by Lockhart for his team. Even Garstino's indomitable nature was starting to wear thin under the strain, but he and his eternal stock of optimism were far from exhausted yet. He had recently met the scandalous Alexandra Kollontai, the promoter of 'Bolshevik marriage'. Contrary to the lady's reputation, Garstino had thought her a 'little quiet woman in an untidy dark flat, full of Bolsheviks'. He had interviewed her in a tiny bedroom: 'I told her why I disagreed with Bolshevism, and asked her, as one propagandist to another, to explain many things.' He was impressed by her answers, and found her charming. 'She isn't pretty and she isn't young,' he declared, 'but she bowled me over.'[31] The meeting had scandalised the bourgeoisie of Petrograd; a British cavalry captain in a tête-à-tête with a commissar – especially one with such a sensational reputation – whatever next?

Completing the trio of captains at the party was Hicks, who was quickly becoming the third man of the British mission, after Lockhart and Cromie. Lockhart, the sole civilian among the men, composed doggerel verses for everyone, Cromie made a lighthearted speech, and Moura served endless rounds of the traditional Maslenitsa blini* with caviar, washed down with shots of vodka and accompanied by gales of laughter and good fellowship.[32]

It was the last hurrah of the British players in Russia; from now on, the stakes would rise so fast they would have to fight to keep up. Before the summer had reached its end, two of the people present at that party would be dead, and the other three would be in a Cheka prison, wondering if at any moment they might find themselves in front of a firing squad.

The transfer of power to Moscow had begun. Lenin was the first to make the move. The following Saturday, 16 March, Trotsky followed. He went on a special train, escorted by seven hundred Latvian soldiers – 'the Praetorian Guard of the new Red Napoleon'.[33] Also accompanying him were his staff and, in places of honour, Robert Bruce Lockhart and Captain William Hicks. They dined with him en route, and he continued to assure Lockhart that he intended to fight the Germans. He had just been appointed Commissar for Military and Naval Affairs – or Minister of War, as everyone called it – and said he wouldn't accept the post unless Russia was going to fight. Lockhart, for the time being, still chose to believe him.

Left behind in Petrograd, Moura was lonely. She had her children, but that couldn't last for long. It was too dangerous for them in the city, and Moura reluctantly took the decision to allow Kira, Pavel and Tania to go to Yendel and be cared for by Djon.

With the border closed and Estonia under German control, it was a risky venture. The children were smuggled out of Petrograd in one of the fast horse-drawn troikas† which were still the backbone of Russia's postal service. Micky went with them. She would face the greatest danger, a British subject going into a German-controlled nation. She was provided with a false passport and enjoined not to utter a word of English until they were settled in at Yendel.[34] Micky's command of Russian had never been very good, so it was a journey beset by risks. In addition to Micky, the children were accompanied by their

---

* Russian pancakes.
† A vehicle (sleigh or carriage) drawn by three horses.

grandmother's two fox terriers. Food was so short in the capital, Madame Zakrevskaya could no longer feed them.

Equipped with a day's provisions and accompanied by a Swiss escort who had made a living out of smuggling people over Russia's borders, the little party of fugitives boarded the postal troika and departed. Micky, daring as she was, feared for the children. Her own tongue she could control, but the children had been brought up speaking English, and at their ages – Tania three, Pavel five, and Kira seven – who could tell what they might blurt out, no matter how strictly they were warned not to?

After a long, weary journey – there was still snow on the ground, which slowed the wheeled troika – they reached the Estonian border. The children kept silent, and they crossed without being challenged by the guards. They eventually made it to Yendel, where they were greeted by Djon.

Under German protection, order had been restored to Estonia, and the Benckendorffs – Djon, the children and all their relations – settled down to a life of peace and safety. But the children were now stranded. The border between them and their mother was a frontier between hostile nations, and they could never go back.

Moura had explained her reason for staying in Russia – her mother was here, and couldn't travel. But she had a much more pressing reason. Free now from her most important responsibility, she was looking forward to the moment when she could travel the four hundred miles to Moscow to be with Lockhart.

6

Passion and Intrigue

April–May 1918

A young woman lay face-down on the carpet, surrounded by the smashed fragments of expensive china and broken champagne bottles. The gorgeous Aubusson carpet was soaked with wine and pools of blood, and the drawing room's silken walls were pocked by bullet-holes. Yakov Peters, deputy head of the Cheka, pushed the toe of his boot under the woman's midriff and turned her over. She had been caught through the neck by a bullet, and her dishevelled hair was matted with a mass of congealed purple blood.

'*Prostitutka*,' Peters muttered, and shrugged dismissively. She wasn't one of the intended victims of the battle that had seared through this house and dozens of others in the district – just a casual associate of the Anarchists who had made their dens in the abandoned homes of Moscow's wealthy elite. But still not worth anyone's concern.

Lockhart looked down at the woman's rigid, mottled face. No more than twenty years old, he estimated. He glanced around at the bullet-holes in the walls and ceiling, and the wreckage of what appeared to have been some kind of orgy. There were other bodies lying about the house, some cut down defenceless, others heavily armed.[1] The Cheka had begun wresting control of the new capital from the counter-revolutionary rabble, and this was their first large-scale operation.

It had been a strange and unsettling day for Lockhart, a shocking but also thrilling interlude in a monotonous first month in Moscow.

In the weeks that had elapsed since the move from Petrograd, life had become an almost ceaseless train of meetings and interviews. Often he had to force himself to concentrate. As day followed day and grew into weeks, his thoughts of Moura grew ever more distracting. When wou' she come to him, as she had promised, as they had planned? How long would he be able to bear the waiting? It had been four weeks. The journey was long, permits were required, she had her work and he his . . . but even so, the suspense was hard to bear. It hampered his work. He had written, sent telegrams, telling her so. Her hasty, tantalising replies were pored over and carefully preserved, as every note from her would be until the day he died. One visit had already been promised and cancelled. Then Denis Garstin returned from a trip to Petrograd with a letter and the news that Moura was unwell.

'Dear Lockhart,' she wrote, maintaining the formality they had cultivated: 'Again it's only a letter and not my own person. Garstino will explain how and why. But I hope you will soon see the red sweater again and do a little more and better work . . . Best love, Moura Benckendorff.'[2] The mere thought was enough to set him itching for her.

In the meantime there were meetings, and still more meetings. Most of them – with Lenin, Trotsky or the other commissars – he had to go to himself, but sometimes the mountain, in the form of fellow diplomats and agents, would come to Mahomet. Lockhart had set up his headquarters in a suite at the Elite Hotel, a refined but rather squat block which took up the whole of a side road off Petrovka Street. The Elite was one of the very few quality hotels still functioning in the city.[3] It seemed that everyone in Moscow needed to quiz, cultivate or sound out the British agent, or be sounded out by him – Russians, British, French, Americans, representatives from every part of the old Russian Empire had to speak to him, for either their benefit or his. Favours were asked or offered, information exchanged and opinions shared.

That was the daylight hours taken care of; after dark he wrote his reports and messages, labouring over the ciphers himself because his mission had no staff. Just a secretary (who wasn't entrusted with ciphers), Lockhart himself, Hicks and occasionally Garstin. There was a loose collection of other Britons in Russia – businessmen, journalists, military men, who weren't attached to Lockhart's mission but had special concerns of their own, often on orders from the British government – yet more of Lloyd George's multifarious roulette chips. Lockhart had little or no knowledge of their business, yet the Russians regarded them as his responsibility.[4] There were only a few he had direct dealings with. Cromie and some of the intelligence fellows in Petrograd were regularly in touch, and sometimes visited. Then there was the military mission in

Petrograd and Murmansk, whose job was to prevent the huge stores of British supplies left over from Russia's days as an ally falling into German hands. (There was constant back-room talk about the mission forming the nucleus of an invasion force – an idea which Lockhart strenuously resisted.) He also had a lot to do with the *Manchester Guardian* journalist (and later children's author) Arthur Ransome, 'a Don Quixote with a walrus moustache' who was very friendly with the Bolsheviks and a good source of intelligence. Lockhart liked him a lot.

Lockhart was occasionally invited to attend meetings of the Central Committee, held in the restaurant of the Metropol Hotel. The whole building had been requisitioned as a parliament and dormitory for Bolshevik delegates, renamed the Second House of Soviets.[5]

At one of these meetings in early April he had been introduced for the first time to the man who was regarded as the embodiment of Bolshevik terror. A slender, impeccable villain from a well-to-do Belarusian family, with a goatee streaked with grey and a nose like a scimitar, Felix Dzerzhinsky was the founding head of the Cheka. A lifelong radical with years of imprisonment and exile behind him, he'd served in the military arm of the Bolshevik Party in the October Revolution. He was highly regarded by Lenin, and already had a reputation for utter ruthlessness in annihilating anything that smelled of counter-revolution. The meeting made a profound impression on Lockhart. Although Dzerzhinsky had twinkling eyes and his thin, delicate mouth tended to twist into a slanted smirk, Lockhart sensed no trace of humour in him.

Accompanying the Cheka boss was a rather short, thickset man of about forty, with a long nose resting on an abundant black moustache; below his dense thatch of combed-back hair, a pair of narrow, intense but faintly humorous eyes stared out. Lockhart was introduced to him and shook his hand, but neither man spoke. The fellow was called Josef Dzhugashvili, a name that meant nothing to the British agent. He gathered that the man was ambitious, but not taken very seriously. 'If he had been announced then to the assembled Party as the successor of Lenin,' he would recall, 'the delegates would have roared with laughter.'[6] But already Dzhugashvili was cultivating a chilling, steely persona and going by his revolutionary pseudonym, *Stalin*.[7]

Dzerzhinsky, having built a ring of security around Lenin, was looking outward at the threats massing against the Bolshevik stat After months of disorder, the regime was beginning to imp discipline on the city of Moscow. Counter-revolutionary plotters were to be eradicated, and the Anarchists were high on the list. They had been valued comrades of the Bolsheviks during last year's revolutions, but the Anarchist Communists had broken away when the Bolsheviks abandoned their ideal of obliterating the state and began setting up their own tyranny. The Anarchists, driven underground, had evolved into a strange and frightening hybrid of subversive political movement and criminal plague, their ranks made up of an unholy mix of ex-soldiers, radical students and criminals. Their leaders had tried to disavow the criminal element, but the Bolsheviks had made up their minds that the Anarchists might once have been allies but had now become counter-revolutionary bandits, and had to go. The Cheka embarked on a campaign to clean them out.

The first big strike against them began on 12 April. It had its origins in an incident a few days earlier, when a motor car belonging to Raymond Robins, Lockhart's American counterpart, was stolen, allegedly by Anarchists.[8] In the early hours of the morning, over a thousand Cheka troops mounted raids on some twenty-six locations known to be Anarchist strongholds, many of them in the opulent houses of Povarskaya Street in the western district where Moscow's wealthy merchants had formerly lived. The Anarchists were well armed, and the gun battles went on for hours, from house to house and room to room. Dozens of Anarchists were killed,[9] and another twenty-five summarily executed by the Chekists.[10] More than five hundred were captured alive and herded away.

In the afternoon, Dzerzhinsky sent a car to collect Robins and Lockhart, and arranged for his deputy, Yakov Peters, to give them a conducted tour of the scene of the raids.

Peters was an unforgettable character. Latvian by birth, he was a fanatical revolutionary. He had lived in exile in England for some years, and stood trial at the Old Bailey in 1911 as one of the participants in the Sidney Street siege, in which three policemen had been shot dead by a gang of radicals. Peters was acquitted of murder and in 1917 returned to Russia to take part in the Revolution. He had a broad, round face with an upturned nose and a downturned mouth like a sickle blade, and looked on the world with an intense, burning stare. As a Chekist he was utterly implacable, entirely without pity or passion. He would execute and torture freely if needed, but took no delight in it. The security of the state was what counted, and like both Lenin and Dzerzhinsky he believed that terror was the most effective way to achieve it.[11]

But he had a civilised side, and was soft-spoken. Later that year, Lockhart would be forced to get to know Yakov Peters much more closely, and despite everything he knew about the man, and the people he had summarily condemned to torture or to death, and everything Lockhart himself suffered at his hands, he found it difficult to dislike him.

Peters had a soft spot for the British and Americans, and rather liked Lockhart and Robins. He seemed to enjoy taking them from house to house along Povarskaya Street, exhibiting the corpses and the devastation that resulted from the Cheka's merciless handling of counter-revolution. Lockhart couldn't summon up much feeling for the dead and the punished; the squalor they had created and in which they had lived in these luxurious, comfortable houses − filth everywhere, paintings slashed, faeces on the carpets − disgusted him.[12] This district had once been his home, during his days at the Consulate. He'd shared an apartment with Jean just one street away from this very spot. These houses, soiled and degraded, had belonged to his neighbours and acquaintances.

But the woman shot dead in the drawing room of the Gracheva house was different. Prostitute or not, she was young, and presumably innocent. Peters commented coldly that perhaps it was for the best that she had died, but whether he meant because she was a prostitute or merely that she wasn't a very attractive one, he didn't say.[13]

This was a day that would remain in Lockhart's memory forever. It proved one thing − that the Bolsheviks, for all their vacillating over the war, were fully capable of screwing down a steel clamp on their cities. They might create a powerful nation yet. It wasn't clear at this moment whether that was a reassuring or a terrifying prospect.

Sunday 21 April 1918

Russia was green again. The snows had thawed and the leaves were budding on the trees that flickered past the train window.

Moura had been stuck so long in Petrograd, it was strange to be in motion again. About this time last year she had travelled to Yendel hoping that the revolutionary madness was over and the world might settle down again. Now Yendel was cut off and the world had tumbled back into an insanity without cure. She wondered if she would ever see her children again. Moura was willing to admit that she didn't have much of a maternal instinct, but by her own reckoning she loved her children. Whether she loved them enough to sacrifice herself for them hadn't yet been put to the test.[14]

It was a long haul to Moscow, all day and overnight, bringing back memories of the interminable trek to the family estate at Beriozovaya Rudka when she was a child. That was almost twice as far as Moscow – about eight hundred miles – and after the death of her father there was never any joy at the end of it. How different things were now, in every way. Every mile was bringing her closer to the moment when she would see Lockhart at last.

When the train slowed through the northern suburbs of Moscow, Moura's heart beat a little faster. As soon as it jolted to a halt in Nikolayevsky station* in a cloud of steam and smoke she collected her valise, straightened her skirt, and stepped down onto the platform. She was gallantly assisted by Commander George Le Page, a heavily built, bearded and genial naval officer who had travelled down on the same train. Le Page, a Guernsey islander by birth, was a member of Francis Cromie's mission, and had come to Moscow on urgent business with Lockhart.

Naval affairs were not going well for the British or the Russians. Cromie – 'old Crow', as Moura called him – had been depressed for the past two weeks, having finally had to destroy his beloved submarine flotilla. At the beginning of April it had been confirmed that Germany was sending an army division to take control of Finland, where the conflict between Red and White Finnish and Russian forces was still spluttering away. The Royal Navy flotilla, still sheltering at Helsingfors after the retreat from Reval, was under threat. With no operational crews, there was no way to mobilise the submarines. Cromie travelled up to Helsingfors on 3 April. The business community there, who had helped sponsor the German invasion, offered him £50,000 if he would prevent the Red Russian fleet from intervening in the German landings. Had he been a mercenary, Cromie

---

* Now Leningradsky station.

could have become a rich man – just recently the anti-Bolshevik Russian White Guard had offered him five million if he would hand over the flotilla to them.[15]

Whatever their value on the open market, the subs would be priceless to the Germans. Cromie ordered his second-in-command, Lieutenant Downie, to destroy the flotilla. Over the next five days, while the German division landed and closed in on Helsingfors, the subs were towed out into the ice floes, charges were set and detonated. Each sinking was followed a few minutes later by a titanic explosion as the sea water rushed into the breached hull and blew up the massive batteries.[16] Cromie stayed on in Helsingfors to carry on the scuttling of three British merchant vessels.[17] Exhausted after days of 'hard labour as engineer, stoker, deck hand and skipper combined, with a crew of useless army officers', he 'got out of Helsingfors in the nick of time' with the help of his White friends.[18] He was deeply upset by the loss of the submarines, and felt he would never forgive the White Finns for it.[19] With the flotilla scuttled, the last vestige of Captain Cromie's naval role had ceased; from now on, he was wholly a diplomat and intelligence agent.

Moura, working every day in the offices of the British Petrograd mission, took it all in. Intrigue thrilled her, and she was always hungry for information. Some of her inquisitiveness came from a need to understand what was happening to her country and what its future might be, but it was also exhilarating to feel oneself a part of world-shaping events.[20] Her interest had attracted notice, and one or two members of the British mission were worried about her friendship with Lockhart – 'Have Lockhart warned if there is any suspicion of Benckendorff,' one of them wrote.[21] But Moura never gave them any real cause for suspicion, and was allowed to continue in her job.

She and Le Page took a cab to Petrovka Street. Moura, who wasn't very familiar with the city, looked curiously at the passing streets. It was less European than Petrograd – more onion domes and squat Asiatic arches, slightly fewer Palladian façades – yet it wasn't vastly different. But as she would soon learn, the atmosphere was changing, becoming more controlled, with fewer radical dissenters, less crime and an intense climate of fear.

So this was the new nest of the Bolsheviks. Moura wondered how she would like it. It was like a different country from Petrograd. She

wondered whether it had changed Lockhart, and how she might feel
about him when she saw him again after so many weeks of anxious
waiting.

A week had passed since the attack on the Anarchists, and Lockhart's
workload showed no sign of letting up. He was still having to manage
almost all of it alone.

He had been without Captain Hicks since a few days after their arrival
in Moscow. Lockhart had despatched him to Siberia to investigate
reports that there was a German bandit army running loose, made up of
former prisoners of war who'd been armed and mobilised by the
Bolsheviks. The report came from SIS, and its claims were flatly denied
by Trotsky, who happily gave his blessing for an investigation. Hicks had
been gone over a month now, and had travelled all over Siberia, visiting
prison camps in company with an officer from the American Red Cross.
Not a single armed German had been found.[22] Lockhart laid the blame
for this farce at the door of his enemy, Foreign Secretary Arthur Balfour
and his ludicrous policy-making – 'what we are playing at God alone
knows,' he wrote tartly in his diary, 'but one cannot expect much with
a Foreign Minister of 74'.[23]

Hicks was due back any day now, and Lockhart would be very glad
to see him. 'Hickie' had become an indispensable colleague and friend.
He was also much more of a dab hand with ciphers.

Meanwhile, there was work. Sunday morning was entirely taken up
by meetings in his rooms at the Elite. Nothing unusual in that. What
was unusual was the feeling of suppressed excitement tingling away
under his skin. At ten o'clock, Le Page arrived from Petrograd.[24] There
were fears on all sides about the Russian Black Sea fleet, which was
vulnerable to being seized by the Germans operating in the Ukraine.
The British were worried for obvious reasons, and the Bolsheviks wer-
en't sure of the loyalty of the sailors.[25] Le Page had served with the fleet
before the Revolution, and knew it well. He needed Lockhart's opinion
on the political situation and access to Trotsky (who had taken up his
post as war commissar despite Russia's continuing failure to reopen the
war against Germany).

There was other worrying news from Petrograd. Major McAlpine, a
member of the military mission that was evacuating supplies who fancied himself an expert on the Russian situation, was sending reports to

London criticising Lockhart's policy of 'blindly backing' the Bolshevik government.[26] McAlpine wasn't the only one stirring up trouble, either; several officers (thankfully not Cromie or Garstin, who remained loyal) were campaigning against him. 'Stupid idiots,' Lockhart commented acidly in his diary.[27] But with the continuing peace and the imminent arrival of a German Ambassador in Moscow, it was getting harder to resist the view that the Bolsheviks were not to be trusted.[28]

Lockhart spent a long time in conversation with Le Page, but inside he was boiling with impatience. He was only interested in the visitor who had arrived with Le Page. After the disappointment of the letter Garstin had brought last week, Lockhart had been thrilled to get a second note, scribbled hastily on a page torn out of a pocket pad: 'Dear Lockhart, Just a few hurried lines in the office to tell you am better . . . Do write again and keep a room for me in the Elite for about Sunday. Best love, Moura B—'[29]

After Le Page had gone, there were still more meetings to be got through. Would they never end? On and on they went. Moura was here, in this very building, and he was being kept from her. It was nearly one o'clock when the last visitor shook hands and was ushered out of the door. Lockhart paused in front of the looking-glass, adjusted his tie, pushed back his hair, shot his cuffs, then dashed to the landing. Gathering himself, he descended the stairs soberly to the next floor, where there was a suite set aside as the mission's living and dining room. He paused outside the door, took a breath, and let himself in.

The room was aglow with midday spring sunshine. Standing near the window, her dark, waved hair alive with light, was Moura. Lockhart paused, then walked towards her in silence, so overcome he couldn't trust himself to speak. When those eyes turned on him, and she smiled that smile, he knew that this was a bond unlike any other, that this was a woman he could never let go. 'Into my life,' he would recall, 'something had entered which was stronger than any other tie, stronger than life itself.'[30]

From this moment on, there would be no more pretence, no more stolen kisses, no more formality. For Lockhart it would be a passionate adventure; for Moura it would begin as a struggle to accept the feelings that he had woken in her.

That evening they went to the ballet, a performance of *Coppélia* at the Bolshoi.[31] Lockhart had once sat in a box here and watched Kerensky whip the aristocratic audience into a frenzy with his swoon-inducing oratory. (He had little idea that the woman sitting close beside him now had been Kerensky's mistress for a short time.) *Coppélia* was a much calmer affair. The aristocrats in the boxes had been replaced by high-ranking Bolsheviks, but the ballet was the same as it had ever been, and it was possible to forget that the Revolution had ever happened.[32]

Whether Lockhart was conscious of any irony in the subject of the ballet – and if so, whether he identified at all with Franz, besotted with a woman brought to life in his own imagination, or wondered if there was a Dr Coppélius pulling strings anywhere behind the scenes – he never recorded it. His adoration of Moura was complete. For her part, Moura still didn't know quite what to make of her feelings. She wasn't a woman who loved, any more than Coppélia was. Or at least, she had not been until now. When she looked back on this time, she came to believe that she was waking up, coming to life.

The illusion that they were back in the pre-revolutionary era was dispelled when the curtain came down and the orchestra struck up the 'Internationale' instead of the old '*Bozhe, Tsarya khrani*'.

Walking out of the theatre into the chill spring night, Lockhart and Moura headed back to the Elite. There was nowhere else to go now that the city was being brought to heel. During their first few weeks in Moscow, Lockhart, Denis Garstin and visiting SIS agent George Hill had gone to an illegal cabaret, appropriately called the Podpolye,* in a cellar beneath the Okhotny Ryad, a street linking the Bolshoi Theatre and Red Square, just a block away from the Kremlin itself. In this underworld, champagne could be had and a rich, anti-Bolshevik audience listened to radical, decadent songs performed by the actor, composer and film star Alexander Vertinsky, who incorporated into his art the gypsy music that Lockhart found irresistibly sensuous. Vertinsky's melancholy style struck a deep resonance with the audience, a class demoralised and without hope. One night the Podpolye was raided by a gang of bandits – former Russian army officers reduced to thieving. While filling their pockets with the clientele's cash and watches, the bandits, noting Hill and Garstin's uniforms, declined to take their belongings – 'We do not rob Englishmen,' said the bandit leader to Lockhart, and apologised on behalf of his country for the contemptible state it had got itself into.[33]

---

* Lit. 'underground'.

There were no more cabarets now. The Bolsheviks had already crim-inalised them, and the purges which destroyed the Anarchists had also cleaned out the city's underground nightlife.

With the music of *Coppélia* still dancing in their heads, Lockhart and Moura arrived back at the Elite. With Hicks still away, Lockhart had the suite of rooms all to himself. He had booked Moura a room of her own, but she was in no particular hurry to retire. During the week that fol-lowed her room was destined not to be used very much.

He wrote her poetry, just as he had for his Malayan princess. Moura was delighted by it. There were more evenings at the ballet, and outings. Lockhart had a motor car at his disposal, and he made full use of it. With the coming of spring, a favourite destination was the deserted palace at Arkhangelskoye, a few miles west of Moscow. The former country retreat of the Yusupov princes, it was an idyllic spot, a bijou palace set in woodland on a bend of the Moskva river. Although the estate lands had been taken over by peasants, the house had been left miraculously untouched. No looters, no squatters; just an elegant peach-coloured palace unlived-in and stuffed with priceless furniture and art. Hardly anyone in Moscow had transport, and for this brief springtime the place could be enjoyed in tranquil solitude.[34]

By the time that week came to an end, Lockhart and Moura had crossed the boundary where romantic flirtation turned into a physical bond, and left it far behind. They had become lovers.

My dear . . .

Moura paused, her pen hanging over the note paper. How should she address him? Not as 'Lockhart', certainly, not now. But he never went by any other name. Her pen inscribed a hesitant line, and at the end of it wrote . . . *Locky*. She smiled.

She was back in her own apartment in Petrograd after a week spent in Moscow, and still trying to make sense of things.[35] She couldn't even decide on the proper tone to take in a letter. 'A hurried line to tell you I miss you so very very much . . . Thanks so much for my week in Moscow. You don't know how much I enjoyed it.'

This was hopeless – was she writing to one of her Benckendorff in-laws? Or was she speaking to the man who excited her above all others, the man she had just opened herself up to, whose body she had welcomed into hers?

'All this is fatuities,' she went on impatiently, 'that with natures like mine exist to hide the real true feelings. But you know I care for you very very much, or all that has happened wouldn't have happened.'

But what exactly *had* happened between them? Why could she still not work out what these feelings were? She wrote on, swinging erratically between the roles of friend and lover. She promised him 'a deep, great friendship for the man who "likes Russia, has a great big brain and a kind heart"'. She implored him, 'do not class me with the rest, will you, with the rest who trifle and with whom you trifle – but keep a separate little place for me, where I will remain a long time'.

Still it wouldn't come out right. She was like a singer trying to master a new, elusive tune, and the notes were all wrong.

Abandoning sentiment, Moura fell back on her first instinct – inquisitiveness. She mentioned the worrying rumours that a German invasion was imminent, and that Petrograd would be unable to resist it. Did Lockhart know whether the Germans would come?

Stumbling on, she resumed the casual tone that was her accustomed voice, the one she used with all her friends. 'I hope to be able to come some time during Easter week.[36] I am looking frightfully forward to it . . . Well – good-bye – or better au-revoir. Take care of yourself. Tell me what I should bring with me, I cannot get your hat, you never gave me the key.'

She signed off with 'Love and a kiss from Moura'.[37]

It would be some time before she discovered how to sing this unfamiliar song, how to express what she was feeling. And as for the feelings themselves, she would never quite master them or fully understand them.

While the bond between Moura and Lockhart drew tighter, the taut relationship between their countries was beginning to approach snapping point.

On 23 April, the second full day of Moura's stay in Moscow, the new German Ambassador, Count Wilhelm von Mirbach, had arrived in the capital to take up his post. Lockhart had been incensed to learn that the Bolsheviks were requisitioning forty rooms in the Elite for Mirbach and his staff – most on the same floors as Lockhart's. 'White with passion' (and perhaps moved by the intense feelings inspired by Moura's presence), he went to see Trotsky's deputy, Chicherin, to complain. Getting apologies but no satisfaction there, Lockhart contacted Trotsky himself (who had to be dragged out of a commissars' meeting to come to the telephone), and threatened to terminate his mission and leave Moscow if Mirbach stayed in the Elite. Trotsky relented, and the Count and his staff were relocated to an inferior hotel.[38]

For the time being, Britain had the diplomatic edge over Germany. When Mirbach had his first official meeting, it was with a deputy rather than Lenin himself, and the tone was 'acidly polite'.[39] Meanwhile, Lockhart wired London to say that the Bolsheviks were willing to agree to all the British proposals for military access to Germany's Eastern Front via Russian territory. An Allied force might enter via Archangel in the north, or from the east via Siberia. There were only a few sticking points needing to be smoothed out.[40] While in his moments of free time Lockhart bathed in the joy of Moura's presence, in his working hours he negotiated with Trotsky and with Whitehall. He and Garstin had cooked up a list of proposals for the British government to consider, including the possibility of dealing openly with the Bolsheviks if, as Trotsky was intimating, they were conducive to the Allied military expedition through Russia. It seemed that Lockhart and Garstin might have discovered the solution; even Balfour, the Foreign Secretary, was beginning to come round to the idea.[41]

What Lockhart did not openly admit was that he was starting to lose faith in his own policy of friendship with the Bolsheviks. The presence of Mirbach shook him, and he knew that the SIS was intriguing to force the issue. It had come to Lockhart's attention, through his intelligence contacts, that anti-Bolshevik elements in Russia, led by Boris Savinkov, former Minister of War in the Kerensky government, were plotting a coup.

Although he denied it later, Lockhart made contact with Savinkov, and knew of his plans.[42] The date set for the coup was 1 May. The Foreign Office was deeply wary of Savinkov (he'd been an anti-government terrorist in the days of the Tsar), but British intelligence were secretly planning to support his coup, and had been funding him. If the coup succeeded, it would blow Lockhart's mission to pieces.

But when May Day dawned, Savinkov's coup failed to materialise. The Cheka had learned of it, and the organisers were forced to postpone. Instead, May Day was marked in Moscow by the first of the triumphal Red Army parades in Red Square.[43]

It was never discovered exactly who warned the Bolsheviks about the coup. Perhaps one of the commanders of Lenin's Latvian 'Praetorian Guard', whom Savinkov had tried to bribe. The Germans seemed to be extraordinarily well informed about the affair, and it was from their news service that the announcement of the aborted coup came.

One person who had known in advance was Moura. She had talked about it with Lockhart during her stay in Moscow, and referred to it in that halting letter to him after returning home – 'One expects all kinds of things on the 1st,' she wrote anxiously, apparently fearing that a German invasion might result from an anti-Bolshevik uprising.[44] At about this time, one or two members of the British mission in Petrograd – none from among her circle of friends, of course – began to wonder again about the trustworthiness of Madame Benckendorff. Nothing was done, and she continued in her job. Almost all British officials trusted her, and she was regarded by the Foreign Office as reliable. Although the head of Britain's naval intelligence was appalled by the use of Russian women as clerks (having learned of it from Cromie) and advised that the practice be halted immediately, the Foreign Office suggested that the ban should only apply to 'other ladies besides Mme Benckendorff'.[45]

Whoever the informant had been, with his coup stillborn, Boris Savinkov evaded capture, and went on to conspire again. Another man who fled Petrograd at this time was Hugh Leech, financier, SIS agent and Moura's main employer. Not only had he been helping to channel money to the anti-Bolshevik conspirators, he had been losing their trust through some shady financial dealings. Also, the Cheka were on his tail. How his name came to their attention was another obscure matter. Perhaps through disenchanted White rebels, perhaps through somebody inside the British mission . . . Leech grew a beard, hid out for a while at Tsarskoye Selo, and then escaped to Murmansk, where he took refuge with the British military mission.[46]

While British operations in Russia appeared to be unravelling, the Germans, with Count Mirbach to the fore, made the most of Savinkov's failed coup, seeing the possibilities of levering apart the British and the Bolsheviks and securing for themselves a controlling interest in Russia. The war being fought in Europe had acquired a new front – its trenches were in Moscow, and Mirbach and Lockhart were the combatants. And in keeping with the spirit of the war, it was a contest in which one of them would end up dead.

7

Old Enemies, Strange Alliances

May–June 1918

Their lives were defined by impatience and anxiety. Moura in Petrograd, Lockhart in Moscow, lived for their next meeting. Letters and telegrams flew back and forth between them, hasty notes scribbled in the moments between meetings and reports, letters brooded over in the long hours of the night. Their bond was still uncertain – far beyond ordinary intimacy, into the realm of obsession, but still not something that Moura knew how to put a name to. He had become 'Locky' and she sent him kisses rather than the 'best love' that her friends received, but she was still struggling to untangle her feelings. She cared for him deeply and spoke of a special friendship, but the word 'love', having disappeared from her greetings, had yet to reappear in a more meaningful form.

She simply didn't know quite how she felt about her British lover, other than that she wanted to be with him.

In May they had a chance to meet again, and seized it gladly. Commander Ernest Boyce, head of the SIS section in Petrograd, was travelling down to Moscow for a meeting with Lockhart. Moura took the opportunity to travel with him,[1] and on Thursday 9 May, two anxious weeks after their last meeting, she boarded the train. Her old friend Miriam went with her.

Perhaps Moura had a shrewd idea of what she was involving herself in by taking Lockhart as her lover, and perhaps it affected her feelings – heightened her trepidation, enhanced the exhilaration and her feeling of self-worth. Whether she suspected it or not, the train speeding towards Moscow was carrying her to the greatest peak in her life. Intense emotion and intense danger would be her constant companions from now on.

When she and Lockhart were reunited in Moscow, the passion that reignited marked the beginning of a new phase in their affair, and in her life. She began learning how to love.

Lockhart had awaited the arrival of the Petrograd train with acute anxiety. His eagerness to see Moura – the emotional flutter and the physical yearning – was only a part of it. Matters were approaching a crisis in Moscow, with almost every day bringing a new and unsettling surprise. He was impatient to see Boyce, whom he had magisterially summoned two days ago to explain the sudden arrival of a new British secret agent in Russia.[2]

Earlier that week, Lockhart had been disconcerted to learn from a member of the Bolshevik foreign ministry that an Englishman apparently calling himself 'Reilli' had turned up at the gates of the Kremlin, claiming to be an envoy of Lloyd George and demanding to see Lenin.[3] 'Reilli' had been interviewed, and the Bolsheviks wanted to know whether Lockhart could vouch for him. Presuming that 'Reilli' must be some itinerant madman – but also aware that there was no nonsense that could be put beyond the British secret services – Lockhart summoned Boyce, who came on the next train.

To Lockhart's astonishment, Boyce confirmed that the man, code-named ST1, was an SIS agent. In fact, as of his arrival, he was *the* principal field agent in Russia, alongside Captain George Hill. He had arrived in the country a few weeks ago, settling initially at Petrograd before heading for Moscow. His name, misspelt as 'Reilli' on the pass he'd been given by Litvinov (the very same diplomat with whom Lockhart had lunched at Lyons), was Sidney Reilly. His mission, ostensibly, was to be an unofficial envoy in the same vein as Lockhart. In reality he had been sent to take charge of Britain's covert efforts against the Germans. At least, that seemed initially to be his mission. As time went by, it became increasingly unclear just what Sidney Reilly was doing in Russia, and whether it matched up with what he had been officially briefed to do (which in itself was equally unclear). He was, apparently, yet another of the miscellaneous roulette chips that the British government was scattering on the Red baize.

When Lockhart met him, he hardly knew what to think. Reilly was middle-aged and dark-eyed, with a slight build and thin face; some thought him Greek, others Jewish. His fellow secret agent George Hill found him 'well-groomed, very foreign-looking' and noted his foreign-sounding accent.[4] Wherever he came from, Sidney Reilly was clearly not Irish.[5] Lockhart, furious with him for the trouble he'd caused at the Kremlin, 'dressed him down like a schoolmaster and threatened to have him sent home'.[6] Reilly took it well, fending off the hostility with a barricade of preposterous excuses. Lockhart couldn't help liking Sidney Reilly, although if he'd had an inkling of the deadly trouble he would get him into before the year was out, he might have tolerated him less. But he'd still have admired the man's sheer brass-necked audacity.

Having failed in his attempt to penetrate the Kremlin via the front door, Reilly assumed his regular disguise – a Levantine Greek called 'Mr Constantine' – and went back to Petrograd. There, through an old Russian acquaintance, he managed to get himself a post as an agent in the criminal investigation branch of the Cheka. Thus equipped, he had total freedom to move around Russia and engage in whatever covert activity took his fancy.[7]

Meanwhile, Lockhart turned his attention to his proper business, and to Moura. The two strands of his life – love and intrigue – were slowly, insensibly becoming entangled, and Moura was willingly binding herself up in the cords.

20 May 1918

Just outside the city, the Moskva river took a great bend to the southwest. Lining the river's edge was a band of low, wooded hills, known as the Vorobyovy Gory – the Sparrow Hills. In the dark before sunrise, the first twitters of the dawn chorus were interrupted by the whine of an engine. The lights of a motor car glanced among the trees as it climbed the gentle, winding slope.

At the summit it parked and two figures got out. Arm in arm, they walked into the woods. On the far side, under the trees, they stood in the chilly air, drowsy with love and lost sleep, and waited for the sun to come up.

Lockhart and Moura were both tired and more than a little drunk. They had been up all night celebrating with their friends – the little circle of Britons who clustered around Lockhart in the increasingly unsettled environment of Moscow. Lockhart had a young fellow he'd taken on to his staff, an artillery lieutenant called Guy Tamplin, who'd been born in Russia and spoke the language perfectly.[8] The previous day had been Tamplin's twenty-first birthday, and Lockhart had decided to throw a party. The venue was the Strelna night-restaurant in Petrovsky Park, outside the city. The Strelna, one of several such establishments in the park, was an incredible place – a great glass conservatory in which tropical plants grew, even in the depths of a Moscow winter, where customers dined in grottoes and cabins built within the glazed enclosure. It had been a favourite haunt of Lockhart's in his days at the Moscow Consulate. It was presided over by Madame Maria Nikolaievna,[9] a beautiful middle-aged lady who was a captivating singer of gypsy songs – the very music most inclined to stir Lockhart's blood. Somehow her cabaret-restaurant had escaped closure by the Cheka.

Her days were numbered, though, and everyone knew it. So too were the days of the British in Moscow, it seemed. Tamplin's birthday party was – or so it seemed at the time – a valedictory hurrah for the Lockhart mission. And for Lockhart himself it was also a farewell for Moura, who was travelling back to Petrograd the next day, after ten days with him.[10]

It had been an intense ten days, for a multitude of reasons. Shortly after Reilly had stolen away, another mysterious individual surfaced in Moscow and made contact with Lockhart. This time it was a person known to both Lockhart and Moura. Fearing for his life after his efforts to raise a military resistance to the Bolsheviks, the surprise visitor was none other than the former premier of all Russia and darling of the people, Alexander Kerensky. He was travelling disguised as a Serbian soldier, and was desperate to get out of Russia before the Bolsheviks could catch and murder him.

His only hope was through the British route, via Vologda and Murmansk. He had approached old Wardrop, the Consul-General (the last sagging remnant of the British ambassadorial presence in Russia), to ask for a visa, but without success; Wardrop would take no action without consulting London. Lockhart wasn't authorised to issue visas, but he cobbled one together anyway, marking Kerensky's false Serbian passport with a signature and a rubber stamp.[11]

It was enough. Kerensky, with his handful of loyal companions, headed north for the bleak British outpost on the Barents Sea coast. A few weeks later, with a blaze of publicity, he surfaced in London, claiming to have come 'straight from Moscow' but refusing to elaborate how.[12]

As Kerensky left the shores of his homeland, the Bolsheviks were overturning one of the most popular measures of his provisional government – on 16 June the government newspaper *Izvestia* announced the reintroduction of the death penalty, a measure Lenin had been pushing for for months. Trotsky had noted Lenin's reaction upon learning of Kerensky's abolition: 'Nonsense,' he said. 'How can one make a revolution without firing squads?'[13]

Lockhart's relationship with Trotsky was falling apart also. During the period of Moura's visit, Cromie came down twice from Petrograd, and the two men met with Trotsky to discuss the destruction of the Black Sea fleet. These were to be Lockhart's last meetings with the man himself; from now on he would see only deputies.

Britain's star seemed to be falling, and so the mood in the Strelna restaurant that night was that of the eve of departure. Madame Nikolaievna's gypsy songs filled the summer night with melancholy longing, the rhythm of the guitars and the depths of her contralto voice having their everlasting effect on Lockhart. 'How it all comes back to me,' he would write, 'like every experience which we cannot repeat.'[14] Aside from himself and Moura, there were five people at that party. Young Tamplin, the birthday boy, was one. Hicks was another – back from his long trip to Siberia – as well as another assistant of Lockhart's called George Lingner. Denis Garstin added good cheer as always, and Captain George Hill, the extraordinary SIS agent, was there, taking a moment out of his life of espionage.

They got drunker by degrees, and took turns to wander outside under the lime trees to clear their heads. Only Lockhart stayed indoors, wreathed in music, along with Moura, who had a powerful resistance to alcohol and could drink strong men into oblivion without showing more than a slur in her voice.

Lockhart persuaded Madame Nikolaievna to repeat one particular song over and over; it was called 'I Cannot Forget', and was 'in tune with my own turbulent soul', 'a throbbing plaint of longing and desire' about a man reputed to be a faithless philanderer but who has been transfixed by one woman – '. . . why do I forget the rest / and still remember only you . . .'[15]

After the party, in the early hours before dawn, he and Moura took the car and drove out to the Sparrow Hills. The wooded slopes gave a spectacular view eastward over the city. The two lovers watched the sun rise, spilling a pool of fiery light over the Kremlin's spires and gleaming domes. Looking back, it seemed to Lockhart like a portent of the violent mood of vengeance that had already been seeping, and would soon begin to flood through the city.

Moura finally knew, finally understood, how she felt. It was a revelation. As soon as she was back in Petrograd she rushed to put her feelings into words. 'I am caught at last and for good,' she wrote to him.[16] Only one thing mattered to her now: 'my love to you, my Baby-boy. I am childishly happy about it, so confident in the future'. Along with love came anxiety, and a yearning to be with him always. But there were so many obstacles; they were both married, and the tide of the Revolution was in spate and forcing them apart. Soon he might be forced to leave Russia, while she was trapped here, and her children stranded beyond the German border in Estonia. She had tried, foolishly and incoherently, to express her feelings to him when he came to see her off from the station after their dawn vigil in the Sparrow Hills. But he hushed her. There was nothing they could do but hope that they would conquer fate somehow.

Love might either see them through these terrible times, or it might destroy them. But one thing was certain – Moura would do whatever she had to in order to survive. In that respect she hadn't changed. The complications of her tender feelings towards Lockhart were minor compared to the contradictions in the other activities she was being drawn into.

It was never recorded when they first approached her. History also failed to note exactly how they approached her, or who was responsible. Neither is it known what inducements were offered or what threats. All that ever came to light – and only to a handful of people – was that Moura began to spy on Lockhart and his colleagues on behalf of the Cheka.

The rumours that arose later were misinformed and inaccurate. What they omitted was that spying on Lockhart was only a small part of what she did. What nobody seemed ever to suspect was that the person who primed and prepared her to spy, who laid the path that took her into the Cheka, was Lockhart himself.

In those weeks of spring and summer, he was ever more preoccupied with the state of his mission: concerned with Bolshevik policy, the position of Germany in it and the multiple conflicting strands of British activity in Russia. Would there be military intervention, covert subversion or diplomacy?

He was so preoccupied that Moura began to worry when she returned to Petrograd that he might not love her as much as she did him. She would do anything for him, and she yearned to be with him; she wanted 'happiness, peace, love, work' and railed against fate and the 'thousand and one things that come between me and all that'.[17] 'I want you to come to me,' she wrote, 'when you are tired, to tell me, when you want my help . . . and I want to be your mistress, when you want passion.' But for now all they could do was wait, hope, and snatch what time they could together – 'And you will have to see, whether you really love me.'[18]

Perhaps it was that uncertainty which made her push back the bounds of what she was willing to do for him.

It began with gossip. Her letters, their pages blooming with love, were topped up with snippets of information and hearsay about the comings and goings of the other British missions in Russia. She knew them all well, personally and professionally. General Frederick Poole, who was heading for Archangel with a British military force of uncertain size and purpose, was a major concern. Moura warned Lockhart that there were rumours that Poole was 'coming with greater powers', that he might take full charge of all British operations, and bend them all towards military intervention. But Moura added darkly that if it were necessary to discredit Poole and his mission, 'there is nothing easier than to expose him'. He was 'in with the Jews', she said cryptically.[19] As an employee of Hugh Leech, she knew something of the underhand financial deals that several senior British officers with backgrounds in Russia had been involved in. Their purpose had been to fund anti-Bolshevik White forces and scupper German banking interests in Russia, but there were signs in Leech's evasive behaviour that there might have been some misappropriation of funds going on;[20] if so, Moura would be the person to sniff it out. He had fled once already to Murmansk and worked his way back.

She was able to reassure her beloved that Francis Cromie and Le Page were true to him (for which she took a little credit for herself), and the

SIS chief Ernest Boyce had a high opinion of him. But there were concerns. Cromie worried her deeply one day by taking her aside and asking her quietly, 'You're friendly with Lockhart, and you don't wish him any harm?'

Startled, she replied, 'Of course not, why should I?'

'Well, don't go to Moscow again,' said Cromie. 'It might harm him, he's got many old enemies in Moscow.'[21]

She wrote asking Lockhart what Cromie could possibly mean. 'I don't see it at all, but of course in some ways I have the psychology of the ostrich.' Her psychology was actually the opposite of ostrich-like, but Cromie had alarmed her. It was only too clear that he was referring to the jealous diplomats and businessmen who resented the young upstart with his pro-Bolshevik policy and might take any opportunity to mar his reputation.

There was another cloud on Moura's horizon. It took the bluff, moustached form of Colonel Cudbert Thornhill, an SIS officer who had come out to handle intelligence for General Poole's mission in the north. He'd been in Petrograd before, at the British Embassy in 1915. For reasons she didn't specify, Moura neither liked nor trusted Thornhill. The feeling seemed to be mutual, though again she didn't elaborate on the reasons. 'I am so suspicious of him in every way,' she wrote to Lockhart. 'If he comes here and suspects something between you and me and even without that – he will be sure to try and blacken me in your eyes.' Perhaps this was some lingering rumour from the time of 'Madame B' and her salon. She worried in case Lockhart believed whatever it was that Thornhill might tell him. 'Perhaps not,' she mused, 'but it will raise doubts in you – and there is nothing I deserve less.'[22] Quickly she assured him that Thornhill was a fractious type who generally didn't get on with people.[23] This was true; there had certainly been friction between him and General Knox, and he'd had a strained relationship with Sir Mansfield Smith Cumming (the original 'C'), the head of SIS.[24] According to Moura, Thornhill and Poole didn't like each other, which could spell doom for the Archangel mission, whatever it turned out to be.

But there was more to Moura's role than gossip. Lockhart's diplomacy was entering a new and dangerous phase. He could see intervention coming, and the mood among the British in Petrograd and Murmansk was all for it. He was feeling more than ever that the government at home didn't value his work. As the last days of May passed by, he began to take on a more militant mood, and much of it was focused on the Germans.

In this respect his antipathy was matched by the Bolsheviks' fears and suspicions of the occupied Balkan provinces and the much bigger threat of the Ukraine. In their lightning advance in February and March, the German army had overrun the Ukraine, and under the terms of the Brest-Litovsk treaty they took possession of it – ostensibly as an autonomous protectorate – and began shaping it to suit their own purposes.

On 29 April a coup brought down the Ukraine's democratic socialist government. The coup was led by General Pavlo Skoropadskyi,* a Ukrainian Cossack aristocrat, and backed by the German army. Before the rise of Bolshevism, Skoropadskyi had been one of the biggest landowners in the Ukraine, a loyal Russian imperialist who had served as a staff officer in the Russian army and aide-de-camp to Tsar Nicholas II.[25]

A new government was set up, supported by Germany and composed of Ukrainian landowners, many with Cossack heritage. Skoropadskyi was installed as ruler, taking the traditional Cossack title *Hetman* – an autocrat presiding over a council of ministers. The first act of the Hetmanate government (as it became known) was to reverse the redistribution of land implemented by the socialist government, returning the Ukraine's great estates and farmlands to their former owners. Strikes were banned, dissent crushed and peasant revolts violently subdued.[26] The Ukraine became a client state of Germany, a rich source of grain for the German war machine, and a kind of sanatorium for German army divisions worn down by service on the Western Front; they were set loose to live upon the land and rebuild their strength and morale at the peasants' expense.[27]

In Moscow, the Bolsheviks were appalled. Not only by what the Hetmanate stood for – a typically heinous bourgeois repression of the proletariat – but also by the terrifying feeling that this was the true face of Germany. Might this be how they intended to treat Russia? The coup in the Ukraine had occurred only three days after the arrival of Count Mirbach as German Ambassador in Moscow, which underlined the Bolsheviks' fears.

Lockhart was privately delighted. In his eyes, the Germans were driving a massive Ukraine-shaped wedge between themselves and the

---

* Ukrainian sp.; Russian sp.: Pavel Skoropadski.

Bolsheviks. On 6 May he noted in his diary that the Bolsheviks 'regard this as a direct menace to their government'; it was seen as an attempt to initiate counter-revolution, 'not only for Ukraine but for all Russia'. When he and Cromie met Trotsky a week later to discuss the German threat to the Russian Black Sea fleet – which was in Ukrainian hands – they were told that war with Germany was 'inevitable', and that he was ready to listen to any proposals the British might have.[28] Even Lenin, the determined isolationist, was starting to see war with Germany as a possibility. He told Lockhart that he saw a future in which Russia would become a battlefield on which Germany and Britain would fight each other. He was willing to do whatever it took to prevent it.[29] Lockhart took that cryptic assurance as encouragement – not realising that Lenin had his own secret plans for settling the situation.

For Lockhart and his inner circle, the Ukrainian crisis offered hope. Anti-British, anti-French, anti-American feelings were reaching a simmering point in Russia. The valedictory mood at Tamplin's birthday party had reflected the belief that the feeling would grow, that it would take over the Central Committee, and finally drive the British out of Russia. But if the German threat were seen to overshadow the British threat, that would all change. With the token British force at Murmansk, however, and a new force on its way to Archangel, intervention against the German eastern frontier without approval from the Bolsheviks was looking increasingly likely. Direct intervention against the Bolsheviks themselves could not be ruled out.

There was still a chance to win the Bolsheviks over, Lockhart believed, but time was running out and his government was giving him nothing tangible to offer Trotsky.

The Bolsheviks – or rather elements among them – began to support guerrilla action in the Ukraine. Captain George Hill, Lockhart's SIS friend, had close cooperative links to the Cheka and was trusted by the Bolshevik leadership, having helped Trotsky set up his military intelligence organisation, the GRU. Hill was central to the operation. He and his Canadian friend Colonel Joe Boyle had built up a network of agents, couriers and saboteurs which had been active in the Ukrainian mining regions for months, causing huge damage to its ability to contribute to Germany's war economy. Starting in May he reactivated his agents, organising attacks on German army rest camps.[30]

Quite how Moura became caught up in the Ukrainian intrigue was never set down in writing – at least not in any form that survived. But the reasons for bringing her into it were clear enough, as was her role – not as a saboteur but as a gatherer of intelligence.[31] Not only was she close to Lockhart, she was absolutely trusted by him, and eager for his approval; she had some experience of espionage – albeit of a genteel, domestic kind; and she knew the British secret intelligence people. That included George Hill. If anyone could secure her a place in the Cheka – which would be needed in order to acquire the necessary travel rights – it would be him.

The Chekists had still not shaken out all the wrinkles of their newborn organisation; they were hungry for personnel, and didn't subject recruits to particularly intense scrutiny. Sidney Reilly, after all, had been able to gain a post. Also, there were elements within the Cheka who had a particular interest in undermining Germany's standing in Russia and the Ukraine, and were already taking steps to bring matters to a head. Around the core of Latvian Chekist deputy Martin Latsis and Ukrainian Jakov Bliumkin, a counter-espionage section was set up to penetrate the German Embassy in Moscow, in cooperation with George Hill.[32]

In this environment, it would be easy to insert a friendly agent into the Cheka.

Crucially, Moura was a Ukrainian. She came from a prominent land-owning family, bred into the very class that was now ruling the country (just as it had in her childhood). If you wanted a spy to penetrate the heart of the Hetmanate, you'd have to search a long time before coming up with a better candidate than Moura Ignatievna von Benckendorff. Few could match her for persuasive charm, and none could beat her for courage.

At about the same time, Lockhart expressed a private worry that the Cheka might have obtained a copy of the cipher he used to encrypt his messages to London.[33] It was said, many years later, that they were acquired by Moura, as part of some unspecified arrangement with the Cheka.[34]

The wolves were running, but this time she was running with them – and pursuing with the hounds as well. There was something in her which answered to the call of the game – the intrigue, the danger, the sense of knowing things that others did not – and it would never quite leave her as long as she lived.

In June the game began in earnest.[35] Moura made the trip from Petrograd to Kiev. It was a journey she had last undertaken when visiting the Zakrevsky family estate. How long ago that seemed now – a different world, a different girl. It was over two days by train. If she hadn't had official Bolshevik authorisation on the Russian side of the border and a mission to the leaders of the Hetmanate on the Ukrainian side, it would have taken much longer – and a good deal of dangerous subterfuge – to cross the frontier.

The familiar dull flatness of the Ukrainian Steppe matched a bleak patch in Moura's heart. She had tried to get in touch with Lockhart before leaving, but he hadn't replied. She read in the papers that he had gone to Vologda at the end of May to meet the Allied Ambassadors holed up there. 'No news from you,' she wrote to him, 'and I want you very badly. I may have to go away for a short time, and would like to see you before I go.' She had heard – not from him – that he was coming to Petrograd. 'Do try and come as soon as you can,' she pleaded, 'I feel so lonely without you.'[36]

Lockhart arrived in Petrograd on 2 June to consult Cromie about the situation at Archangel. But he didn't meet Moura; by the time he reached the city, she had gone. She had begun her journey; not just the literal one to Kiev, but the longer, more insidious journey into the service of the Bolshevik secret state.

In Kiev she lost no time making contact with the Hetmanate. She had a powerful *entrée* to their circle, besides merely her birth and class. Those things would make her trustworthy in the Ukrainians' eyes, but she also had a direct connection. In early May, Hetman Skoropadskyi had appointed one Fedir Lyzohub* as both minister for internal affairs – giving him responsibility for state security – and prime minister. As the right hand of the Hetman, Lyzohub took the traditional Cossack title *otaman*.† Like Skoropadskyi, Lyzohub was a rich landowner. He had been prominent in the regional government of Poltava before the war,[37] where he had known Moura's father, Ignatiy Zakrevsky.

Moura approached Lyzohub – a solemn, dignified old gentleman with a steep forehead and a neat white beard – and offered her services as a spy against the Bolsheviks. He believed in her wholeheartedly (for

---

* Ukrainian sp.; Russian sp.: Fyodor Lizogub.
† Chieftain.

why should he not believe in the daughter of a fellow noble, especially when she had such irresistible magnetism?) and immediately ordered the Ukrainian intelligence service to employ her.[38]

Moura was introduced to Skoropadskyi himself, and to Foreign Minister Dmytro Doroshenko.* For the best part of the next month, and intermittently thereafter, she made journeys back and forth between Kiev and Russia, passing intelligence to both sides.[39] What she was most skilled at was social espionage – listening for gossip, encouraging indiscretion. There is no underestimating the vanity of semi-powerful men, and their willingness to display their importance to an attractive young woman by telling her secrets. It wasn't until much later – far too late for them to do anything about it – that the Hetmanate realised that Moura – daughter of their own kind – had been betraying them to the Bolsheviks. By then, Moura herself had more important things to worry about, and had left the province of her birth behind her, never to return.

During that summer of 1918, that was still in the future; in the meantime, during her trips back and forth to the Ukraine, Moura realised that she was facing a problem that eclipsed all others. She was pregnant.

---

* Ukrainian sp.; Russian sp.: Dmitri Doroshenko.

8

A Hair's Breadth from War

June–July 1918

Lockhart had changed his mind. Almost overnight, he had utterly transformed his beliefs and his attitude. His faith in the Bolsheviks, which had been eroding throughout April and May, finally expired in June. They couldn't be relied on, couldn't be persuaded to support a British intervention against Germany. In that case, intervention must come whether the Bolsheviks willed it or not.

During his visit to Petrograd in early June, he had met an officer visiting from Archangel, who had convinced him that intervention would come, but not for a long while.[1] This was typical of the British government – they pushed for intervention, but were dithering and dilatory in providing it. Well, that would have to change.

On his return to Moscow, he fired off a startling message to London: if they were going for military action in north Russia, it must come in the immediate future. If not, he would resign.[2] Foreign Secretary Arthur Balfour clucked like a kicked hen at this astonishing about-face. Lockhart must learn to understand the subtle complications of international diplomacy, Balfour insisted. But Lockhart had neither time nor patience for the subtle complications of diplomats. He had enough of his own, and they were becoming increasingly risky. He had been secretly in contact with Savinkov's anti-Bolshevik movement in April, before its abortive coup; now he began to involve himself more deeply.

His hope that he could swing the Bolsheviks against Germany was falling to pieces – and had been doing so since the arrival of Count Mirbach in Moscow. On 15 May – the very same day that Lockhart and Cromie had met Trotsky and were told that war with Germany was inevitable – Lenin had been meeting Mirbach and proposing a deal.

Germany must accept Bolshevik policy in Russia and promise not to interfere in Russian internal affairs; in exchange, Russia would promise friendly and lucrative trading relations with Germany.[3] Lenin had told Lockhart that he would do whatever was necessary to prevent Russia becoming a British–German battleground; Lockhart hadn't guessed that this was what he had in mind. If the agreement was ratified, it would end all hope for Britain in Russia, other than the vain hope of beating both Germany and Bolshevism by military action.

On 12 June, while Moura was still engaged in spying, a peace treaty between Hetmanate Ukraine and Bolshevik Russia was signed.[4] It wasn't the end of hostility between them, or spying, but it all but obliterated Lockhart and Hill's – and Trotsky's and the Cheka's – hope of a terminal breach.

Into the middle of this tangle of politics intruded the most basic, most pressing of human crises. A month on from their last passionate spell together in Moscow, Moura discovered that she was pregnant with Lockhart's child.

As soon as she could, in the last days of June, she travelled to Moscow to tell him the news. The jokes they had concocted about an imaginary little boy Moura would give him, who would be fed on raw meat and be good at football, had suddenly become real.

Again Moura was surprised by her own feelings. It confirmed for her that Lockhart was the man she wanted to be with, and without whom she could not live. 'All the day the thought of you never leaves me and I feel lost without you – why Baby, what have you done to me, the little callous icicle!'[5] She was thrilled to be able to give him a son; there was no doubt in either of their minds that it would be a boy, and they christened him 'little Willy' – or 'little Peter' if they were in a more serious mood. The welfare of both Moura and the baby were added to the towering stack of worries that overshadowed Lockhart night and day.

Together they faced the question of what was to be done about little Peter and about the future. There was a wife in England and a husband in Estonia to consider, not to mention Moura's other children. What would become of them? It was decided that Moura must go to Yendel – with her freedom to travel and her experience of crossing borders, it should be little trouble. Her purpose there would be to contrive to have Djon sleep with her. Thus, when the baby was born, his legitimacy could not be disproved, and the two lovers could do what they wished without a stain on their little boy's character.

It was a desperate plan, and a dreadful prospect. Unusually, Moura shrank from acting on it, and she delayed her departure from Moscow. After a month without his arms, his kisses, his presence, she clung to Lockhart. But eventually she had to detach herself from him. His situation in Russia was becoming more precarious by the week, and when Moura boarded the train for Petrograd on Thursday 4 July, it was with the possibility that he might not still be here when she returned.

Moura arrived in Petrograd to find a letter waiting for her. It was from Djon. She had contacted him to suggest a visit, but would he still wish to see her now? The last time they had been together, at the beginning of the year, it had been in a state of frigid dislike. Did he know about Lockhart? Tearing the letter open and racing through it, she was relieved to find that he wanted her to come to Yendel.[6]

The relief was tinged with guilt. Moura fretted about the impending plot. 'I love my kids very dearly,' she wrote to Lockhart from Petrograd, 'and placing them in a false situation apart from losing them . . . will be very very painful to me.' But her resolve held – 'not for a moment does it interfere with my decision, not for a moment does it make me think: "is it not better to give him up – return to the old life again" – I might as well think of giving up light – air'.[7]

Whatever her feelings, she could do nothing immediately. There were no trains between Petrograd and Estonia, so she intended to travel by the same mail troika that had taken the children in March, with the same escort. But her delay in leaving Moscow had made her miss the departure. She would have to linger in Petrograd and wait for the man's return.[8]

It had become a miserable place – 'dying a natural death' from poverty and starvation.[9] There had been outbreaks of cholera, with more than three hundred new cases each day.[10] Everything was short, and Moura and her mother had become dependent on flour sent by Lockhart or Denis Garstin from Moscow, where food was plentiful if you had the money to pay the rocketing prices.

While she slipped back into her usual life – working, seeing Cromie and the other embassy people, gathering gossip, writing letter after letter to Lockhart – the situation took a sudden dramatic turn. In Moscow on Saturday 6 July, two days after Moura's return to Petrograd, Count

Wilhelm von Mirbach, German Ambassador to Moscow, Lockhart's nemesis, was assassinated – shot and bombed to death in his own embassy. The reports were confused, but the Red papers in Petrograd claimed that the killing had been instigated by British and French imperialist agents. A horrified Moura wondered what repercussions might ensue for Lockhart.[11]

The assassination had been a long time in the planning. And whatever the Red papers might be saying in Petrograd, the plot had originated, hatched and been executed from within the upper ranks of the Cheka.

It came to a head during the Fifth All-Russian Congress of Soviets, the great policy-making gathering of the governing parties of the Russian Soviet Republic.[12] The Congress was held in the Bolshoi Theatre in Moscow, and began on Thursday 4 July, the same day Moura departed for Petrograd.

In the spirit of revolutionary openness and egalitarianism that still lingered in summer 1918, all parties, all opinions, all dissenting voices, were allowed to be heard. and the representatives of foreign missions were encouraged to attend as observers. Lockhart, accompanied by Captain George Hill and some members of his mission staff, found himself allocated a box on the left side of the stage, along with the French and American missions. Directly opposite were the boxes of the Central Powers – the Austrians, the Hungarians, and the Germans, presided over by a serene and self-satisfied Count Mirbach.[13]

The entire Congress – delegates, audience and chairmen – crackled with tension and hostility from the very beginning. There were over one thousand two hundred delegates in attendance, from all over the Soviet Republic. They represented the only two parties still surviving from the informal coalition that had fought the October Revolution – the Bolsheviks and the Left Socialist Revolutionaries. Lenin's Bolsheviks were unquestionably the party of power. Having dominated, purged and destroyed most of the others – including the Anarchists and Mensheviks – they now outnumbered the Left Socialist Revolutionaries two to one, and were set on establishing a total monopoly on power. The Fifth Congress of Soviets quickly turned into the prelude to the final, fatal showdown between the two parties.

Their mutual loathing came into the open on the second day, when the leadership of the Left SRs began laying their grievances at the feet of the Bolsheviks – from the reintroduction of the death penalty to the continuing poverty of the rural peasantry. The foremost speaker was a slight, pale young woman called Maria Spiridonova. Utterly dedicated to the socialist cause, in her youth she had gained fame by shooting dead a brutal landowner and local government enforcer. Her courage was indomitable, and from the stage of the Bolshoi she berated Lenin from pillar to post. 'I accuse you of betraying the peasants, of making use of them for your own ends'. In Lenin's philosophy, she said, the workers were 'only manure'. Her voice was monotonous and grating, but her spirit was potent, and she promised that if the Bolsheviks continued to humiliate and crush the peasants, she would deal out the same retribution she had delivered to the Tsarist enforcer twelve years earlier.[14]

While the theatre erupted in wild cheering, Lenin sat quiet, with an air of such self-confidence that Lockhart found it almost irritating. Lenin believed in his own power, his own security. He had the Cheka, and also the Latvian rifle regiment who were his loyal 'Praetorian Guard' – the entire theatre was surrounded and infested by them. He was safe from fanatics' pistols, he believed, and his new regime was secure against political radicals.

Spiridonova was not finished; she also lashed the German party in their box, shaking her fist at them and insisting that Russia would never become a colony or vassal of Germany. Sitting next to Lockhart, George Hill had to restrain himself from cheering.[15] Lockhart, knowing that the Left SRs were no more friendly to British intervention than the Bolsheviks, felt less encouraged.

The anti-German theme was taken up by Boris Kamkov, another Left SR and superb orator. He too addressed the German box, and thundered at them: 'The dictatorship of the proletariat has developed into a dictatorship of Mirbach.' He denounced Lenin's shameful kowtowing to the German imperialists, 'who have the audacity to show their faces even in this theatre'. While Lockhart marvelled at Kamkov's passion and suicidal foolhardiness, the Left SRs in the audience cheered and yelled 'Down with Mirbach!'[16]

Again and again the German occupation of the Ukraine and the Skoropadskyi Hetmanate government were cited as evidence of Germany's nature and its intentions for Russia.

Mirbach seemed unfazed by the denunciations. Like Lenin, he regarded the threats of the Left SRs as nothing but oratory. Both were making a grave error. Neither realised that, away from the theatre, Spiridonova and her comrades had been getting ready to put their principles into action. They had already taken over the requisite sections of the Cheka and were ready to strike.

At about three o'clock in the afternoon of Saturday 6 July, the third day of the Congress, two Cheka officers arrived at the German Embassy in Denezhnyy pereulok,* a well-to-do street in the west of the city. The senior of the two was Yakiv Blyumkin,† head of the counter-espionage section of the anti-counter-revolutionary department. Blyumkin, a Ukrainian Jew from Odessa, was young – just turned twenty – but had an impressive record of service in the armed forces of the Revolution, and had been given one of the most powerful positions in the Cheka. His official role was to keep watch on the activities of foreign agents and diplomatic missions, principally the Germans. Like several other key officers of the Cheka he was also a member of the Left Socialist Revolutionaries and a close comrade of Maria Spiridonova. She had helped plan the operation that Blyumkin was here to carry out.[17]

Blyumkin and his partner brought with them a document authorising them to consult with the German Ambassador, signed and sealed with the full authority of the Cheka and its head, Felix Dzerzhinsky (the very same blade-faced villain to whom Lockhart had taken such a dislike). Count Mirbach's aide, impressed by the warrant, ushered the two men straight into the Ambassador's presence, in the drawing room of his residence.

In fact, Dzershinsky's signature was forged, the seal used illegally, and the warrant had been written out by Blyumkin himself, using an official form.

The two Chekists exchanged a few words with Mirbach, then Blyumkin drew a revolver and, without hesitation, fired several shots at the Count. Wounded, Mirbach tried to escape, and German guards returned fire as Blyumkin and his comrade clambered out of the window. Blyumkin fractured his leg in the escape and was hit by a German bullet, but still made sure of his victim by lobbing a hand grenade into the room. The two Chekists made it out of the embassy grounds and were picked up by a waiting car which rushed them to their headquarters.[18]

---

* Money Lane.
† Ukrainian sp.; Russian sp.: Yakov Blumkin.

They had done their job well. The death of Count Mirbach was announced later that day. Immediately the Cheka and the Bolshevik government started to detonate from within. Dzerzhinsky himself attempted to arrest Blyumkin and the Left SR Chekists, but was instead arrested by them and held captive.

So began the uprising of the Left Socialist Revolutionaries. Despite the violence, it was never intended as a coup, but rather an attempt to force the Bolsheviks to rescind their policy of appeasing Germany and exploiting the peasants.

On the very same day, apparently unconnected to the events in Moscow, Boris Savinkov, the anti-Bolshevik militant leader who was being secretly backed by the Allies, finally launched his long-delayed uprising. Following the abandonment of his May Day coup, he had prepared a new strike against the Bolsheviks, and on 6 July his forces seized control of Yaroslavl, a small but strategically important city on the Volga on the road between Moscow and Vologda. Savinkov's uprising was being funded by the French mission at Vologda to the tune of millions of roubles, with the full knowledge of Lockhart.[19]

The Bolshevik press had a field day with allegations that Britain and France had helped both Savinkov and the Left SRs, whose uprising spread the next day to Petrograd. In the early hours, appalled by the possible repercussions from Germany, Lenin telegraphed his deputy, Stalin, about the implosion within the Cheka. 'The assassination is clearly in the interests of the monarchists or the Anglo-French capitalists,' he claimed, and with cold fury condemned the perfidious Left SRs: 'We are about to liquidate them mercilessly tonight and we shall tell the people the whole truth: we are a hair's breadth from war.'[20]

In Petrograd, Moura witnessed the uprising of the local Left SRs with a mixture of contempt and fear. Contempt for its poverty of spirit, and fear for the danger that Lockhart must now be in. Hearing rumours of riots in Moscow, and the tales that were being put about that the Allies were involved in the assassination, she postponed her already delayed trip to Yendel, and wrote to him, pouring out her fears. 'You know what that might mean,' she said, referring to the rumours of Allied involvement. 'I am terrified, terrified.'[21]

On Sunday evening, the day of the Petrograd uprising, Moura and Francis Cromie went together to look at the scene of insurrection. For anyone anticipating the downfall of the Bolsheviks, it was a disappointment.

The Pazhesky Korpus* was a prestigious military academy in the centre of the city, off the Nevsky Prospekt, about half a mile from the British Embassy. It had been commandeered after the Revolution as the headquarters of the Left SR military wing, who were supposed to defend Petrograd against German and White Finnish attack.[22] The building was occupied by a confused band of several hundred soldiers. Most were young, many were mercenaries. Their ranks were depleted by the number of dedicated Left SR fighters who were away serving against counter-revolutionary forces in remote parts of Russia – the Caucasus, Siberia. When the Red Army approached the building and threatened them with arrest unless they handed over their weapons, the Left SRs – who had little idea of what had actually been going on in Moscow – fought back. A siege began. The Red Army attacked in strength, mounting guns in a shopping arcade across the street and hitting the Pazhesky Korpus with artillery fire. The Left SRs shot back with rifles.[23]

Standing with Cromie among the terrified but enthralled onlookers as the smoke of battle drifted in the streets, Moura was unimpressed – 'after 40 minutes their courage failed them and they surrendered,' she wrote to Lockhart, 'it was ludicrous to look at'.[24] Some of the defenders gave themselves up; others fled across the rooftops. By nine o'clock it was all over. So ended the Left SRs in Petrograd, while in Moscow, more organised and better led, they struggled on.

Cromie didn't take it quite as lightly as Moura. Since hearing the news about Mirbach, he had begun destroying his official papers; a crisis was approaching, and he deemed it unsafe to keep records.[25] This business was all new to him. Accustomed to commanding at sea, he was navigating unfamiliar waters now, sailing into the dark realm of conspiracy and espionage, dealing daily with SIS agents, propaganda and anti-Bolshevik movements in the Baltic provinces, and it made him edgy.

He wasn't entirely cut out for this sort of affair, Moura believed; he hadn't the natural discretion for it. She took advantage of his gossipy temperament and his susceptibility to her charm, and made him her

---

* Pages School.

most prized source of information about the British missions. She passed her discoveries along to Lockhart, warning him of any hostilities and backbiting, and reassuring him that the most important people – Cromie himself, for one – were true. Even while she fretted over the dangerous aftermath of the Mirbach murder and counted the days until her departure for Yendel, she continued to gather intelligence.

One item alarmed her. A story was told by Major McAlpine (a member of the military mission who was anti-Lockhart) that Moura had been 'seen in Moscow walking about with a member of the German Embassy'. She ridiculed the idea: 'As I have not been with any male person except the 6 Englishmen,' she told Lockhart, 'I wonder who of you has been taken for a German. It is really funny.' Despite making light of it, she was rattled by the story, and made sure to point out that her friend Colonel Terence Keyes of the SIS knew how anti-German she was – he had joked about her having murdered Mirbach herself before fleeing to Petrograd. 'In my national inner self,' she wrote, 'I wish it were I . . .'[26]

With boundless, reckless courage, Moura rarely accepted the true gravity of any situation. But Lockhart, under extreme stress as conflict and danger flared around him – and around the future of British interests in Russia – was less inclined to be flippant. Missing her sorely, concerned about the baby, and startled by what sounded like a lot of extremely loose gossip going on in the British mission in Petrograd, he arranged to speak with her on the telephone, both to reassure her and to upbraid her.

Moura was thrilled speechless. 'I am moved to tears at the thought that you are there on the other side of the line,' she wrote immediately after, 'and I cannot take your head in my hand and kiss your eyes and your lips and let you take me in your arms'.[27]

He grilled her about what she had been saying to people, what she had been hearing. The situation in Moscow was more delicate than ever; Lockhart and Cromie were beginning to involve themselves in covert anti-Bolshevik activities which Moura didn't yet know of; activities which Lockhart was not even telling his superiors in London the whole truth about. He demanded to know what she had said to Cromie, and warned her to be careful in her conversations. She too was involved in covert operations in the Ukraine which could put her in a difficult situation if her British companions in Petrograd learned of them and misconstrued their purpose.

She chided him in turn for mistaking her levity for carelessness. 'You funny Boy,' she teased him afterwards, 'first of all getting anxious when I spoke of letters being searched – what did you think? – that I put Cromie in the confidence, or what? You are extraordinary!' She assured Lockhart that she only believed half of what Cromie told her – 'and am more careful with him than you think'. Indeed, it was Cromie who had a problem with discretion – 'he is a kind of a gramophone for all the infernal gossip in the Embassy,' she said. 'That's why I cultivate him.'[28]

It was a strangely cynical way to refer to a friend for whom she felt real affection, but Moura, despite her lightness of tone, was shocked and indignant that her beloved Baby-Boy could doubt her. And perhaps slightly alarmed that she was a little less immune to scrutiny than she had believed.

But the one thing that worried her deeply was Lockhart's safety. In Moscow the Bolsheviks, who were regaining control of the Cheka and vigorously purging the Left SRs, were falling over themselves to make amends to the Germans – although they drew the line at having a battalion of German troops guard the Embassy. Despite the propaganda being spread that the Allies had been behind the assassination, however, the foreign ministry offered Lockhart a bodyguard to protect him from German reprisals.

Moura wasn't very reassured.[29] She could sense the anti-British feeling rising on the streets of Petrograd. Her journey to Yendel – the subterfuge to protect her unborn child from shame – could not be cancelled, and it seemed increasingly possible that Lockhart might have left Russia or been caught up in some new conflagration by the time she returned. She wrote him letter after letter during those days in Petrograd, until she could delay no more.

'If I remain there longer than a week,' she wrote, 'I pray I will not – but if – you *must beleive** that it will only be if there is some difficulty about trains and passes. Please please, Baby, don't think of anything else.'[30]

By the eve of her departure her hopes had sunk, but her defiance and courage had risen to meet them. 'How I hate it all,' she wrote, dreading the deception she was about to foist on her husband, 'when I just want to cry for you and let all the world hear, that I love you so . . . Do you know what your love has done? It has changed me from being a woman

---

* Despite her linguistic gifts, Moura never mastered the spelling of 'ie' words.

to be a man, with a man's sense of decency, sense of honour, sense of what is fair and what isn't. No lack of determination about me now sir. I know what I want and I'm jolly well going to get it.'[31]

With that thought she went to sleep, knowing that she would have to be up at dawn to begin the irksome journey.

9

Across the Border

July 1918

Monday 15 July, Narva, Estonia

In its way, this was a harder journey than any she had made before, harder even than her duplicitous, dangerous trips into the Ukraine. Danger was a thing that Moura could take in her stride; humiliation and debasement wounded her to the soul. She could never have imagined, even a year ago, that the journey to Yendel could be anything other than a pleasure. Now the thought of what she would have to do there filled her with loathing.

It had been a long, weary day. Rising in the dark before dawn, she had gathered her minimal luggage – for once she would have to travel as lightly as possible. At 5.30 she boarded the mail coach – the same antiquated troika that had taken the children to Estonia, and still the only reliable transport between Petrograd and the border zone. It had once been considered fast, but in an age of steam and combustion it was an infuriatingly slow relic. Hour after hour it trundled along behind its three horses, stopping at every hamlet, changing the beasts, and starting off again at what felt to Moura like walking pace.

West of the little town of Yamburg,* the marshy coastland began – the band of lakes, wetlands and dykes that joined Estonia to Russia. Tantalisingly, the now-disused rail tracks ran beside the road, straight across the marshlands. Here began the border zone, the demarcation line. Here the mail troika stopped, and those crossing from Russia to Estonia – or Germany as Moura thought of it now – were met by an escort of German soldiers. Moura felt insulted, soiled even, by their proximity. She felt a profound shame that her people could be so pitiful

---

* Now Kingisepp.

as to submit to German occupation – they were 'utterly lost like children, letting themselves be bullied by these swine'.[1]

As the travellers plodded along the straight marsh road towards the
border town of Narva, one of the soldiers took a fancy to her, and sidled
up beside her. Moura kept her head averted, shuddering. '*Sind sie
deutsch?*' he asked.

Moura turned a hard, blank gaze on him, trying to control her
feelings and attempting to give the impression of not understanding
the language. The soldier stammered awkwardly, '*Vy russkiy?*' he
asked.

'*Da,*' she confirmed coldly and (she hoped) defiantly. Yes, she was
Russian – how could anyone have the gall to think she was German?
Did she *look* German? How dare he.

At last she was safely across the border, vouched for by the same
friendly official who had helped Micky cross with the children. In Narva
she headed for the railway station. Now at last for some properly civilised transport! In the waiting room she sat down and wrote a letter to
Lockhart, pouring out her feelings in blunt pencil on the single sheet of
thin paper she had with her.

'If there is any telepathy worth speaking of,' she wrote, 'you, my Baby
– must feel the agony I am going through. I don't know how I have
been able to bear this day.' She struggled to express how besmirched she
felt – as if having to deal with Germans was somehow a betrayal of
Lockhart and his country – 'my personal pride crushed to the ground,
trampled upon every second of the day'. Only the thought of little Peter
helped her cope with it.

Already she was dreading the weary journey back, but not as much as
she dreaded the arrival at Yendel, and what she had to do there.
Cramming words into the remaining margins of the paper, she pleaded:
'Baby, good-bye, my baby love, my love for ever, take care of yourself
and be with me. God bless. I kiss you. Moura.'

She folded the thin sheet and stowed it away, hoping for an opportunity to send it. Most likely it would have to wait for her return. Would
she even make it back? Would Lockhart still be in Russia? For all she
knew, he might be ejected from the country or forced to flee – beyond
her reach forever – or thrown into a Bolshevik prison. Moura didn't
even like to think of the possibility that he might be killed.

Diplomacy was as good as dead. Lockhart continued to meet with his contacts in the foreign ministry, but all pretence of cooperation had been dropped. Their negotiations and discussions had become those of two nations on the verge of hostility – still civil, even personally cordial, but each with his hand on the hilt of his sheathed sword.

Lockhart had become wholly committed to Allied intervention. The only way to reopen the fight against Germany on the Eastern Front was in the face of Bolshevik opposition. So be it. The problem he faced now – the constant, stumbling obstruction that made him want to tear his hair out – was the dithering of the Foreign Office. The very people who had derided or hindered his plan to get Russia back in the war through diplomacy, who had pushed the strongest towards direct intervention, now dragged their feet over a thousand and one logistical and political sticking points.

Uprisings and anti-Bolshevik conflicts were flaring all over Russia. The Whites, the Mensheviks, the Left SR regiments in the field, all were giving the Red Army a hard time, and by midsummer virtually all of Siberia was in anti-Bolshevik hands. And still the Foreign Office, the War Cabinet and General Poole struggled to decide how to take advantage. Having pushed for intervention, they found that they didn't have enough troops.

The key to it all was the Czechoslovak Legion. A huge corps of tens of thousands of seasoned troops, the Legion had served in the Tsar's army against the Germans. After the signing of the peace, as an independent corps the Legion had been granted clearance by the Bolsheviks to leave Russia and go to France, there to continue fighting alongside the Allies. With Germany controlling the northern and southern sea routes, it was decided to let them go the long way round, via the Trans-Siberian railway to Vladivostok. It wasn't an easy route. Rail transport was patchy, and much of it was being used to transport German and Austro-Hungarian ex-prisoners of war from Siberia back to their home countries. There were constant delays along the route, and the Czechoslovak soldiers grew increasingly restive and more and more difficult to handle – both for the Bolsheviks and for their own commanders. Trotsky ordered that they be forcibly disarmed, which added to the friction. The Legion stopped heading east, and starting heading west again, fighting as it came.

In Murmansk, the British wanted the Czechoslovak Legion like they wanted breath. Such a huge corps would solve the problem of the shortage of Allied troops at a stroke, and enable intervention to go ahead. Plans were drawn up for seizing the vital Archangel–Moscow axis and thereby controlling northern Russia; all the plans involved using Czechoslovak regiments and coordinating them with local anti-Bolshevik forces, such as Boris Savinkov's little army of rebels.

In Moscow, Lockhart monitored the situation and helped as he could, at the same time badgering Whitehall to get on with the job. Anti-British feeling was growing in Moscow, and Moura's letters reported a similar deterioration in Petrograd.

It was in early July that the British scheme began to go badly wrong. In Murmansk, General Poole, despairing of the arrival of either the Czechoslovak Legion or an American force, had postponed his main landing at Archangel until August. But communications between Moscow and Murmansk were intermittent, and Lockhart – who had been secretly monitoring the rebels – had been unable to warn Savinkov in time to prevent him launching his uprising at Yaroslavl (a key point where the Moscow–Archangel route crossed the Volga) on the day of the Left SR action in Moscow.[2] His few hundred fighters were embattled in the city by the Red Army, and were now being relentlessly whittled down.

Elsewhere there was still hope. A Red Army general in southern Russia came out in support of the Left Socialist Revolutionary Party, and turned his troops against the government, with the intention of creating a breakaway republic of the Volga and declaring war on Germany. The Red Army was being pulled to pieces from outside and in, and meanwhile the Czechoslovak Legion aggressively continued its long journey westward, heading towards the next great turning point in the revolutionary war.

In the Legion's path stood the Urals city of Ekaterinburg. It was a flat, drab place, unremarkable; but it was about to become the most infamous and haunted city in Russia. In a blockish, dullish but quite comfortable merchant's house in the centre lived the former Tsar Nicholas II, his wife and their five children, eking out the eventless months of their imprisonment, with no knowledge of what would eventually be done with them. That question was inadvertently decided by the approach of the Czechoslovak Legion. As its regiments began to surround Ekaterinburg, on the night of 16/17 July the head of the local Cheka took the decision to execute the entire family – parents, children and their few remaining servants. The murders were carried out inside the house that very night, in a single violent onslaught.

The news reached Moscow the next day, and Lockhart was the first person to telegraph it to the appalled outside world.[3]

His own situation was growing graver by the day. The British alliance with the Czechoslovak Legion was a given – which put Britain in the position of being indirectly at war with Russia – and the Bolsheviks' view of Lockhart was now downright suspicious. Only the friendly relationships he had developed with certain middle-ranking members of the government, together with his reputation (no longer accurate) for being pro-Bolshevik, protected him. All British personnel in Moscow and Petrograd had been forbidden to travel, and there was no longer any secure way of communicating directly with the outside world. It seemed an age since he had heard anything from Moura. His concerns about her safety were beginning to turn desperate.

20 July, Yendel

She wouldn't be able to go through with it. It was worse than she could ever have imagined. The feelings she had had on the approach to the border, when the German soldier tried to flirt with her, were nothing compared with the indignation and disgust she felt now.

Djon, her so-called husband, the former officer and diplomat of the Tsar and loyal son of Russia, had gone over wholeheartedly to the Germans. He had transformed himself, effectively, into a German. As if there weren't already enough of them in Estonia; their soldiers were everywhere. There was even a German officer staying at Yendel – here in the place that had once been her home, the playground of her British friends! Rather than being shunned as an enemy occupier, he was welcomed by her husband, lunching and dining with the family. Moura was appalled.[4]

Whether the officer was aware of her disdain or not, Djon certainly noticed it. Soon they were back to their old ways, arguing about politics. Djon accused her of being on the side of the Allies, which was half-true, but also rich; he had been their friend too until it suited him not to be. And what of his loyalty to Estonia? The master of Yendel's new allegiance would win him few friends among the local people. The

German occupiers in Estonia were behaving in much the same way as those in the Ukraine. Baltic Germans were favoured over ethnic Estonians in the government, workers were being laid off and wages reduced, newspapers and Estonian cultural societies were suppressed, and colonists from Germany were being offered farmland by Baltic German landowners, many of whom wanted Estonia to be fully incorporated into Germany.[5] This former province of the Russian Empire, which had lacked independence but at least had some cultural identity of its own, was being thoroughly Germanised, and it made Moura sick.

Djon offered her a choice – either him or her convictions.[6]

Even if she had been capable of subjugating herself to any man, she could not have done so for Djon. Before coming here, she had worried about the morality of using and deceiving him in the way she was planning to. Above all, it would involve deceiving her children too. But now she felt unable to go through with the deception for entirely different reasons. Moura shrank from her husband's touch. This man, who had been her romance, her life, for whom she had borne two children, repelled her physically and morally.

She wrote to Lockhart: 'I want to scream and say I am not going to bear it any more. It's only the thought of him, of our little boy that stops me – but I don't know, Babykins, if I'll be able to stick to it after all.'[7] All she wanted was to abandon everything and hurry back to Russia, to her one and only love.

The single shred of comfort was that the children were safe so long as Estonia was under military rule. The countryside had been brought to order, and the peasant bandits and saboteurs were gone, for the time being. But she missed her children, missed being able to embrace them, and she worried about their future. But even they weren't a strong enough tie to hold her at Yendel against the pull of Lockhart, all those hundreds of miles away in Moscow.

Casting her plans aside, throwing Djon's ultimatum back in his face, and laying down her maternal duty, she departed from Yendel, heading back towards the border. The future could take care of itself; for the present, she wanted freedom. And Lockhart.

The days of the British mission in Moscow were numbered. The future of the Allies in Russia was grim – unless they stiffened their backbones and came marching in as conquerors. The Czechoslovak Legion was dominating central Russia, but the Allies had nothing to match it with. In between, isolated at Yaroslavl, Savinkov's uprising was withering. It had spread to nearby towns, but failed to build up the support and weaponry needed to hold out against the Red Army. On Sunday 21 July, after two weeks of battle, Savinkov's few hundred surviving fighters surrendered.[8] Once again, Boris Savinkov himself escaped, and would rise again to trouble the Bolsheviks, but the Allies' plans had taken a debilitating blow. Any force landing at Archangel now would have little chance of getting through to Moscow. Unless it came in sufficient numbers.

On 25 July, in a panic move, the British, French, American and Italian embassies which had been impotently holed up at Vologda since the spring, monitoring the situation but playing little direct part in any actual diplomacy, suddenly struck camp and fled to Archangel, where two ships were waiting to evacuate them. The move was prompted by a message from General Poole indicating that his force would be landing at Archangel imminently. The Ambassadors were keen to avoid becoming hostages of the Russians, and their urgency was so great, some British stragglers arrived late, and had to run down the quay and clamber aboard as the ships were pulling away.[9]

'So here ends the Vologda episode,' Lockhart noted sourly in his diary, 'a thoroughly stupid one at best.'[10]

Lockhart and his handful of staff were now isolated in Moscow, while Cromie and his little group were similarly cut off in Petrograd. Neither Lockhart nor Cromie had been given any warning of the Ambassadors' departure, and the Bolsheviks certainly had not; they guessed correctly that military intervention must be imminent. Despite reassurances from Georgy Chicherin, Commissar for Foreign Affairs, Lockhart knew that he and his people had effectively become potential hostages against Allied action. They could be seized at any moment.[11]

Following his meeting with Chicherin, Lockhart returned to his rooms at the Elite and began preparing everyone for departure. It was agreed that after he had gone, Captain George Hill and Sidney Reilly would stay on in Russia and continue their counter-revolutionary missions under cover.[12] Everyone else must leave.

It was ten days now, Lockhart calculated grimly, since Moura had left Petrograd bound for Estonia, and still he had heard nothing.[13] *Ten days.* He had one of her last letters with him. 'If I remain there longer than a

week,' she had written, 'you *must beleive* that it will only be if there is
some difficulty about trains and passes. Please please, Baby, don't think
of anything else.' She had promised that as soon as she was back in
Russia she would come straight to Moscow – 'if it is possible still'.[14]

If it is possible. She knew as well as he did the risk that he might not
be here that long. Ten days of silence, of not knowing; three whole
weeks since he had last seen her and held her. It was unbearable. Could
he depart without seeing her again? How would he ever find out what
had happened to her if he left now?

While preparations for departure went on around him, Lockhart sank
into a torpor. He delayed setting off. The next day there was still no
word from Moura, but still he lingered. A form of madness was taking
him over. He couldn't sleep, he couldn't deal with official business,
couldn't concentrate on any thought but her. He sat in his room for
hours on end, dealing out hand after mindless hand of patience and
'badgering Hicks with idiotic questions'.[15] The ever-patient, ever-loyal
Hicks understood. He was fond of Moura, and had his own romantic
interest in staying – in the form of young Liuba Malinina; along with
Moura she had become part of the little intimate circle around Lockhart
and Hicks.[16] But patience and devotion must reach their limit. Another
day came, and still there was no news. Departure could not be delayed
forever; soon Lockhart would have to make the decision to go.

On Sunday afternoon, three days after the flight of the embassies
from Vologda, a week since the collapse of Savinkov's uprising, the telephone rang in Lockhart's room. He picked it up, and with a rush of
exquisite joy heard a familiar voice crackling down the line. It was
Moura, and she was back in Petrograd, safe and sound and breathless
with adventure. She was catching the train to Moscow that night. She
would be with him tomorrow.

Lockhart's depressed lassitude fell away from him. 'The reaction was
wonderful,' he would recall. 'Nothing now mattered. If only I could see
Moura again, I felt that I could face any crisis, any unpleasantness the
future might have in store for me.'[17]

As soon as she was back in Lockhart's arms, Moura poured out her story.
The journey from Estonia had been a dreadful ordeal – a full six days
from Yendel to Petrograd, some of it on foot through terrible danger
and hardship, sneaking or charming her way past German border guards.

(She heard months later that the official who had helped her cross the border had been arrested for abetting an English spy, and was shown a dossier about her.)[18] But here she was – safe and as full of love as ever. In celebration, the couple drove out to dine at the Yar, another of the opulent night-restaurants in Petrovsky Park.[19]

Overjoyed to have her back, Lockhart perhaps didn't think to query her tale. Six days was a long time to travel two hundred miles, even with the certainty that she must have had to walk the twenty-two versts* from Narva to Yamburg, which she had known beforehand she would have to do ('won't I be nice and thin,' she wrote).[20] An air of mystery would always surround this journey. In later life she would magnify the account further, claiming that she had walked the entire way from Yendel to Petrograd.[21] Any possibility that she might have been anywhere else en route, or spent less time at Yendel than she claimed, was never raised by Lockhart – at least not that he ever wrote down. He was the only source for her having told this story upon her return.[22]

The final leg of her journey had been as quick as could be. She had boarded the train for Moscow immediately, whereas before she had always had to wait for passes and tickets to be obtained through her diplomatic friends. Now, with the authority of the Cheka behind her, she could travel however she wished within Russia. It was all the more surprising, then, that the journey between Yamburg and Petrograd should have taken so long.

No doubt it was wholly coincidental that the day after Moura's arrival in Moscow, a stunning and unsettling event took place hundreds of miles away in Kiev. On Tuesday 30 July, Field Marshal Hermann von Eichhorn, the detested commander-in-chief of the German forces in the Ukraine, the man who was in effect Hetman Skoropadskyi's overlord, was assassinated. A bomb was thrown into his car from a passing taxi, mortally wounding both him and an aide. The aide, a Captain Dressler, bled to death; Field Marshal Eichhorn, with multiple wounds, lingered for a few hours in hospital before dying of a heart attack.[23]

The reactions to the murder were varied and interesting. The assassin, a twenty-three-year-old student from Moscow named Boris Donskoy, was arrested at the scene. When he was interrogated by the German

---

* 1 verst = ⅔ mile.

military authorities, the first question the interrogator asked him was, 'Do you know Lockhart? Do you know who I mean?' They relayed a report on the interrogation to Moscow, where Commissar for Foreign Affairs Chicherin gave a précis to a startled Lockhart. Chicherin and his deputy, Lev Karakhan, were gleeful about the whole business – in their personal view it served the imperialists right for acting against the wishes of the proletariat.[24] One could almost imagine that there were elements within the Bolshevik government who had wanted the German Field Marshal dead.

At first Donskoy denied any connection to Lockhart or anyone British. He was a member of the Left Socialist Revolutionary Party, acting in response to the crushing of his comrades in the wake of the Mirbach assassination. But by Saturday 10 August, when he was publicly hanged in Kiev on the orders of a German military court, Donskoy was claiming that his group of Left SRs had been 'bought' by representatives of the Allies.[25]

Both Trotsky and Lenin were furious. Despite what some commissars might be saying behind closed doors, Lenin valued Russia's peace with Germany, and had already begun making speeches declaring that Germany was Russia's only friend, and that 'Anglo-French imperialism is now threatening the Soviet Republic on a large scale'; he now spoke out against Eichhorn's assassination, calling it an Allied attempt to pro-voke German intervention in Russia.[26]

At the same time, George Hill – whose agents had been active in the Ukraine since the spring – had one of his occasional meetings with Trotsky, with whom he had long enjoyed a cordial and fruitful relation-ship. In front of the British officer's eyes, the furious Trotsky tore up Hill's travel passes and dismissed him from his office. The breach didn't end there. Later that evening, Hill received a tip-off from one of his contacts in the Cheka: Trotsky had ordered his arrest. An experienced agent and survivor of two attempts on his life by German assassins, Captain Hill was prepared. Leaving behind most of his possessions and taking only his trusty sword-stick, he slipped away from the Elite Hotel and made his way to one of the safe apartments he had secretly set up. He had become a hunted man, and from now on would be living on his wits – a form of subsistence he was thoroughly used to.[27]

If Hill or his Ukrainian agents had any connection with the Eichhorn assassination, he never admitted it in print. Likewise, if Lockhart knew of it, or if Moura did not spend all her time away shuddering at her husband's touch or walking long distances, they both thoroughly covered their tracks. One person who hadn't quite erased every trace was Francis Cromie, who was busy cooking up intrigues against the Bolsheviks on every front. On 26 July he wrote to Admiral Hall, head of naval intelligence, that he had 'sent a trusted agent to Kiev to keep in touch with Black Sea intrigues'.[28]

According to the Western press, Bolshevism was doomed. Even Lenin's own speech to the Central Committee on 28 July was laden with darkness. He spoke of the 'hard and humiliating peace' with Germany, and of how the imperialist Allies and the White and Left SR counter-revolutionaries were beginning to 'forge an iron ring in the East, in order to suffocate the Soviet Republic'. Even German newspapers were predicting that 'Bolshevism must collapse'.[29]

Moura, keeping both eyes open and her dainty fingers on every pulse, would be ready if it did. And equally she would be ready if it did not. Whoever prevailed, whoever perished, she would be sure to survive. She had come a long way since her naive attachment to Kerensky – the ruler turned fugitive turned exiled pariah. (Moura had been faintly amused to read in the Red papers lately that Kerensky had been 'beaten by the workmen' in London when he appeared there publicly for the first time.[30])

She had learned how to keep pace with the tide – to run with the wolves and with the hunters. What she had not yet learned was how not to suffer a broken heart.

PART 2

Love and Survival: 1918–1919

Those were exceptional times, when life was the cheapest of all commodities, and when no one could see twenty-four hours ahead. We had flouted all conventions. We had gone everywhere together, sharing our dangers and our pleasures during a period in which months were equivalent to years.

Robert Bruce Lockhart, *Retreat from Glory*, 1934

10

The Lockhart Plot

August 1918

If Bolshevism was going to collapse, now was the time for the founda-
tions to crack and the cornerstones to give way. The British military
force, which had been the subject of rumour and speculation for two
months and more, finally began landing at Archangel on Friday 2
August. The Allies were determined to open up their Eastern Front
against Germany, and would fight their way through the Bolsheviks to
do it.

Through that hot summer weekend, the news leaped from town to
town and from newspaper to commissary office like a fire-front, growing
as it went. General Poole had landed with ten thousand men, it was said
– no, twenty; no, fifty; no, *one hundred thousand* Allied troops had come
ashore and would soon be swarming down the Vologda–Moscow route
to join up with units of the Czechoslovak Legion on the Volga. At the
same time, seven Japanese divisions were coming through Siberia;
together the Allied force would hammer the few loyal divisions of the
Red Army and throttle Bolshevism in its cradle.

Some of the less level-headed commissars began to panic, and moves
were made to prepare to destroy the Bolshevik archives. Lev Karakhan
at the foreign ministry told Lockhart that the government would go
underground and fight if necessary. In the meantime, they looked to
their new friend for help. At a meeting in the German Embassy, the
new Ambassador, Karl Helfferich, turned down the Bolsheviks' urgent
plea for a Russian–German military alliance to meet the British offensive. Instead he secretly wired Berlin to suggest that Germany act now
to destroy Bolshevism. His suggestion went against official German
policy, but received a sympathetic hearing from many in the

government. But it was impossible. Germany was reeling from the
failure of its spring offensive on the Western Front, and hard-pressed to
resist the enemy advances there; chaos and war on its eastern borders
would be unthinkable. And so, unwilling to share his predecessor's fate
or be caught in Moscow by an Allied invasion, Helfferich departed for
Berlin, having spent barely a week in Moscow.[1]

The Bolshevik leaders began to know real fear, and struck out more
harshly than ever against anything they perceived as a threat. A few days
after the Archangel landing, the arrests of British nationals in Moscow
and Petrograd began. Overnight, Lockhart and his people had become
enemies of the state.

Since her return to Moscow from Yendel, Moura had begun living with
Lockhart, held at his side by the force of events as much as by her reluc-
tance to be parted from him.

It would always be believed afterwards that there were other ties
holding her in Moscow. Her days of spying in the Ukraine were over,
but the Cheka had a more pressing use for her.[2] Possessing the heart of
the British agent made her an ideal spy; living with him placed her in a
perfect position. It would later be believed – though never proven – that
she passed information from inside Lockhart's mission to the Cheka.

If she was guilty, her motives were deep and complex, and sprang
from the will to survive. Her love for Lockhart was profound, and it
both excited and bewildered her. But for Moura the survival instinct
was more profound still, and she was learning to lay her bets with cunning and caution.

Survival was a powerful imperative, and for a woman of the aristocratic class living in the Red surge of 1918 it was a difficult trick to pull
off. Other people of her class and kind – aristocrats, bourgeoisie, the
wealthy, the propertied and landed – were a monster that Bolshevism
was determined to slay. And they were willing to do it literally. Those
who hadn't the will or the wit or the means to escape Russia were dis-
possessed and became enemies in their own homeland. The campaign
against them had been slow to rise, but was gathering momentum as the
spring of 1918 turned to summer. The Declaration of Rights of the
Working and Exploited People had been drafted by Lenin in the wake
of the Revolution and passed by the Third Congress of Soviets in
January 1918. It gave the new state a name – the Russian Soviet Republic

– and was its first functional constitution.[3] It conjured the Red Army and the Soviet bureaucracy into existence, repudiated Russia's sovereign debt and abolished private ownership of property and capital, bringing all of Russia's land, industry and banks into state ownership. Most rural lands and city buildings had been seized by the state before the end of January, under an earlier decree, but private homes and personal wealth were mostly untouched, aside from widespread incidents of robbery and squatting. But from the spring of 1918 onwards, that began to change.

Members of Moura's class were officially termed 'former people'. They had lost their power and lands, and now the time had come to dispossess them of everything that was left. By the height of the summer more and more were homeless or living jam-packed into shared rooms, and consigned to forced labour; there was even talk now of putting the more troublesome elements, such as priests and landowners, into concentration camps.[4]

Owners of safe deposit boxes were forced to turn over their contents. The more foresighted among the wealthy had hidden their valuables in sealed-up walls in their homes, or buried them in their gardens.[5] Living in Petrograd, Moura had been severely pressed for money to pay the astronomical prices for food, fuel and clothing to sustain herself and her elderly, ailing mother. In the spring she had raised cash by selling shares through her employer, Hugh Leech, and had borrowed 10,000 roubles from Denis Garstin to tide her over; Lockhart had been appalled when he learned of it. 'Don't be cross that I didn't ask you,' she wrote to him, 'because I purposely don't want any questions of money between us, Baby Boy, don't you see?'[6] But she would put pleas for flour and sugar in the margins of her letters, and her mother's health was a constant worry.[7] Maria Zakrevskaya knew about her daughter's friendship with Lockhart and thought him rather young; 'What a clever face – but he looks 18!' she had said when Moura showed her his photograph. When Moura went away to Yendel, filled with foreboding, she had arranged that if necessary her mother could wire Lockhart and he would look after her financially.[8] (The fact that she felt it necessary to make such a provision could be taken as evidence that she expected something more dangerous than a journey to see her husband – such as a side-trip to Kiev perhaps.)

Moura had managed to avoid the worst of the living conditions that people of her class were being reduced to. She no longer had her own (or rather Djon's) home, but she had managed to save her mother's apartment at 8 Shpalernaya ulitsa,* close to the river and the British Embassy. How she achieved this, she never revealed.[9]

More terrible than the dispossessions was the hostility of the Bolshevik state and the Cheka. As their hold on power looked like it might be broken, their attitude to the 'former people' grew ever more intolerant. The era of the Red Terror was beginning, and its atmosphere was already growing in the summer heat. Later that year, one senior Cheka officer would declare: 'We are exterminating the bourgeoisie as a class. During the investigation, do not look for evidence that the accused acted . . . against Soviet power. The first questions that you ought to put are: To what class does he belong? What is his origin? . . . And it is these questions that ought to determine the fate of the accused.'[10] Class war was the way forward, even if the class was already all but defeated. 'There is no other way to liberate the masses,' said Lenin, 'except by crushing the exploiters by violence. That is the occupation of the Cheka, and therein consists their service to the proletariat.'[11]

And somehow Moura avoided the forced labour, the theft of personal belongings, eviction, and arrest and interrogation. All this despite her prominence, her background and her known closeness to the British imperialist missions in Petrograd and Moscow, who by the summer of 1918 were believed by the Cheka to be involved in counter-revolutionary activities. She herself had been a servant of the Cheka, but following the Left SR uprising of July, the organisation was purging itself of potential counter-revolutionary infiltrators. Moura must have looked like a potential candidate.

Something saved her. History would conclude that she had struck a deal, over and above the arrangement that had sent her spying in the Ukraine. Men at the very top of the Cheka – its leader Felix Dzerzhinsky and his deputy Yakov Peters – were watching Captain Francis Cromie and Robert Bruce Lockhart very closely and very quietly, and as July gave way to August and Moura settled in Moscow, they were beginning to penetrate the British agents' innermost dealings.

Lockhart's mission and domestic ménage had altered since Moura was last with him. All that remained was Lockhart himself, his secretary

---

* Tapestry Street.

George Lingner, young Lieutenant Guy Tamplin, and of course his loyal right hand, Captain Will Hicks. George Hill had gone into hiding, and Denis Garstin had long departed, ordered north to join the military establishment at Archangel several weeks prior to the landings.

The scene had changed too. At the beginning of August Lockhart had been notified by the authorities that he could no longer stay in the Elite Hotel. It was being requisitioned for Soviet use – in this case by the General Council of Russian Trades Unions. He had already been forced to find premises for his diplomatic business, and had ended up with an office in a building on Bolshaya Lubyanka ulitsa,* cheek by unneighbourly jowl with the Cheka headquarters (there really seemed to be no escaping their presence).

There was a hidden, accidental significance in both the Russian security service and Lockhart's mission occupying this ancient street. If you followed the Bolshaya Lubyanka out past the northeastern suburbs, you would find that it became the main road which led to Yaroslavl, Vologda and Archangel. If the Allied army came to Moscow, the Bolshaya Lubyanka was the road upon which they would march.

For domestic quarters, Lockhart struck lucky, managing to secure his old apartment, the one he had shared with Jean during his days at the Moscow Consulate. It was on the fifth floor of an apartment block at 19 Khlebnyy pereulok,† in the district of Moscow where the violent raids on the Anarchists had taken place in April. It was now more or less safe again. Lockhart and Moura moved in on 3 August, and Hicks moved in with them.[12]

It was that very weekend, while they were moving in, that the news came to Moscow that the British had landed at Archangel – the news that threw the Bolsheviks into a state of near-panic.

At precisely the same time, Lockhart was busy opening up a new dimension to his business in Russia. Having begun as a friend to the Bolsheviks, he was starting to involve himself in a dangerous plot designed to bring down the Bolshevik regime from within, by infiltrating the ranks of its 'Praetorian Guard' – the Latvian rifle regiments.

Lockhart never quite told the truth about his involvement, and it would be decades before Soviet and British archives would yield up the

---

* Great Lubyanka Street.
† Bread Lane.

facts that he covered up – about his own activities, and by implication those of Moura too. He never ceased loving her or protecting her, nor she him, in spite of what they did to each other that summer.

That weekend, while his household was settling into its new accommodation and the news of the landing was still on its way from Archangel, Lockhart was visited at his mission office by two men identifying themselves as Latvian officers.[13] They gave their names as Smidkhen and Bredis and said that they had been sent from Petrograd by Captain Francis Cromie, who was planning to raise a rebellion among the Latvian regiments by playing upon the discontent that was already building within their ranks.

Everybody knew that the Latvian regiments were the most loyal in the Red Army, the mainstay in the defence against counter-revolution and the only reliable barrier against Allied invasion. But their morale was low and their loyalty becoming doubtful. Like other regiments they had been subjected to purges, many were unhappy about the Bolsheviks' failure to live up to their socialist promises, and about permitting the Germans to take control of the Baltic provinces, including their homeland of Latvia. In July, believing that Bolshevism had run its course, they negotiated an amnesty with Germany which would allow them to return home. But their repatriation had not come about. There were many disaffected officers, said Smidkhen (the senior of the two, who did most of the talking), who would be amenable to raising a mutiny if given the right encouragement.[14] When news of Archangel came through and the Bolsheviks began openly panicking, it looked still more promising.

But how could Lockhart know that these two men had really come from Cromie? He had been out of all contact with Petrograd for some time now, and had no way to check. They could easily be *agents provocateurs* sent by some element within the Bolshevik government. They had brought a note of introduction, allegedly written by Cromie. It was this, Lockhart would later claim, that convinced him they were genuine. In it Cromie wrote that he expected not to be in Russia much longer – 'but I hope to bang the dore before I go out'. Poor old Crow was a great naval commander, but he never could spell. No forger would get such a detail right.[15]

It was true that Smidkhen and Bredis had come from Cromie. He and Sidney Reilly had been dealing with the two men for weeks, plotting how they could use them, sending tentative feelers into the officer corps of the Latvian regiments in the hope of finding sensitive spots, and spreading propaganda about the behaviour of the German occupiers in the Baltic states.[16] On 29 July Cromie and Reilly met with Smidkhen in a hotel in Petrograd. Cromie furnished the letter of introduction for Lockhart, and the two Latvians were despatched to Moscow with a brief to facilitate the plot there. The key was to foment an uprising among the Latvian regiments in the garrison at Vologda, the main barrier between the Allied force and Moscow.

The note was genuine. The Latvians really did come from Cromie. And yet, in telling his tale of the misspelt word (which there is reason to believe he invented), Lockhart was covering up his real reason for believing in the two men. Somebody – some unidentified person – vouched for them. There were only two people in Moscow whom Lockhart could trust *and* who had been in Petrograd recently and close to Cromie. One was Sidney Reilly himself, but Lockhart would have no reason to obscure his involvement. The other was Moura.[17] It was entirely likely that he would cover up her connection, especially in view of what it led to.

However the two Latvians were vouched for, Lockhart was still not wholly satisfied, either by the men themselves or by the prospects of stirring up mutiny. He told Smidkhen and Bredis that he would get involved if they managed to find a more senior Latvian officer who was willing to help. When they had done so, they should come back and see him again.

It would be more than a week before he saw them, and by that time the situation in Russia had changed dramatically and the need for a Latvian mutiny had become all the more urgent.

On Monday afternoon, while the Bolsheviks were still panicking over the news from Archangel, Lockhart and Hicks paid one of their occasional visits to the British Consulate. It was housed in the former Volkov-Yusupov Chambers, a miniature palace a few streets away from Moscow city centre, a remarkable place to choose for a diplomatic office – a marvel of bright pink and mint green, with a pink-and-white chequerboard-tiled roof; the interior was like the inside of a gilded musical box, florid with Art Nouveau and a forest of gold leaf.

Here Consul-General Oliver Wardrop and his small staff conducted their formal, ineffectual business in fretful peace while Lockhart and

Cromie did the real work of diplomacy, espionage and propaganda. Wardrop was a slender, gentle-eyed fellow with a scholarly manner, who was in a frail state of health. He and Lockhart got on well, having the same view of Allied intervention – like Lockhart, Wardrop had opposed it; he understood the inevitability of revolution in Russia, but he differed from Lockhart in believing that interference would be futile.[18] Now both men were caught up in the Bolshevik whirlwind.

Before dawn that morning, the Consulate had been raided by a group of ten armed men from the local Cheka; after forcing their way inside at gunpoint, they had eventually gone away again. An apology was given. But later that morning, Wardrop began to hear of arrests of British subjects around Moscow – businessmen, clergymen, journalists, and a woman from the consular staff. Then, in the afternoon, the Cheka came back in force, and this time they had a warrant. They surrounded the building with armed guards, and marched in, seizing control of every office and every chequer-tiled, gold-laced lounge and bijou state-room. The officer in charge came into Wardrop's office, where he was in a meeting with Lockhart and Hicks, and announced that everyone in the building was under arrest.

Lockhart and Wardrop begged to differ. The officer showed them his warrant, but Lockhart countered it with his own pass, signed by Trotsky, which made him and Hicks effectively immune from arrest. The officer turned to Wardrop, who shook his head and declined to recognise the warrant: 'I shall yield only to force,' he declared. The Cheka officer hesitated, realising the gravity of manhandling a senior diplomat, and held back. Pressing his advantage, Wardrop mentioned that Commissar Chicherin had promised that consuls would not be subject to arrest in any circumstances.[19]

Chicherin's promise did nothing to protect the consular staff. While Lockhart, Hicks and Wardrop were held under guard in Wardrop's office, the Chekists were going from office to office, sealing cupboards, safes and drawers and arresting the staff. Upstairs, British intelligence clerks were frantically burning their secret papers before being placed in custody. Wardrop had already destroyed his confidential papers. Eventually Lockhart and Hicks were allowed to go, leaving Wardrop under effective house arrest, alone with his guards in his defunct chocolate-box Consulate.

Lockhart and Hicks went straight to their mission headquarters in Bolshaya Lubyanka. It too had been raided, and his staff arrested. Lingner and Tamplin had been taken away and thrown in prison. There had also been raids and arrests at the French Consulate and mission office.[20] A few days later, the Petrograd Cheka followed suit, and began arresting diplomatic staff and other Allied citizens and imprisoning them without charge or explanation.[21]

It was perfectly plain what was going on. 'I do not regard failure to arrest myself and Mr. Lockhart as evidence of intention to treat us better than our staffs,' Wardrop wrote on the day of the raid, 'but rather the contrary.' The fate of the prisoners was to act as hostages. 'I do not regard Bolshevik detention of our nationals as aimed at deterring us from vigorous action'. Rather it was for the safety of the Bolshevik leaders. 'They are converting houses in centre of the city into impro-vised fortresses in the belief that there will be soon a serious rising, in which their Allied prisoners will serve as centres. Finally, if they regard all as lost they will probably hound populace on to massacre these prisoners.'[22]

Such was the sense of doom hanging over the government that a rumour sprang up that there was a yacht anchored at Petrograd in which Lenin would escape into exile.[23]

In this atmosphere of oppressive tension, Lockhart and Wardrop did what they could to succour the prisoners. There were nearly two hun-dred in all, British and French, crammed into a small set of rooms and given no food other than bread.[24] The diplomats of neutral nations – chiefly Sweden, Denmark and the Netherlands – negotiated with the Bolsheviks for the prisoners' release. It came gradually. First the women were let go, then, after three days of captivity, the last of the consular staff were freed. They all remained under close guard, and plans were made to evacuate them to Petrograd.

Lockhart was left now with just Hicks and Moura, plus occasional contacts with Sidney Reilly and the prospect of another visit from his two Latvians – assuming they managed to find a more senior officer to support them. It didn't look promising – a week had gone by and still there was no further sight of them.

All thought of insurrection was driven from Lockhart's mind by the terrible blow that fell a few days after the release of the prisoners. Accurate intelligence is always outpaced by wild rumour; finally, on the weekend of 10 August the truth came through to Moscow about the size of the force General Poole had landed at Archangel – the army that had been rumoured to be tens of thousands strong. It turned out to be rather smaller. Lockhart heard the news with disbelief, which quickly gave way to disgust and anger. Britain and her allies 'had committed the unbelievable folly of landing at Archangel with fewer than twelve hundred men'. He called it 'a blunder comparable with the worst mistakes of the Crimean War'.[25] Lockhart, who knew the Russians well, knew how it would be perceived. As Cromie expressed it, and as the atmosphere during the past week proved, 'a Russian only understands a big stick and a big threat, anything else is mistaken for weakness'.[26]

That afternoon, Lockhart called on Lev Karakhan at the foreign ministry, and where before there had been an air of despondency and doom, the deputy commissar's face 'was wreathed in smiles'.[27] He knew, as did Lockhart, that the White Guard and the Czechoslovak Legion had strength, but it was unlikely to suffice in the absence of a strong Allied force.

Having been in two minds about Cromie and Reilly's plan to suborn the Latvian regiments, Lockhart decided that he must do his best to put it into action. The Allied and anti-Bolshevik causes needed all the help they could get. He had come a long way since the beginnings of his mission. All friendly feeling towards the Bolshevik government had gone, and he had become implacably committed to bringing it down.

A few days later, at his flat, Lockhart received a second visit from the young, sallow-faced Latvian officer, Smidkhen. This time his young comrade was absent; in his place was an older man, 'tall, powerfully built' with 'clear-cut features and hard, steely eyes'. He introduced himself as Lieutenant Colonel E. P. Berzin, commanding officer of the Latvian Special Light Artillery Regiment, one of the 'Praetorian Guard' units whose job was to guard the Kremlin. He had talked with Smidkhen and agreed that his fellow officers could be persuaded to act against the Bolshevik government, given the right inducements. Moreover, they certainly had no intention of fighting against Allied forces.[28]

The next day, Lockhart consulted his remaining Allied counterparts, the American and French Consuls-General, DeWitt C. Poole and Fernand Grenard. (Although they were as much part of the Entente alliance as Britain, the Bolsheviks had reacted much less harshly against them, especially the Americans.) Both men approved the plan, and that same day Grenard and Lockhart met with Colonel Berzin. Also present was Sidney Reilly, who had returned to Moscow from Petrograd, his bogus position in the Cheka still intact. He was now going by the name 'Constantine'.

Berzin was asked what it would take to subvert the Latvian regiments. His answer was simple: money. Between 3 and 4 million roubles should do the job. Lockhart and Grenard agreed to consider the amount. They also promised, despite lacking their governments' backing, full self-determination for Latvia in the event of the defeat of Germany and the fall of Bolshevism.[29] Berzin's task would be to prevent Latvian units being used against General Poole's force; without their contribution, even that pitiably small formation ought to be able to link up with the Czechs and take Vologda. With that aim, Lockhart provided Berzin with signed documents to be used by picked Latvian officers as passports to the British lines, so that Poole could be informed of the plan.

If it occurred to him that with those small slips of paper, bearing his signature, he was potentially putting a lethal weapon into the hands of his enemies, it didn't deter him.

Reilly suggested an additional scheme – to suborn the Latvian regiments within Moscow and the Kremlin, stage a coup and place Lenin and Trotsky under arrest. Lockhart and Grenard flatly refused to have anything to do with such a dangerous plan. Or so Lockhart later claimed. He would also claim that this was the last time he saw Sidney Reilly, and that his involvement with the Latvian scheme, having set it in motion and handed it over to Reilly to manage, ended here.[30] In fact, Reilly went back undercover, bringing his fellow SIS agent George Hill – still in hiding in Moscow – into the plot. They began building up an intelligence-gathering network in and around Moscow and planning to use the Latvians to stage the decapitation coup which Lockhart had supposedly forbidden. Lockhart remained fully in contact with Reilly and Hill and their agents, and was equipped with the secure SIS cipher system in order that they could communicate with him.[31]

Lockhart was playing an extremely dangerous game. His role in the plot to subvert the Latvians would later, from the viewpoint of history, become almost invisible. But at the time he lacked the luxury of concealment which Reilly and Hill enjoyed. He was starkly visible, dependent on secrecy and on the hope that the remaining threads of his diplomatic status would keep him safe. But if the Bolsheviks discovered what he was involving himself in, it would offer him no protection at all.

While all this was going on, Moura remained in the background. The blanket of secrecy that was being tucked in around everyone involved covered her completely. If she was present in the flat while Lockhart was meeting Reilly, Berzin and Smidkhen, nobody ever recorded it. Neither was it ever noted whether her keen nose for intrigue detected what was going on. Still less was there any intimation of whether she was still connected to the Cheka, and if so, whether any information from within the flat at 19 Khlebnyy pereulok was ever passed to the grim offices at 11 Bolshaya Lubyanka by her pretty hands.

She and Lockhart continued to live their private life of romance in the spaces between political upheavals. There were days of relaxation in the gardens of the defunct British Consulate, where the men, English, French and American, played football.

And there was still nightlife. One evening, in an attempt to relive the memory of Guy Tamplin's birthday party, Lockhart and Moura, together with Hicks, went out to Petrovsky Park, where the night-restaurants were. Sadly, the Strelna had been closed down. They found the maîtresse, Lockhart's old and dear friend Maria Nikolaievna, living in a dacha nearby. 'She wept over us copiously,' Lockhart would recall, and having sung them some of their favourite gypsy songs in a faint, mournful voice, pleaded with them to stay with her – 'She saw tragedy ahead of us.' Lockhart was chilled by her words and her mood, and haunted by the memory of their parting, 'beneath the firs of Petrovsky Park with the harvest moon casting ghostly shadows around us. We never saw her again.'[32]

While Lockhart and Moura indulged their passion and looked forward to their life together with their unborn baby, while he and his associates plotted, they were being closely watched.

After the conspirators' meeting in Lockhart's flat, the Latvian officers Smidkhen and Colonel Berzin had gone across the centre of Moscow to a certain notorious office in the Bolshaya Lubyanka ulitsa, where Berzin reported in full to deputy chief of the Cheka and fellow Latvian Yakov Peters. The truth was that Colonel Berzin was not a disaffected officer at all; he was an honest and scrupulous one, entirely loyal to the Bolshevik government. It was upon the orders of the Cheka that he had gone with Smidkhen to meet with Lockhart.

Likewise, Smidkhen himself was not a mutineer in waiting but an officer of the Cheka, real name Jan Buikis. Both he and the accomplice with whom he had first approached Lockhart – the man identified as 'Bredis', whose real name was Jan Sprogis – had been primed from the beginning by Peters and his boss, Felix Dzerzhinsky.

All three Latvians were what Lockhart had feared they might be – *agents provocateurs*. Their mission had been in train for months. Smidkhen and Bredis had been briefed to make contact with the British mission in Petrograd, and after two months of careful preparation had succeeded in getting themselves 'cultivated' by Captain Cromie, to whom they suggested the idea of subverting the Latvian regiments. Cromie was impressed and believed in them. Putting the plan into action, he sent them on to Lockhart. As soon as they arrived in Moscow, they reported to their chiefs in the Cheka, and continued to do so throughout the conspiracy. When Lockhart asked for a senior officer, the Cheka picked out Colonel Berzin from the Kremlin guard and briefed him to go along with Lockhart's scheme.[33]

The double-cross had been slow to bear fruit, but as the summer of 1918 waned towards the harvest season, it looked like bringing in a large crop of British, French and American diplomats and agents. Quite what the Cheka hoped to achieve with their entrapment, and what they would have done with the fruit of the harvest, was never discovered, because out of the blue the whole scheme was blasted by two lightning bolts.

On the morning of Friday 30 August, Moisei Uritsky, the head of the Petrograd Cheka, a man with a reputation for cruel retributive justice, was shot dead on his way to his office. The assassin was Leonid Kannegisser, a young army cadet with a reputation as a poet and intellectual. All that was known about Kannegisser's politics was that he had been a keen supporter of Kerensky.[34]

The news of the murder flashed through immediately to the Moscow Cheka and the Kremlin. Lenin personally ordered Felix Dzerzhinsky (now firmly back in control of the Cheka after the Left SR revolt in early July, but technically in a sort of semi-retirement) to set aside all current business and go straight to Petrograd to investigate.

Having despatched his top man to deal with the case, Lenin carried on with his programme for the day. In the evening he spoke at a public meeting of workers at the Mikhelson armaments factory in Moscow. His theme was the poison of counter-revolution and how it must be purged from the system. 'There is only one issue,' he declared, 'victory or death!'

At about eight o'clock in the evening, Lenin left the building through a dense press of people crowding the hallway and the roadside. Just as he got outside, a woman accosted him and began to berate him about the injustice of flour being confiscated from the people by the government. Lenin denied the accusation – then, as he was in mid-sentence, another woman in the crowd produced a revolver, aimed at the leader and fired three shots. The first bullet hit Lenin in the shoulder; the second hit him in the neck; the third missed and hit a woman standing nearby. Lenin's driver, who had been preparing the car, pushed through the fleeing, screaming crowd towards the sound of shooting, and found the leader lying face-down on the ground.[35]

The arrests began immediately. Sixteen people were seized at the scene and taken away to the Cheka headquarters in the Lubyanka. Lenin was lifted into the car and taken to the Kremlin. He was still alive, but barely.

Felix Dzerzhinsky heard the shocking news when he was still en route to Petrograd to begin his investigation into the Uritsky assassination. Immediately he turned back to Moscow. During his absence, the investigation was begun by his deputies, principally Yakov Peters, who began the interrogation of suspects. In the early hours of the next morning, Peters extracted a confession from the most likely person – a young Ukrainian Jewish woman who went by the name of Fania Kaplan. 'I was the one who fired at Lenin,' she declared, and admitted that she had been planning it for months. But beyond that, she would say nothing about her motives, her political affiliation or her accomplices.[36]

The Bolsheviks were stunned and enraged by the two shootings; coming within hours of each other, they looked like the first rockfalls of a landslide. It became all the more urgent that the forces of counter-revolution be exterminated, root and branch, without mercy. Until now, the Cheka had been ruthless in putting down the enemies of the state, but now a new movement burgeoned – instantaneously, almost while the gunshots were still echoing. It was a movement based on fear, constant suspicion, and violent summary justice. They called it the Red Terror.

'Without mercy, we will kill our enemies in scores of hundreds,' declared the popular paper *Krasnaya Gazeta*. 'Let them be thousands, let them drown themselves in their own blood. For the blood of Lenin and Uritsky let there be floods of bourgeois blood – more blood, as much as possible.'[37]

During that last day of August, while Uritsky's body lay in the morgue and Lenin's life hung by the frailest of threads, the British in Petrograd and Moscow wondered what would happen to them. Inevitably, the assassinations were being blamed on all kinds of counter-revolutionary movements – the Anarchists, the Socialist Revolutionaries, the White Guard – but the recurring theme uniting them all was the Anglo-French imperialists. They must have a hand in it somewhere, and the time had come to sever the hand from the arm that controlled it.

I I

The Knock on the Door in the Night

August–September 1918

Saturday 31 August 1918, Petrograd

In Britain they called it murder, the incident that occured that day. The people who were actually there were less certain about what had occurred, but the British press and politicians, in their righteous indignation against all things Bolshevik, called it cruel, cold-blooded murder of a fine and gallant man.

Whatever they called it, it was tragic, and left an indelible mark on Moura. She wasn't there when it happened, but when she saw the scene weeks later and found the bloodstains, still there on the floor in the deserted, haunted building, it wrung her already breaking heart. The men in her life – the three very dearest of them – were being violently torn away from her, one by one, by forces which she struggled to understand. The tangled chain of events stretched back a long way, but the final act of the tragedy began on that last August day in faraway Petrograd.[1]

It was a strange day from the very beginning. The summer was dissolving in a chilly dampness, and the atmosphere of hate and dread that followed the shootings of Uritsky and Lenin affected everyone. The Bolshevik press was full of furious demands for imperialist blood.

The British who worked in the old Petrograd Embassy felt the atmosphere keenly. Those who were most alert – such as Francis Cromie – seemed to sense that a blow was about to fall. What Captain Cromie did not know was that it already had. He was vaguely unsettled that his invaluable right hand, Commander George Le Page, had not turned up for work that morning. Something was afoot. Perhaps it was connected with the shootings of Uritsky and Lenin; on the other hand, with the almost total lawlessness on the streets, it wasn't unusual for foreigners to be murdered by robbers and their bodies dumped in the Neva. Cromie was also aware that Sidney Reilly was back in Petrograd, full of plots and delighted with the progress he was making with the Latvians in Moscow. It was all rather unnerving. As Cromie stood in Le Page's office, some impulse made him open the desk drawer and take out the revolver that was kept there. For some unaccountable reason, he had left his own pistol at home, despite his life having been threatened more than once during the spate of arrests and anti-British reprisals earlier that month.[2] He put Le Page's pistol in his trouser pocket and closed the drawer.

At that moment, the pistol's owner was in a cell in the Petropavlovskaya fortress across the water, having been arrested and interrogated by the Cheka during the night, along with several other British subjects. The Red Terror was already in action, and turning its angry attention on the foreigners who were known or believed to be up to their imperialist necks in counter-revolution.

At some time after four o'clock, several motor cars approached Palace Quay and stopped outside the British Embassy. A party of Cheka officers, backed up by a squad of Red Guards, got out. They quickly surrounded the building. Ignoring the notice pinned to the front door stating that the former Embassy was now under the legal protection of the neutral Netherlands Legation (which had taken over the job of representing British subjects since the arrests in early August), they forced their way in. They believed they would find evidence inside linking the British to the assassination of Uritsky.[3]

On the first floor, where the naval and military offices were, Cromie was conducting a meeting with some of his secret agents. A car was heard in the courtyard. At the same time the handle of the locked door was rattled by someone out on the landing.

Cromie glanced out of the window. Simultaneously, one of his agents, a man called Hall, went to the door. Cromie had guessed immediately what was happening. 'Don't open the door!' he called, but it was too late – Hall found himself confronted by a man levelling a pistol at him. He slammed the door shut instantly. Cromie crossed the room in a couple of strides, drawing Le Page's revolver from his pocket. 'Remain here,' he said, 'and keep the door after me.'

Flinging the door open, he pointed the revolver at the startled Chekist. 'Clear out, you swine,' Cromie snarled, and stepped forward. The man backed away, and Cromie drove him at gunpoint back along the passage towards the main landing. At the far end was a corridor leading to the chancery offices; on the right was the grand staircase curving up to the upper floors; on the left was the long, straight, broad staircase leading down to the front door. In the chancery corridor were more armed Chekists, taking control of the offices and herding the staff at gunpoint.

It was never determined who fired first, but it was certain who made the first kill. As Cromie reached the landing, he collided with a Chekist coming up the stairs from the hall. Cromie shoved the man aside, and turned to head down the stairs towards the entrance. That was when the shooting started.

One Chekist was killed instantly; a second was hit in the stomach. Furiously shooting back and screaming for help, the Chekist crawled back through the door into the chancery, where the horrified embassy staff were being held. Cromie ran for the main door, taking the stairs two at a time, bullets striking the walls around him and shattering the glass in the main door.

Young Nathalie Bucknall, the wife of one of the staff, had been sitting in the reception office. Startled by the shooting and afraid for her husband, who had just gone upstairs, she hurried into the hallway and saw Captain Cromie racing down the stairs towards her, Russians firing at him from the landing. Suddenly, he seemed to stagger; he twisted, and fell backwards down the last few stairs, his head striking the last step.

Nathalie ran to him and raised his head. His eyelids were fluttering, and she could feel warm blood running over her hand.

Before she could so much as speak, she was seized violently by one of the Chekists who had been shooting; he slapped her hard and drove her forcibly up the stairs, shouting angry abuse at her and hitting her in the back. She was put with her husband and the rest of the embassy staff in the chancery. After being searched, they were all herded out of the building. As they passed down the stairs and through the hallway, Nathalie saw that Cromie's body had been shoved to one side, under the coat stand. Several people, including the embassy chaplain, had tried to tend to him, but were refused by the Chekists.

The prisoners were marched through the streets to the Cheka headquarters. Some of the women were let go the next day – including Nathalie, who had been interrogated throughout much of the night – while all the rest were moved to cells in the dungeons of the Petropavlovskaya fortress. Meanwhile, the Cheka completed their breach of the law of extraterritoriality by ransacking the Embassy from top to bottom, looking for evidence linking the British to the shootings of Uritsky and Lenin, and all the other counter-revolutionary activities they were suspected of being involved in.[4]

It would be some time before Moura learned what had happened to her dear Crow. Communications between Petrograd and Moscow were intermittent, and she soon had more than enough trouble of her own to cope with.

While the lethal drama unfolded in Petrograd, in Moscow the Bolsheviks moved more slowly but more deliberately against the Allies. Since hearing the news about Lenin, Lockhart and Hicks had been debating what to do. Leaving Russia was not an option – even if they were allowed, which they wouldn't be, Hicks had to consider his Russian fiancée, Liuba, and Lockhart had Moura. Neither man had the skills or resources to go underground as Hill and Reilly had done. So they stayed up late into the night talking it over and over, but got no closer to a solution. There was nothing they could do, nowhere they could hide.

Sunday 1 September 1918, Moscow

At around two o'clock in the morning, a motor car turned in to Khlebnyy pereulok. It drove slowly along the narrow, unlit lane; near the end a grey six-storey apartment block loomed into the headlight beams. The car stopped and three men got out: two in plain clothes, the other a uniformed police officer.

The younger of the two plain-clothes men was Pavel Malkov, Chekist and Commandant of the Moscow Kremlin. He walked up to the front door of the block. In the wash of the car's lights he could make out the number – 19. This was the right building. This was where the British agent Lockhart had his nest.

Malkov had been summoned to the Lubyanka headquarters just after midnight by Yakov Peters, deputy head of the Cheka. Peters always spoke slowly with a heavy Latvian accent, as if picking his words with difficulty. 'You are going to arrest Lockhart,' he said simply.[5]

The young Chekist took the order calmly. He had met Lockhart a few times: first when he was head of security at the Smolny Institute in Petrograd during its time as the Bolshevik headquarters, and later on the train to Moscow in March. He'd been impressed by the British agent but didn't like his air of superiority. He would later recall him as 'outwardly calm, with a military bearing; a dry, energetic person under a thick cap of dark brown, slicked-back hair', who had an air of experience despite his youth. He spoke Russian fluently, with no trace of an accent. Malkov and Lockhart had carefully cultivated each other, pretending friendship and pumping each other for intelligence.[6]

'Remember,' said Peters, 'we have to act decisively, but . . . diplomatically. Try to be polite to him. But you will conduct a thorough search, and if he tries to resist, well then . . .'

Malkov shook his head. 'He will not resist.'

Peters nodded. 'Perhaps not. It isn't his style. And he's a coward; makes himself out to be saintly, and gives all the dirty work to his assistants. But be prepared, understand?' Malkov understood. He was accustomed to violent action, and he was prepared for anything.

Glancing up at the black windows of the darkened apartment block, he checked the Colt semi-automatic tucked in his back trouser pocket, then, gesturing to his Cheka comrade and the policeman to follow, he stepped inside the pitch-black hallway. By the glow of cigarette lighters, the three men made their way cautiously up the stairs, pausing to note the door numbers as they went. Finally, on the fifth floor, they came to number 24.

Moura was woken by a thunderous hammering on the front door. Heart racing, she listened in the darkness, wondering if she had dreamed it. The knocking sounded again. She switched a light on. Beside her, Lockhart was sound asleep, oblivious. The poor Baby-Boy; so anxious, so full of stress. He and Hickie had stayed up talking things through until long after midnight; eventually he had crashed into bed beside her utterly exhausted, falling instantly into the sleep of the dead.

Again the knocking. *Bozhe moy!** Moura pulled on her peignoir and padded out into the hall. There was no sound from Hickie's room. The knocking came again, reverberating through the apartment. Whoever was out there wasn't going to give up. What time was it?

She unlatched the door and opened it an inch. Peering out, she couldn't see a thing in the black hallway, but she could sense the presence of people. Before she could open her mouth to speak, hands

---

* My God!

gripped the edge of the door and pulled hard (the door was eccentrically fitted to open outwards).[7] It only moved a few inches before it was stopped by the chain that Moura had cautiously left in place. Out in the gloom a male voice cursed, and a figure stepped into the shaft of light spilling out from the apartment.

Moura recognised the face – long and blockish with close-set eyes – and felt a chill. She didn't know the man's name, but she knew he was Cheka.

'Who are you?' she asked, thickening her heavily English-accented Russian and feigning incomprehension. 'What do you want?' The Chekist quickly jammed his foot in the door. 'I have come to see Mr Lockhart,' he said.

'What could anyone want with Mr Lockhart so late?' Moura demanded.

'I will state my business to Mr Lockhart alone,' he growled.

Moura could sense the Chekist's patience rapidly eroding, but she stood her ground, assailing him with questions and refusing to release the chain.

There was a sound behind her, and she turned to see Hicks coming out of his room. Bleary and dishevelled with sleep, he peered out through the gap. At the sight of the Cheka officer he stiffened and turned pale. 'Mr Mankoff?'[8] he said, summoning a polite smile and taking the chain off the door. 'What can I do for you?'

Immediately, Malkov pulled the door open and, pushing Hicks aside, strode into the flat, followed by his two companions. His Chekist assistant was a burly, rough-looking middle-aged man with black dirt ingrained in his skin – the indelible tattoo of years of factory work.

'Take me to Lockhart,' Malkov demanded.

'Pardon me,' said Hicks. 'Mr Lockhart is asleep; I'll have to wake him.'

'*I'll* wake him,' said Malkov.

Hicks showed him to Lockhart's room. The Chekists and the policeman all strode in. Malkov glanced around, his proletarian soul faintly offended by the figured Karelian birch wardrobe and cupboard, the dressing table laden with Moura's trinkets and jewellery, the pair of easy chairs, the deep patterned carpet, and in the centre of the room the ottoman bed, draped with a beautiful tapestry rug and containing a recumbent British agent – still soundly sleeping despite the sudden intrusion of three armed men and the light being switched on.

Malkov crossed to the bed and pushed gently at Lockhart's shoulder.

Lockhart was dimly aware of his name being called by a rough-sounding voice. Slowly he clawed his way upward from the deep, black pit of sleep he'd fallen into. Opening his eyes, he got the blurry impression that the room was full of people – at least ten, it seemed to him at first, all armed. But the thing that focused his attention and snapped him wide awake was the muzzle of a pistol pointing steadily at his face from a few inches away. The face behind it was hauntingly familiar – he had seen it at the Smolny, and a few times since, and knew its owner's chilling reputation. 'Mr Mankoff!' he mumbled nervously.

'Mr Lockhart,' said the rough voice, 'you are under arrest by order of the Cheka. Get dressed, please, and come with me.'[9]

While Lockhart dressed, Malkov and his comrade went through to the study to begin their search. Again Malkov's soul was struck by the opulence of the furnishings – a mahogany desk, expensive plush armchairs and a thick carpet. Sending his helpers to search the other rooms, he began going through the desk. Riffling through the letters and papers, he uncovered a revolver and ammunition, together with great bundles of banknotes, ranging from old Tsarist roubles to new Soviet issue, and even some *kerenok* – Kerensky notes. Everything was gathered up and taken as evidence.

As soon as Lockhart had finished dressing, he and Hicks were taken down to the car. Sitting with an armed guard either side of them, they were driven away. It was around five o'clock now, and dawn light was beginning to seep over the pallid buildings and deserted streets. They passed the Kremlin and turned down Bolshaya Lubyanka ulitsa, drove past the building where Lockhart had had his office until a month ago, and pulled up at number 11, the squat, forbidding headquarters of the Moscow Cheka. The prisoners were marched inside and left in a tiny bare room, with just a rough table and chairs.

They had been there only a few minutes when Lockhart was taken out again and marched down a corridor to an office. Behind the desk sat a man with a sickle-blade mouth compressed in a hostile arc, and eyes that glinted in the lamplight. Lockhart had last seen him in the role of guide amidst the carnage of the raids against the Anarchists in Povarskaya Street. To Lockhart's bewildered mind, Yakov Peters resembled a poet, dressed in a loose white shirt, his long black hair brushed back from his forehead. On the desk in front of him lay a revolver.[10]

After dismissing the guards, Peters stared at Lockhart in silence for a long while, then opened a folder. 'I am sorry to see you in this position,' he said.

He ignored Lockhart's protests and demands to see the Commissar for Foreign Affairs. 'Do you know the Kaplan woman?' Peters asked.

'You have no right to question me,' Lockhart replied.

'Where is Reilly?'

The mention of that name gave Lockhart his first real jolt of fear. Peters took a piece of paper from his folder and held it out. 'Is that your writing?' With another jolt, Lockhart recognised the pass he had given the Latvian officers to identify themselves to General Poole. He felt queasy. He had expected to be inconvenienced by a fruitless attempt to link him to the shooting of Lenin; he'd had no idea that they had uncovered his involvement with the Latvians. How deeply they had penetrated it, he had not the slightest conception.

'I cannot answer any questions,' he said carefully.

'It will be better for you if you tell the truth,' Peters replied softly.

Lockhart was silent. Peters summoned the guards and told them to take the prisoner back to his room.

He and Hicks were left alone together. Aware that they were being listened to, they confined themselves to trivial chat. Lockhart was scared; the Cheka knew about the Latvian conspiracy; in the light of that, there was no predicting what they might do with him. Diplomatic protocols might count for nothing; he had dishonoured his side of the diplomatic bargain; could he really expect the Bolsheviks to honour theirs?[11]

It was even worse than he had thought. During the night the Cheka had been swooping upon all the leads their Latvian informants had given them, and Lockhart was not the only catch.

After dropping the prisoners at the Lubyanka headquarters, Malkov had hurried back to the Kremlin to find out how Lenin was and check on his guards. On his way home a couple of hours later, he called in at the Cheka to see Peters. He found him fast asleep on a sofa, exhausted after three days on constant alert. Lockhart wasn't the only one who'd been on edge since the shooting. Peters had left instructions that he was to be woken, and Malkov had to almost drag him off the sofa to rouse him.

There had been a new development. Cheka officers had remained at Lockhart's flat to continue the search. A woman had turned up at the door, attempting to deliver an unmarked package, and had been arrested on the spot by a female Chekist. She had just been brought to Peters for interrogation when Malkov arrived, and he sat in on the interview. The lady proved to be young, well dressed and, to Malkov's eyes, remarkably beautiful. She gave her name as Maria Fride, but refused to give any further information. Peters opened the package she had been attempting to deliver to Lockhart's flat. Inside was an incredible, unsettling document – a thick report detailing the dispositions of Red Army regiments on the front lines. The whole thing had been written by a single roving individual. It was headed 'Report No. 12', and even included details of German forces culled from Soviet army intelligence.[12]

Maria Fride claimed she knew nothing of the document, or of the occupant of the flat in Khlebnyy pereulok; she had been out shopping for milk (she did in fact have a can of milk with her) and had been given the package by a stranger and asked to deliver it to flat 24. She even described the stranger in detail – medium height, wearing a military uniform.

Peters listened for a few moments, then quietly interrupted: 'You lie.'

But although he pressed her hard, she stuck to her story. 'I swear to God,' she insisted.

'Do not swear to a God we don't believe in. Do you have any relatives here? Family?'

She admitted to having two brothers who worked for the government, but claimed not to know which ministry. Realising he was going to get nothing more from this obstinate woman, Peters sent her to solitary confinement.[13]

Later that day, Maria Fride's brothers were traced. One of them, Aleksandr Fride, was a former colonel in the Tsar's army, now working in the intelligence section in the Commissariat for Military Affairs. He had used his position to obtain secret documents, which he had passed to Lockhart and Sidney Reilly, sometimes using his sister as a courier. They furnished exactly the kind of information that would be useful to counter-revolutionary rebels fighting the Red Army, and by agents trying to stir up mutiny among loyal regiments. Aleksandr Fride was quickly arrested and made a full confession.[14] Maria's flat was searched (it was on the far side of the city, which undermined her story about having been out buying milk, despite the can she had been carrying). At the same time as the raid on Lockhart's flat, the apartment rented by Sidney Reilly and his mistress had been raided and searched. Reilly himself, having gone to Petrograd to see Cromie, avoided being caught.

With Colonel Fride's confession, together with the statements of other people swept up in the dragnet, the Cheka had a full and profoundly incriminating picture of the network of British, French and American spies, agents and couriers operating in and around Moscow.

The spy ring, grave and insidious as it was, had been merely an intelligence-gathering operation. By comparison, Lockhart's involvement in the attempt to suborn the Latvian regiments – the men who held the safety of the Soviet government in their care – was altogether more heinous. And now Uritsky was dead and Lenin possibly dying. Was this Lockhart's doing? Now was the time to discover the connection between Fania Kaplan and Robert Bruce Lockhart.

The Cheka knew of one possible but tenuous connection. The Ukraine. Kaplan was a Ukrainian, as was Moura Benckendorff, the Bolsheviks' spy in Kiev, and Moura was Lockhart's mistress. They had known this all along, while the British secret agents and the Cheka conducted their uneasy cooperative projects and spied on each other at the same time. But was there a hidden connection there too?

Kaplan was questioned obliquely about whether her motivation had anything to do with the Hetmanate government, or if she knew of the terrorist network linked with the counter-revolutionary Boris Savinkov. She denied both charges.[15] At every turn the Cheka seemed to find indications that there might be Party insiders connected to the attempted assassination, and backed off, to their intense frustration.[16] There was something here that was beyond the ken of the Cheka – they were a new organisation, skilled in terror and summary justice but still inexperienced in investigation and plotting. The only way they could see to connect Kaplan to Lockhart would be to bring them face to face and see what happened.

Lockhart and Hicks had been in custody for several hours, trying not to think what would be done with them.

Summary executions were already going on. Everywhere in Moscow and Petrograd sporadic outbreaks of gunfire could be heard as the death squads went to work on any Russian who was so much as suspected of counter-revolutionary activities or sympathies. The bourgeoisie were the main targets, and anyone loyal to them – families and servants alike. And in both cities it looked like the British prisoners might be next up against the wall.

Lockhart wondered what had happened to Moura. Had she been left behind at the flat? Or had she found somewhere else to go?

The door opened, and Lockhart and Hicks were surprised to see a young woman led into the room, dressed all in black. The guards went out and left her there. Lockhart regarded her with interest. 'Her hair was black, and her eyes, set in a fixed stare, had great black rings under them.'[17] She was bizarrely calm and composed; ignoring the two Englishmen, she went over to the window and stood looking out, with her chin on her hand. After a long interval of strange, awkward silence, the sentries came and took her away again. Lockhart guessed she was the woman who'd been charged with Lenin's shooting, and guessed the reason for bringing her face to face with him. Presumably Peters had been hoping for some sign of recognition between her and Lockhart. Well, he hadn't got it. If they had ever seen each other before in their lives, neither showed the slightest indication of it.

Lockhart and Hicks had been in custody for about six hours when, suddenly and surprisingly, they were told they were free to go.

Outside, they found the weather 'wet and beastly'. Managing to find a cab, the two men made their weary, dejected way home.[18]

Yakov Peters was frustrated. He had been advised by Commissar Chicherin − Lockhart's sole remaining friend in the government − to release him on the grounds of diplomatic immunity − despite the fact that the government was even now arguing that the same immunity should be stripped from the French and American consuls.

When Malkov learned of Lockhart's release, he was incredulous. Peters shrugged it off. Now that Lockhart had been arrested and most of his co-conspirators were locked up or under observation, he was no longer dangerous. He could always be picked up again. He would be under close watch, and if he still had agents not yet known to the Cheka, they might try making contact, and then . . . more counter-revolutionary fish in the net.[19]

Arriving back at the flat in Khlebnyy pereulok, Lockhart and Hicks found it turned upside-down, drawers hanging open, belongings strewn about. There was nobody home. Lockhart's manservant, Ivan, and his cook, Dora, were gone. So was Moura. The building's porter, who had watched all the morning's proceedings, told Lockhart that the servants and the lady had all been taken away by the Cheka.

12

Sacrificial Offering

September–October 1918

Wednesday 4 September 1918, Moscow

A rrested! How could they? How could these beasts arrest *her*? After what she had risked on their behalf, putting herself in mortal danger, betraying her very people, to gather information for the Soviet state. And now arrested! It was the Bolshevik way – they recognised no obligation beyond their present needs, no loyalty other than to Vladimir Ilyich Lenin and the Revolution.

They accused her of being sympathetic to the Allies – an echo of the accusation Djon had thrown at her, and no less dangerous for being only half-true. They said she had a 'pro-English orientation'. She had worked for the British, her friends were British, and her lover was British.[1] That hadn't troubled them before – indeed, it had made her invaluable to them. But now her associates had been revealed to be elbow-deep in counter-revolutionary plots. The Chekists, shaken by the July rebellion and the killing of Uritsky, were suspicious of their own shadows, and apt to execute first and not worry about asking questions at all. And Moura, daughter and darling of the aristocracy, was a natural enemy.

From the Lubyanka headquarters they had moved her to the notorious Butyrka prison-fortress. This hexagonal ring of beetling brick cell blocks guarded by four squat round towers resembled a cross between a factory and a castle. It had long been the place for political prisoners – Felix Dzerzhinsky had been held here during his days as a revolutionary outlaw, and had been freed during the February Revolution. Now he ruled the organisation that sent its victims here, none of whom was likely to be saved as he had been. Moura was not alone. Many British and French citizens had been rounded up, along with the Russians who had collaborated with them. Sidney Reilly's mistress was in the women's section along with Moura.

Conditions in the prison were foul – dirty, verminous and over-crowded. Rations consisted of water and a half-pound of black bread per day, sometimes supplemented with a little thin soup or horse meat. In these conditions, prisoners would grow rapidly thinner and their health would deteriorate. Some could be here for months without charge. Over all of them hung the fear of death (a bullet to the back of the head was the Cheka's preferred method), brutal interrogation or deportation to the new concentration camps.[2]

Where was Lockhart? Where was her love, her life, her darling boy? She had seen him led out of the flat, and hadn't heard anything since. He might have been shot for all she knew. They had come back with another car and taken her and the servants. Nobody would tell her any-thing. She wouldn't be able to bear it if anything had happened to her Lockhart – the Baby-Boy whose baby boy she was carrying inside her this minute.

She had been in this wretched, filthy place four days now, and still no news came. It seemed to Moura that her courage was a frail thing, which would give way sooner or later. If she could only have her beloved, she could stand anything. She hoped he was still alive.

Lockhart had bought a newspaper on the way home from the Lubyanka. Between the bulletins about Lenin's condition were furious impreca-tions against the bourgeoisie, the counter-revolutionaries and the Allies.

Over the next few days, the papers sang the same shrill refrain. Some were openly calling for the murder of British and French citizens. Official reports claimed that some five hundred people – mostly Russian men and women of the bourgeois classes, including shopkeepers, army officers and businessmen – had been summarily executed in the three days since the death of Uritsky, and more were to follow.[3] Dozens of foreign prisoners – mostly British and French, plus a few Americans – were being held in Moscow and Petrograd. Among them was Moura.

After shaving and cleaning himself of the stink of the Lubyanka, Lockhart went in search of information, making the rounds of the for-eign agencies that still clung on in Moscow.[4] The Allies had been revealed as enemy conspirators; as a result, all further responsibility for their citizens had been placed in the hands of the representatives of the neutral nations – which for Britain meant the Norwegian and Dutch Legations. Lockhart met W. J. Oudendijk, the Netherlands Minister, who was visiting from Petrograd. He was an amiable, generous man, and Lockhart found him in a terrible state of anxiety; from him Lockhart first heard the dreadful, shocking news of the raid on the British Embassy and the death of Cromie.

His anxiety redoubled, Lockhart went to the head of the American Red Cross, Major Allen Wardwell, to ask if he could find out about Moura and, if possible, plead for her release. Wardwell was a calm, assured fellow, and Lockhart was comforted by his promise that he would do what he could. He had been promised an interview with Chicherin the next day, and would bring the subject up then.[5]

The feeling of reassurance didn't last long. By the next day, Lockhart could no longer bear the suspense. He wasn't used to relying on others to negotiate with the government, so he went to the foreign ministry himself and demanded to see Lev Karakhan. Despite being officially a pariah, he was granted admittance right away. Regardless of what they had against him, he pleaded, it was inhuman of the Bolsheviks to strike at him using Moura as a hostage. He begged Karakhan to have her released. All the commissar was able to give him was another *I'll-do-what-I-can* promise. It counted for little, but it was better than nothing.

Despondently, Lockhart made his way home through the quiet streets. The atmosphere was like the days leading up to the Revolution the previous year – soldiers guarded every street corner, and the few citizens who were out and about went with their heads bowed and didn't linger. Terror was in the air.

Back at the flat, Hickie made them both a supper of black bread, sardines and coffee. It was Lockhart's birthday; he was thirty-one years old and had never felt less like celebrating.

The next day he sat with nothing to do but read the papers, which were now full of the most lurid accounts of what was already being called the 'Lockhart Plot'. Not only was he said to be trying to stir up mutiny among the Latvian troops; he and his agents were also planning to help the White and Allied armies conquer Russia by blowing up key bridges and subjecting the Russian people to starvation. Once they had taken control they would appoint a new imperialist dictator. *Pravda** led

---

* The official Bolshevik newspaper (*pravda* means 'truth').

the way in calling for the Red Terror to be applied to all enemies of the Revolution, including the British.[6]

By the next day Lockhart was unable to sit still any longer. He decided to go straight to the source of the problem. If the Dutch and the Red Cross and even the Bolshevik foreign ministry couldn't help Moura, he had no choice but to go directly to the Cheka. The thought of going back within their orbit was terrifying, but he must do it. He saw Karakhan again, and asked him to set up an immediate one-to-one meeting with Yakov Peters. Karakhan consented, but wasn't hopeful of the outcome.[7]

The encounter took place at the Lubyanka headquarters. Moura had now been in prison for four days. All the while the Terror was rising. Just the day before, Fania Kaplan had been taken from the Lubyanka to the Kremlin, where without trial or further questioning she was shot – a single revolver bullet to the back of the head, in the Cheka style – and her remains destroyed without burial. Her executioner was the man who had brought Lockhart and Moura to the Lubyanka – Commandant Pavel Malkov. In this climate, nobody was safe.

Yakov Peters regarded Lockhart impassively. Before stating his business, Lockhart insisted on a gentlemen's agreement – the meeting must be treated as unofficial, off the record and entirely secret. Peters agreed. Lockhart launched immediately into an impassioned plea for Moura's release. He claimed that the reports about the Latvian conspiracy were untrue – but even if there was *some* truth in it, Moura was completely innocent.

Peters listened patiently, and promised to give Lockhart's words due consideration.[8] Then he changed the subject.

'You have saved me some trouble in coming here,' he said. 'My men have been looking for you for the past hour. I have a warrant for your arrest.'

By the next day, everyone was saying that Lockhart was going to be shot. Moura heard the news of his release and re-arrest from Major Wardwell, the heroically kind American Red Cross man who came regularly with food for the Allied captives in the Butyrka prison.[9] The Bolsheviks, he said, were executing people in their hundreds, and Lockhart was likely to be among them.

Her love, her life, her all was going to die.

It would always be a mystery how she survived those days without going mad with worry. Moura was nothing if not tough – for all her pampered upbringing, she was capable of withstanding physical discomfort (although not without complaint if she had someone to complain to). But mental anguish was different. This period of gnawing worry would age her and alter her, take away some vital element of her personality that she would never quite recapture. Believing that she was about to lose Lockhart forever would leave a wound that would never heal. She would do anything to see him, to keep him, and if that failed, at least to save him from death or confinement in a dreadful Cheka prison.

Lockhart was kept in a room in the Lubyanka headquarters, a grubby, ill-furnished office used by junior clerks. It contained a dilapidated sofa on which he was sometimes allowed to sleep while the clerks worked and two sentries watched over him.[10]

At all hours of the night, Peters would have him brought to his office for interrogation. The questioning was persistent but calm. Lockhart was exhorted to confess to his crimes, as some of his fellow conspirators allegedly had; otherwise he would be handed over to the Revolutionary Tribunal for examination. Lockhart denied that he had done anything other than what his government had ordered him to do and insisted that the claims that he was the instigator of a counter-revolutionary conspiracy were false. But the Cheka had the hard evidence of espionage and the witness evidence of conspiracy, and Lockhart was in it over his head.

Oudendijk, the Netherlands Minister, lobbied the foreign ministry and the Cheka to spare Lockhart's life. He reported to his British contacts that the Russian government had 'sunk to the level of a criminal organisation'. It seemed to him that the Bolsheviks 'realise that their game is up and have entered on a career of criminal madness'.[11] Oudendijk warned Commissar for Foreign Affairs Georgy Chicherin that Britain was more powerful than Russia, and would not be deterred even if hundreds of Britons were executed.

In his report on his negotiations, Oudendijk gave his views on the political situation in Russia, and on Bolshevism. He was regarded by everyone as a kindly, honourable and good man, and what he had to say wasn't at all out of step with the times; but it was a chilling foreshadowing of Europe's future. He felt it his duty to tell the governments of the world that 'if an end is not put to Bolshevism in Russia at once the civilisation of the whole world will be threatened . . . I consider that the immediate suppression of Bolshevism is the greatest issue now before the world.' He believed that the infection was 'bound to spread in one form or another over Europe and the whole world, as it is organised and worked by Jews who have no nationality, and whose one object is to destroy for their own ends the existing order of things. The only manner in which this danger could be averted would be collective action on the part of all Powers.'[12] Oudendijk noted that the Germans and Austrians were thinking it too. What none of them could have imagined was the solution that would eventually be conceived to tackle the imagined threat.

While the Dutch and Swedish diplomats negotiated with the Bolsheviks, the neutral Norwegian Legation became a refuge for Moscow's Allied outlaws. Will Hicks and Lockhart's assistants Tamplin and Lingner, along with many other British, American and French fugitives, had gone into hiding there. The building was besieged by the Cheka; unwilling to force an entry into neutral diplomatic territory this time, they hoped to starve the criminals out. It would be a long siege – the building had previously been the headquarters of the American Red Cross, and its basement was well stocked with food supplies.

Unhappily, the same couldn't be said for the prisoners in Petrograd – confined in the dungeons of the Petropavlovskaya fortress, they were being slowly starved to death in cells without functioning toilets; many were suffering chronic diarrhoea but were refused medical care.[13]

When Oudendijk returned to Petrograd after two days of bargaining, he had been promised that Lockhart would be released, but he wasn't reassured – 'his position is precarious in the extreme,' he reported.[14]

And then, quite suddenly, everything changed.

The cause of the change would never be entirely clear, because those who were involved – Lockhart, Yakov Peters and Moura – took steps to blur the record.

First the circumstances altered. On 6 September it was announced that Lenin was out of danger. The mood of vengeance among the Bolsheviks gave way briefly to one of relief. At the same time, a deal with the British was being considered. In reprisal for the death of Captain Cromie, the British had arrested the Soviet Ambassador in London, Maxim Litvinov. He and his staff were being held in Brixton prison. An exchange of prisoners was being talked about. Lockhart might be one of them. But whatever the mood, and regardless of the diplomatic situation, there was no getting around the enormity of the crimes Lockhart was accused of – espionage, counter-revolutionary sabotage, and an implicit threat to the lives of the heads of the Soviet government. The author of such a plot couldn't possibly be let go, could he?

Lockhart had been in custody for three days when he was told that he was to be moved from the Lubyanka to the Kremlin. Peters had summoned Pavel Malkov and ordered him to prepare accommodation for the prisoner. The last person Malkov had taken there from the Lubyanka had been Fania Kaplan, whom he had executed five days earlier. Lockhart's fate would be different – for the time being, at least. He was to be held until a decision had been made about what to do with him.

Malkov wasn't particularly pleased about having to take responsibility for Lockhart again. He set aside a suite of rooms in the Freylinsky corridor of the Grand Kremlin Palace, which was still mostly empty. The rooms appeared to have been some kind of lady-in-waiting's quarters – small and with no windows. With unconscious irony he selected guards from the Kremlin's Latvian regiment – the very 'Praetorian Guard' whom the Lockhart Plot had tried to suborn.[15]

Lockhart was alarmed to find that he had a companion living in his apartment: Smidkhen, the Latvian officer who had come to him from Cromie just over a month ago – the man who had led him to get involved in the plot, and who had brought Colonel Berzin to see him. Lockhart guessed that this was an attempt to prise some indication of guilt from him, and for two days he didn't dare speak a word. Eventually Smidkhen was removed. Lockhart never learned his fate, and suspected that he had been shot. He never knew that the Latvian had been a Cheka plant from the beginning.[16]

Lockhart kept pressing both Peters and Malkov about Moura. He protested her innocence, accused Peters of making war on women, and demanded that she be set free. Peters agreed to let Lockhart write Moura a letter – provided it was in Russian so that he could censor it if necessary.

This was the moment at which the situation began to change rapidly and dramatically, and none of the persons involved ever gave a clear or consistent explanation of how or why. They kept silent, or lied.

'My dear, dear Baby,' Moura wrote. 'I have just received your letter through M. Peters. Please don't be anxious about me.'[17] After more than a week in the squalid, overcrowded Butyrka prison, his note had brought exquisite relief, a glimpse of blue sky in the darkness of her captivity. He was alive, and that was all that mattered.

What Peters thought when he met Moura, what he felt, what was said between them, went unrecorded. All Moura would say in her reply to Lockhart, written on the headed Cheka notepaper that Peters had given her, was the astonishing news that 'M. Peters has promised to release me today'. But her freedom meant little without Lockhart:

> I don't mind waiting at all as long as you are not free. I will be able however to send you linen and things and perhaps he will arrange for me to see you. I love you my dear Baby more than life itself and all the hardships of the past days have only linked me all the more to you for life. Forgive this incoherent letter – I am still bewildered, anxious about you and so lonely but hoping for the best.
>
> Bless you my beloved.
>
> Your Moura.

Her bewilderment was so great that, when she stepped outside the gates of the prison, she turned and walked a long way before realising she was going in the wrong direction. She eventually made her way back to Khlebnyy pereulok, trudging along under the fading early-autumn trees – Russia was succumbing early to wintry weather – then up the five flights to the apartment. There she sat in utter solitude. The servants were still in prison, Hicks was besieged in the Norwegian Legation, and Lockhart was in the Kremlin.

Moura knew the fear that was attached to that name. Some said that prisoners who were taken within the walls of the Kremlin never came out again. But Moura had faith, and just knowing that her beloved was still alive was enough.

The next morning she began gathering things to take to him, as Peters had promised she could. Clothes and books went into her basket, along with tobacco, some coffee and a fantastically expensive ham she had managed to procure. And she wrote another letter, trying to convey her confusing feelings of love and despair.

Baby, baby – all this has wrought a great change in me. I am now an old, old woman and I feel I will be able to smile again only when God will grant me the joy of having you again . . . Oh, my Baby – what is freedom without you. My imprisonment was nothing while I thought you were free, then it became an agony of incertitude and anxiety. But I know we both must be brave and think of the future. There is one thing – Baby – all the details of life – all the small petty things I used to talk to you about – all have vanished. I only know I want to make you happy and this to me will be everything. Baby – no woman has ever loved anyone as I love you, my life, my all. I cannot write any more – my misery is too great and my longing for you too infinite.[18]

It was too much to hope that she would be allowed to see him – she just had to trust Peters' word that Lockhart would receive the letter and the basket of gifts. The Chekist honoured his word, and Lockhart was uplifted by the confirmation of Moura's freedom and profoundly grateful for her provisions.

Knowing his habits when under stress, Moura had inserted a pack of cards in the bundle. He began a ritual of playing hand after hand of Chinese patience, just as he had when she was away on her dangerous mission to Yendel in July. This time, he felt he was gambling his life on the game, reasoning superstitiously that if he could win a hand each day, he would be safe. Although he no longer feared execution, he expected to be handed to the Revolutionary Tribunal and given a long term in prison. A real prison, not like this.[19] The news from outside wasn't encouraging. The Red Army was recovering its strength, growing week by week and beating back its enemies on the Volga, regaining ever more territory from the White and Allied forces.

While Lockhart turned over his cards, immersed himself in books and pondered his fate, did he wonder how Moura had worked this trick? He never said, but it must have played on his mind. She was an aristocrat, the known consort and paramour of an alleged enemy spy, a long-time friend of the British . . . Regardless of any service she had given the Bolsheviks in the past, it was a marvel that she had been allowed to live, let alone been set free. And how extraordinary it was that she should be allowed to come to the Kremlin each day and deliver food and gifts for her lover – and exchange letters too. Sometimes Peters insisted that the notes be in Russian so that he could check them, but sometimes he allowed them to pass in English.[20] How had she achieved all this? Did her past service to the Cheka count for so much? Or was there something else?

There were a few gossips in Moscow who believed they could supply an answer. Yakov Peters was as susceptible as any other man to the magnetism of Moura, and as willing, given the right encouragement and the right manipulation, to succumb to her powers of persuasion. (Pregnancy had evidently not diminished her attractiveness.) The young lady had been seen, said the gossips, riding about the city on the pillion of Peters' motorcycle. It was all too clear that she had sold herself to the deputy chief of the Cheka, become his mistress. There were others who thought it more likely that she had allowed herself to be recruited, body and soul, into the Cheka itself.[21]

Moura never spoke of this time, except to admit, some years later, that she had found Yakov Peters 'kind'.[22] Also muddying the waters, Lockhart would try to claim that he had secured Moura's release by giving himself up as a kind of hostage.[23] The true events – the compromises and bargains – were obscured forever; all that remained was the evidence of the results.

There was more to come. Diplomacy had saved Lockhart from the executioner's bullet; Moura's arrangement with Peters had won her release from prison and the ability to bring provisions and gifts to Lockhart. But her beloved was still a prisoner, still facing an unguessable sentence from the Revolutionary Tribunal. And she was beginning to realise that even if by some miracle he were released, he would be ejected from Russia. Either way she was going to lose him. And what would happen to her and her unborn child then? Would she be able to abandon everything and follow him? Would she even be allowed?

'Don't think me an hysterical coward,' she wrote, tormented by the inability to see Lockhart and touch him. 'I cry bitter scorching tears and I feel so small, so helpless, so utterly miserable. But I try so hard to be brave, Baby. We both need it so in order to keep all our strength and build a happy future.' As the days went by, she worked away at Peters, and felt she was having some success. 'I pray so hard that God should let this dreadful time for us pass quickly and I feel He is gradually answering my prayer.'[24]

The first real sign of an answer came during the second week of Lockhart's captivity, when Moura was at last allowed to see him.[25] Peters escorted her to the apartments in the Grand Palace. The corridor was now serving as a cell block for several high-grade prisoners, including the former commander of the Imperial Russian Army, General Brusilov, and the Left SR conspirator Maria Spiridonova.

From the moment Moura stepped into the room and her eyes met Lockhart's and saw the joy there, every detail remained in her memory as vivid as life itself. 'The sofa with the little blue cushion I sent you, where your dear curly head rests – and the litter of books; and the patience – and you, you, my Baby, there, alone . . .'[26] They weren't allowed to touch or speak to each other. Peters kept between them. He was in a garrulous mood, and sat and talked to Lockhart, reminiscing about his life as a revolutionary.

While Peters' attention was occupied, Moura stood behind him, pretending to browse some books piled on a side table. Catching Lockhart's eye, she held up a note and slipped it between the pages of Carlyle's *The French Revolution*. 'My heart stopped beating,' Lockhart recalled. 'Fortunately, Peters noticed nothing or else Moura's shrift would have been short.' As soon as he was alone again, Lockhart rushed to the table and leafed through the book until he found the little slip of paper. On it were just six words: 'Say nothing – all will be well.'[27]

Whatever price Moura was secretly paying, it seemed to be working. Peters promised to bring her to Lockhart again, and continued to let her communicate with him and bring him provisions. Her life at the flat was lonely and miserable. The servants, Dora and Ivan, had been released and come home, but Dora was ill and both were traumatised – 'they worry the life out of me,' Moura wrote, 'crying and remembering their prison experiences'.[28]

Despite her belief that her efforts, her sacrifice and her faith could see her through this awful time and make everything come right with Lockhart, the next time she saw him she had dreadful, heartbreaking news. She had miscarried. They had lost little Peter. Lockhart, who rarely mentioned his intimate feelings in his diary, wrote, 'Moura brought very sad news yesterday. I am much upset and wonder how everything will end.'[29] Moura tried to lift his spirits: 'Don't be sad about what I told you yesterday as it may make it more difficult to bear.'[30]

Amidst her own grief, Moura was on the verge of panic, worrying that Lockhart's love for her would falter now that there was no child to bind their futures together. They had been making tentative plans to escape together via Sweden if he were released, but now he seemed to be wavering. 'I am very depressed that you are so grieved,' she wrote to him. 'You probably care for me less now?' She promised to make up for the loss: 'Don't worry, Baby. Pray God I will be able to give you later on a dear sturdy boy.'[31]

Peters was still predicting that Lockhart would be put on trial, but Moura didn't give up. Whatever devices and persuasions she had at her disposal (and her powers were quite magnificent, as everyone who ever knew her could testify) she exerted now. Three days later, Lockhart was officially informed that he was to be freed. Ambassador Litvinov and his staff were being released from Brixton prison and sent back to Russia, and Lockhart would be part of the exchange.

Despite the news, he was still depressed and sleeping badly. The loss of the baby, the prospect of leaving Russia without Moura, and the third anniversary of his younger brother's death on the Western Front combined to keep his spirits and courage at bay.

The only thing that lifted him was another visit from Moura. Again she was brought by Peters. On this occasion the Chekist appeared in full duty gear in a leather jacket with a Mauser pistol on his belt; he brought confirmation that Lockhart would be set free in a few days. More importantly, he brought Moura, and this time he let them talk.

'The reunion was wonderful,' Lockhart wrote in his diary.[32] During his last few days in the Kremlin, she was allowed to spend real time with him – whole days. Moura would recall those precious hours with exquisite affection: 'How close we were to each other – how nothing existed except you and me in the whole world.' They took long walks in the Kremlin gardens, talked at length and sat in cosy silence – 'sitting very close and so happy with the sheer joy of being together after all the terrible ordeal. How happy I was, how happy.'[33]

It soon became clear why Lockhart was having doubts about their plan to go to Sweden. He was giving serious thought to staying on in Russia. Peters, who had become fond of Moura and seemed to regard Lockhart with an odd mixture of natural enmity, jealousy and friendly affection, couldn't understand how he could even contemplate leaving Moura and going back to the corrupt, decaying capitalist world. Lockhart shared his disbelief. He had been profoundly unimpressed by his country's behaviour during Russia's crisis, and like other young people of his era he was still attracted to the fleeting ideal of democratic liberty that the Revolution had seemed to offer and might yet deliver. Peters observed Lockhart's indecision with interest, but for the moment kept his thoughts to himself.

Having been pushed to clear the way for Lockhart's release, Peters had to attend to the details. He was in charge of the Cheka investigation into the Allied plot. Lockhart stood accused of – indeed had been caught red-handed at – the most heinous conspiracy against the Soviet govern-ment. His name was blood throughout the Bolshevik press. And yet his release had to be justified to the public and (on behalf of the Cheka) to the government. It was too late to remove him from the frame alto-gether – he was acknowledged as the leader and mastermind of the plot that bore his name. But as Peters compiled his dossier on the case and wrote his report, he began systematically manipulating the evidence, snipping the cords that tied Lockhart to his eponymous conspiracy, minimising his involvement and diluting the wickedness of his character.

Peters was already falsifying the report anyway, in order to make the Allied missions seem more culpable and the Cheka less guilty than they were. He covered up Dzerzhinsky's Latvian *agent provocateur* scheme, which had been a breach of the law of diplomatic immunity. Peters wrote that the plot had been wholly authored by the Allies, and had been exposed as a result of the loyalty of Colonel Berzin, who had been approached by Smidkhen ('Lockhart's agent') and immediately blew the whistle. Given this false premise, a few more lies and misrepresentations wouldn't be out of place.[34]

The simplest task was to separate Lockhart from the espionage ring centred on Aleksandr Fride, perhaps the most damning of his activities. That was achieved by claiming that Maria Fride had been caught deliv-ering her package of secret documents to the flat rented by Sidney Reilly and his mistress, rather than to Lockhart's. By the time Peters had finished describing the Frides' role in providing military and economic intelligence to the conspiracy, it appeared as if they'd had dealings with just about every Allied agent and consul in Moscow *except* Lockhart.[35]

To an impartial mind Lockhart's apparent non-involvement would look bizarre. And this was only the beginning of the lies and omissions. Peters wasn't a particularly skilled dissembler or fabricator, and in his efforts to unite his de-Lockhartised version with what was already pub-licly known, he produced a report that was full of contradictions.

Lockhart appeared as both arch-manipulator and hapless dupe, auda-ciously daring agent and feeble coward.

Peters' baldest lie was that Lockhart had been arrested by mistake – contradicting the statement in the same report that the raid had been targeted and that Lockhart and his people had been under observation for some time (this again was to cover up the breach of diplomacy).[36] And yet when Lockhart was interrogated (voluntarily, of course, so as not to breach diplomatic rules) he was said to have admitted everything and claimed to have been ordered by his government to enact the plot. Peters portrayed him as an unwilling tool of his own government; he had reluctantly set in motion the plot to subvert the Latvian regiments, but then stepped back and had little or no further involvement. Despite the fact that the conspiracy was known within the Cheka as 'Kalamatiano-Lockhart & Co' (after the captured American agent Xenophon Kalamatiano, a principal conspirator in the espionage ring), Lockhart barely featured in Peters' narrative of it.

And as for Lockhart being re-arrested when he met Peters to plead for Moura's release – why, that was merely a formal reprisal for the arrest of Litvinov in London. This was an impossible claim: the Soviet government was only told later that day that the arrest of Litvinov had taken place, and besides, the reason stated at the time of Lockhart's arrest was that the Cheka had discovered documents signed by him guaranteeing British diplomatic protection for members of the conspiracy.[37]

Peters compromised his report still further, denigrating Lockhart's character. He exercised his own emotions here – there was a sense of betrayed friendship in Peters' writing. He and the Bolshevik leaders had truly believed that Lockhart was sympathetic to their cause. When Peters showed Lockhart the aftermath of the destruction of the Anarchists, he had imagined he was dealing with a friend. But now he believed (wrongly) that he had been fooled; the duplicitous Lockhart had been conspiring to destroy the Soviet dream. To a committed ide-ologue like Peters it was unthinkable that a man might act pragmatically, following the policy that seemed best at the time. Therefore Lockhart must *always* have been plotting. 'Prior to his arrest, Lockhart would proclaim from every housetop that he was conducting a campaign for the recognition of Soviet power,' Peters wrote, and 'cloaked by this trust, Lockhart conducted his secret activities.'[38]

Quite likely there was jealousy in the demeaning portrait Peters drew of Lockhart – jealousy about Moura. The man he described seemed a most unlikely arch-conspirator. Peters declared that 'not one of the criminals who passed through the Cheka presented a more pitiable spectacle of cowardice than that of Lockhart'.[39] Having been caught red-handed, 'like a wretched coward, Lockhart protested that he had not acted on his own volition, but on suggestions made to him from his government'. Thus Lockhart appeared to be merely a diplomat, not the dangerous plotter he was widely believed to be.

Belying Lockhart's own fond recollection of their private dealings, Peters described Lockhart's personal crises over what he should do with the future as the writhings of self-interest:

> Lockhart was a wretched individual, several times even taking up a pen in order to write down everything that had transpired . . . and about his government. But being the pathetic careerist that he was, he stood like a mule caught between two bales of hay, drawn to the one side by British and world imperialism, and to the other by a new, burgeoning world. And each time he spoke about this new burgeoning world . . . Lockhart would seize a pen in order to set down the whole truth. Then, after a few minutes had passed, the wretched donkey would be drawn once more to other bale of hay, and toss the pen away.[40]

Nobody who knew Lockhart would have recognised this withering portrait. But it had one crucial thing in its favour: nobody could possibly object to releasing such a pathetic, feeble creature. Nobody could believe him dangerous.

While Peters cooked and spiced his report, Lockhart and Moura discussed the future. Despite his desire to stay with Moura, when it came to it Lockhart couldn't bear to cut himself off from his mother country or make his home in the corrupt, cruel place that Russia had become. The only solution was for Moura to come with him to England. There they would brave the opprobrium of society and make a new life for themselves. She would divorce Djon and he would do likewise with Jean.

But how could it be achieved? Moura couldn't leave her ailing mother; there was nobody else to look after her. Moura's brother was dead (another mystery – he was possibly killed in one of Russia's wars, but whether it was the Patriotic War or the civil wars isn't recorded), her wayward sister Alla, having divorced Engelhardt, was living in Paris with her second husband, and Alla's twin Assia lived in the Ukraine. And there were the children: Pavel, Tania and Kira, in Estonia with Djon. It was all so desperately complicated.

Inflicting a terrible emotional wound on herself, Moura made her decision: she could not leave now. Everything must be done properly. For the time being, they must part. She would work to secure the money she would need from her father's estate in the Ukraine (what was left of it), obtain a divorce from Djon, and acquire the necessary permits, passports and visas to get herself and her mother out of Russia.[41]

At the same time, Lockhart would pull whatever strings he could with the British and Swedish diplomatic services in Finland and Sweden. They would meet in Stockholm, and then go to England.

Perhaps Moura was light-headed when she agreed to this plan. She wasn't well in those last days. With the effects of the miscarriage, the stress and her privations in prison, she had fallen ill and her temperature was flying steady at 39°C. But she still struggled to the Kremlin on his final day of captivity for their priceless last hours together.[42]

Wednesday 2 October 1918

At 9.30 in the evening, Lockhart was taken from the Kremlin in a motor car provided by the Swedish Consul-General. He was driven directly to the station, where a train was waiting to depart for the frontier.

He wasn't alone. Other foreign prisoners had been released in exchange for Litvinov. They included Hicks, who was accompanied by his new Russian wife, Liuba. At her request, Lockhart had arranged, through Peters, for Hickie to be allowed out of the Norwegian Legation a day early so that the couple could get married in time to depart together.

There was no such possibility for Lockhart and Moura, and their friends' happiness rubbed the wound raw.

The train was waiting in the darkness some distance from the station, guarded by a platoon of Latvian soldiers. The passengers walked in subdued silence along the tracks to get on board; they felt they wouldn't be able to breathe easily until they were out of Russia. Some friends had come to see them off – relations of Liuba, Wardwell, the American Red Cross man, and Moura.[43]

For the second time in less than a year Moura found herself standing beside a train in the cold, saying goodbye to dear British friends. This time there were no tears – the shock and pain were too deep. She and Lockhart talked little, and only about meaningless trivialities, both trying to avoid breaking down. Moura dreaded appearing a coward, and fought to hold herself in. 'Remember,' Lockhart said to her, 'each day is one day nearer to the time when we shall meet again.'[44] While the train waited to depart, she was escorted back to the station by Wardwell. Looking back and seeing the train recede into the darkness, she felt that her real self, her soul, was aboard with Lockhart, and that the person walking along with Wardwell, going home through the Moscow streets, teeth and fists clenched tight, was just an outer shell, a half-stunned automaton, 'repeating to itself that one mustn't break down, that one must fight the obstacles and be confident in the future'.[45]

13

The End of Everything . . .

October–November 1918

Autumn 1918, Petrograd

One by one they were being taken from her, the men she had loved and cherished. Lockhart was gone, perhaps forever (although she wouldn't allow herself to think that). Cromie was dead. Now, on her return to Petrograd from Moscow, Moura learned that Denis Garstin – her dear, darling Garstino, the prince of good fellows – had been killed in action at Archangel.

It had taken nearly two months for the news to filter through the tenuous channels that connected Petrograd with the outside world, and still longer for the full story to be told. Like Francis Cromie, Denis Garstin had died in a blaze of martial valour – or purposeless folly, depending on how one saw it. Having received his marching orders while he was with Lockhart's mission in Moscow, Garstin had made his way north on foot, passing through the Red Army lines disguised as a peasant, and reached the British forces at the end of July. A veteran of the Western Front, he threw himself into the fighting with the same verve that he brought to every aspect of life. When his unit was engaged by Soviet machine guns and armoured cars, he led a charge against them. Single-handedly capturing one armoured car, he made a second charge; on the brink of reaching his objective, he was hit in the neck by a rifle bullet and killed instantly.[1]

What a futile death, but also how strangely fitting. In the last weeks before he went away, he had lost much of his characteristic optimism, worn down by the depredations of the Soviet state and the continued suffering of the poor:

I . . . have been damnably disappointed in all I've tried to do out here, have had chance after chance and seen all swept away by that ruthless

fate that seems to dwell in these wide lands and twist the little schemes
and hopes of man into malignant shapes, or else wipe them bewilder-
ingly right away. But it's perhaps for this reason that I shall never be able
wholly, or even partially, to wipe Russia out of my life.[2]

As his friend Hugh Walpole wrote, 'it is one of the tragic ironies of life
that he should have been killed by the people whom he loved, believing
in the future of that land as many of its citizens did not'.[3] He had recovered his spirits in the north, with a clear task before him, but going
home was the one thing he had been dreaming of when he died – 'it's
home, home, home, for me at the first chance'.[4]

Moura didn't know if she could go on bearing all this. 'The dear,
brave, loyal boy – who made such wonderful plans for the future – the
dear old idealist.'[5] She felt terrible guilt that she had sometimes treated
him spitefully – 'a regular pig'.[6] Along with a mass of his papers, Garstino
had left his dog, Garry, in Moura's care when he went away. Moura
diverted her love to the dog, and he went everywhere with her – 'we sit
and look at each other and remember him'.[7]

She managed to sustain her courage in spite of everything, but it was
hard. If Cromie and Garstino could be taken so violently, how could she
expect any process of natural justice to reunite her with Lockhart?
Nothing could be relied on any more in this world.

The grief was brought still closer when she visited the former British
Embassy. She went there looking for some letters that had been sent to
Cromie by Meriel Buchanan and Edward Cunard.[8] The building was
being used as a left-luggage store and occasionally as a refuge for desperate British expatriates still trapped in Russia. Princess Anna Saltikoff,
the owner of the building, was still living in one wing, but the rest was
now deserted, and it was easy for a person with connections to gain
entry. The only person remaining from the old embassy days was
William, Sir George Buchanan's chasseur and butler, now the building's
caretaker. He had once been a proud figure, but now he was aged and
sad, reduced by loneliness and hunger.[9]

It was a desperately melancholy visit. There were boards over the
broken windows, and a piece of paper still pinned to the front door
declaring that the place was under the protection of the Dutch Legation.

Stepping inside, Moura found herself at the foot of the long staircase
that led up to the first landing. Less than a year ago she had ascended

those stairs on the arm of her husband to attend the Buchanans' Christmas party, the weirdly mournful-convivial gathering where there had been bully beef for dinner, impromptu national anthems, and rifles stored ready for use in the chancery.

On the hall floor and the bottom step was a dark, rusty bloodstain. Moura guessed whose it was, and it cut her to the heart. Cromie had fallen here with the Cheka's bullets in his back – there on the bottom step was where his head had lain. Poor dear old Crow. Only a few days ago, Moura had been sorting through old letters and books when she came across the copy of Stevenson's *Virginibus Puerisque* that he had given her 'to remember him by if he was killed'. It brought on a rush of pain and regret.[10] She had immersed herself in the book's lavish, heart-felt essays, and their moods and thoughts permeated the letters she wrote during those last months of 1918.

What had Cromie had in mind when he selected this particular volume to give to Moura, the lady who returned his affection but not his love? Almost every other page seemed to contain something that spoke about himself and Moura. Perhaps he hoped she might be struck by Stevenson's suggestion that 'A ship captain is a good man to marry if it is a marriage of love, for absences are a good influence in love and keep it bright and delicate'.[11] Yet what about Cromie's wife, Gwladys, the Welsh cousin he had married in Portsmouth over a decade ago – what had she felt about being wife to a ship's captain? What was she feeling now?

And what of Moura's own husband? How staid and tedious Djon seemed in comparison to the men Moura admired and loved. Here again was Stevenson, so apt to the moment:

> To be suddenly snuffed out in the middle of ambitious schemes, is trag-ical enough at best; but when a man has been grudging himself his own life in the meanwhile, and saving up everything for the festival that was never to be, it becomes that hysterically moving sort of tragedy which lies on the confines of farce.[12]

There was Djon to a T – hiding away at Yendel, saving up his life for a doomed Germanic future and for the imperial social order that would never return. If he were to die violently, like Cromie (some hope!), the comparison would be complete.

But it was in the book's third essay, on falling in love, that Stevenson's words truly cut into Moura's heart and spoke to her innermost soul:

> Falling in love is the one illogical adventure, the one thing of which we are tempted to think as supernatural, in our trite and reasonable world. The effect is out of all proportion with the cause. Two persons, neither of them, it may be, very amiable or very beautiful, meet, speak a little, and look a little into each other's eyes . . . They fall at once into that state in which another person becomes to us the very gist and centre-point of God's creation, and demolishes our laborious theories with a smile ; . . . and the love of life itself is translated into a wish to remain in the same world with so precious and desirable a fellow-creature. And all the while their acquaintances look on in stupor, and ask each other, with almost passionate emphasis, what so-and-so can see in that woman, or such-a-one in that man? I am sure, gentlemen, I cannot tell you.[13]

Neither could Moura explain how love had caught her so unexpectedly, changed her, made her act against her innate self-regard. 'The fact that you are far away,' she wrote to Lockhart, 'hurts with an acute pain that is almost unbearable and theories of courage and reason are swept away.'[14]

Her heart quailed at the sorry sight of Cromie's blood, and the ghostly atmosphere of the old Embassy. Every room was a mess; the place had been looted for valuables by Red Guards and ransacked for evidence by the Cheka. In the ballroom Moura found damaged furniture and des-patch boxes piled up, their locks broken, and a safe, also broken open. 'What a pitiful sight,' she wrote. 'Even for my half-British heart it was too much and lifted a storm of indignation in me.' She found Cromie's letters and left. 'My heart fell so . . . all my world contains you alone and how all the rest has lost any importance.'[15]

All she could do was work to bring about their reunion. It would have to take place in Stockholm, and would require a bewildering array of permits, passes, visas, documents and money. Putting forth all her charm, Moura acquired a permit to travel between Moscow and Petrograd, and cultivated the diplomats of every neutral nation, as well as Soviet ministers. She visited Yakov Peters, and relied on his influence to keep her safe from further arrest; she was concerned that the Petrograd Cheka (which now had a female chief, a fact that worried Moura) might have suspicions about her and take it upon themselves to snatch her. She had only just learned that the Estonian official who had helped her cross the border in July had been arrested by the Germans.[16] This kind of talk made her nervous.

There was gossip about her of a more trivial nature too. Everyone, from Moscow to Petrograd to London, knew about her affair with Lockhart, and her husband's 'high-falutin relations' had begun 'rather turning up their noses' at her. Her friend Miriam wasn't permitted by her parents to be seen in public with Moura. 'I don't mind one little bit, really,' she wrote to Lockhart. 'And it will all blow over sometime.'[17]

What worried her far more was that he might have heard damaging gossip about her from people he met on his way home through Finland and Sweden. The dreaded, spiteful Thornhill, who had been with the British force at Archangel, was abroad again, with his inexplicable grudge against her. Now that Lockhart was beyond her reach, it terrified her that something might happen to lessen his love for her. 'I'd go like a shot to Stockholm for a week and come back again,' she wrote, 'if it weren't that gossip clings to me like flies to Tanglefoot paper – and people would surely call me a spy on either side.'[18]

It hurt her that he seemed to write so rarely. Weeks and months went by with no word. She knew perfectly well that their letters could only pass in and out of Russia when a friendly diplomat was available to carry them, but the long silences pained and worried her.

Lockhart's journey home had been long and fraught. He had travelled in a group with his surviving comrades – George Hill (who had evaded capture and resumed his own identity), Lingner, Tamplin, and of course Hickie and his new wife Liuba. They talked over their experiences, trying to make sense of it all.

The recriminations started coming at them as soon as they were out of Russia. Their fellow refugees blamed Lockhart for their plight, and let him know it to his face. It was a foretaste of the hostility he would experience when he got home.

In Sweden he succumbed to the Spanish flu pandemic which had been killing people off at a rate to compete with the war. He survived it, just as he had survived his brush with the epidemic of Bolshevism, and arrived in England by way of Aberdeen on 19 October. At King's Cross he was surrounded by reporters before he'd even got off the train

– they got into his compartment and questioned him excitedly, demanding to see the revolver with which he had shot Lenin.[19]

He was more worried about the interrogation he was going to receive from his wife and family. His affair with Moura was known about at the Foreign Office, and his enemies would have spared no effort in spreading it more widely. The person he most feared, though, was his formidable Scottish grandmother, who was a more effective investigator than any Chekist. She would inevitably subject him to a stern dressing-down, 'richly illustrated with Biblical metaphors, on the inevitable consequences of sowing in the flesh'.[20] His concern was practical – he would be dependent on this old lady for financial support if he failed to get a new posting from the Foreign Office.

That seemed a likely outcome – his cosying-up with the Bolsheviks, his collusion with Lloyd George behind Balfour's back and his nefarious dealings with intelligence agents had made him deeply unpopular in the Foreign Office.

While he waited for the future course of his career to reveal itself, he recuperated from the effects of his ordeal and his illness. He went through the motions of patching up relations with Jean, and spent time at Bexhill-on-Sea and Exmouth, where he fished and played golf. He wrote a long, detailed report on Russia and Bolshevism, and recommended that if Britain were to continue its intervention, it must do so in proper numbers. The war with Germany had ended now, and the required troops would be available – he suggested two forces, each of fifty thousand men, invading by way of the Black Sea and Siberia. His report was received well in the Foreign Office (whatever they thought of his diplomacy, Lockhart couldn't be faulted for his knowledge and his intelligence), but his proposal was dismissed.

As he convalesced, as he dined out with Jean, clubbed with his friends, paced the golf courses, and politicked with the intelligence services and the Foreign Office, he thought constantly of Moura. He loved her still. He recalled how she had sustained him during his imprisonment, and saved him from despair. 'Had this cataclysm of our arrest not intervened, I think I would have stayed in Russia for ever. Now we had been forcibly torn apart . . . For all I knew I might never see her again.'[21]

He wrote to her, and experienced the same frustration she did at the long intervals caused by their reliance on the travels of friendly diplomats. Moura's letters kept him going – 'the mainstay of my existence'.[22]

He hoped that either Moura could get out of Russia or the Bolsheviks would fall. There was no telling which of those possibilities was the more remote.

Some believed that Bolshevism must end soon; others (including British conservatives and King George V) feared that it would spread throughout Europe. Germany looked a likely next victim. Lockhart thought so too, but noted that 'I think Germany, too, will have her Bolshevik phase, although it will be different from the Russian process.'[23] He hadn't wholly lost his ideals, and his sympathies were with the fledgling Labour Party. Lunching with some friends at his club, they realised that they wouldn't know which side to take if it ever came to war between the 'White' and 'Red' sides in England. 'Decided that we should all prefer to remain in bed.'[24]

One way for him to be reunited with Moura would be if he were to return to Russia in an official capacity. In late November the Foreign Office proposed to give him a posting to Petrograd as 'assistant commercial attaché'. But it was more a calculated insult than an opportunity, and completely unthinkable.[25]

It would also have been fatal. The furore over the Lockhart Plot hadn't gone away. Despite the efforts of Yakov Peters to downplay Lockhart's involvement, on 25 November the Revolutionary Tribunal formally indicted him, along with a batch of other counter-revolutionary agents and agitators, on charges of espionage and conspiracy. Lockhart and Sidney Reilly, along with their French colleague Grenard, were found guilty *in absentia* and sentenced to death. If they were ever apprehended on Soviet soil, the sentence would be carried out.[26]

Lockhart could never return to Russia as long as the Soviet state endured. And Moura couldn't come to England – at least not yet. Their only hope in the meantime was a reunion in Stockholm; and then, in time, Moura might succeed in arranging all the prerequisites for their permanent reunion. She needed money, she needed to be free of Djon and ensure the safety of her children and mother. It all looked insurmountable.

In the meantime, Lockhart fought with the chronic ill health that had dogged him since his return, hoped for a career opportunity which would make him an independent man again, and wrote his letters to Moura.

The impenetrable ring around Russia was growing stronger by the month. Lenin, who was now well enough to resume making speeches, declared that the Red Army would soon be three million strong. Although there were still rumours that the Allied force in the north would win through to Moscow and Petrograd, nobody with any sense believed it any more. Moura certainly did not. (Her sources, while belying Lenin's grandiose claim, confirmed that the army now numbered many hundreds of thousands of effective troops.) And as the Bolsheviks, whose position had seemed so precarious a few months ago, strengthened their hold it became all the more imperative – and all the more difficult – to get out.

Moura had most of the documents she needed. The one thing that eluded her was a permit for her mother to cross into Finland. Without that, it would be impossible for the elderly Madame Zakrevskaya to leave Russia, and therefore impossible for Moura to join Lockhart in England. As soon as she could she would go to Estonia (provided she could get across the border) and begin divorce proceedings. She had received a letter from Djon, who claimed that his friends the Germans were 'making things unpleasant to him' because of the belief that she was spying for the Allies. So great was the inconvenience she had caused him, she joked that he might try to kill her if he had the opportunity.[27]

Now that Germany had lost the war the Red Army was fighting its way into the Baltic provinces against resistance from nationalist armies, and Moura's children in Estonia were in the path of the fighting.

Her mother was unwell and vulnerable. Without Moura's influence, her home would be requisitioned and Madame Zakrevskaya would starve. In early October the flat had been searched by government officials and all their provisions seized, supposedly for redistribution. In the 'new burgeoning world' (as Yakov Peters had called it) you were only entitled to eat if you were a member of the working classes. Moura had had to take a job as an office manager, which shortened the time she could spend on oiling the wheels for her departure.

She put prodigious energy into cultivating foreign diplomats. The most important was Asker, the Swedish Consul-General. He was also the friendliest, and had negotiated heroically on behalf of Lockhart and the other prisoners. He was a small, neat man with precise manners and a pretty young wife. He liked Moura, and delighted her by addressing her effusively as 'Baroness', but she puzzled him; he had the sort of mind which 'likes to register all he sees – and somehow he cannot register me and that perplexes him'.[28]

Even in the shambles of the new Russia Moura managed to scrape together a social and intellectual life, forgetting her troubles in books and concerts – she went with her Red Cross friends to hear Feodor Chaliapin sing, and accompanied the elderly Princess Saltikoff to a Wagner concert in the Winter Palace – 'it was such a pleasure to sit with the old lady and listen to fine music. And Wagner is just restless enough to suit me, now.'[29]

And all the time she laid her plans for Stockholm and the reunion with Lockhart. Every month the plan altered as the political situation changed or belated news of his health came through. And each time the meeting got delayed, Moura lost a little of her stock of hope.

One December evening she walked home from work by way of the Palace Quay and the Summer Garden. The Russian winter had returned, and everything was covered in soft white snow. The great park was deserted, and she sat down on a bench, dreaming of Lockhart and their sleigh-rides along the banks of the Neva. Moura always remembered those joyful, playful rides when she walked through this part of the city, near the Embassy and the river – that period had been the bright morning of their love. 'What children we were then,' she recalled sadly, 'what old, old people we are now. But how infinitely thankful I am to Providence that I have met you, my Baby, what happiness you have given me, how you have taught me to love.'[30] But as the weeks had gone by, her nerves had frayed. Now, sitting on the bench amidst the snow and the loneliness, she could feel herself coming apart. Just that morning she had been sorting through some of her belongings and had come across her children's old baby clothes. 'Those tiny things brought back such a longing for little Peter,' she wrote to Lockhart, 'for a child that should be yours and mine.'

But the prospect of Lockhart fulfilling his promises to her seemed frail and unreliable now. 'I am nervous and jumpy and morbid and my glorious confidence in you sometimes gives place to the most utter depression and torturing surmises,' she wrote. 'And I am jealous, Baby. But you will be true to me, Baby, won't you? If you fail me – it will be the end of everything for me . . .'[31]

14

Se Mettre en Quatre

December 1918–May 1919

There were two Christmases again this year. The first came on 25
December. Russia ignored it – despite the Bolsheviks' anti-reli-
gious stance, the Church kept to the Old Style calendar. Moura marked
the date – the anniversary of the embassy party – in private silence. She
knew now for sure that the English would not be coming back to Russia
to save her. Intervention was dead. The Allies, still holding on at
Archangel, would never beat the growing Red Army, and the rumour
of a British fleet steaming through the Baltic was nothing but a myth.
Russia would have to steer its own course into the future.

Moura noted sardonically the Bolsheviks' perplexity at the Tory victory in the recent British general election. They had been convinced
that socialism must spread throughout Europe, and couldn't understand
why it wasn't happening. But guided equally by wishful thinking, Moura
convinced herself that a new revolution must occur in Russia within the
month and sweep away the rotten Bolsheviks.[1] She was usually more
astute than this.

Perhaps the stress and privations of her life were degrading her per-
cipience. She was getting thinner all the time, plagued by a persistent
cough, and the temperature indoors hovered around 6°C. Firewood
cost up to 500 roubles a bundle (a month's wages for a workman), and
was difficult to get even at that price. Moura sometimes spent whole
days trekking through the snowbound city looking for fuel.[2] The
authorities were shutting down the tramways and the electricity supply
to homes. 'No food comes from anywhere,' Moura wrote, 'and from
to-day they are giving oats and bran-smash instead of bread. So gradually we will all develop into little cows and horses.' To her horror,

shops had begun to appear in the city selling dog meat; Moura took extra care when she was out with Garry, frightened that he might be snatched.[3]

Two visitors came calling during that British Christmas, one less welcome than the other. One was a Red Army officer who knew of her contacts with British intelligence. He claimed to represent a network of White Guard infiltrators who were preparing to betray the Red Army to the Allied forces. Three quarters of the artillery were ready to go over to the White side, and many infantry regiments. Moura asked him if he didn't think that Russians could overthrow the Bolsheviks without foreign help. 'It revolted me to see this man refusing to admit that anything could be done without foreign intervention and I don't believe he is right either.'[4] Neither did she think there was much substance in his claims, but she passed the information to Lockhart, as she did with every rumour and snippet of political news that she thought might interest him.

Perhaps unconsciously she was repeating what she had done in the early months of their relationship, when, responding warmly to his admiration for her intellect and insight, she sought to impress him with opinions and information. She stoked up her consumption of literature in all her various languages – 'I'll read and read and read,' she had promised him, 'and become such a blue stocking that all your knowledge will be nothing next to mine.'[5] She also enrolled at the university to study for a diploma – as 'a tonic . . . in order to keep a more or less balanced mind – which otherwise would go to pieces in this atmosphere'.[6]

Her endeavours began to pay off. The other visitor in late December was much more promising. The literary critic, satirist and anglophile Korney Chukovsky, mop-haired and thickly moustached, called on her with an offer of work translating English poetry. Like Moura, Chukovsky had worked for the British missions as an interpreter.[7] He was now involved with a new venture which had been set up to publish Russian translations of the greats of English literature. Thrilled, Moura decided immediately to accept, but kept him dangling. Next day she called at his office to discuss the proposal. There she was introduced for the first time to the man who was heading the publishing house – novelist, poet, dramatist, essayist and contender for the title of greatest living Russian, Maxim Gorky. Aside from Lenin, there was probably no man in Russia more well known or more admired.

He had just turned fifty, and the intense, glaring good looks of his youth were starting to give way to the haggard, drawn features of his age – the razor cheekbones were hollowing out from beneath, the moustache was thickening, greying and drooping as if it too felt the weight of age, but his piercing black eyes still glittered brightly under the crinkling lids.

To a woman of Moura's literary pretensions, it was a remarkable achievement to be noticed and offered work by this man. But she played it cool in her letters to Lockhart. 'We talked of English authors,' she wrote, 'of which, strange to say, he knows a good deal, even the modern ones. He asked me to give him a list of books I thought would be interesting to translate! It all amused me rather and I will go there twice a week to kill time. The whole atmosphere there is very bohemian – but rather stimulating.'[8]

She was curious about Gorky's politics; although he was a socialist he was protective of his aristocratic acquaintances and used his influence to save them from the Bolsheviks. Moura guessed cynically that he was motivated by a wish not to be 'compromised abroad'. He told her that his ideal was 'to have the world ruled by people of creative thought . . . without any distinction of class. He thinks himself a d'Annunzio of Russia.'[9]

Perhaps in another, earlier time in her life she might have been more impressed by this turn in her fortunes. Now, though, she felt that Russia must change itself or lose her. She wanted freedom and comfort, she wanted her children, and most of all she wanted Lockhart. 'How I wish I had news from you oftener, Baby-Boy. It would have been such a comfort in these terrible days to know more about you.' To a woman who lived on attention, thrived on knowledge, it was unbearable. 'I feel stupid to-day and can't write. Sometimes the longing for you, for the certainty of you, for the feeling that you belong to me is so great – that writing becomes a torture and words cease to mean anything.'[10]

Nonetheless she took it as a good omen when the first book she was given to translate (at a fair wage of 10 kopeks a line) was the biography of Walter Scott by John Gibson Lockhart. Perhaps that meant something.[11]

The official Russian Christmas came in early January. Although she had never felt less like celebrating, Moura bought a bedraggled tree from the market and struggled home with it through the cold streets.

It was now three months and two days since she had last seen Lockhart.

(She kept count.) As she did every evening, she sat and wrote to him, pulling together little scraps of news, gossip, political intelligence, all held together with her inner thoughts. She was in the middle of describing a rumour that the charismatic head of the Petrograd Soviet, Grigory Zinoviev, had been arrested by Lenin 'for disobeying orders about provisions' when her mother's voice cut in on her train of thought.

'Are you writing again to *that man*?' she said.

Moura paused. 'Yes,' she admitted, tight-lipped.

'Quite useless – I am sure he has forgotten all about you by this time.'

Ugh. Moura went on writing, and a few minutes later came another interruption. '*He* has been eating pudding for his Christmas,' said Madame Zakrevskaya bitterly, 'while we here have to suck our thumbs and grind our oats. But he doesn't care!'

Staring down at the page, shaken, Moura copied down her mother's words, and added, 'Do you, Baby?'[12] Did he care? Would he come to Stockholm when it was time? Would he take them both out of this nightmare? She was beginning to lose faith in the future, and sometimes hated writing to him: 'Letters are such horrible – unsatisfactory things. And you seem so unreal – out there in the darkness – where these little slips of paper perhaps never even reach you.'[13]

The Christmas season bore upon her for other reasons. As she decorated the tree and prepared her mother's presents, her heart ached for her children – 'when I think of my kiddies far away, perhaps in danger, and I not able to put toys in their little stockings. Babykins – I'm having such a terribly hard time – altogether. Riga has been taken to-day by the red army and they are advancing on Reval.'[14]

And it was two months since Lockhart had last sent her a letter.

Later that month, the Bolsheviks came at last for the remaining Benckendorff wealth. Moura was notified that her husband's safe deposit box at the bank was going to be broken open and its contents seized. (Other wealthy people who had less influence with the regime had gone through this robbery nearly a year ago.) Moura insisted on being present when the 'few un-washed boys who are dictators of my bank now' broke the safe open. She used all her charm and persuasion on them, and managed to keep the contents for herself. These youths presented little challenge for a woman who had seduced statesmen and won her way out of a Cheka prison. 'One really has such a tremendous privilege over them all,' she wrote, 'for even the cleverest ones are perfect infants in arms as far as any training of the mind goes. They . . . continue looking at life from the point of view of the little third-class restaurants in Switzerland where they used to meet.'[15]

Again she had to use her influence and charm – *se mettre en quatre*,* as she expressed it – to save the apartment from being requisitioned. She succeeded, but this constant struggle to avoid destitution was a drain on her energy.[16]

All through what was left of that winter her emotional fortunes rose and fell with the flow and retreat of Lockhart's letters. After long interludes of silence they would come through in batches, months out of date but bringing floods of joy. 'Your dear, dear letters – how splendid they are. You tell me all what I could have wished to hear, my Baby, that you love me – that you beleive in me – that you want me.'[17]

His letters to her did not survive in the historical record, but even in her breathless appreciation of them his misgivings echo. She brushed away his recital of the social awkwardness of their getting together, assuring him that she knew the risks and the shame better than he did, and that she was willing to face anything. She shut out any notion that he might not be so willing, and focused only on his protestations of love.

She concocted a plan. Even if they couldn't yet be reunited permanently, they could come together for a short time – their meeting in Stockholm, proposed months ago and continually put off, could be just a brief reunion, an affirmation of their love in advance of the moment when they would be reunited permanently in England. Moura worked out how the visas could be arranged by way of the Swedish Consulate and Lockhart's diplomatic contacts in Helsingfors and Stockholm.

As the weeks went by, she began putting it in motion, looking for the opportunity to make her move. At the same time, she proposed to enter Estonia to initiate her divorce proceedings – an extremely risky prospect, given the war for independence that was going hammer-and-tongs not far from Yendel and Reval, not to mention her reputation in some quarters as a spy. It would be safest, she reasoned, to go via Finland and make the fifty-mile sea crossing from Helsingfors to Reval.[18]

The plan was postponed in February, when she learned that Lockhart had been ill and needed an operation to remove cartilage from his nose.

---

* Bend over backwards (lit. 'go on all fours').

He wrote complaining of feeling tired and run-down. His health worried her dreadfully – not just the thought of him suffering but the idea that his wife might win him back by nursing him to health (after his influenza she'd been tormented by a dream in which Lockhart told her that he was giving her up in gratitude to Jean).[19] It worried her too that she had failed to give him the son he wanted, and promised that it would be 'the aim of my life – as something necessary to your happiness'.[20]

Her feelings were starting to take on a fatalism, her optimistic faith taken over by a darker, heavier sense of the future. 'I love you,' she assured him. 'With a grave, sublime love, that is stronger than death.'[21] Her words were more than mere effect. Death was all around her – not only the friends she had lost to the Bolsheviks but to disease and starvation too. Spotted typhus had broken out again in Petrograd, and by February several acquaintances had died from it. There was a constant fear that the Finns, whose border was just a few miles away, would invade the city. 'Oh Baby-Boy,' she wrote, 'what I would give to have you here, near me, with your arms round me, and have you comfort me and cuddle me and make me forget all the nightmare.'[22]

On the eve of her birthday, Moura received the best possible present – a letter from Lockhart inquiring whether their meeting was still going to take place. 'My little one, my dearest,' she replied, 'of course I am coming . . . perhaps in a week or ten days from to-day I will be in your arms. My beloved, my Baby – what happiness, what joy it is going to be.'[23]

The actual day of her birthday was bittersweet. It was a year since the party at her own apartment, with all her men – Lockhart, Cromie, Garstin – when there had been caviar, blinis and vodka. Now there was bran-smash and oats in the bitterly cold flat, and a sad letter from Garstino's mother, who knew what a friend Moura had been to her boy. There were new people in her life, but they seemed unimportant – even the august, fascinating Gorky was little more than an employer. Frazier Hunt, the *Chicago Tribune* journalist and Gorky's rapturous admirer, gave her Walt Whitman's *Leaves of Grass* ('as a young American democrat should'), and there were chocolates and wine from Folmer Hansen, head of the Danish Red Cross, who had also brought a letter from Lockhart and joked about being the *postillon d'amour*.[24]

She was now twenty-seven years old, but felt older.

Everything was blotted out by the prospect of being with Lockhart himself, in the beloved flesh. It was going to happen soon – unbearably, impossibly, happily soon. Theirs, she believed, was a love like no other – greater and more potent than Walt Whitman's 'unspeakable passionate love', his 'sobbing liquid of life'.[25] It must and would be fulfilled.

Saturday 12 April 1919, Helsingfors, Finland

The Hotel Fennia was supposed to be one of the best in the city. It towered grandly over the wide boulevard adjoining the railway station, seeming to promise luxury and comfort. But Finland had suffered from its civil war just as Russia had, and Moura's wealth had long since been exhausted. Her room was tiny and horrid; it had no bath, and the bed was alive with bugs.[26] In a way, this was the perfect place in which to consider her situation.

The reunion had not taken place.[27]

Moura had made it out of Russia and into Finland – crossing the frontier into what was effectively enemy territory. At Helsingfors she had found herself trapped. In order to reach Lockhart in Stockholm she needed a Swedish visa. But the Swedes in Helsingfors, despite her and Lockhart's good relations with Asker, the Swedish representative in Russia, wouldn't give it to her without a *British* visa. Lockhart had been supposed to wire a consular friend (either in Helsingfors or Christiania,* it wasn't clear) to arrange it. The whole plan, which Moura had worked out in every detail, should have fallen neatly into place, and she should have been able to cross into Sweden and fall into the arms of Lockhart. To feel his warming, consoling presence again, to see his dear face, plan the next stage of the bureaucratic game which would let them come together permanently.

But the visa hadn't been arranged. Not only that, but she discovered that Lockhart wasn't waiting for her across the border in Stockholm. Instead there was a telegram for her. He was ill again. He couldn't travel. He pressed her, as he had before, to abandon everything and come straight to England.

It wasn't a question of resisting temptation – even if she had been able to abandon her mother and any prospect of seeing her children again,

---

* Now Oslo.

she couldn't pass through Sweden without that visa. And now the Finns were putting pressure on her to go back to Russia.

The disappointment was bitter. She was haunted – 'with a poignancy which leaves me cold and numb' – by the thought that Lockhart might think her a coward for lingering in Russia instead of coming to England. That he might not care for her any longer; that he might not want her. It was a worry that had dogged her always, and he had stoked her concerns. She had been reminded of this a few weeks ago, when she heard Gorky lecture on French poetry, and she remembered how Lockhart liked to recite Maurice Magre's '*Avilir*', which seemed to resonate with him:

> J'ai le besoin profond d'avilir ce que j'aime . . .
> Je sais que la candeur de ses yeux ne ment pas,
> Qu'elle m'ouvre son coeur quand elle ouvre les bras,
> Je sais à voir ses pleurs que sa peine est extrême
> Et malgré tout cela j'affecte de douter.
> Je cherche avec une soigneuse cruauté
> Ses erreurs, ses défauts, ce qui fait sa faiblesse,
> Et m'en sers pour froisser, déchirer sa tendresse[28]

> (I have a profound urge to demean that which I love . . .
> I know that the candour in her eyes doesn't lie,
> That she opens her heart to me when she opens her arms,
> I know by the sight of her tears that her suffering is great
> And despite all that, I affect to doubt.
> With careful cruelty I seek out
> Her errors, her faults, her weakness,
> And in so doing, crumple and tear her affection)

Was that how he felt now? Would he misinterpret her actions? Did he share Magre's urge to destroy his love and escape from it?

There was no option but to go back to Russia. She must free herself from all ties – then she would travel from Helsingfors to Stockholm and England, 'having put a full stop on all my obligations of the past'.

One obligation, one particularly irksome tie, was her marriage. Well, that could be dealt with immediately. Only a narrow waist of sea separated her from Estonia and Djon. She had been there before, and now was the time to go there again. Here was one part of her plan that could not go wrong.

The events of the days that followed grew into one of the most insidious mysteries of Moura's life.

Saturday 18 April, Yendel, Estonia

The Germans had gone from Estonia, and anarchy had returned. Peasant bands were roaming the countryside again, the violence exacerbated by the nationalist war that had broken out.

At Yendel the Benckendorff family had suffered more raids, even worse than the one over a year ago, in which Moura had had to hide in the garden with the children. One day, while Djon was away, a group of bandits got into the manor and rampaged through the living rooms, plundering and vandalising.

It had become too dangerous to stay there, and at the end of March Djon made the decision to move the family to another part of the estate. On the far side of the south lake was a much smaller house, named Kallijärv, where Djon's mother had once lived (this was the lair from which she had sourly observed Moura and her disreputable friends sporting in the lake in summers past). It was more modest and much more removed from the main roads, and therefore less likely to attract the attention of raiders.

On the Saturday before Easter, Djon left Kallijärv to walk up to the Red House to check that everything was in order, and to see to some estate business. He had talked about taking four-year-old Tania – his 'little woman' – with him, but her nurse forbade it, so he went on his own. He promised the children and the servants he'd be back in time for lunch.[29]

The hours ticked by, and he didn't return. Lunchtime came and still there was no sign of him. It would later be recalled by several people that three gunshots were heard during the morning, but nobody could remember exactly when. Gunshots were not at all unusual in the countryside around Yendel, and nobody thought anything of it. Except for Micky – afterwards she would claim that the sound had given her a presentiment of calamity. But she didn't do or say anything at the time.

At one o'clock it was decided that they'd better go looking for him. The three children were dressed up in their coats and hats by their Russian nurse, Mariussa. (Micky was more than ever a member of the family rather than a servant, and childcare was no longer her task.) Leaving the cosy little house with its smell of cooking and oil lamps and paraffin heaters, Kira, Pavel, Tania and Mariussa set out along the lake shore towards the Red House.

Winter was receding – the deep snow was melting and the frozen lake breaking up into floes. The children prodded at the ice with sticks as they passed. Beyond the second corner there was a lane that went uphill, while the footpath carried on between two hills. The lane crossed between the hills on a little span known as the Devil's Bridge. It was a secluded spot, hemmed in by trees and always shadowy. As the party approached, they could see the shape of a man lying across the path where it passed under the bridge.

It was clear at a glance that it was Djon. Mariussa shrieked and tried to shoo the children away, but they had already seen, and even the youngest had realised that something dreadful had happened. Mariussa knelt beside him and tried to raise him up. It was no use; he was dead.

Djon von Benckendorff had been shot. As for who had done it, there was no trace – not a sign, not a footprint, not a whisper. Only the memory of those three gunshots heard at some unremembered time in the morning.

Easter Sunday, Terijoki, Finland[*]

It was a strange little town, Terijoki. Standing in the angle where the Russian frontier met the Gulf of Finland, it was where the Finns regulated border crossings. The town had been carved out of thick forest, and woodland took up most of the space between the streets.

Moura had been stranded here for a couple of days, trying to make her way back into Russia after the travels and travails of the past few weeks. She felt that Lockhart was slipping irretrievably away from her. She had phoned the Hotel Fennia to find out whether he had sent her any more telegrams, but there was nothing.

---

[*] Now Zelenogorsk, Russia.

Today, it being Easter Sunday, she went to Terijoki's little church. When the service was over she set out to walk back to the little *pension* she was staying in. She had quickly grown to loathe her terrible room there, with its geraniums and white lace curtains, where at night the moon shone in on her. She was in no hurry to get back, and she walked slowly.[30]

The path from the church led – as most paths in Terijoki did – through a wood of tall, tall trees. The weather was warming – so much that the thawing snow was making rivers in the main streets. There was green grass underfoot, and blue sky in the gaps at the tops of the trees. As she looked up, Moura recalled strolling arm in arm with Lockhart in the tree-lined avenues of Sokolniki Park in Moscow. Suddenly, with the blue sky in her eyes, it was as if he were there. She felt his real, physical presence as powerfully and vividly as a hallucination . . . and then, just as suddenly, he was gone.

As soon as the moment passed and she felt the return of her perpetual, crushing loneliness, she broke down. For the first time in all the months since he had gone away, Moura abandoned herself to the ferocity of her grief. She threw herself on the wet, cold ground and sobbed her breaking heart out.

When the fit had passed, she picked herself up and went back to her room. A few days later she crossed the border into Russia. It closed behind her with a finality that must have been almost audible.

Less than two weeks after her return to Petrograd, Moura found herself suddenly free of the two ties which had held her back. On 7 May she received the news that Djon had been murdered. She wrote Lockhart a short, frantic letter – 'My husband has been killed on the 19th of April by some Estonians out of revenge'.[31] At the time she was writing, Moura was struggling to keep her feelings under control in front of her mother, who was in hospital, scheduled for an operation the next day. 'Can you see what a strain it is?' Moura wrote to Lockhart. 'I can make no plans, I cannot think of anything yet, Baby. I must try and get the children away from that place as soon as possible'.

Why had there been no word from him, no letters, no telegrams?

> I don't understand your silence, Baby. For God's sake
> be frank with me, Baby, play fair with me as I always
> have and always will with you.

May God keep you safe and well.
And remember, Baby, how much I love you.
Yours for ever
Moura

She never received a reply. Within the week her mother died. Moura was utterly alone.[32]

Who killed Djon von Benckendorff? Was Moura present? Did she pull the trigger? On 18 April, the day of the murder, she wrote to Lockhart from Terijoki and added the postscript: 'I have started my divorce the day before yesterday.'[33] To do so, she must have met with Djon – either in Reval or at Yendel – to obtain his signature. Two days later he was dead.

Moura certainly had a powerful motive to wish herself rid of Djon quickly before the political situation, together with her reputation for espionage, trapped her permanently inside Russia. But there must have been many around Yendel who hated the master of the estate for his Germanism. He might well have been one of those Baltic German land-owners who turfed out ethnic Estonian peasants and gave tenancies to Germans.

Moura's letter from Terijoki on the day of the killing was a kind of alibi, but not a very strong one.

But even assuming she didn't fire the shots that killed him, she could have wielded an influence. Few people knew the political situation in Estonia better than Moura; she knew the people of Yendel and would have understood their grievances. And she was extremely skilled in per-suasion and manipulation, as she had proved with the commissars at the bank – 'One really has such a tremendous privilege over them all, for even the cleverest ones are perfect infants in arms as far as any training of the mind goes.'[34] If there were locals with a grudge against Djon, she would have been quite capable of influencing them. And having spent most of the past year in the company of men who habitually armed themselves with revolvers, she might even have been able to supply the means.

In the end, the truth – whatever it might be – was never discovered. Moura's close family – her children – never suspected her. And only the most tenuous evidence remained of her ever having been in Estonia in April 1919. The letter she wrote Lockhart from the Hotel Fennia, which would have marked the eve of her crossing to Reval, has a page missing – a page which appears to be about to mention her visit: 'The worst, the longest bit in our parting is over,' she wrote, still trying to convince herself that it was worth going on with the plan, 'we have only a little more to wait. I hope to get . . .'[35]

What did she hope to get? Did Lockhart remove the page to protect her from suspicion? If so, it would not be the only letter of hers where he appears to have excised indiscreet pages.

At the end of 1919 Lockhart left England for a new posting. He had been appointed commercial secretary in the British Legation in Prague. He had turned down a second (more serious) appointment in Russia, on the grounds that 'I had better leave Russia for a bit'.[36] Either the Foreign Office didn't know about the death sentence hanging over him there, or thought he would be safe from it.

There had been no letter from Moura for months – the last word from her was the disturbing news of the death of her husband. Now, with the closing down of Russia's relations with the outside world, there were no friendly diplomats who could be relied on to get letters in and out.

He still loved Moura, but in his mind their impossible affair was at an end: 'She had left a wound in my heart, but it was healing.'[37] Perhaps he was thinking of Magre, as Moura had guessed he would, unconsciously echoing the words of the poem in his recollection – 'C'est une tache au coeur dont aucune eau ne lave. / Je voudrais oublier, je voudrais m'en guérir' (It is a stain on my heart that no water can wash away. / I want to forget, I want to be healed).

At the same time, Moura was setting about trying to heal herself. For her, it would be a lifelong quest.

No man would be allowed to come so close to her again; no man would be loved or idolised; and no man would ever be allowed to possess her.

Except Lockhart. No matter where she went or what she experienced, she would never regain the part of herself that belonged to him.

PART 3

In Exile: 1919–1924

Her I loved naturally and necessarily and – for all the faults and trouble . . . she has satisfied my craving for material intimacy more completely than any other human being. I still 'belong' so much to her that I cannot really get away from her. I love her still.

H. G. Wells, 'Moura, the Very Human' in *H. G. Wells in Love*

15

'We're All Iron Now'

1919–1921

Late September 1920, Petrograd

The city was all but dead; its heart had stopped beating and yet it was still somehow breathing and stirring.

When H. G. Wells arrived in Petrograd in that autumn of the third year of the Revolution, he could scarcely believe the transformation. He had last visited in 1914, before the start of the war, when the imperial capital was still a teeming, thriving metropolis of well over a million souls, with glittering palaces and streets packed with shoppers and strollers. That had all gone, and in its place was desolation.

A Russian acquaintance in London had suggested that Wells, well known to be sympathetic to the spirit of the Revolution (although emphatically not a Communist), would be interested to see how things were working out since his last visit. And so, near the end of September 1920, he had set off with his nineteen-year-old son George Philip (known as 'Gip') for a two-week tour of the new Russia.

It was a profoundly dispiriting experience. The palaces were still there, but most stood empty. Perhaps because of his family background in shopkeeping, it was the closed shops that struck Wells' heart most keenly. He reckoned there were no more than half a dozen still functioning in the city. The rest were dead. They had 'an utterly wretched and abandoned look; paint is peeling off, windows are cracked, some are broken and boarded up, some still display a few fly-blown relics of stock in the window, some have their windows covered with notices . . . the fixtures have gathered two years' dust. They are dead shops. They will never open again.' It had killed off the city streets. 'One realises that a modern city is really nothing but long alleys of shops . . . Shut them up, and the meaning of a street has disappeared.'[1]

Eschewing the Hotel International, where foreigners usually stayed, Wells was put up by his old friend Maxim Gorky. He found himself entering a peculiar domestic scene, a sort of commune in which Gorky presided over a ménage of writers, artists and intimate friends, all crammed together in a huge apartment on the fourth floor of a block on Petrogradsky Island, overlooking Alexander Park.

Among the inhabitants was a young woman who was apparently Gorky's live-in secretary and (though Wells didn't realise it) his mistress. Despite her drab, makeshift clothing and a rather unsightly broken nose, she was an attractive, captivating creature, and Wells was pleased to learn that she had been approved by the authorities to act as his guide and interpreter during his stay. Her name was Maria Ignatievna Zakrevskaya, but everybody knew her as Moura.

Wells, who was almost as prolific a womaniser as he was a writer, would always remember this meeting as one of his life's great encounters.[2]

How Moura came to be living in the Gorky commune, and how she had passed the sixteen months since her last contact with the world outside Russia, is mostly a blank page. Or, to be more precise, blank with a few daubs and doubtful sketches on it, and only a few definite impressions.

After her desperate final letter to Lockhart in May 1919, in the wake of Djon's murder and on the eve of her mother's death, with the Estonian nationalist forces pushing the Red Army back to the very outskirts of Petrograd, Moura slipped into obscurity. Not a written word in her own hand survived, and few contemporary accounts. Most of what was handed down to posterity was hearsay, much of it wrong.[3]

By the end of that May, Moura was alone in the world. Lockhart was beyond her reach, and her mother dead, either from surgical complications or from the illness which the surgery was intended to treat.[4] With her children in Estonia, she had no other family left in Russia.

Moura's plight grew desperate when she finally lost her struggle to hold on to her mother's apartment. Now that the elderly lady was dead it would no longer be possible to work on the sympathies of the government officials. Moura found herself on the streets, forced to throw herself on the charity of acquaintances. She said later that she was given accommodation for a time by the elderly General Aleksander

Mosolov, who had once been head of the Court Chancellery under Tsar Nicholas II.

When the summer of 1919 drew to an end, a full year had passed since her last period with Lockhart – the nightmare of their imprisonment and the last few blissful days together in the Kremlin. Winter was approaching and she still had no proper home. She had found extra work as assistant to her old friend Korney Chukovsky, who, in addition to his publishing work, ran a studio, library and children's theatre for the House of Arts.

Then another mystery occurred. In late summer she was arrested and held by the Cheka. The reason is unknown, but people were being arrested constantly for crimes as slight as being out late at night or failing to carry the requisite identification papers. Chukovsky was concerned about her, and when Maxim Gorky came to him one day in an incoherent rage about a friend of his who had also been arrested, Chukovsky asked him to use his influence to help Moura too. Gorky threatened to make a scandal and repudiate the Bolsheviks if the prisoners were not released.[5]

Once Moura was free, Chukovsky took her, as he had done the previous December, to see Gorky. She already knew the great man quite well through her translation work for his World Literature publishing house.[6]

This meeting took place at his apartment. It was a peculiar place, on the fourth floor of a block at 23 Kronverksky Prospekt, a vast crescent on Petrogradsky Island (where Moura and Lockhart had liked to come on their sleigh-jaunts). The block itself was a rather ugly alpine-looking conglomeration of rustic stone and stucco, with hefty arches and hexagonal windows, reminiscent of the manor at Yendel. The atmosphere within was a world apart. Gorky had become a saint-like figure. Since the Revolution, he had been one of the mainstays – perhaps the principal saviour – of the arts in Russia. He had used his influence to help found the House of Science and the Houses of Literature and Art – institutions which fostered the intellectual life of the new Russia. And on his own initiative he had begun the World Literature publishing venture, which sought to import the fruits of foreign authors into the Russian language.

Within his domain he was like a baron in his manor, surrounded by companions and supplicants. His appearance had become eccentric.

One of Moura's contemporaries, the poet Vladislav Khodasevich, described him as looking like 'a learned Chinaman in a red silk robe and motley skullcap' which set off his sharp cheekbones and Asian eyes. His formerly thick hair had been cropped to the scalp, his face was deeply lined, and he wore spectacles on the tip of his nose. There was always a book in his hands. 'A crush of people filled the apartment from early morning to late at night,' Khodasevich recalled. 'Each of the people who lived there had visitors, and Gorky himself was positively besieged by them.'[7] Living in or passing through were writers, scholars, publishers, actors, artists and politicians. People in trouble flocked to the apartment to plead with Gorky to protect them from Grigory Zinoviev, the powerful head of the Petrograd Soviet and Northern Commune, or to help them get food, transport or countless other favours. Gorky listened to every plea, and was tireless in his efforts to help.

In an echo of her first meeting with Gorky at the office of World Literature, Chukovsky brought Moura to see him in the afternoon. Weak tea was served from a samovar in the large, well-furnished dining room. This was the only public room in the apartment – all the rest were bedrooms belonging to the many residents.[8]

Gorky had been charmed and intrigued by Moura ever since their meeting nine months earlier. 'He was a brilliant speaker,' she would write years later, recalling that first meeting, and 'in the presence of a strange, new young woman, he displayed a special eloquence'; Chukovsky had whispered to her afterwards that Gorky had been 'like a peacock spreading his beautiful feathers'.[9] He gave her a permanent position as his secretary and interpreter, and invited her to move into the apartment.

Moura reverted to her maiden name, and became Maria Ignatievna Zakrevskaya once more. Perhaps she wanted to erase the memory of Djon; perhaps she hoped that by registering officially under that name she might break the ability of the Cheka or of intelligence agencies abroad to keep track of her. Many people came to believe that she was still in the service of the Cheka, and was briefed by them to spy on Gorky and pass back information about his attitudes and contacts.

His relationship with the government was a rocky one. His politics were leftward and pro-revolutionary, but he was neither a Communist nor a Bolshevik. Having supported the Revolution and helped work towards it for decades, Gorky's views had altered. He had seen the behaviour of the common people during the battle and did not like it. 'You are right 666 times over,' he wrote to a friend who had predicted this; the Revolution was 'giving birth to real barbarians, just like those that ravaged Rome'.[10] The government that had emerged was a government of corrupted rabble and tyrants. He wrote a series of essays in his newspaper, *Novaya Zhizn*,* roundly condemning the Bolsheviks as enemies of free speech: 'Lenin, Trotsky and their companions have already become poisoned with the filthy venom of power,' he wrote; they were no more friends of democracy than the Romanovs had been. Following a shooting of demonstrators by Red Army soldiers in January 1918, he lamented the blood and sweat that had gone into bringing about the precious idea of revolutionary democracy in Russia, 'and now the "People's Commissars" have given orders to shoot the democracy which demonstrated in honour of this idea'.[11] That he could publish such statements with virtual impunity was a measure of his stature in Russia.

Anger, regret and dissatisfaction were mingled in Gorky's character. His surname had been chosen with feeling – born Alexei Maximovich Peshkov, as a young man he had assumed the name *Gorky* (meaning 'bitter') – although perhaps *Kisly* (sour, acidic) might have been equally apt.

He dreamed of a republic of the arts and sciences; neither a democracy nor a socialist state (he feared and disliked the peasant class), but a society governed by intellectuals, artists and creative thinkers, with himself at its heart. As Moura had commented dryly to Lockhart some months earlier, 'He thinks himself a d'Annunzio of Russia.'[12] Gorky had been close to Lenin for many years, but had an antagonistic relationship with him, and a hostile one with some powerful figures, including Zinoviev. But such was his stature and popularity, none dared touch him directly. Although *Novaya Zhizn* was closed down on Lenin's orders in July 1918,[13] his person was inviolate, and most commissars – even his enemies – judged it politic to grant any favours he cared to ask.

In this climate, it would not be surprising if the regime chose to spy on him. And Moura might have been their agent. On the other hand, the rumour that she was their eyes and ears in the Gorky household might just have been more of that gossip that clung to her 'like flies to Tanglefoot paper', as she put it.[14] And yet, her occasional complaints

---

* New Life.

about the gossip could equally have been the natural indignation of a guilty conscience.

Although Moura had been given a start as a translator of books into Russian, Gorky used her mainly as a translator-secretary, concerned mostly with business matters.[15] Thus she began to acquire the all-round knowledge of the publishing and translating businesses that would be her principal means of subsistence throughout her life.

There were twelve rooms in the apartment, of which four small chambers were reserved for Gorky's private use – bedroom, study, library, and a little museum where he displayed his collection of Oriental artefacts. The rest of the apartment consisted of the communal dining room and bedrooms. Moura shared a room with a young medical student called Maria Geintse (or Geynze), nicknamed 'The Molecule' and described as 'a wonderful girl, the orphaned daughter of some old acquaintances of Gorky's'.[16] The population of the commune changed over time, but the main long-term inhabitants included the artists Valentina Khodasevich, her husband Andrei Diderikhs (known as 'Didi') and Ivan Rakitsky, and at a later period the poet Vladislav Khodasevich (Valentina's uncle) and the writer Nina Berberova, who were also a couple. There were many others who came and went.

Moura, whose closest experience of communal living had been in Lockhart's lavish apartment, shared only with Hicks and the servants, had to adapt to an entirely new mode of living. But she had been doing that for two years now, and sharing a room in a crowded apartment was better than starving on the freezing streets. Most of the other 'former people' of the wealthy classes were now crammed into shared rooms in squalid conditions, and living by forced labour. In Gorky's household there was warmth in the air and food on the table.

At some point – perhaps immediately, more likely over the course of months – Moura became Gorky's mistress. It would be a troubled affair; she was young enough to be his daughter, and had a flighty, fiery temperament that irked him, but like all Moura's men, he fell in love with her.

Gorky's relationships with women were like his relationship with politics – erratic and idiosyncratic. He liked to be in control; he could be madly jealous, and when jealous, violent. There had been many women who had fulfilled the role of *de facto* wife to Maxim Gorky, but only one to whom he had been legally married – Yekaterina Peshkova (née Vozhina), a fellow revolutionary. He met and married her in Samara on the Volga in 1896; he was a young man then, and Yekaterina was eight years his senior. She bore him a son, Maxim, and a daughter, who died in childhood.[17]

By 1902 he was gaining a reputation as a dramatist and worldwide fame as an author to rival Tolstoy (who knew and admired him). His play *The Lower Depths* was staged by the Moscow Art Theatre, the best in the country, and was taken around the world. One of the theatre's top actresses, Maria Fyodorovna Andreyeva, became his lover.[18] She was a dark-eyed beauty with reddish-golden hair and an outspoken manner. She was a political radical, and captivated Gorky. She was married to a government official, but Gorky the *littérateur* and revolutionary suited her better. In 1903 Gorky left the distraught Yekaterina and went to live with Andreyeva. They never divorced, and he provided financially for her and their son.

Gorky and Andreyeva joined the revolutionary exiles on the Italian island of Capri after the failed uprising of 1905, and toured the United States. The puritan Americans hounded them and when no hotel would accommodate the unmarried couple they were forced to return to Capri.[19] Andreyeva called herself 'Countess' and was disliked in the exile community, who believed she was only after Gorky's money and status.

Their relationship was strained. Andreyeva's obstinacy and domineering nature began to irritate the egotistical Gorky, who wanted to have things his way. He considered returning to his wife but Andreyeva had nowhere to go and Gorky did not have the heart to leave her. He wrote to Yekaterina, 'I beseech you, do not call, do not rush me . . . At the present time I do not possess the energy to take a decisive step.' All he wished for was 'peace in which to work, and for this peace I am prepared to pay any price'.[20] In 1912 Andreyeva made her peace with the government and returned to Russia. Still a political exile, Gorky was unable to go with her.

In 1913 amnesty was granted to the exiles as part of Tsar Nicholas II's celebration of three hundred years of Romanov rule. While Yekaterina and their son, Max, returned to Moscow, Gorky settled for a while in a small town nearby. He saw Andreyeva regularly although they no longer lived together. Eventually Gorky moved to Petrograd, where he took the flat at 23 Kronverksky Prospekt. From the windows he could see Alexander Park, and beyond it the Petropavlovskaya fortress, where he had once been imprisoned.

Shortly after the start of the war with Germany, Andreyeva, along with her new young lover Pyotr Kriuchkov, a lawyer, came to live in the apartment. Kriuchkov took on the role of Gorky's secretary. After the February Revolution Andreyeva moved out again. She joined the Commissariat of Enlightenment, which was charged with promotion of the arts and preservation of artworks. With Lenin's backing she became Commissar of Theatres and Spectacles in the Northern Commune in 1918, and in 1920 became head of the Arts section of the Commissariat for Education.[21] Maria Andreyeva was becoming a woman of power and influence.

With the founding of the Kronverksky commune, at last a kind of stability had entered Gorky's life. But the picture was incomplete without a woman.

There had been others before Moura came along in the autumn of 1919. Other women had served tea to guests, shared Gorky's bed and been referred to as his 'wife', but Moura, officially his new secretary, would become the one to whom he was most deeply attached, and who was his most constant. Everyone liked Moura. She became head of household duties, supervising the two elderly servants and generally organising things. Gorky's son Max was pleased with the change when he next visited, commenting, 'the boss-free days are over'.[22] She became known in the commune as *Titke* – Aunt.

Her love of Lockhart was undiminished, and could never be supplanted or equalled, but in time she would develop a deep fondness for Maxim Gorky, a fondness which could only be called love.

Under Gorky's roof she survived the winter of 1919/20, but by February she had begun to feel restless. Something – some unidentified feeling or motivation – prompted her to make an attempt to escape from Russia.[23] In February the temperature in northwest Russia drops to its lowest: an average of $-10°C$. In 1920, as in almost every other year, the Gulf of Finland was frozen over, from the shores of Russia to the coast of Finland. Moura, by her own account, set out one day from Petrograd and attempted to walk across the ice to Finland.[24]

It was a desperate, confused and, by her own admission, foolish thing to do. What her motive was, and where she hoped to go, is unclear. She claimed that she was trying to reach Estonia to be with her children. But in that case, why not head directly for Estonia? The war with Russia was over, and Estonia had won its independence. Perhaps she believed that

1. The Russian Orthodox Church, Ennismore Gardens, the principal church for Russian émigrés in London.

2. Berezova Rudka, (formerly Beriozovaya Rudka), Ukraine, the country seat of the Zakrevsky family, where Moura spent much of her childhood.

3. Moura with her husband Djon von Benckendorff, at the Berlin races, 1913.

4. Meriel Buchanan during her time as a nurse at the war hospital in Petrograd. *c.* 1916.

5. The Red House, Yendel (now known as Jäneda Manor). Built by Djon von Benckendorff in 1910–15 based on William Morris's Red House at Bexleyheath, London.

6. (Above left) Second Lieutenant (later Captain) Denis Garstin *c.* 1915.

7. (Above right) Captain Francis Cromie *c.* 1918.

8. (Bottom left) Cromie enjoys a sleigh ride with Moura (left) and Baroness Fairy Schilling.

9. (left) Moura with Captain Fenner, Captain Cromie and Meriel Buchanan, skiing in Estonia.

10. (below) Kallijärv, the lakeside house on the Yendel estate in which Moura's family lived from 1918.

11. Felix Dzerzhinsky, September 1918.

12. Yakov Peters.

13. H. G. Wells, Maxim Gorky and Moura, 1920.

14. Robert H. Bruce Lockhart aged about twenty-two.

15. H. G. Wells by George Charles Beresford, 1920.

16. Moura around the time she moved to Britain.

17. Timosha (Maxim Gorky's daughter-in-law), Yekaterina (his legal wife) and Moura in Sorrento, 1925.

18. Moura and her family at Kallijärv, 1930. Back row from left: Hermann von Benckendorff, R. Knupffer, Hans-Ernst von Maydell. Moura, Tania, Micky, Ilse von Hoyningen-Huene, Kira, Sophie Benckendorff, Alexander Benckendorff, Paul. Front Row: Mitja von Stackelberg, Marina von Stackelberg, Alexandra Benckendorff, Natalie Benckendorff.

19. Kay Francis as Moura in the film *British Agent*, 1934.

20. Moura and Wells in Brighton, 1935.

21. Returning from a Picnic at Yendel. Left to Right: Princess Zoya Galitzine, Kira, Moura, Zoria, Paul, Count Contantine Benckendorff and his daughter Nathalie.

22. Maxim Gorky and Genrikh Yagoda, NKVD director 1934–36 *c.* 1934.

23. Sir Robert Hamilton Bruce Lockhart by Howard Coster, 1936.

24. Guy Burgess.

25. Anthony Blunt (bottom left) with fellow members of the Cambridge Apostles while a fellow of Trinity College, 1932.

26. Sir Alexander Korda with Alexandra Boycun, soon to be his third wife.

27. Baroness Moura Budberg in her Cromwell Road flat. This photograph was taken for *Knobs and Nosh*, a book to which Moura contributed.

by getting to Finland she might give herself more than one choice. She might repeat the journey she had made from Helsingfors to Reval the previous year. Or perhaps she might find an opportunity to cross Sweden and make it to England, and thus find her way to Lockhart.

The place she chose was the narrow neck of the gulf west of Petrograd, in the middle of which stood the island fortress of Kronstadt, the base of the Russian Baltic fleet.

She didn't get far. Along with several other refugees she was apprehended on the ice by a Russian patrol, and brought back to Petrograd. The group of prisoners with their military escort made quite a spectacle passing through the city streets. Moura was recognised by the porter of an apartment block where she had once lived, who was among the crowd of spectators. From him, word of her plight reached Gorky.

The prisoners were locked up in the Cheka headquarters on Gorokhovaya Street. Moura was recognised as Maria Benckendorff, and her nefarious past brought her under deep suspicion. She had never had any direct ties to the Petrograd Cheka, and the circumstances of her arrest, in combination with her known foreign sympathies, rang alarm bells. When Gorky lodged an earnest plea for her release, the answer was a firm *no*. This was remarkable – Gorky was on good terms with the Cheka, and was an old and valued friend of Felix Dzerzhinsky.[25] But his pleas were blocked by the head of the Northern Commune, Zinoviev, who was Gorky's enemy and thoroughly suspicious of young Madame Benckendorff.

Moura's release, when it came, was prompted by a surprising intervention. Maria Andreyeva, Gorky's former mistress and presumably therefore Moura's rival, wrote to I. P. Bakaev, head of the Petrograd Cheka, making a startling blood commitment: 'I respectfully ask you and the Commission of the Cheka to release into my custody Maria Ignatyevna Benkendorf . . . I will bet my life that, having given me her word, she will not attempt to repeat this desperate undertaking, even for her children.' If the worst should happen, 'I give you my word to shoot me: knowing this and seeing my signature here, she will not lift a finger without your knowledge. She is a mother and a very good person.'[26]

The Cheka released her, and she returned to Kronverksky Prospekt.

How could a mere commissar of the arts and education wield such an influence with the almighty Cheka where the great Gorky had failed?

There was probably more to Maria Andreyeva's government role than was officially admitted. Since 1918 she and Gorky had been principal agents in a scheme to preserve Russia's cultural heritage – its artworks and antiques. A registration commission was formed to collect (by seizure if necessary), store and catalogue objects previously in the hands of private owners. But unknown to Gorky, Maria Andreyeva, far from working to preserve Russia's artworks, was involved in a secret programme to dispose of them for cash.[27]

The Russian economy was in a desperate situation, and needed hard currency to prop it up (and to promote international revolution). The *valiuta** programme was initiated to supply the need. It liquidated the assets which had been seized from the aristocracy and bourgeoisie, ranging from jewellery and gold to works of art, selling them abroad for foreign currency. Maria Andreyeva was an agent of the programme. Hence her influence with the Cheka. It seems that an unspoken part of the deal over Moura was that she be brought in as a subordinate agent. Her status, her contacts abroad, her experience of covert activities, her cultured background would suit her perfectly for such a role.[28]

Released from prison, Moura settled back into her life with Gorky, chastened but unbowed. If anything, her experience had hardened her. Gorky might be powerful, but in this affair Moura was the one with the strength. In his previous relationships, he had ruled – sometimes with violence – but here it was Moura who wielded the power. She acted as if she needed nothing from him. It bewildered him, and on one occasion he challenged her over her hardness, comparing her to Alexander Pushkin's famously unyielding mistress, known as the 'Bronze Venus'.

'You're not bronze,' Gorky told Moura with a penetrating glare, 'you're iron. Nothing in the world is stronger than iron.'

'We're all iron now,' she replied. 'Would you like us to be lace?'[29]

When H. G. Wells arrived near the end of September 1920, Moura had been a member of the commune for a year, and was accustomed to the inflow of artists and intelligentsia who came to pay homage to her patron.

Wells wasn't the only eminent Englishman to visit that year. Bertrand Russell had come to Russia in the early summer, and called at the apartment on Kronverksky Prospekt. Gorky was unwell, and their interview

---

* currency.

took place in his bedroom, where Moura served tea and interpreted.[30] (Russell found it a little difficult to concentrate; he was fascinated by this young woman.) There was a good deal of sympathy between the two men. Both had supported the overthrow of the old regime, but both were troubled by the brutality of Bolshevism. Unlike many apologists, Russell wasn't willing to excuse it as a product of the 'peevish and futile' interference of the Allied nations; 'the expectation of such opposition,' he reasoned, 'was always part of Bolshevik theory', and 'was both foreseen and provoked by the doctrine of the class war'.[31] Like many of his Russian counterparts, Russell had served time in prison for his principles – an admittedly short term in Brixton in 1918 for his anti-war activities.

Russell was shocked by Gorky's appearance: 'apparently very ill and obviously heart-broken'. 'One felt in him a love of the Russian people which makes their present martyrdom almost unbearable,' he wrote. He was deeply worried by Gorky's illness and what it might portend for the future of the arts in Russia – 'Gorky has done all that one man could to preserve the intellectual and artistic life of Russia. I feared that he was dying, and that, perhaps, it was dying too.'[32]

H. G. Wells was among the many who read Russell's impressions and worried about Gorky's impending death. When he arrived in September, he was relieved to find his old friend well. 'Mr. Russell was, I think, betrayed by the artistic temptation of a dark and purple concluding passage.' Indeed, 'Gorky seems as strong and well to me now as he was when I knew him first in 1906.'[33]

Lifting his eyes from Russell's purple passages and Gorky's rude health, H. G. Wells gazed for the first time in his life on Moura Ignatievna Zakrevskaya, secretary, translator and – for the duration of his stay – his guide. And he was smitten.

All his life he would be at a loss to comprehend why she affected him so. Her appearance was against her. She was thin and starting to look careworn. Clothes were virtually unobtainable in Russia, and everyone had to make do. The lady who had danced at the Sanssouci Palace at Potsdam in the company of the Tsar and the Kaiser, the lady whose extravagant couture, even with so much competition, had prompted a crown prince to exclaim, '*Quelle noblesse!*',[34] was dressed for poverty. She wore a British army waterproof coat over a plain black dress which had seen better days, and a rudimentary hat made from a twisted piece of black fabric – apparently an old stocking or a scrap of felt. But whatever her appearance, no matter how degraded her situation, in Wells' eyes, 'she had magnificence'. Her attitude and bearing hadn't been eroded by what she'd been through. 'She stuck her hands in the pockets of her waterproof, and seemed not simply to brave the world but disposed to order it about.'[35]

Lockhart had been captivated by her brilliant, incisive mind, Gorky by her charm and talents, but Wells was taken by her audacious survivor's pride and – as with all her men – the intense sexual allure she radiated. 'She was now my official interpreter,' he recalled. 'And she presented herself to my eyes as gallant, unbroken and adorable.'[36]

How Moura perceived Wells, she never recorded. Perhaps she noted his resemblance to Djon. He had the same blunt, stolid features and sad eyes, the same lank lick of hair across a domed forehead, the same soup-strainer moustache. Whatever she saw, and however she felt, she began their acquaintance as she meant to go on – by dealing him a hand from the ready pack of lies she was beginning to accumulate. Her uncle, she claimed, had been Russia's Ambassador in London, and she had strong personal ties to England herself, having been educated at Newnham College, Cambridge, and since the Revolution she had been imprisoned *five times* by the Bolshevik government.

Each of these untruths was tethered to reality, but by a severely overstretched length of elastic. When Wells published his account of his visit to Russia, he faithfully and innocently repeated Moura's falsehoods as proof of how honest and open the Russian government had been with him. With her aristocratic background, her Englishness and her bad relations with the Bolsheviks, Moura would be 'the last person likely to lend herself to any attempt to hoodwink me'. He had been warned in Britain (and in Russia) that 'the most elaborate camouflage of realities would go on, and that I should be kept in blinkers throughout my visit'.[37] The fact that such a lady had been approved as his guide showed that the Bolsheviks were not out to deceive him.

The one true thing she told him was that she had been confined to Petrograd because of her arrest on the Finnish ice. It deepened his sympathy, and he promised to try to get a message to her children as soon as he left Russia.

Wells, like Russell, had come to see Bolshevism in the flesh, and with Moura as his companion he spent his days touring Petrograd, visiting schools and other state institutions. As well as the dead shops and deserted streets, he learned that all of Petrograd's wooden buildings had been demolished the previous winter to feed the desperate need for firewood, leaving behind gap-toothed streets and piles of discarded masonry. There were holes in the roads where the wood-block paving had been torn up for fuel. The government appeared to be better prepared for the coming winter, and huge stacks of timber lined the quays and the centres of the main streets.[38]

The trams were now running again during the day. At six in the evening, when the electricity supply was switched off, the service stopped. Although the population had halved as citizens fled abroad (if they could) or migrated to the countryside, the trams were always full to bursting, with people clinging to their outsides. There were frequent accidents. Wells and Moura witnessed a crowd gathered round the body of a child who had fallen and been cut in two.[39]

It seemed that the most profitable class of person to be in Russia nowadays was a peasant. The Bolsheviks still had little power in the countryside, so while the workers and former aristocrats starved, the peasants – freed from their tyrannical landowners and the debilitating taxation of the old regime – lived easily and ate well. They came to Petrograd and Moscow to sell food on the street corners. This was illegal (food distribution was state-controlled) but the authorities rarely took action, for fear that the peasants might stop bringing food at all. When the Red Guards did try to curb the black-marketeering, there were armed clashes in which the peasants typically trounced the soldiers.[40]

In Wells' opinion, the blame for Russia's privations lay not with Bolshevism but with capitalism – this was the inevitable outcome. Unlike Bertrand Russell, Wells did blame the interference of the Allies. The Bolsheviks, he reasoned, were the inevitable form of government that must arise in the wake of a revolution. And yet he hated it with a passion, and hated Marx as the conjuror and figurehead of it all:

Wherever we went we encountered busts, portraits, and statues of Marx. About two-thirds of the face of Marx is beard, a vast solemn woolly uneventful beard . . . It is not the sort of beard that happens to a man, it is a beard cultivated, cherished, and thrust patriarchally upon the world. It is exactly like *Das Kapital* in its inane abundance, and the human part of the face looks over it owlishly as if it looked to see how the growth impressed mankind.[41]

In Marxist Russia everyone starved and froze and dreaded falling sick. Medicines were unobtainable. 'Small ailments develop very easily therefore into serious trouble . . . If any one falls into a real illness the outlook is grim.'[42]

The commune at Kronverksky Prospekt was spared the worst of these privations. In the evenings the inhabitants and their guests would gather in the dining room, where in the middle of the table stood a large kerosene lamp; in its glow, people would sit and talk art and politics, or listen to Gorky's tales of his life, which he turned into the bravura performance of a gifted storyteller and dramatist.[43]

Gorky accompanied Wells and Moura on one of their outings. It was a doubly meaningful one for Moura – a visit to the Petrograd storehouse of the art and antiques commission. This was the state organ which seized and evaluated works of art, whose secret purpose was as a resource for the *valiuta* programme. Gorky was probably ignorant of the programme; neither would he have known that Moura was now involved in it. But the visit had an extra meaning for her. The building that had been taken as the commission's storehouse was the old British Embassy on Palace Quay.

Two years had passed since Cromie's death, and almost as long since Moura's last visit, when the place was a clutter of broken furniture. Now, to Wells' eyes, it was 'like some congested second-hand art shop':

> We went through room after room piled with the beautiful lumber . . . There are big rooms crammed with statuary; never have I seen so many white marble Venuses and sylphs together . . . There are stacks of pictures of every sort, passages choked with inlaid cabinets piled up to the ceiling; a room full of cases of old lace, piles of magnificent furniture.[44]

It had all been catalogued, but nobody seemed to know what would be done with 'all this lovely and elegant litter'. While Gorky could only hope for it to be preserved, Moura probably knew that a good portion of it would end up sold abroad.

As the days passed, Wells' relationship with Moura was nurtured and persistently cultivated by him until she agreed to consummate it. 'I fell in love with her,' he would recall, still bewildered many years later, 'and one night at my entreaty she flitted noiselessly through the crowded apartments in Gorky's flat to my embraces. I believed she loved me and

I believed every word she said to me. No other woman has ever had that much effectiveness for me.'[45]

But for the time being, it was no more than a fling. After just a couple of weeks' stay, Wells and Gip departed. After a visit to Moscow, they returned by way of Petrograd and travelled on to Reval to catch the boat to Stockholm on their way home to England.[46]

Reval and Stockholm. How those names must have struck a chord in Moura, and what a dissonant, unsettling chord it was. The country where her reunion with Lockhart had failed to occur, and the land where her children were still living, beyond her reach. Wells agreed to pass a message to them on his way through Estonia, letting them know that she was alive and well. And *England*, where Lockhart had his home. It was now two years since she had seen him, more than a year and a half since she had last heard word from him. And it was over three years since she had last seen her children.

The time was coming – again – to try to put all that right.

The days of the Gorky commune in Petrograd were numbered. By the end of 1920 Gorky's relationship with Zinoviev, the head of the Northern Commune, was getting worse by the day. 'Things reached a point where Zinoviev ordered searches of Gorky's apartment,' recalled Vladislav Khodasevich, who had joined the commune in November, 'and threatened to arrest certain people who were close to him.'[47] Moura, whom Zinoviev suspected of all manner of espionage, was among those he had an eye on.

She had told Wells that she was happier now than in the old days before the Revolution, because 'now life is more interesting and real'.[48] She always had a tendency to say what seemed suitable to the moment. Perhaps she meant it a little, thinking of her stifling marriage to Djon. But in reality, Russia was a nightmare, and she was waiting for something to wake her from it.

It came in the spring of 1921. Life for Gorky in Russia was becoming untenable. Lenin was finding him more and more of a liability and put pressure on him to go abroad, ostensibly for the good of his health. Indeed, the extreme conditions in Petrograd were making him ill. The destination settled upon was Germany.

Moura had been forbidden to leave Petrograd as a condition of her release from jail the year before. And yet in April she was granted a passport and given a permit to travel to Estonia. She always remained silent about how this was achieved. Perhaps Gorky intervened, as he did for many would-be émigrés – but if he did, no trace remains of it.[49]

Gorky had settled on Berlin as his new home, and preparations were made for his move. His son Max, his personal secretary Pyotr Kriuchkov and Maria Andreyeva went ahead to prepare a home for him.

Moura was notionally included in this party, but she would be travelling via Estonia. Maria Andreyeva, now working openly for the Commissariat for External Trade, had a purpose in Berlin – saleswoman *par excellence* with the wealth of imperial Russia in her carpetbag. So it may be that Moura's potential as an agent in the *valiuta* programme, which had won her Andreyeva's protection, was also the reason for her being allowed to leave Russia. Under the terms of the peace treaty of 1920 Russia had full use of Estonia's railways and the port of Reval, which was needed for shipping antiquities and precious metals abroad (Petrograd's port facilities had been damaged in the Revolution). Reval had already become a major artery for Russian gold flowing out to Stockholm.[50] An additional agent who had friendly contacts with foreign diplomatic services would undoubtedly be valuable there.

On the day before Moura was due to travel, she received a piece of news that almost prostrated her with shock. Who it came from is unknown, but it was news of Lockhart, the first she had heard in two years. She had been looking forward excitedly to the freedom of communication that she would enjoy abroad, and anticipated bombarding her beloved with telegrams and letters as soon as she reached Estonia. But on that last day in Russia, word reached her that Lockhart had achieved his heart's desire without her. His wife had given him a son.

All Moura's hopes were blasted to pieces; it would be a month before she could master her feelings sufficiently to write to him.

> There is no use asking you why, and how and when, is it? As a matter of fact, of course, all this stupid letter is of no use at all – only that there is something in me that aches so intensely that I must shout it out to you.
>
> Your son? A fine boy? Do you know – as I write those words – it seems to me that I will not be able to live with that thought. I am

ashamed of my tears – I thought I'd forgotten how to cry. But there
was 'little Peter', you know.[51]

There was a poem by Burns – 'A Red, Red Rose' – that Moura and
Lockhart had once shared and which they had sworn by when they
parted in Moscow.

> . . . Till a' the seas gang dry, my dear,
> And the rocks melt wi' the sun:
> I will luve thee still, my dear,
> While the sands o' life shall run.
>
> And fare thee well, my only Luve
> And fare thee well, a while!
> And I will come again, my Luve,
> Tho' it were ten thousand mile.

'The rocks, for me, have not melted wi' the sun,' she wrote. 'And
never will.'

Lockhart was gone from her – he had broken the bond, and her heart
with it. 'But if we meet again,' she wondered, 'in this small and rather
disgusting world – how shall I greet you?'

It was fitting, perhaps, that the close of the Russian period of her life
should coincide with the door closing on Lockhart's love. It had been
born of Russia, and tempered and pulled asunder by the forces of Russia.
And yet she would never, until the sands of life had run, be able to give
him up.

16

Baroness Budberg

1921–1923

May 1921, Estonia

The Narva train steamed into the Baltic station of Reval. Or *Tallinn* as Moura must now learn to call it. In a display of nationalism, the old Finnish-Germanic name had been abolished, and the traditional Estonian one revived. The train had passed through the tiny stations at Yendel and Aegviidu, tantalisingly close to home, but Moura hadn't alighted. Although she yearned for them and hadn't seen them for three years, the time hadn't yet come for her to be reunited with her children. Her movements were no longer hers to control. There was business to attend to.

Still, it had been an easier journey than either of her previous entries into the country: easier than the crossing from Helsingfors or the long walk across the frontier zone with German soldiers as an escort. This time she had everything – a passport, a visa to enter Estonia, a permit to leave Russia and semi-official work to do.

Moura stepped down from the train and found a porter to carry the single battered suitcase which contained all her worldly belongings – her felt hat, her threadbare fur coat, her old-fashioned slippers, and a few odds and ends. Walking out of the station, she glanced around the square, looking for a cab. Before she could so much as raise a hand, two uniformed men stepped up either side of her. 'You're under arrest,' said one of them in Russian. They gripped her arms and pushed her into a carriage. While one got in with her, the other climbed up on the box and whipped up the horse.[1]

This was becoming almost a way of life for Moura. She didn't panic or berate the policeman. Calmly she said, 'Everything is in order.'

'What is in order?'

Moura listed her passport, visa, permits – all the official documents that authorised her presence in Estonia.

The officer was unimpressed. 'You've violated the law. You're under arrest. Keep quiet.'

She was put in a cell and left for hours. She was fed, which cheered her up. The meal – a fatty meat soup with white bread – was better than anything she had eaten in Petrograd in a very long while.

The interrogation, when it came, was no surprise and no great ordeal for a woman who had twice seen the inside of Cheka jails. She had heard about the arrest of the official who had helped her cross the frontier in 1918, and the dossier the Germans had put in front of him, itemising her alleged work as a spy. Now she saw for herself the dossier the Estonians had on her. She was known to be an associate of Gorky; she had previously been the mistress and agent of Yakov Peters.[2] She was undoubtedly a Bolshevik spy, and had entered Estonia for that purpose.

Moura knew they could have no hard evidence of any of this. But what they told her next shook her profoundly. News of her arrival had preceded her. The brother and sister of her late husband, Djon von Benckendorff, had petitioned the authorities, demanding that Moura be deported back to Russia and that she be barred from visiting her children. They regarded her as a Bolshevik agent, and some even suspected her of complicity in Djon's murder. Several other Benckendorff and Schilling relatives had lent their voices to the demands.

Immediately she asked for a lawyer. The police provided her with a list of names to choose from. Moura studied it with a sinking feeling; some of the names were Russians – they would probably be old Tsarists who would be prejudiced against anyone with Soviet connections. The other names were all those of the Teutonic families who had ruled the Baltic region since the Middle Ages. They would all be against her; indeed, many of the men on the list were related to the Benckendorffs. She hadn't a hope.

There were just two other names, both of them Jews. Moura was infected with the casual anti-Semitism that was virtually universal in her world; like most of her class and kind, she viewed Jews with a sort of sardonic tolerance, not unlike her view of peasants,[3] and she picked a name despondently. Her lawyer, as it turned out, was a good one, and a kindly man who sympathised with her plight.

The police released her, apparently for lack of evidence. They were content to let her be passed, according to custom, to a court of Baltic barons – an *Ehrengericht** of the so-called *Gemeinnutz Verband*.† Despite the nation's independence, the upper class of Estonia was still profoundly Germanic, and despite the socialist reforms and the redistribution of land that had occurred since 1918, the nobility still had influence. The court was convened under Count Ignatiev, the elected head of the Baltic nobility.[4] Its purpose was to determine her connections, if any, to the Soviet regime. With the help of her lawyer, Moura began to make her case. The proceedings would drag on for months.

Meanwhile, she was more or less free. Time was running out; as a Russian citizen she was only allowed a three-month stay. At first, while the court deliberated, her Benckendorff relatives would not allow her near her children. They had their own suspicions about her story. Why had she not left Russia with the children in 1918? Why had she not taken her mother out via Finland the following year? Why had she visited Estonia and not stayed with her husband and children? And what precisely was the nature of her relationship with the Bolsheviks? The Benckendorffs, like all their Baltic ilk, had been almost religiously devoted to the old imperial order, and 'regarded the Communist regime which had murdered the Tsar as a criminal conspiracy'.[5]

With a mixture of truth, omissions and lies, she offered up her story. She had to remain in Russia to care for her mother; truthfully she told them that the Bolsheviks had continually refused her mother a permit, and that there had been a hundred and one difficulties with Swedish and British visas. This was all true. But she flatly denied any relationship with the Soviet state or its spies, and kept resolutely quiet about her relationship with Lockhart. If the Benckendorffs thought it suspicious that Djon had been murdered at a time when Moura was seeking a divorce and had visited Estonia, they didn't voice it.

Finally, reluctantly, she was allowed back into the Benckendorff fold. She could visit the children. She left Tallinn and made the short journey to Yendel.[6] At least one person at Yendel was looking forward to Moura's return. Micky, who loved her like a daughter, had been growing

---

* court of honour.
† Association for the Common Good.

increasingly excited as the days passed, and her excitement had passed to the children.

Moura arrived at night. On the journey from the station, along the familiar arrow-straight driveway, she passed by the estate farm and the manor house. Neither belonged to the family now. Along with all the other landholdings in Estonia, Yendel had been taken over by the state, and was now an agricultural college. The family had been left with a small farm and the quaint little lakeside lodge of Kallijärv.

After Moura had arrived and been greeted by Micky, she went to bed – her own soft bed in her own room, in a quiet, secluded country retreat. After the life she had led during the past few years, it was the answer to a prayer. She would be reluctant ever to rise from this bed. As she grew older, her bed would always be dear to Moura – the centre of her world.

The morning after, Micky took the children to see their mother. They were full of anticipation, caught up in Micky's enthusiasm and curious to know what this unfamiliar mother might be like. Only Kira was old enough to have clear memories of her. Of Moura's own children, Pavel had been four when he last saw her. For Tania, who was now six, it was as if she were meeting her mother for the first time.[7]

They were taken into Moura's room, where they found her sitting up in bed. Tania didn't recognise her at all. She felt nothing for this complete stranger. She would recall that her mother 'was larger than I had expected', and she felt a little disappointed that 'this rather healthy-looking person did not correspond to the stories of hunger and privation we had been told'.[8] Micky had told them that Moura had caught burrowing lice during her time in prison in Moscow, but Tania could see no sign of them on her skin. The children weren't allowed to ask questions about why she had been in prison; it was 'all finished and done with'.

There was no glad reunion – everyone was awkward and embarrassed. Micky clucked and fussed around Moura, and shooed the children out once they had taken a good look. Their mother had been through an ordeal, they were told, and was exhausted physically and emotionally.

Moura barely rose from her bed during that first week at Kallijärv. Anyone she wanted to see was brought to her. Nobody in the household or the extended family would speak about Moura's past in front of the children, but Tania heard enough snippets and whispers to make her mother sound mysterious and wicked. The little girl was fascinated and puzzled.

Not long after Moura's arrival, all the family went together to church – one of the big Russian Orthodox feast days that followed Easter, either Ascension or Pentecost. Moura went with them. When Tania trooped up with the others for communion, she noticed that her mother stayed behind, at the back of the church. To Tania's mind, only those who had the blackest sins on their conscience – those which one wouldn't dare admit to in confession – would refuse the sacrament, and she wondered if Moura had committed murder or robbery.

Moura's conscience might well have been troubling her. She took her religion seriously – at least her personal faith in God had been invoked many times in recent years as she struggled through her ordeals and crises. And yet she sinned with a defiance that bordered on bravado. Maybe her faith had taken a blow; she had prayed hard for everything to come right with Lockhart, and had got nothing but heartache in return. And yet that needn't stop her making an insincere show of taking communion. That she refused must have been a measure of her state of mind and conscience.

Looking back at her mother, and wondering what crime she might have committed, Tania felt her first pang of affection. 'I felt that whatever it was I would protect her,' she recalled. Returning from the altar, she stood beside her and stroked her fur coat, 'to reassure her that I was on her side'. The little girl was rewarded with a smile.[9]

After a period of rest at Kallijärv, Moura began spending time in Tallinn. What she was up to, Tania didn't know, either then or later. All she knew was that her mother was put up in a flat owned by friends of the family, Baron and Baroness Bengt Stackelberg. She spent the middle of every week there, returning to Kallijärv only for weekends. She made contact with the other members of Gorky's advance party in Berlin, reporting on her arrest by the Estonian authorities. At Gorky's request, she was wired a sum of money from Berlin.[10] Presumably it was trade ministry money, and the sender would have been Maria Andreyeva. It never occurred to Tania in later life to wonder why Moura spent the working week in Tallinn and the weekends at Yendel. If her business there was connected with Maria Andreyeva's in Berlin, she was well placed.

Only once in her life would Moura allude to her work in Tallinn; many years later she admitted that she was employed by a Dutchman selling gold and diamonds.[11]

Since the previous summer, Tallinn had been the nexus of a gold-laundering scheme. Russian gold was transported there from Petrograd and shipped to Stockholm, where it was melted down and sold. Swedish, German and British companies were buying into the extremely lucrative scheme, and hard currency and industrial products ranging from locomotives to pharmaceuticals were flowing back to Moscow. As starvation and unrest grew worse in Russia, the trade goods were increasingly military – especially rifles and ammunition. And while British firms were profiting from the gold-laundering, the British and American governments and their intelligence agencies were trying to prevent illegal Russian gold from entering their markets.[12]

Perhaps it was this that made Moura an asset in Tallinn. She knew many of the foreign diplomats and intelligence agents from the old days in Russia, and she must have had inside knowledge of the bank schemes that were being run in 1918 by her then boss Hugh Leech. There weren't many in Russia who had Moura's talents and knowledge, and it must have made her valuable enough for Maria Andreyeva to guarantee her freedom. There was clearly some influence working for Moura now; later that summer she even managed to make a flying visit to Petrograd to meet with Andreyeva.[13]

It was also around this time that MI5 first decided to open a file on her.[14]

Regardless of her connections, Moura's time in Estonia would be severely limited. Her visa allowed her three months, and then she would have to go back to Russia.

It wasn't an attractive prospect. After the comforts of Kallijärv, the thought of going back to Petrograd was appalling, especially now that Gorky had moved on and she would no longer have a secure refuge. Moura's lawyer suggested that she might try fleeing to some other country, perhaps Switzerland. But that would probably lead to arrest again. He added thoughtfully that maybe the best thing she could do would be to get married.[15] Marriage to an Estonian citizen would free her from Russia's clutches for good. The lawyer even had a candidate in mind, and introduced her to him.

Baron Nikolai Budberg was twenty-six years old, a little younger than Moura. He had much in common with Djon. Like the Benckendorffs, the Budbergs were a large and powerful old Baltic-Russian landowning family. And Nikolai – known to his intimates as 'Lai' – had, like Djon, attended the military academy in St Petersburg in the days before the war. But in every other way Baron Nikolai Budberg was as unlike Djon von Benckendorff as he could be. Whereas Djon had been staid, responsible and sensible (if dull), Nikolai was the archetypal aristocratic rake. He was a notorious duellist, and had fought four duels, in the last of which he had killed his opponent.[16] He was also rumoured to have been an agent for the Okhrana, the Tsar's secret police.[17] Having inherited his title and his wealth at a young age, he had squandered it on dissipated living and gambling. He was in a delicate situation; he had debts and wanted to leave the country, but his creditors would not allow him.[18]

An arrangement was negotiated between Moura and Nikolai. They would marry, on condition that she pay his gambling debts. She arranged the money out of funds channelled to her from Russia via Berlin – possibly taken from the proceeds of the *valiuta* scheme. In return, Moura acquired the prestige of the title 'Baroness' (which delighted her) and, most importantly, Estonian citizenship and a passport. At last she would have the freedom to go where she wished.

In later life, Moura would bristle indignantly at any suggestion that this was a marriage of convenience. She developed a sympathetic fondness for Nikolai, and believed that he loved her after his fashion. She felt that she had 'found the only reason that could make me want to go on living – to be of use to someone. It is but a poor reason, I admit, and I think I am too much of an egoist to be satisfied with it'.[19]

Moura didn't undertake the marriage lightly. In late June, after bottling up her feelings for a month, she had finally written to Lockhart to express her grief and dismay at the news of his baby son.[20] And there were her feelings about Gorky (and his about her) to be considered. On the day she left Petrograd, she had left a letter for him (he was away in Moscow at the time). Smarting and bewildered by the previous day's news about Lockhart, she tried to kindle a feeling deeper than that between a great man and his mistress.'I want you to feel that intense inner feeling that I think happens only a few times in life,' she wrote, 'that the love of this girl from Kobelyak will be with you throughout the difficult, anxious, boring and dark hours of your life . . . You are my joy, my big true Joy, if you only knew how much I need you.'[21] Even in this seemingly heartfelt letter, she was sustaining a fiction. Kobelyak, a town in the Poltava region of the Ukraine, was not where Moura came from; she had been born on the Zakrevsky estate at Beriozovaya Rudka, near the town of Pyryatyn, more than a hundred miles from Kobelyak. The purpose of the deception is unknown, but its juxtaposition with her declaration of love seems not to have troubled her. Throughout that summer she wrote to Gorky reminding him of her love for him, expressing her annoyance at his constant silence, and urging him to hurry up and leave Russia to escape the Bolsheviks' latest campaign of repression.[22]

In October, in the last weeks before the wedding, Moura travelled to Finland to meet up with Gorky, and told him about Budberg. The lessening of the stresses she had been under had mellowed her, Gorky found, and she had 'generally become somewhat nicer'. As for Budberg, Gorky's disapproval of the match seemed to be largely on ideological grounds: 'She tells me that she intends to marry some kind of a baron, but we all protest with energy – let the baron find himself some other object of fancy – this is one of us!'[23]

The wedding, held in November in the Russian Orthodox church in Tallinn, was conventional enough, but made sombre by the melancholy gloom of Moura's Estonian relations, who compared it unfavourably with the glorious wedding to Djon in St Petersburg almost exactly ten years earlier.

Moura's close family were even more unhappy. Tania and Pavel had been very upset about the marriage – they didn't like the look of Nikolai Budberg, who 'was ugly and had a bald, egg-shaped head'. They attempted to run away from home in protest. Micky too disapproved. But nothing could stop the process or obviate the need for it. The wedding reception, held at an aristocrats' club in Tallinn, was more convivial, with everyone – even the Benckendorffs – abandoning themselves to the inevitable and deciding to enjoy themselves.[24]

Magically, the disapprobation that had surrounded Moura since her entry into Estonia vanished as soon as the knot was tied. She had become a part of a different branch of Estonia's relic nobility, and was accepted into society. There was still gossip about her. But it wasn't to last. Moura and Nikolai each had plans, and a few months after the wedding they

left Estonia for Berlin. Again the children had to get used to being virtual orphans.

Berlin was the centre for Russian émigrés. There were three hundred
thousand of them living there when Gorky joined the throng in 1921.
There was a Russian theatre, publishers, scores of newspapers and
Russian restaurants. The old Russian intelligentsia met to discuss politics and their wish for a return to the past.

Gorky didn't fit into this community, even the intelligentsia.
Surrounded by these relics of the *ancien régime*, and no longer seeing the
new regime's atrocities first-hand, his natural sympathy for the Bolshevik
cause began to return. From this safe distance he wrote to Lenin to let
him know he was planning to write a book which would be 'an apology
of Soviet power'; it would argue that Soviet Russia's successes 'completely justify its sins, intentional and unintentional'.[25] Perhaps he really
believed this wholeheartedly, but probably not. However, he relied on
Lenin to allow the despatch of his royalty payments, so it was as well to
keep on his good side.

Moura was yearning to join Gorky in Berlin – a city she had last seen
in 1914, when she was the pampered wife of a young diplomat. Politically
she was more consistently socialist than Gorky; she was also more adaptable, capable of immersing herself in foreign languages and foreign
politics, handling both with a light touch. But like Gorky, now that she
was back in Europe, with its obnoxious, unreconstructed aristocracy –
even in Estonia where their wings had been clipped short by reforms
– she began to feel more affinity with Bolshevism. She wrote to Gorky
from Tallinn: 'I want so much . . . to speak to you about Russia, which
now, from a distance, I feel and see better than before.' Arguing against
Gorky's pessimism, she insisted, 'No, no, it will not perish. It is terrible,
it is horrible, that many Russians are dying, but Russia will not die. It is
going through a severe, cruel trial. But, in a rotting Europe, is not what
is happening in Russia better?'[26]

It was no doubt easier to believe in the ultimate rightness of the cause
when one was no longer likely to be its next victim.

While Gorky sought a cure for his health (bad in Russia, it had
become worse in Berlin), he made preparations for Moura's arrival. At
Christmas he wrote to Lenin suggesting that Moura be given an official
role alongside Maria Andreyeva raising funds for Russia, commending

her as 'a very energetic and educated woman who speaks five languages'.[27] He didn't know that Andreyeva was already acting in this
capacity, let alone that his latest love was already involved.

Having completed a 'cure' in the Black Forest by May 1922, Gorky
rented a house for the summer at Heringsdorf on the Baltic coast, four
hours from Berlin. Moura, having parted company from Budberg,
joined Gorky there and resumed her role as his principal 'wife'.[28]

Moura was now thirty years old. She had grown her hair long –
going against the current fashion for short bobs – and wore it in a low
knot tied at the back of her neck, carelessly pinned up, with stray locks
falling fetchingly on her cheeks and brow. In further defiance of mod-
ishness, she went without a hat. Nina Berberova, who began her
acquaintance with Moura around this time, recalled her vividly: 'Her
lightly pencilled eyes were always eloquent . . . Her body was straight
and strong; her figure was elegant even in simple dresses.' She was
growing accustomed to the comforts of life again, buying good clothes
imported from England and expensive shoes. Her style was comfort and
quality over fashion. She wore no jewellery other than a man's wrist-
watch. (Who had it belonged to? Lockhart, perhaps? Cromie?) 'Her
fingers were always ink-stained, giving her the look of a schoolgirl.'[29]

Moura had realised her predicted 'blue stocking' destiny, and was
becoming ever more deeply immersed in her career in books. Using the
experience and connections she had acquired, she established a small
publishing house in Berlin – Epokha Verlag – which published German
translations of Gorky and other foreign writers from an office on the
Kurfürstendamm.

Not long after her arrival in Germany Moura was forced to rush back
to Estonia. Micky had been taken ill and needed Moura to take care of
the children. They had outgrown their nanny, Mariussa, and Micky was
approaching sixty now. A permanent solution was needed.

Having them to live with her in the commune was impossible, especially as she spent so much time in Berlin on business, so Moura decided
to put them in boarding schools. Her first thought was England. She
lodged an application for a British visa, stating that she wished to find a
school for her children in London. As referees she gave the names of
Commander Ernest Boyce and Colonel Thornhill, her two British SIS
associates from Petrograd (presumably she had resolved her doubts about
Thornhill's suspicions of her). She was interviewed by Colonel Ronald

Meiklejohn, the new SIS station chief at Tallinn, who had served with the British intervention force at Murmansk. After considering her case, Meiklejohn reported that 'this lady does not really desire to proceed to the UK but merely wishes to use the visa, if granted, for the purpose of convincing the Estonian Authorities and other persons who are not satisfied with her bona fides'.[30] Her application was refused; she was never told why, but did discover that her referees hadn't been consulted.[31]

Moura brought the children back to Germany with her, and by the end of 1922 they were lodged at a school at Dresden. It was planned that they would go back to Kallijärv for their holidays, and Moura would join them there.

Gorky didn't feel settled in Heringsdorf and wished for somewhere warmer for the winter, so in late 1922 the household moved again to Bad Saarow, a lakeside spa town in Brandenburg, where he set up his entourage in a set of rooms in the Neues Sanatorium, a huge white villa on the lake's edge.[32] It was an idyllic spot, with sailing on the lake. Moura took over the running of the household once more.

The days were regular. Rising at eight Gorky took a breakfast of coffee and two raw eggs, and would work until one o'clock. His friends would try to persuade him to take a break, but he would usually avoid it, rushing back to his work and sticking at it until supper time. Vladislav Khodasevich recalled Gorky's working patterns; he loved the implements of writing – 'good paper, different coloured pencils, new pens and holders' – and kept a ready supply of cigarettes 'and a motley collection of mouthpieces, red, yellow, and green'.[33] He not only wrote tirelessly, he read and answered the countless letters in all languages that poured in from all over the world (one of Moura's jobs was to help with the translating). He was always being sent books and manuscripts, which 'he read with astonishing attention, setting forth his opinions in the most detailed letters to their authors'.[34] He annotated every book and manuscript with comments, even correcting spellings and punctuation with a red pencil. 'Sometimes he would do the same with newspapers – and then throw them away.'[35] And he appeared to remember everything he read, in the smallest detail.

Moura would recall that to Gorky 'every human being aroused his curiosity, his sympathy, his attention'; he believed that 'all instruments, all voices were needed in the great orchestra that humanity would hear when it got the world it deserved'. He had 'an obsessive faith in work, goodness and knowledge, the three fundamental features of tomorrow's human society'.[36]

The closer she got to him, the better Moura understood Gorky's art, and how intimately it was bound up with his own self. Moura found resonance and encouragement for her own approach to her life history in Gorky's dramatic art. Commenting, as everyone did, on his ability to tell tales and bring characters to life, she believed that 'In his memories all events acquire a character of history, of permanence. Artistic truth is more convincing than the empiric brand, the truth of a dry fact.'[37] Thus Moura – her own impulsive self-invention, her shaping of her own tale, her magpie borrowing of incidents that belonged to others but which she made her own, all in the cause of making her life a thing of artistic veracity.

In recalling Gorky she seemed to be speaking of herself as much as him: 'like a tall, knotty tree, which had grown in spite of all the inclemency of the weather . . . This man, corroded through and through by a cruel life' who nonetheless found joy in living, and had hope. 'Born a poet, he became a teacher, not because he liked teaching but because he liked the future.'[38]

From time to time Gorky would allow indulgences. Every Sunday, if the weather was not too cold, the coachman was sent for; everyone wrapped up in their warmest clothes and set off for the cinema. Moura and Gorky would sit together on the back seat of the coach while the others crammed in wherever they could, the girls sitting on the men's laps.

But despite the volume of work and the social pleasures, the commune was never really the same now it wasn't hemmed in by a deprived, dangerous outside world. It was riven by enmities, as it hadn't been in Petrograd. When Maria Andreyeva visited, which was quite often, she tainted the atmosphere with continual complaints. Her movie director son sometimes accompanied her, and she treated him and the rest of the company with 'scornful condescension'.[39] Yekaterina, Gorky's estranged legal wife, also visited, but never at the same time as Andreyeva; the two disliked each other vehemently.

Moura divided her time between Gorky's personal life, his work and holidays with her children at Kallijärv, as his peregrinations and their school holidays dictated. Meanwhile, she attended to the other men in her life – Budberg and H. G. Wells. Making full use of her new state-sponsored wealth, she had set her husband up in a flat in Berlin, where he could happily gamble the evenings (and her money) away.

Young Baron Budberg seemed to believe 'that earning money is a job suitable only to those who can do nothing else,' she wrote to Wells.[40]

With an abiding ambition to go to England one day, and conscious that Wells would be a valuable, influential friend to have, Moura had struck up a correspondence with him as soon as she was free of Russia, and had been feeling her way ever since. At such a distance and having had so little physical contact with him, she played him uncertainly – sometimes he was 'My dear Mr Wells', sometimes 'Dear H. G.'. She began enticing him to move from his previous German publisher to Epokha Verlag, promising that 'we pay better'. She also invited him to contribute to a literary and scientific 'Russian Review' journal Gorky was setting up.[41]

Throughout this time, Moura was disquieted by what was happening in the world, particularly in Germany, with its unrest, its national shame and proliferation of aggressive workers' parties. The world, she wrote to Wells, was 'again preparing to bring to life a Bastard'. She couldn't have worded it more presciently. 'How naughty of it!' she added.[42]

As Europe began building its stack of powder kegs, England must have looked all the more inviting, if only it would let her in. Moura cultivated Wells' interest in her and minimised her relationship with Gorky; she was here to help with his publishing, she said, because of his ill health. Moura flirted with Wells, alluding to their night together in the Kronverksky apartment and anticipating a similar liaison during an upcoming visit to Italy. 'It would be delightful if you really came to the Riviera – for you surely would allow *me* to find you in your *ermitage*, wouldn't you?' she teased, referring to the hotel in which he planned to stay.[43]

But by late 1923 she was becoming irritated with him. He wasn't replying to her letters as diligently as he ought, and there was intense competition from his other lovers. Wells' womanising was legendary – a friend of Lockhart (who had no idea at the time about Moura's relationship with Wells) wondered at the man's energy, with four new novels and five mistresses every year.[44] Wells, who was still married to his wife, Jane, was trying to end his long-standing relationship with Rebecca West. And in summer 1923 he had a fling with an Austrian journalist, Hedwig Gatternigg, who had offered to translate some of his work into German. It was a brief encounter, but she began to stalk him. He was disturbed but incapable of resisting her sexually. The affair ended with her being taken away by police after invading his house and threatening to kill herself.[45]

Instead of trying to rekindle his affair with Moura, Wells embarked on a difficult relationship with Dutch journalist and traveller Odette Keun, an extremely volatile woman whom he met in France and with whom he would be painfully entangled for the next nine years. All the while, however, the special, inescapable hold that Moura had established in Petrograd three years earlier was still there.

Moura, despite the practical importance of Wells for the future and her irritation at his inadequate responses, didn't worry overmuch about him. Throughout 1923 she had been kept warm by one thought – the possibility of a reunion with Lockhart. The old flame was still burning, and now they were back in touch.

17

One Perfect Thing

1923–1924

Despite all the ways in which Lockhart had let her down and hurt her, she couldn't free herself from him. She had tried to cut him out of her thoughts, and seemed to be succeeding. But at the beginning of 1923 she heard word of him again. And yet again he managed to hurt her.

He had never stopped thinking of her, he wrote, and professed to believe that she had shied away from coming to him in 1919 – that she had lost her nerve. 'Knowing me as you do,' she wrote back indignantly, 'how could you think I would run away, afraid to face you?' And how, she asked, could he wonder what her feelings were now? 'It seems useless to say that I love you just as much as ever – for love does not even seem to be the right word at all – it is just that with you I have known happiness which I did not know either before or after and in the long run – it is always only that that counts.'[1]

She told him how she had lived through the years since his departure, sometimes despairing, sometimes 'finding a thousand reasons for hoping . . . I still lived, feeling sure, somehow, that you were there. Do you know what that means?' And then, just as she was leaving Russia, believing that she would now be free to find him again, there came the heartbreaking news of the birth of his son. 'I had to face the future without you,' she wrote. 'It was as I suppose death is to those who suddenly lose faith in life after death. And, to face it, I had to build myself a reason for facing it at all.'[2] Moura was a woman of high drama, seemingly unconscious of the point where she crossed the line from real emotion into high-sounding fiction; for example, her statement that in marrying Budberg she had been motivated by a profound need to be of use to someone, and that this gave her her sole reason for living.

Maybe it was that step too far that caused Lockhart to go on doubting her. In his view, it had been entirely a marriage of convenience. Or perhaps his doubts came from Magre's 'urge to demean that which I love' – 'I know by the sight of her tears that her suffering is great / And despite all that, I affect to doubt.'

Unable to help herself, she urged him to come to her now – to meet in Berlin. He must write immediately to let her know when he would be coming. She advised caution, and begged him to be patient with her this time while they worked out the best, least harmful way to get her out of the commitments she was tied up in.

Sober reflection could have told her that it was hopeless, that Lockhart would not come to Berlin, that there would be no way out. And yet she continued to hope. While she lived her life that year, working, cultivating Wells, looking after Gorky, holidaying with the children and enjoying the narcotic of gaiety which 'kills the consciousness of other things of which I know the value',[3] she waited for an opportunity to find her way back to Lockhart's embrace.

Just like before, there was a husband in the way. But this time the husband was entirely dependent on her. She sent Budberg to Rio de Janeiro – about as far away as could be – where he would be forced to earn his living giving bridge lessons.[4] They would never see one another again. Now that she had hopes of Lockhart, she had little use for her professed 'reason for facing it all'.

As time passed, nothing came from Lockhart – just silence. The months dragged slowly by in the quiet little town of Bad Saarow.

In the summer Moura travelled to Paris. Her sister Alla was there, now married to her third husband, a man named Trubnikov. They had both become hopelessly addicted to opium, and Moura had been called upon – not for the last time – to try to help her sister. She wrote to Gorky to tell him that this time she thought Alla was cured.[5]

Moura spent time in Estonia too, but her visits there were frustrating. She loved being with her children, but she missed being in the orbit of Gorky. She was jealous that other people could be with him and she couldn't. When the British sculptor Clare Sheridan, who had sculpted the likenesses of Lenin, Trotsky and Dzerzhinsky, came to visit Gorky in August 1923, Moura was detained in Berlin by business (she was managing his struggling Berlin-based magazine, *Beseda*) and by dental work (she was forever troubled by her teeth). When she was away from Gorky, she felt distanced from him emotionally too, and his cold, unsentimental letters unsettled her. She was particularly piqued by the thought that Sheridan ('that Englishwoman') might be spending too much time with him.[6]

In December she was forced apart from him again – back in Paris, en route to join the children in Estonia for New Year. Alla was not cured after all and had been admitted to hospital for her nerves. Between her mother and now Gorky and Alla, Moura's life seemed to be defined by waiting upon chronically sick people. After Christmas Moura herself became ill with influenza, and was stranded at Kallijärv when Kira too fell sick.

By February 1924 she was back in Saarow. It was a year since her letter to Lockhart, and still there seemed no sign of him coming back to her.

Her path had very nearly crossed with H. G. Wells' in Paris before Christmas. 'So we missed each other again,' she wrote to him, 'And I would like to see you so much. Well – let us be patient.'[7] Her letters to 'dear H. G.' were always warm, and seemed to hint at the possibility of romance, but for the time being she maintained a distance, always signing off with 'Best love to you and Gip' from 'Moura Budberg'. As in the early days with Lockhart, Moura's 'best love' was reserved for men she had hopes for but whose worth was yet to be proven.

Gorky's stay in Saarow was over. He and his household were moving on to Italy. Gorky had lived in Capri in the days of his pre-revolutionary exile, and longed to return there. But Mussolini was in power, and like all ideologues jealous of their position and their cults of personality, he was wary of Gorky. After persistent lobbying, permission was given for Gorky to stay in Italy, but not to return to Capri. Instead he settled for Sorrento, where he and his entourage moved into a villa called Il Sorito.[8]

Set just outside the town on the Capo di Sorrento, it was enchanting. It had a large garden filled with cypress trees and a terrace where they could eat supper, drink wine and tell stories. Gorky's room on the top floor overlooked the Bay of Naples and Vesuvius, the climate suited his health and he was soon a local celebrity. But despite his love of Italy he couldn't speak the language and never tried to learn – Moura, who spoke it fluently, helped him out. He also missed his homeland, but there was nothing anyone could do about that.

But Gorky was happy. Among the commune he now had his son, Max, and his wife, Timosha, as well as Moura. They were the three most important people in his life. But Max had an ulterior purpose in joining his father's household – he had been briefed by Lenin to try to change Gorky's political orientation, which he half-heartedly attempted to achieve.[9] Max loved to spend his father's money and had no real purpose in life; no real job or occupation. He was supposed to be his father's assistant and yet it was Moura and Pyotr Kriuchkov who did the work while Max took up tennis, motorcycling, stamp collecting, devouring detective novels and going to the movies. He longed to go back to Russia because the authorities had promised him a motor car.[10]

While living in Sorrento, Moura realised that she and Gorky were being watched by the Fascist authorities. Given that Gorky's visa had been approved by Mussolini himself, Moura was indignant on his behalf. She managed to engineer a meeting with Il Duce and challenged him over it. Gorky was in the country legally, she pointed out, and deserved to be treated with respect. 'Oh it's not Gorky, it's you,' he told her. A Russian émigré had denounced her. The Fascists thought it strange that a baroness should be on close terms with a socialist like Gorky. Moura riposted, 'Well, don't people change?' She reminded Mussolini that he had once been a socialist, and had edited the left-wing newspaper *Avanti* (after his conversion to Fascism, his blackshirts set fire to the newspaper's offices). He saw the irony, roared with laughter, and ordered the surveillance terminated.[11]

Although Moura had settled into the routine of the commune, she was restless. The abiding longing was nagging at her, and she decided that the time had come to seize her chance. In the summer she made her regular trip to Estonia to visit the children, and on the way she stopped off in Vienna, where her old friend Will Hicks and his wife Liuba were living. Hickie had left the diplomatic service and taken a job heading the Cunard office there. Moura asked him if he would contact Lockhart on her behalf.

Lockhart's career with the Foreign Office had not lasted long. The salary for his modest post at the Consulate in Prague had not been enough to cover his lifestyle. In early 1923 he had taken up a much more lucrative job as 'industrial director' at a bank in Prague that had been taken over by a British firm.

He was despatched to London for three months to learn the business. While he was there he made the acquaintance of Lady Vera Rosslyn, known in society as 'Tommy', the wife of the Earl of Rosslyn, who was a notorious drinking, gambling rake.[12] Lockhart and Tommy began an affair. Besides appealing to his powerful sexual needs, Tommy widened Lockhart's social horizon, introducing him into the circle of the Prince of Wales. She was also a Catholic, and her influence on him was so great that he converted to the faith.

They were both Catholics with elastic consciences that allowed them to indulge in the sins of the flesh as they pleased. Lockhart's life was going out of control – the very same pattern of wild, self-destructive behaviour that had nearly ruined his career in Russia before the Revolution, and which his marriage to Jean had been supposed to cure. He was still married to her, and his new religion forbade them the divorce they needed. Jean had a nervous breakdown in July 1923 and had a spell in a nursing home.[13] And yet the marriage limped on. Lockhart didn't know what to do with his life. He'd had some success as a journalist after coming home from Russia, but his ambition was to write books. Inspired by fatherhood, he'd proposed a book of fairy tales, but it had been rejected. And he was in debt.

Banking in Prague was the only way forward. That and a regime of hard work and abstinence from sinful pleasures. He had done this before, and it never lasted long. By the height of summer 1924 he was hating every moment of his job. He found the meetings 'overwhelmingly tedious', and life generally uncongenial. 'For six days a week I sat dutifully in the bank, doing my best to keep my end up and praying silently for the Sunday'.[14] On Sundays he went shooting or played golf; in the evenings he worked half-heartedly on a book about Czechoslovakia. 'For ten weeks I led the life of a saint.'

He was in this state of mind one Tuesday afternoon at the end of July. He was in a meeting with a man named Geduldiger (who was ostensibly his adviser on local industry but who actually did all the work) when the telephone rang. It was Will Hicks, calling from Vienna. They chatted for a minute or two, and Lockhart wondered why Hickie would make an expensive international call just to talk trivia. Suddenly Hicks paused and said, 'There's someone here who wants to speak to you.'

The phone was passed over, and Lockhart experienced another of those moments that would live for him forever. The voice that came down the line from Vienna was 'slow and musical' and sounded 'as if it came from another world'.[15] It was Moura. It was the first time he had heard her voice since their parting in the darkness on the railway tracks in Moscow in October 1918. The receiver shook in his hands, and he found himself asking inanely, 'How are you, my dear?' The memories took hold of him – Geduldiger and the office disappeared, and he was back in the flat in Moscow: the endless games of patience, the unanswered phone calls to Petrograd, while Moura was on her mission to Estonia and he feared they might never see each other again. And the ecstatic relief when the phone rang and he heard her voice and knew she would be back with him that night. He didn't realise it, but that had been six years ago to the very day – 29 July 1918.[16]

Listening to the familiar, measured voice relating the tale of her life since then, Lockhart had just one thought. Stammering, he asked Moura to put Hickie back on the line. 'May I come for the weekend?' he asked. 'Can you put me up?'

Then he left the bank and 'went home in a stupor of uncertainty'.[17]

During all the years in between, as he followed the path of least resistance back into his old life and his old ways, he had never stopped loving Moura. He preserved every one of the letters she wrote him during those dreadful months in Petrograd after he left. It had been easy to doubt her commitment, and to believe that her failure to follow him to England indicated cold feet. But hearing her voice again made it much more difficult, and brought vividly to mind the unparalleled strength of the love that had held them together through the dangerous summer of 1918.

Perhaps the time had come to make a break from England – the break he had shied away from in his last days in the Kremlin. But he was approaching middle age, divorce was out of the question, and there was four-year-old Robin to consider.

On Friday, after four days of agonising and still undecided, he took an evening train for Vienna, arriving early on Saturday morning.[18] Before he'd even checked into his hotel, he sought guidance by going to mass at St Stephen's Cathedral. It didn't help. He had several hours to kill before his rendezvous with Hicks at his office, so he sat in his hotel, drinking coffee, chain-smoking and trying to read the paper. Eventually he stubbed out his last cigarette and began walking slowly along the Kärntner Strasse, looking in shop windows to waste more time. The weather was glorious, the sun so hot in the blue sky that it softened the asphalt underfoot. At the end of the street, he turned into the Graben, where Cunard had its offices above a bookshop.

Moura was there. At the foot of the stairs he saw her standing alone in the streaming sunlight, waiting for him, just as she had been on that April morning in 1918 when she first came to his hotel in Moscow and he raced down the stairs to greet her.

What a difference six years had made. She looked different – a little older, more serious, and with a touch of grey in her hair. With marvellous self-control, she greeted him calmly and led him upstairs to the office, where Hickie and Liuba were waiting.

'Well,' said Moura, 'here we are.'

To Lockhart, in that moment, it was 'just like old times'.[19]

The four old friends caught the electric train up to Hinterbrühl, the idyllic forest resort in the hills outside Vienna, where Hickie and Liuba had a villa.

Lockhart's mind was still in turmoil. As they were leaving the office, Hickie had whispered to him to be careful, and Lockhart understood. Although Moura had changed a little in appearance, it was he who had changed the most, 'and not for the better'. He was nervous, Hickie and Liuba were nervous; they all talked too much and laughed too much on the journey; of the four of them, only Moura seemed entirely self-possessed.

After lunch at the villa, Lockhart and Moura took a long walk together up into the hills. He dreaded to speak his mind, and by the time they reached a high rocky crag beside a splashing stream, he was sweating with nerves and exertion. She told him the rest of her story – from Petrograd to Sorrento. He was amazed by her calmness and her strength of character, just as he had been since their very first meeting. 'I admire her above all other women. Her mind, her genius, her control are all wonderful,' he wrote in his diary. 'But the old feeling has gone.'[20]

It wasn't just the feeling that had gone – she had moved beyond and above him, gone through years of ordeals and trials, and had survived, maturer, stronger. 'Her tolerance was equalled only by her complete mastery of herself. She had a new attitude towards life, which I found wholly admirable and which I myself was incapable of imitating.'

They sat down on the crag beside the stream to rest. He stumbled through his own story, which sounded sterile and barren in his own ears by comparison with hers. 'I had lost even my old impudent self-reliance,' he noted miserably.[21] Broaching the awkward subject of his wife and son, he admitted that he had become a Catholic, and confessed 'like a schoolboy pleading guilty to his housemaster', the litany of 'my debts and my follies'.

'Oh God,' she whispered. He was expecting reproaches, but she gave him none. She just listened silently, 'her brows knitted, her chin resting on her hand, and her eyes fixed on the valley below, half-hidden by the heat haze'.

What she was thinking while he talked, she never recorded, but she seemed to be wondering how the man of six years ago had become the man that sat beside her now. And in that moment she realised at last that the love of 1918 could never be recaptured.

When he had finished talking, she said to him thoughtfully, 'You will be thirty-seven on the 2nd of September – the anniversary of Sedan and Omdurman? You see I remember the date. At thirty-seven one is not the same – men are not the same – as at twenty-seven.' Then, squashing down the feelings that had burned in her all these years, the longing for this man who sat beside her now, she made a plea that must have cost her dear, an act of superlative control. 'Don't let us spoil something – perhaps the one thing in both our lives – that has been perfect,' she said. 'It would be a mistake, would it not?'[22]

Lockhart didn't know what to say. 'There was a mist before my eyes, and my temples throbbed violently. I knew that she was right, that she had gauged my character exactly.'

She stood up and took his hands, and said firmly, 'Yes, it would be a mistake.'

They had been talking for hours, and the sun had lowered in the sky. As its fading light reddened the trees, Moura turned and, with Lockhart following, began making her way down the mountain path.

PART 4

England: 1924–1946

She was H. G.'s match, mentally. With her quick wit and unexpect-
edly wide knowledge . . . she could hold her own with him. More
than that, she could handle him in his sometimes querulous moods
– with a laugh or a joke or even a regal snub at his expense.

Moura was a Catherine Parr to H. G., a tower of strength to
him, a fount of spiritual consolation.

Lord Ritchie Calder, friend of Moura and H. G. Wells

18

Love and Anger

1924–1929

Indignant at the way Moura had been treated, H. G. Wells gave his opinion that Lockhart was 'a contemptible little bounder'.[1] Not that his behaviour was very different from Wells' own towards lovers who were too troublesome to keep but too compelling to discard; but he felt a jealous protectiveness towards the one woman who had the least need of it. After all the mis-steps and ordeals of her life so far, she was quite capable of dealing with any eventuality, in her own time and on her own terms.

When they descended the mountain that evening and returned to the villa, the air was clearer. Four old friends together, Moura, Lockhart, Hicks and Liuba talked late into the night, as they had done so often in the flat in Moscow when it felt as if they held the future of Russia in their hands. Now none of them, save perhaps Moura, had even a fingertip hold on the destinies of nations. So they made predictions.

'Moura prophesied that the economic system of the world would alter so rapidly,' Lockhart recalled, 'that within twenty years it would be closer to Leninism than to the old pre-war capitalism.' She predicted that it might be a compromise combining the best features of both systems, but 'if the capitalists were wise enough, it would come about without revolution'.[2]

When Lockhart wrote down that memory in 1933, he still had little idea how accurate her prophecy was, but he did guess that no radical changes would be wrought by their generation. They had sold their ideals after the war and gone back to the trough.

It was a pleasant but melancholy weekend of discovering that youth was gone for good. They tried playing rounders, as they did when killing time in the gardens of the British Consulate in Moscow in the long summer when the Cheka was itching to arrest every Briton and Frenchman in Russia. They couldn't keep it up for long; Lockhart's health, never good, had been ruined by overindulgence, and the others weren't much fitter.

On Sunday evening, Lockhart had to return to Prague. Moura was heading to Estonia via Berlin, so they travelled together for the first leg. There were no sleeper cars, and the train was overcrowded. They sat together in a crammed first-class compartment and talked through the night. Speaking Russian for privacy, they reminisced about their months together in Russia – about Trotsky and Chicherin, Yakov Peters and the Reilly plot, and 'Bolshevik marriage'.

They parted at Prague station at six o'clock in the morning. As Lockhart walked home he felt ill at ease and wondered whether he had made a wrong decision. He asked himself, 'Was my indecision due to lack of courage, or had the flame of our romance burnt itself out?'[3]

Lockhart – or rather his obtuse male vanity – believed that Moura had seemed 'a little bitter' at their parting.[4] In fact, if her manner with him was tight-lipped, it was irritation at his inability to understand what it was she wanted from him. After their conversation at Hinterbrühl she had suggested that they avoid seeing or communicating with each other for five years, and at the end of that they would come together again.[5] He felt that she was trying to bind him to an impossible promise. Always thinking in terms of romance and sexual adventure, he failed to see the importance that their love had had for her – how it had given her life and sustenance and hope for the future. A few days later in Berlin, she wrote to him, trying to explain herself.

She chided him for having expressed his trivial regret for 'the thrill that is gone, never to be revived'. To her mind it seemed 'like sexual hysteria – and I should have thought you were above that'.

> During all these years I have chiefly been doing my duty towards my own self-respect, or my children, or your memory . . .
>
> I do not think you quite understood my plan of the other day. I had not meant to bind you in any way – I told you I didn't. All I wanted was to have an illusion to live for – while for you – it would have given a certain satisfaction to your better self . . . But don't let us mention it again.

I will not tell you, what seeing you again has meant to me, I will not speak of the triumphant feeling of knowing love that was stronger than death – all this is something which from now on belongs to me alone.

But I think that this – should be good-bye for ever. It is not because you may not want to kiss me that I prefer not seeing you again, don't think that. But it would disturb your peace of mind . . . and as for me – it would, perhaps, spoil something which was, before God, really 'the most beautiful romance in the world'.

So good-bye, my dearest; I am going out of your life never to return. May God give you – yes, happiness – I say it from all my heart.

Moura[6]

It would never be known how much it cost her to write that letter, to compose herself, to guide her often wild hand to produce the neat, flowing script of a lady at peace with herself. There was artistic truth in the letter, and some dry fact. But in the real truth of life, although she had kept her dignity, she hadn't wholly retrieved her heart from Lockhart's possession, and never would.

In Berlin, Moura immediately threw herself back into her work, writing a torrent of letters to Gorky about the parlous state of his literary magazine *Beseda* and its publisher. The whole project was close to bankruptcy due to the refusal of Soviet Russia to allow the magazine to be sold there.[7] By the end of August she was in Estonia with the children.

Her relationship with Gorky was turning around. Just a year ago, she had been troubled by not being with him, by the insufficiency of his letters to her; now *he* was berating *her* for not writing often enough. She told him that her health was poor, that she needed to settle the children, and assured him that whenever she was away from him, she left a part of herself behind.[8] Gorky knew nothing of her meeting with Lockhart, but his legendary jealousy was stirring anyway.

Gorky's life had entered a new phase that year, as had that of every Russian. On 21 January 1924, while Gorky was still awaiting his visa to enter Italy, Vladimir Ilyich Lenin had died. The death forced him to re-evaluate his relationship with Lenin the man and Lenin the ideologue. He sent a wreath with the simple inscription 'Farewell Friend'.

And yet, only a few days earlier, he had written to his friend and fellow writer Romain Rolland, lamenting that he was unable to return to his homeland and that his arguments with Lenin had 'awakened a spiritual hatred for each other'.[9] Gorky tried to express his complicated feelings for the dead leader: 'I loved him. Loved him with anger.'[10]

Moura worked with Gorky to produce his reminiscences of his friend, which would be published around the world in many translations. The death of Lenin, he wrote, had 'painfully struck at the hearts of those who knew him':

> And if the storm cloud of hatred toward him, the storm cloud of lies and slander around his name grows thicker, it would make no difference: there are no forces which could darken the torch raised by Lenin in the sweltering pitch darkness of a panic-stricken world.[11]

In publishing this statement, Gorky irritated the Soviet government and scandalised Russian émigrés everywhere. How could he have written such words about the man who had forced so many of them to flee for their lives, instigated butchery, locked up their people? The government continued to send Gorky money, but he was beginning to feel the pinch, and due to the animosity of his fellow Russians he felt more of an outcast than ever. He was earning a healthy $10,000 a year in royalties, and although he spent little on himself, he had a lot of dependants, and never refused anyone's entreaties.[12]

Gorky's former wife Yekaterina was sent by Dzerzhinsky to Sorrento to try to persuade young Max to return to work for the Cheka back in Moscow. Gorky guessed that they were using Max as bait to try to lure him back. 'They think I will come after him,' he wrote to Yekaterina. 'But I won't go, not on your life!'[13] Gorky remained at Il Sorito, and the commune continued its existence.

Moura spent most of 1925 apart from Gorky. She spent time in Paris taking care of his literary affairs, and then carried on to Berlin where she met up with Maria Andreyeva. In July she holidayed with her children in Nice, where her sister Assia and her husband, Prince Basil Kotschoubey, had a small apartment.[14]

She had left Gorky behind in a depressed mood after a serious discussion about their relationship. There was friction between them, and a crisis was developing. He could sense that things had changed somehow

and was trying desperately to win her round. It had taken four years
– perhaps because of the circumstances of their day-to-day existence in
a crowded commune – but Gorky was experiencing the same helpless
addiction to Moura that Lockhart had felt and that Wells had already
begun to sense after their first week together.

Gorky told her that she was the first woman with whom he had been
truly sincere, and complained that by way of reward she gave him strife
and argument; he was starting to feel that things could not be put right.[15]
She assured him that although their relationship had gone past its
'youthful' stage, her feelings about him had not altered.[16] But he wasn't
to be placated; he was convinced that she wanted to leave him, and told
her that life without her would be unbearable.[17]

Their relationship was coming under stresses from every quarter. He
was being attacked in the Russian émigré press for his politics. *Beseda*
was still barred from Russia. And Moura was almost constantly away
from him, on business in Berlin, staying with the children at Kallijärv,
or travelling in Europe. The Sorrento apartment had been searched by
the Italian police, and in September Moura had been arrested and briefly
held by them.[18] Gorky's health was declining, he was acutely conscious
of his age and physical deterioration, and he was increasingly unhappy
about Moura's disregard for him and the belief that she was in love with
a younger man – a mysterious entity referred to directly only once in
their correspondence as 'R' – apparently living in Sorrento.[19]

He berated her for the insincerity of her letters – sometimes she
would write frankly, but at other times she seemed to be reaching for an
effect, a dramatic pose. This was her way, and it always had been. When
she wrote directly from her feelings, her letters were rushed, the hand-
writing erratic; but sometimes she would compose carefully, expressing
thoughts and sentiments that were dramatically appropriate to the scene
playing out in her life as she saw it. In Moura's mind, and in her percep-
tion of Gorky's writing, 'Artistic truth is more convincing than the
empiric brand, the truth of a dry fact.'[20] But for Gorky, artistic truth was
for art. In real life he wanted empiric fact; he wanted and demanded
sincerity.

And he got it. On 23 October she laid out the truth about her feelings. She insisted that she had loved him in Russia, and that it had
continued through their time at Saarow. And then, gradually, she realised, 'I was no longer in love with you. I love you but I was not in love.'

She struggled to describe what it was that had gone, and reached into her feelings about Lockhart – 'what makes birds sing and makes you see *God* in your head'. She hated herself for feeling no rapture with Gorky, only tenderness. 'I convinced myself that none of this is important, that this demon can be strangled, but it kept on growing.' And then, being as open as she knew how, she told him that she longed to 'sense my life being illuminated again with that wonderful kind of love that gives everything, but demands nothing, love for which alone it is worth living. I had this with Lockhart and I had it with you – but it's gone'. Without that, she pleaded, 'what am I good for, how can you need me?' To her mind, it was 'insulting to take your rapture of love – and not be in a condition to sing with you as one voice, not feel excitement from your caresses. My dear friend,' she concluded, 'God knows if I have left you to suffer – I have paid for this a hundred times over with my own suffering.'[21]

For a while, the crisis seemed to pass. She had been sincere, and that was all he asked. But by December, the complaints resumed. Moura, deciding that the time had come to be single again, had begun divorce proceedings against Budberg. Believing the situation with Gorky to be settled, and borne down by work and family, Moura had started being 'cautious' again in her letters to Gorky, picking her words, and again he interpreted this as an attempt to hide her feelings. He preferred sincere harshness to false pleasantry. 'I'm no less self-centred than you,' he assured her. 'I want you to be inspired with the philanthropy of a surgeon and not be tormented like you have tormented me this whole past year. In the last few months it has been especially onerous and frivolous.'[22]

She was shaken and hurt by his hostility. In a flurry of increasingly emotional replies, she assured him that she loved him, apologised for the anxiety she had caused him, denied that there was a 'secret corner of my soul' that she kept hidden from him. And she dismissed his accusation of frivolity and torture, and reminded him that it was he who had taught her to be cautious. If he wanted 'the philanthropy of a surgeon', 'would it not be better for you to be just as "surgically" open with me?'[23]

Gorky, who hadn't slept for five nights, was furious. They must part, he decreed; their relationship must end. He was unable to work without the 'basic conditions of peace of mind', and he couldn't achieve that so long as Moura was there to torment him. He could take no more of her 'caution'.

I told you many times before that I am too old for you, and I said this
in the hope of hearing your truthful 'yes!' You did not dare, and do not
dare say it, and this has created both for you and me a completely
unbearable situation. Your attraction to a man younger than I and
therefore more worthy of your love and friendship is completely natural. And it is absolutely useless for you to conceal the voice of instinct
with the fig leaves of 'fine' words.[24]

Her attachment to the younger man – the mysterious 'R' – might have
existed only in Gorky's imagination; an invention to explain Moura's
disaffection. No clear evidence of a relationship survived, and Moura
was never good at hiding her amours. Gorky believed that her travels to
Berlin to take care of his business and to Estonia to see her children were
pretexts. Separation would be better, he told her: 'You will not have to
split yourself in two, not have to resort to thinking up little lies "out of
concern for me", you will not have to restrain and distort yourself.'
Having made his case, having sustained his pride and dignity, at the close
of his letter he broke down: 'After all, I love you, I am jealous and so on.
Sorry, maybe you don't need to be reminded of this . . . How heavy,
how terrible all this is.'

She had pushed him too far. She needed Gorky; needed him personally as a friend and literary mentor, and as a haven in an unfriendly
world. After nursing her feelings for a week, in early January 1926
Moura wrote Gorky a portentous letter. In it she referred to the famous
farewell poem of Sergei Yesenin, the Russian émigré poet who had
committed suicide in Petrograd just two weeks earlier. Young and ach-
ingly handsome, Yesenin had been a hugely popular author of romantic
verse, a young darling of Russia and a prolific lover of women (he had
been briefly married to Isadora Duncan and had lately married a grand-
daughter of Tolstoy). Suffering from depression, he had killed himself in
his hotel room, leaving behind a final poem to a friend. It was said that
for the lack of any ink, he had written the poem in his own blood.

Quoting the poem in her letter to Gorky, Moura implied that she
might seek a similar farewell from him:[25]

> Goodbye, my friend, goodbye
> My love, you are in my heart.
> It was destined that we should part

> And be reunited one day.
> Goodbye, my friend, no handshake, no words.
> Don't be sad, don't frown.
> There's nothing new in dying now
> Though living is no newer.[26]

A silence fell. Gorky in his room above the Bay of Naples and Moura in snowbound Kallijärv brooded on their feelings.

What happened next wasn't recorded. Perhaps a telegram, a telephone call, perhaps merely a simple calming and subsiding of their feelings. A week later, Moura wrote again to Gorky. She had been ill, she said, and apologised for the delay in setting out; she would soon be on her way back to Sorrento.

When Moura returned in early 1926 the relationship continued. Wounds were patched up but not healed. In February Gorky noticed her concealing a letter when he walked into the room.[27] By April she was travelling again, attending to his publishing and reviewing his parlous financial affairs. Payments were not coming through from Russia, which was where his largest audience was. He was in such dire need of cash he had considered selling some of his beloved jade figurine collection.

While Moura was away, the cracks appeared again, and they were soon scolding each other for not writing, not being sincere. Moura told Gorky that she thought she had convinced him, during the winter, that she planned to remain as his 'wife' and had no desire to leave him. She said that she had 'decided not to see R any more'.[28]

Not only did she have to deal with Gorky's paranoia; she had heard that her sister Alla's husband had tried unsuccessfully to commit suicide. Like Alla he was addicted to morphine, and had long-standing problems.

That summer Moura's children finally got to meet the man who had been dominating their mother's life for so long, the august and remote figure from whom they received Christmas presents but whom they had never seen. Tania, who was ten years old now; Pavel, who was eleven; and Kira, sixteen, travelled by train with Micky to Italy. It was hot and stuffy, and after a long journey they reached Sorrento in late afternoon. The children were taken to meet the great man that evening. Tania's first impression was that he was immensely tall and thin but emanated an aura of strength. The children had been nervous, but were soothed by his kind eyes and mild manner, and found that they could relax in his company. He left an impression in their minds of an embroidered Tartar skullcap and enormous drooping moustache, and that he was easily moved to tears and seemed to be working all day. He tried to participate in the children's games but was often forced to give up as too much exertion brought on his coughing. 'There was something so human and even touching about this huge, gruff man,' Tania would recall. 'I thought him quite wonderful, serious and gay, gentle with us children and compassionate to everybody.'[29]

If Moura hoped that introducing Gorky to her children would placate him, she might have been right. But the next rift between them came from an entirely new direction. Gorky had again roused public controversy, and this time Moura was on the public's side.

On 20 July 1926 Felix Edmundovich Dzerzhinsky, the terrifying head of the Cheka, whose health had rarely been good and who had deteriorated after steering the course of the Red Terror, finally died. Gorky had been his friend in their outlaw days before the Revolution, and had remained on good terms. Under pressure from Yekaterina, Gorky was persuaded to write a eulogy. 'I am absolutely overwhelmed by the death of Felix Edmundovich,' he wrote. 'I importuned him about various matters and, because he was gifted with a sensitive heart and a strong sense of justice, we did a great deal of good.'[30] The piece was printed in the Soviet press. Russian émigrés across the world were outraged. This was worse than eulogising Lenin. They or their friends and families had suffered under the fist of Dzerzhinsky's Cheka. A 'sensitive heart'? How many innocent Russians had received bullets in the back of the head from his executioners? How many had starved and died in his prisons?

Moura had been one of those imprisoned. But she tempered her disapproval, only reproaching him guardedly.[31]

The children stayed at the Gorky household for two months, and saw more of their mother than they were used to (usually she stayed only two or three weeks in Estonia and those visits were broken up by trips to Tallinn). Moura seemed oblivious to the fact that her long absences upset them. Every August prior to her arrival, preparations were made in Kallijärv to receive her. Her room was vacated and cleaned and a basin, water jug and portable bidet were set up. Flowers were picked and the house made ready for her presence. On arrival she would throw open a suitcase full of gifts for everyone – a blouse for Micky, silk stockings, coloured pencils, a gramophone, a postcard album . . . After all were opened they would sit down to breakfast. Moura would take the head of the table and dominate the conversation. She expected 'to be adored, and treated as the "oracle from the west", she made the most of the general atmosphere of heroine-worship', Tania recalled.[32]

After a few weeks of playing games and swimming in the lake, the time would come for her departure. Micky would become tense at the impending loss. Pavel and Tania grew depressed, knowing that she was soon to leave. When her bags were packed, according to an old Russian custom, the others would all assemble for a moment of silence to bless the traveller on her way. As Moura always left late, the children would be tired and emotional. Their Aunt Zoria, who together with Micky took care of the children in Moura's absence, disapproved of these emotionally charged, prolonged, almost theatrical departures.

In the late autumn of 1926 Moura's marriage to Budberg was dissolved in a Berlin court without any fuss and in the absence of both partners.

Throughout the rest of that year and into the next, the relationship with Gorky continued to fizzle and crackle, and at intervals blew up in a flurry of complaints and accusations. His letters upset her; he had started accusing her of mismanaging his business affairs, laying the blame for his financial troubles on her rather than where it belonged – on the political situation in Russia and the acrimonious relationship that was growing between him and the émigré community, especially its writers.

But they still couldn't let each other go. All through the Saarow and Sorrento periods, Gorky had been working at his epic tetralogy, *The Life of Klim Samgin*. When the first instalment was published in Russia in 1927, it was dedicated to Moura – or 'Maria Ignatievna Zakrevskaya' as he still called her. This huge, slow, intense story of the life of a mediocre liberal lawyer among the intelligentsia of pre-revolutionary Russia would be his last book. It was intended as a satire on Russian émigré intellectuals – a few years later he would comment on the way in which, living abroad, they 'spread slander about Soviet Russia, foment plots, and in general, behave basely; most of those intellectuals are Samgins'.[33]

Moura, though she would never quite let go, was getting ready to move on. She had continued her correspondence with H. G. Wells. She asked for favours, sometimes satirically, trying to appeal to his humour as well as his politics. She instructed him to contact the 'Rulers of the world whoever they may be' and ask them to help Estonia with its economy and enable it to resist Bolshevism.[34] She talked of Russian and German translations of his work, and flirted coquettishly: 'don't be so entirely business-like. And tell me when I shall see you!'[35] Moura had never let go of the idea of getting to England in some way, and hopefully settling there. Wells knew all the right people and had money, power and influence.

Britain was looking more attractive with every passing year. In 1927 the attentions of the Italian police intensified. They were following her. She also believed that they were opening her correspondence, and indicated this to Gorky with a code, in Russian, 'Mary had a little lamb / And everywhere that Mary went / the lamb was sure to go.'[36] Having been held and questioned by the Italian police a couple of years previously, her paranoia was not without foundation.

The Italians were not alone in their suspicions. MI5's file on her had been active for several years now, and the French intelligence service, the Deuxième Bureau, were taking note of her and listening to gossip among the Russian émigrés. 'This woman seems to be a double agent of the Soviets and the Germans,' their report stated. 'She travels constantly across all of Europe.' It went on:

> Considered as suspect. Reported as having obtained a number of visas for the Western countries and as being the fiancée of Baron Budberg, former secret agent of the emperor, then became the friend of Maxim Gorki and Zinovieff and agent of the Soviets.
> Of very great intelligence and of considerable education – she speaks fluently and without accent English, French, German and Italian – seems to be a very dangerous spy in the service of the Soviets.[37]

Some witnesses claimed that she had been travelling back into Russia, and that a special office in Berlin provided her with 'a special entry authorization, of the kind that no trace of her trip is left on her passport'. The Deuxième Bureau considered it likely that Moura could be turned: 'She returns very often to France on the pretext of visiting her sisters. The Baroness B would work without doubt for us if we would pay her.'

What neither the Deuxième Bureau nor MI5 knew at this time was who the Baroness was spying on. In fact, it was the former members of Skoropadskyi's Ukrainian Hetmanate government, now living in exile in Berlin. She had resumed the double agent role she had begun in summer 1918. Her sister Assia's husband, the Ukrainian Prince Basil Kotschoubey, was an active member of the movement, and Moura used him as a source of information which she passed back to the Soviet Union.[38] The source had dried up by 1929, when Pavlo Skoropadskyi himself had become aware that she had been betraying the Hetmanate in 1918.[39] Her contacts with the Ukrainian exiles ceased.

The truth about Moura's activities was always mingled with hearsay. Some of the gossip she knew about, but some was confined to the files of secret intelligence agencies. And only Moura herself knew how much truth, if any, was in the rumours. If she really did go back into Russia after leaving it in 1921, carrying information on Gorky or her fellow émigrés, she managed to conceal it absolutely from everyone who knew her closely, and Gorky's only suspicions of her were her supposed liaisons with the youthful 'R'.

Moura's life with Gorky – though not their relationship – was gradually moving towards its close. During 1928 Stalin, who had muscled his way to the top of the Soviet leadership after the death of Lenin, began trying to persuade Gorky to return to the country of his birth. If he would not come to live, then he should at least visit. Moura tried to dissuade him; she told him that she was not interested in going back and that he would have to go alone.

Money had become an increasing worry for Gorky. Stalin promised that in Russia he would be given property, cars and a luxurious lifestyle. A bombardment of letters came from all corners of the Soviet Union – Gorky's admirers were distressed by the absence of their famous writer. The letters, which were designed to appeal to Gorky's vanity and timed to coincide with his sixtieth birthday, had been organised at Stalin's request by Genrikh Yagoda, the head of the State Political Directorate – the GPU, which had superseded the Cheka.[40]

Although Moura had personally spoken against visiting Russia, she now joined in the propaganda campaign. In Berlin she politicked with influential figures in the literary and émigré communities, repairing the damage he had been causing with his attitude to the 'Klim Samgins'. Letters came in from all the giants of the literary world – Theodore

Dreiser, John Galsworthy, George Bernard Shaw, Thomas Mann, Romain Rolland, Georges Duhamel and H. G. Wells, among others – all praising him, calling him a 'genius of world literature' and a 'powerful life force in the new Russia', and keeping quiet about the atrocities of the Soviet regime and the fact that Gorky had become an apologist for them. On his birthday, 25 March 1928, the *New York Times* printed an accolade with fifty signatures attached to it.[41]

Gorky was flattered by the attention and the adulation. He liked what he heard about many of Stalin's latest projects, not least the idea of agricultural collectivisation, which he saw as the answer to changing the 'half savage, stupid, heavy people of the Russian villages' into an 'agricultural proletariat'.[42]

But more than anything else, Maxim Gorky – Alexei Maximovich Peshkov – was homesick. In May 1928, after an absence of seven years, in company with his son, Max, he made his first visit to Russia.

During that first summer sojourn he met Stalin and Yagoda for the first time. An elaborate masquerade was set up whereby Gorky and Max were asked to don wigs and make-up to disguise themselves to enable them to take a walk around Moscow. Gorky was unaware that most of those with whom he came in touch during that day were part of an elaborate sham which culminated in a specially prepared dinner at the railway station – supposedly an ordinary meal, but nothing like the normal fare that the average person could eat.

Gorky was willing to be deceived; he wanted to believe that the Soviet Union was a good place to live. His days of denouncing the Bolsheviks were long past. In return, Stalin valued him for his popularity and his potential to unite and placate the common people.[43] So began a courtship that would eventually bring Gorky home from exile for good.

The renewal of Gorky's relationship with Soviet Russia coincided with the end of his intimate relationship with Moura. But she continued to handle all his business affairs – translation rights, film deals, publishing – as well as those of other writers.

At the same time she encouraged the attentions of H. G. Wells.

Wells was gradually disconnecting himself from the ties to the women in his life. Rebecca West was in the past, and his wife, Jane, was ill. He had been in his holiday home on the French Riviera near Grasse with his lover Odette Keun when Gip sent him the news that Jane had cancer. Wells returned home and stayed with her until her death in September. Now that he was free, Odette could see no reason why Wells would not marry her. But with her volatile temper, the demands she made on him and the violent quarrels that had always punctuated their relationship, he had no intention of rushing into marriage. She would often open Wells' mail, and was shocked to find that he had been writing to Moura. Wells knew he should make a clean break from Odette but couldn't summon up the courage or the will.

Moura's motivations for cultivating Wells were complex. He was influential, and as a literary woman she couldn't help admiring him, and as a romantic she was attracted to him, but there was little possibility of really loving him. Unlike Gorky and Lockhart, Wells had only a moderate regard for her intellect or her talents. He thought her bright and shrewd, but believed that she thought 'like a Russian: copiously, windingly and with that flavour of philosophical pretentiousness of Russian discourse, beginning nowhere in particular and emerging at a foregone conclusion'. She was 'a cultivated person who thinks after the manner of literary criticism and not along scientific lines'. He compared her intellect unfavourably with his wife's and his daughter's, who 'had science in their education and think in English forms'.[44] Wells believed strongly in rationalism, even as applied to politics. Some of his younger contemporaries, such as George Orwell, considered this a fatal flaw that blinded him to human nature.

Wells must have given his opinion on this to Moura, for in catching up with her correspondence with him after the whirl surrounding Gorky's visit to Russia, she wrote placatingly that she was trying 'to change my asiatic habits to western ones'.[45] She had always taken it in good humour when he criticised her prose style or her English ('Did I *really* say "publishment"? What a shame!').[46] In later life his pedantry would set her teeth on edge, but for now it just amused her.

In July Moura was back at Kallijärv. There, after an interval of four years, she wrote to the one man who had valued her mind and her talents above all others, the one man who had never reproached her for 'asiatic habits' or treated her with jealous possessiveness.

'Dear Baby,' she wrote. 'How are things with you?' With grim humour she alluded to the breaking of the vow she had made four years earlier: 'The Russian proverb is right when it says that the grave alone will cure

the hunchback.'[47] She wondered if he might be in Paris or Berlin any-
time soon, and if he would care to meet. She was keen to hear what had
happened to the 'famous book' he had been planning to write, and how
he was progressing with his memoirs.

When he replied, the sight of his name seemed to 'sweep away ten
years and transform me into the happy young fool that used to tear open
your envelope with trembling fingers'. On 28 July she wrote again,
reminding him that it was ten years to the day since 'I started on foot
from Narva to join you in Moscow'.[48]

While she continued to flatter, humour and charm H. G. Wells,
Moura reverted to the habit that had marked the beginning of her affair
with Lockhart ten years earlier – passing him information. Gorky was
back in Sorrento after his trip to Russia, and Lockhart, who was now
earning a crust writing a gossip column for the London *Evening Standard*,
had heard a rumour that he had 'quarrelled with the Bolshies'. She
denied it, and described Gorky's ill health and his need to work on
completing the remaining volumes of his epic novel. 'Please don't use
my name when you give this,' she warned.[49]

Moura would prove very useful as a source of high-level gossip for
years to come. But it wasn't the same as it had been in their youth.
Feeding intelligence to an important diplomat involved in great political
events was not the same as passing gossip to a newspaper columnist. And
a rather lowbrow one at that.

With her connections to Lockhart and Wells, Moura worked away at
gaining admittance to the one place she most wanted to go – England.

On 13 June 1928 she applied for a visa. She said she wanted to
escort her adopted daughter Kira, now eighteen, who had been given
a place at Pitman's secretarial college in London. One of her referees
was again her old SIS friend Commander Ernest Boyce (who would
later be rumoured to be a Soviet double agent).[50] After several letters
to and fro between various government departments and the police,
her application was once more declined on the grounds that she was a
security risk.

Gorky, who was considering returning to Russia permanently, asked
whether Moura would contemplate going with him. She turned him
down. It would be impossible to see her children if she lived in Russia.
'And this thought, meaning separating from you, is very, very tor-
menting, my joy, believe me!' she wrote.[51]

In August 1928 she moved Pavel to a school in Berlin. The move proved a bad one as in March the following year a tutor took the fifteen-year-old boy to an inn, where he probed him for his political views and referred to Moura as a revolutionary. Pavel sprung to the defence of his mother and hit the tutor. Both were expelled from the school. Pavel ran away, disappearing for a few days, staying at a hotel and washing dishes to pay for his keep.[52] He was moved to another school in Germany where he stayed until he was called up for military service in Estonia.

By 1929 Moura was living most of the time in Berlin, in an untidy little apartment in Koburger Strasse, a side-street in the Schöneberg district. She spent her time socialising and building up her publishing and translating business. With power of attorney over the foreign rights of Gorky's books she could negotiate freely for their translation.[53] Moura acted as his literary agent and worked personally on the translation of many of his books. She also began organising the foreign publication of books by unknown Russian writers.

In 1929 the opportunity she had been waiting and working for finally materialised.

In the spring H. G. Wells arrived in Germany. He gave a lecture in Berlin entitled 'The Common Sense of World Peace'. As he was about to go on, he was handed a letter from Moura; she had seen the lecture advertised and seized the opportunity to arrange a meeting with him. Afterwards, as the audience dispersed, there she stood, 'tall and steady-eyed, shabbily dressed and dignified, and at the sight of her my heart went out to her'.[54]

She had aged and put on weight, but it made no difference. Wells was sunk. The next day they dined with Harold Nicolson. Afterwards Nicolson told his wife, Vita Sackville-West, that Wells had flirted with Moura most of the evening.[55] They ended up 'in her shabby little apartment', Wells recalled. 'From the moment we met we were lovers, as though there had never been any separation between us.'[56] Moura had got the break she had been waiting for.

Almost immediately after Wells left Berlin, Lockhart arrived. She gave him all the news about Gorky's proposed return to Russia, and confessed that she was intending to leave him while he was away.[57]

They spent a week together, and the encounter relit Moura's flame. The love she had tried to bring to a dignified conclusion at Hinterbrühl was taking her over again. She wanted him back, she wanted to help him climb out of the demeaning, lowbrow literary hole he was in. Most of all, she wanted him back for good. Reaching once more for an artistic truth, she could sense that Europe was on the verge of another conflagration, and that they shared obligations rooted in their past. 'Why not give in to me?' she wrote to him. 'Why not even "sacrifice" yourself? That is done, after all, sometimes, and I want you so much – and so well.'[58]

She would never be able to give him up – only the grave could cure the hunchback.

In the summer of 1929 she got one of her dearest wishes. In June, Ernest Boyce (who had retired from SIS service in 1928) sent a letter to the Passport Control Office, in which he promised to 'personally guarantee that there is no political reason why Baroness Budberg should not visit England'.[59] Finally, after a decade of trying, she was granted a visa to enter the country which was almost her spiritual homeland.

19

Not Such a Fool

1929–1933

Wednesday 18 September 1929, Dover, England

Moura's first sight of England was the inner harbour under the chalk cliffs, its quays crowded with tall-stacked tugs and cross-Channel steamers. The boat from Calais, bluff-bowed and dragging smoke from its funnel, edged in and settled beside the dock.

The little girl, now thirty-seven years old, who had learned the English language in the cradle, whose dearest friends were British, and who had risked her life for British interest, looked at last on the country she had been making her way towards for more than ten years.[1]

She hadn't much time to take it in. The visa she'd been grudgingly issued was valid for just one week, and she had things to do and people to see.

Her principal mission was to see H. G., and having deposited Kira in London (London!) she travelled on to Essex, where H. G. had his country home. Easton Glebe was a pleasant, unassuming Victorian house on the estate of Easton Lodge. H. G. had been renting it from Daisy Greville, the Countess of Warwick, since 1910. This was his arcadian retreat, and many of his books had been written here – among many others, *Mr. Britling Sees It Through*, his novel of humane courage in wartime; its village setting was based on Easton. *Mr. Britling* had been popular in Bolshevik Russia, and was one of two books given by Yakov Peters to Lockhart while he was imprisoned in the Lubyanka (the other being Lenin's *State and Revolution*).[2]

H. G. and Moura spent the week together. Moura got to see the gardens he was so pleased with and which he had sent her picture postcards of. And they went up to London, where Wells kept an apartment: 614 St Ermin's Hotel in Caxton Street, Westminster.

They had a polite, decorous time – or at least Moura attempted to fashion it in that way. She was having to adjust herself to H. G.'s view of her, and she tended to misjudge it. Accustomed to the admiration of brilliant men who treated her as an intellectual equal – or at least as a gifted protégée – it wasn't easy to adapt to a man who appreciated her brightness but seemed to want to regard her in a playfully romantic manner. How should she respond?

She chose levity, loaded with a barb to provoke his jealousy. After her brief interlude in England, she returned to the Continent. Stopping off at the Hôtel Meurice in Paris, she dashed off a brief note to H. G., mentioning that she was awaiting a rendezvous with a 'faithless swain' (presumably Lockhart). More pleasure, she said, was to be had in 'writing to you to tell you how charming, delightful you have made my visit to London, dear'. She belittled herself lightheartedly – 'I am a very grateful little person . . . and will never forget it.'[3]

It was the wrong approach. She was startled by his reply, in which he complained about the brevity and tone of her note; he'd got the impression that having had her entertainment she would now 'go her way'. Alarmed, on her return to Berlin she wrote him a longer letter. She denied that she wanted to cast him off. On the contrary, she insisted, 'I want, in a very womanly, if very "unintellectual" way to feel that I belong to you'. Ever since Petrograd he had meant a great deal to her, and her 'silly letter from Paris' had been intended so that 'you should not feel my heartache'. One quality Wells perceived in her was her strength, apparently, so she played to it. 'Yes, I am strong, I suppose, strong enough not to make a fool of myself.' But she urged him to 'not be *too* strong, H. G. my dear, be a little "weak" . . . if that means thinking of me more than you ought to'.[4]

If her cultivation of Wells cost Moura anything in pride, she didn't let it show. She had learned the importance of pandering to men's vanity in a Cheka prison, with Yakov Peters as her subject, and her 'training of the mind' had been sharpened through years of handling secret policemen, spies, commissars and diplomats. One Englishman, however august, shouldn't be too severe a challenge for a woman of such talent.

There might well have been a hidden motivation: that she was not merely cultivating or seducing him but grooming him. If the rumours about her spying for the Soviet government were true, and the misgivings of the British and French secret services were justified, Britain would be a doubly good place for her to be. H. G. Wells' circle was international; it encompassed royalty and writers, film stars and aristocrats, and politicians at the very top of their countries' leadership. Lockhart too, although not well known like Wells or Gorky, mixed with the rich and famous, including at one time or another Winston Churchill, Oswald Mosley, Lord Beaverbrook, Brendan Bracken, the Prince of Wales and Wallis Simpson. Between these two men, a spy whose métier was political gossip would find rich pickings.

But there was a deep emotional need in her too. Her men were never mere tools, least of all Lockhart. Even her daughter Tania could never illuminate the hidden parts of Moura's character. She could never fathom how 'somebody who had suffered as much, and lost as much, as my mother, could still expect and command such adulation'.

> One way she achieved this, without doubt, was by exerting an emotional pull: she once told a friend of mine that she thought men would remain attached to her if she had slept with them. Yet the question remains of how much this was an egotistical desire to manipulate people, or a response to a deep need within herself. Certainly, once attached she never let go; and yet this seems to have been part of the attraction for those caught in this way.[5]

Having repaired her initial mis-step, Moura began to settle into a regular relationship with Wells. Yet neither of them was either free or constant. Gorky was still living at Sorrento, and Moura was still a part-time member of his household. At the same time she was also settling into an intermittent sideshow affair with Lockhart.

Wells, meanwhile, was still entangled with Odette Keun. She remained tucked away in the Riviera, where he visited in the winter. He refused to see her elsewhere, and kept his new relationship secret from her, for fear of the savage recriminations that would undoubtedly ensue. Despite being quite sure that it was Moura he loved, Wells had never been good at ending relationships cleanly, and now, in his early sixties, was of an age when he couldn't face another upheaval in his routine. After Jane's death, he had gone through a period of anxiety and had felt that his own life was drawing to a close, leaving him with an urgency to complete important work; he was reluctant to do anything that might affect this.

At the same time, Wells made it clear to Moura that he intended to stay with Odette, that he and Moura should not have a child and that he would not expect fidelity from her.[6] Moved to pity by her 'shabby', impecunious existence, Wells settled on her an annuity of £200 a year, supplementing her business income, which was around £800.

H. G.'s conditions suited Moura very well. Gorky was away in Russia in the summers, and Wells was off with Odette in the winters, so everything fitted neatly. And she still had time to dally with Lockhart.

Somehow, Wells did not seem to realise that Moura's relationship with Gorky had been sexual. He still believed her to have been merely his secretary. Neither did he know the extent of her feelings for Lockhart. He thought he was the only man she loved. Yet although she told him that she loved him and belonged to him, she gave him nothing like the wholehearted, abandoned declarations of love she made to Lockhart.

Moura was now past her youth and on the downward slope into middle age. And she was beginning to experience a new and irritating sensation – the presence of a generation of grown women younger than herself.

In October 1929 she took Kira to live with her in Berlin for a while. The apartment was small, and she soon found that Kira's presence irritated her and cramped her style. She was not good at introducing the handsome young woman at gatherings and appeared jealous if any men took notice of her. Moura seemed to resent her presence, intruding into her life and taking away the limelight that she required for herself. Kira's stay only lasted a few months.

In 1930 Gorky's health was worse than usual. His tuberculosis had been particularly bad that winter, and he was unable to go to Russia. Moura left him in Italy and went to spend some time with Alla. Her husband had attempted suicide again, and this time succeeded, and Alla's morphine addiction had taken hold of her once more. In March Moura admitted her to an asylum, but she wasn't ill enough to be held by force, and ran away. Moura wrote to Gorky to apologise for missing his birthday, and continued tending to Alla. In June she moved her to a hospital specialising in treating narcotic dependency. In between, she worked away at translations of Gorky's *Samgin* and attended to her publishing.[7]

She managed to find time to acquire another visa and spent some of June with Wells at Easton Glebe. Anthony West, Wells' son by Rebecca, was staying when Moura arrived. He had been out for a walk when Moura arrived, and when he returned he found the couple sitting on a garden seat in front of a tree. 'Their faces were illuminated by their delight in finding themselves together again, and their evident happiness made the sight an unforgettable one. When my father was happy he was the pleasantest of men to be with.' When Anthony returned home to his mother, bubbling with excitement about the wonderful time he had had, he was met by a stony Rebecca, who was angry that her son could be so disloyal.[8]

They spent time in London, where Moura began to infiltrate Britain's literary and publishing world. She was introduced to the formidable Barbara Back, the boss at Heinemann, a man-eater who was reputed to have slept simultaneously with Somerset Maugham and his secretary and lover Gerald Haxton. She ordered her office boy, the young Rupert Hart-Davis, to partner her at badminton against Moura and Wells. Afterwards they repaired to Wells' new flat in Baker Street for tea. Hart-Davis was impressed by Moura, finding her an energetic, enthusiastic opponent on the badminton court. She refused tea, preferring 'a brandy and soda, accompanied by a large cigar', over which she discussed politics and government with Wells.[9] She had made a deep impression on the twenty-three-year-old. In later life, he would come to admire and adore Moura for her kindness and warmth. 'She hugged you, not just with her arms but with her whole self.'[10]

During the rest of that summer, she worked her way slowly back to the sick Gorky at Sorrento, via Paris, Berlin and Estonia. But by October she was in London again, lunching with Lockhart at the Savoy Hotel prior to leaving for Genoa and Berlin. They had a good gossip – Moura told him that the author Arnold Bennett was bored with his actress lover 'and had lost his inspiration since she made him give up wearing shirts with myosotis flowers on them'.[11] She regaled him with tales of Gorky, who had given away all his money and was only making about £300 a year, despite selling over two and a half million books every year in Russia. Stalin wouldn't let money out of the country, and was making it impossible for Gorky not to return home. Meanwhile, Moura was seeing less and less of him every year, and spending more and longer periods in Britain.

With every journey she widened her social web, gathered new intelligence, added new authors to Epokha's list. And the rumours about her never ceased – that her travels were the cover for spying, either as a Soviet agent or a British double agent. At the same time, her restless and potent emotions drove her to take new lovers.

She didn't lodge with Wells when she was in England; instead she stayed with Count Constantine Benckendorff and his wife. Constantine, a distant cousin of her late husband Djon, was the son of Count Alexander Konstantinovich Benckendorff, the last imperial Russian Ambassador to the Court of St James's. Alexander's widow, Countess Sophie, had settled in England after his death in 1917, renting out her house in London and living in her quaint garden cottage, Lime Kiln, at Claydon in Suffolk, where she cultivated roses. Sophie had died in 1928, and Constantine had inherited Lime Kiln. Boldly citing her Benckendorff connection and exerting her charm, Moura threw herself upon Constantine, presuming his hospitality – and received it.[12] Over the next decade and a half, she would receive a good deal more from him.

Constantine, a political liberal, was married to the harpist Maria Korchinska, and had a seven-year-old daughter, Nathalie. Constantine was twelve years Moura's senior, had served in the Russian Imperial Navy, was captured by the Japanese during the war of 1905, and worked for a while in London with his father. While there he made friends with writer, traveller and socialite Maurice Baring, who introduced him into the political and literary circles that included Arthur Balfour, George Bernard Shaw, King Edward VII and H. G. Wells. Constantine returned to Russia before the Great War to work on the family estate, and shared a flat in St Petersburg with Baring. After the Revolution he decided to throw in his lot with the proletariat and joined the Red Navy. But his career became irksome, marred by the Bolsheviks' suspicions of his background. At various times he was incarcerated in both the Kremlin and the Butyrka – the very same prison in which Moura had spent those two terrifying weeks in September 1918.[13]

As veterans of the Cheka jail, and as progressive nobles who had worked for the Bolsheviks, perhaps there was a fellow feeling that drew Constantine and Moura towards each other. Like Moura, 'Cony' was believed by some Russian émigrés to be a Soviet spy.[14] Some believed that Moura's acquaintance with him pre-dated her arrival on his London doorstep in 1930. He had once served as a border commissioner in Estonia, during the time when Moura was crossing the frontier.[15]

Constantine resembled Djon – stolid, blunt and now tending to be portly. But in temperament he was closer to Moura – progressive, liberal, adaptable to circumstances and cultured. He was a flautist, and on leaving the Navy had joined an orchestra, where he met his wife, Maria. He was forty; she was twenty-seven. They had escaped Russia in 1924 and joined Countess Sophie in England. Like many other Russian émigrés, Cony had little to do in England, and turned to gambling, leaving his wife to earn their money. She spent most of her time in London pursuing her career while Cony lived at Lime Kiln.

Within a few months of her arrival in England, Moura had managed to melt Cony; they began an affair which was destined to last for fifteen years. He was a charming person, well liked and popular.[16] Moura, explaining herself to a friend many years later, said, 'Gorky and Wells I loved. For Constantine I felt a physical passion he fulfilled.'[17] His daughter Nathalie, who knew from family gossip about the affair, grew up loathing Moura.[18] Dragged to Kallijärv for a holiday in 1935 when she was twelve, she was thoroughly embittered by the association, and detested all of Moura's family. Although she found Tania beautiful, she disliked Pavel intensely and found Kira a 'religious maniac, communion daily, queer in the head'.[19]

The extended Benckendorff family, with whom Moura was already on cool terms, were further alienated by the affair. Constantine spent money on Moura, buying her jewellery, escorting her to the theatre and the ballet. Nathalie considered her father a courageous man, but believed he was morally weak and Moura 'devoured him'.[20] Moura even had the gall to take H. G. down to Claydon to visit Cony. Only a woman of Moura's calibre would dare take one lover to visit another for the weekend.[21]

Moura's life was woven with lovers. Gorky at Sorrento, still wavering over whether to give up his beloved Italy and go home for good; Constantine providing passion and intrigue; and Wells, kept in the dark, believing that he was the only one. H. G. judged that Moura was 'not a feverish lascivious woman like Odette' and could only be made love to by a man whom she loved.[22] This was true enough, but as with her intelligence, Wells underrated her capacity to love men.

Through it all, the thread that tied her to Lockhart was still strong. And between them was a secret truth – that if only it were possible, she wished she could be with him to the exclusion of everything and everyone else in the world.

Lockhart's life was a mess. He was still writing his gossip column, still in debt, and agonising over the ruined remains of his marriage. Moura wanted to help him. She tried to inspire him to get a grip, settle his debts, and do some proper writing. 'She is a big-minded and big-hearted woman,' he noted in his diary in early 1931.[23] He knew how difficult he had become, and what a struggle it was for the woman who still unconscionably loved him. She had once told him that he was 'a little strong, but not strong enough, a little clever, but not clever enough, and a little weak, but not weak enough'.[24] Now she urged him to 'stop making such a mess of your life' and take advantage of the opportunities he had in front of him. 'You *must* have time to write and you *must* fight your physical troubles . . . Why don't you listen to me?'[25] From time to time they met and stoked the old flame again, and occasionally – apparently when she had been drinking heavily or had worked herself into a passion – she wrote him wild letters in a chaotic hand, telling him 'my darling, you must know how much I love you . . . all my love is yours', and swearing that it hadn't diminished in any way since 1918.[26]

In 1931 Gorky was well enough to visit Moscow again. Moura busied herself selling his jade collection in order to boost his income in Europe, but was upset at only getting half as much for it as she would have liked.[27] At Christmas 1931 Kira became engaged. Her fiancé was Hugh Clegg, a doctor and editor of the *British Medical Journal*. The couple married in the Russian Orthodox church in London the following year.[28]

By 1932 Lockhart was making good progress with his memoir, based on his career in diplomacy and espionage. Eager to see him produce a proper book, and equally keen to monitor what he put in it, Moura took a close interest, lending him her experienced editorial eye. In March, during an oppressively dull stay at Kallijärv ('this little hut'), she mentioned casually in a letter, in response to some remark from Lockhart that is now lost, that 'R is *not* dead as our friend said'.[29] Another mysterious 'R'. This was clearly a different 'R' from the one Gorky had been incensed about.

Almost certainly Moura was referring to Sidney Reilly, SIS agent and Lockhart's former accomplice in the Latvian plot. Reilly had disappeared during a mission to Russia in 1925. It was presumed that he was dead – shot soon after crossing the border. It would later appear that he had been sent deliberatcly into a trap by Ernest Boyce of the SIS, who was allegedly a Soviet double agent. Some would later come to believe that Reilly's death had been faked, and that the Ukrainian-born agent had in fact defected.[30] If this was true, and if Moura knew it, she must have been every bit as deeply involved in espionage as her accusers claimed.

It was a plausible idea. Reilly had always seemed strongly anti-Bolshevik, but in late 1918 Lockhart, who had just returned from Russia, received a letter from him. At this time, Reilly was staying at the Savoy in London on the eve of a return mission to Russia with George Hill. In his letter, which was kept secret until long after Lockhart's death, Reilly observed that Bolshevism was 'bound by a process of evolution to conquer the world . . . and nothing – least of all violent reactionary forces – can stop its ever-rising tide'. He gave his opinion that 'the much decried and so little understood "Soviets" which are the outward expression of Bolshevism as applied to practical government, are the nearest approach, I know of, to a *real* democracy based upon true social justice'. Furthermore, he believed that 'they may be destined to lead the world to the highest ideal of statesmanship – Internationalism'.[31]

Reilly knew Lockhart quite well, and certainly knew of his sympathy with socialism, his exasperation with British intervention, and might have had some inkling that Lockhart had considered staying in Russia for Moura's sake. He might well have been a defector. If Moura was indeed letting Lockhart know that Reilly's death was a hoax, it was an act of extraordinary foolhardiness or courageous trust. If there was one thing that Moura never learned to resist, it was the impulse to make people aware that she had her fingers on pulses that were beyond their ken.

During 1932 Moura and H. G. were seen out together more and more frequently. They spent weekends with Lord Beaverbrook (Lockhart's boss) at his country mansion, Cherkley Court, and Wells gave Moura a key to his Baker Street flat. In April they holidayed together in Ascot, staying at the Royal Hotel, run by the eccentric John Fothergill, who wore a green suit with brass buttons and buckled shoes, and kept three elephants on the premises. Moura enjoyed feeding them 'epples' as she called them in her affected Russian accent.

It was here that Wells first began to talk to Moura about marriage. Unsurprisingly, she was against the idea. She wanted to go on as they had been and was adamant that she didn't want a change in their relationship.

Wells was on the verge of breaking up with Odette Keun, but despite his talk of marriage to Moura, he had still not ended the relationship. He resented Odette's temperamental behaviour, but seemed afraid to tell her it was over. When Wells had been diagnosed with diabetes the previous year, Odette had turned up in London, took a short course in nursing and demanded to be allowed to look after him, hoping that he would marry her out of gratitude. Wells told her that he was quite able to look after himself and certainly did not want her interfering. Seeing her for the first time in his home environment he realised just how little they had in common and how embarrassed he was by her eccentric behaviour and outlandish dress.

In late 1932 Wells wintered with her at Grasse for the last time. Increasingly suspicious, Odette discovered letters from Moura. She threatened suicide, said she would publish the letters and sell the ones Wells had sent her, and write a book about their life together. Wells and Odette parted in March 1933, and in 1934 she published *I Discover the English*, in which she passed damning comments about Englishmen's attitude to sex. He was calm about it, and told her he was glad things were going so well and that her book was such a success. She told him she had been blackening his name at a party with Lloyd George and Stanley Baldwin. 'I kept them all listening,' she told him. 'About you and your Moura. Do you know I've invented a name for her. It will be all over London. Such a funny name. All London will laugh at you. I call her . . . Baroness Bedbug.'[32] If only Odette had known, the men in the British government had heard worse tittle-tattle than that about Moura Budberg.

Wells was so thoroughly smitten with Moura he didn't care what Odette did. He had always been well aware of her faults (or those which he was able and willing to see, anyway), and yet he loved her. In 1934 he wrote down his thoughts about Moura, struggling to work out what it was that fixated him so.

She is a manifestly untidy woman with a scarred and troubled forehead and a broken nose . . . with streaks of grey in her hair; she is a little inclined to be heavy physically; she eats very fast, taking enormous mouthfuls; she drinks a great deal of vodka and brandy without any manifest results, and she has a broad soft voice flattened perhaps by excessive cigarette-smoking. Generally she is clinging to a distended old black bag which is rarely fastened up properly. She clings to it with very nicely shaped hands which are never gloved and often grubby. Yet I have rarely seen her in any room with other women in which she was not plainly – not merely in my eyes but to many others – the most attractive and interesting presence.[33]

She wasn't photogenic – 'I have never known anyone to whom the camera was so hostile . . . Usually the camera produces plain ugliness; the face of a savage woman with broad nostrils under a squat nose that was broken in her childhood.'[34]

Wells put her magnetism down to her air of courage, her self-possession and quiet confidence. Her hazel eyes were 'steady and tranquil', and her 'broad Tartar cheekbones' made her seem amiable even when in a bad mood.

While Wells struggled with his feelings, Moura continued to travel around Europe, and her absences caused H. G. distress just as they had Gorky.

In 1933 Gorky finally left Italy and settled in Russia. In March, before he left, Moura visited him in Sorrento one last time. It was a momentous visit. She arrived in the midst of a debate over what should be done with Gorky's archive of letters and papers. They contained material that would, in the eyes of Stalin, incriminate their authors – émigré Russian writers and intellectuals who had written to Gorky during the 1920s, trying to persuade him out of his defensiveness about the Soviet government. The letters – filled with anti-Stalinist sentiments and personal information, including remarks about people still in Russia – had all been gathered into a suitcase, but nobody could decide what to do with them. Gorky's son Max knew of the suitcase, and his secretary Kriuchkov probably did too. (And if they knew, Yagoda and his secret police knew as well.) But they couldn't decide between incriminating the people whose names filled the documents (and possibly Gorky himself) or angering Yagoda and Stalin.

A decision was made to entrust the suitcase to Moura, along with the key to a safe deposit box in Dresden which contained other archive material.[35] Moura was now in possession of a dangerous weapon that could result in hundreds of deaths.

A report was filed by MI5 that same year stating that despite being granted a visa Baroness Budberg was considered to be 'politically suspicious' and a Home Office warrant was placed on her. During a one-month stay in Britain just prior to her trip to Sorrento, her post was opened, her movements monitored and her phone tapped. The material collected – none of it conclusive – was added to her MI5 record.

As if she didn't already have enough to occupy her time and trouble her conscience, Moura had become involved with yet another new lover, and another twist was given to the spiral of espionage in which she was implicated.

Paul Scheffer was the London correspondent of the *Berliner Tageblatt*, a liberal, anti-Nazi newspaper. She might have met him through Epokha in Berlin, or through their shared social circles in London. Little would ever be known about Moura and Scheffer other than a few documents held by MI5, which had them both under surveillance.

Scheffer had begun his career as Moscow correspondent of the *Tageblatt*. During his seven-year stint he became an important and influential writer. His commentaries on Russian life under the Bolsheviks were blunt and deeply angered Stalin. In 1928 he wrote of the enforced exile to Siberia of many of the leading figures of the Revolution. And he predicted that Stalin's enforced collectivisation of Soviet agriculture – which Gorky had supported – would have disastrous consequences. Scheffer became *persona non grata* and was barred from the Soviet Union.

Was Moura's interest in Paul Scheffer personal or political? She was keen for inside information about the leading Nazis, who were on the verge of taking real power (she passed this information on to Lockhart, who was keen for 'Hitler stories' for his column, especially if they were sexually discreditable). During the period of their relationship – from early 1932 to at least the end of 1933 – Scheffer's predictions about collectivisation were coming horrifically true in the Ukraine. Mismanagement and conflict with peasants who didn't want to hand over their livestock to the state were bringing on a devastating famine which would eventually kill millions of people. In April 1933 Scheffer wrote a piece in the *Tageblatt* publicising the investigative reports by British journalist Gareth Jones (formerly Lloyd George's political secretary) which exposed the role of collectivisation in causing the famine.[36]

But the Soviet Union claimed that there was a hidden side to it. In 1938 it claimed that Scheffer had been a Nazi spy, and had himself been responsible for causing the famine. He had, the Soviets alleged, been a go-between for Goebbels and the Soviet traitor Mikhail Chernov, the Commissar for Trade for the Ukraine. Chernov had instituted policies designed to cause famine on instructions from the Nazi regime, con-veyed via Goebbels and Paul Scheffer.[37] During the Second World War, Scheffer went to America, where suspicion that he was a Nazi spy led to his arrest and interrogation. He was cleared, and subsequently worked with the Office of Strategic Services (the forerunner of the CIA) and served as a prosecution adviser at the Nuremberg trials.

Was Paul Scheffer secretly a Nazi, or willing to do their work? When they came to power in 1933 they took over ownership of the *Berliner Tageblatt*, and when Scheffer became editor in chief, Goebbels freed him of the obligation to publish Nazi propaganda. He wasn't free from pres-sure, though; eventually he resigned and left Germany.

It may be an extraordinary coincidence that Moura and Scheffer were lovers throughout the period when the Ukraine crisis was going on. Or it might not. They corresponded in German, and some of the letters were intercepted by MI5. Apart from some remarks related to pub-lishing, they were mainly love letters. 'I am sleepy,' Moura wrote, 'but in my sleep I see your sparkling eyes and your lower lip – and I wake up. I am very glad, my dear, that things have happened in the way they have . . . The world is empty around me.'[38]

Another, written on her headed notepaper ('Baroness Marie Budberg, Author's Representative, 3 Willoughby St. WC1'), proposed a driving holiday near London. She told him that she loved him 'tremendously'.[39] In 1933 she took a few moments from a holiday in Salzburg and Vienna with Wells to write to Scheffer: 'I have hardly a moment to myself,' she complained. 'We have seen so many people, Zweig, Freud, etc. And the little old person is pedantic, and exacting like all small greats.'[40]

That she could refer to H. G. so callously and dismissively could be just an attempt to forestall any jealousy on Scheffer's part. Or it might be a glimpse of her real feelings about Wells. He was devoted to her, and it sometimes exasperated her. She could be cruel. H. G. had once taken her to see the shop in Bromley High Street where he had been born in 1866. As the car drove slowly by, he pointed to a modest and shabby little shop and said with some pride, 'That's where I was born.'

Moura looked at the shop, glanced at Wells, and said sourly, 'I'm not surprised.'[41]

By 1933 H. G. was proposing to her at every opportunity, Gorky was pleading with her to go back to Russia with him, she was still involved in a passionate relationship with Constantine Benckendorff, and Paul Scheffer had been added to the list. All were being spied upon by the intelligence agencies of various countries. The only man who was not desperate for her was the one man she really wanted – Lockhart. He enjoyed his friendship with her and their periodic dalliances, and profited from her encouragement to write his memoirs, but he would not respond to her pleas to make her his own.

From time to time Moura saw friends from the old days, including Meriel Buchanan, who was enjoying a steady career as an author; she had already turned her experiences in Russia into three books, the first published in 1918 with Moura appearing anonymously as 'my Russian friend'. Meriel was married now to a Major Harold Knowling of the Welsh Guards, and had a little boy. Moura wasn't impressed, referring to the Major as 'that blasted husband of Meriel's'.[42]

Marriage was a sore subject. While on holiday in Austria, between sightseeing and writing love letters to Scheffer, Moura had to endure Wells' continual barrage of proposals.

'This is only the beginning of our life together,' Wells said to her in Salzburg. 'In a little while we will marry.'

Moura was irritated. 'But why *marry*?' she asked. She could sense that in marrying her he hoped to cage her, keep her by him always – or until he found her too troublesome. 'I'd be a bore if you had me always,' she told him.[43]

It was in this mood that she complained to Scheffer about the pedantic 'little old person'. Lockhart's attitude to Wells was similar; after a dinner party at which Russian politics was discussed, he commented, 'H. G. is not impressive. He is like a board-school teacher who has all his facts marshalled and who produces platitudes with the manner of a great original thinker . . . He is a vain old boy.'[44] There was undoubtedly some jealousy in his summing-up – not a lover's jealousy but that of a struggling writer for a great and successful one, and of a thwarted professional diplomat for a lionised amateur. But Lockhart wasn't alone in his view. The radical thinker of the late Victorian era was looking increasingly out of touch with the modern world, and growing irascible at its refusal to take his advice.

Wells had noticed that Moura was sending telegrams to Russia while they were away, but thought little of it at the time. He didn't know of her other affairs. The more often Moura refused his offer of marriage, the more fixated and obsessed he became. Moura commented to her friend Enid Bagnold (author of *National Velvet*), 'I'm not going to marry him. He only thinks I am. I'm not such a fool.' She wasn't going to be turned into a housekeeper.[45] Enid herself had nearly dipped into an affair with Wells, decades earlier, and was forever captivated by his attractiveness – fixated by his 'extraordinary little blue eyes' smiling in 'that blunt, unmoulded face' with its cocky, Cyrano-like nose; they were 'wildly seablue' and she found it heavenly to be an object of attraction for 'that greedy little boy'. And yet Enid liked Moura, and admired the way she handled him.[46]

At the end of their Austrian holiday in July 1933, leaving Wells to return home alone, Moura rushed off to Istanbul to rendezvous with Gorky aboard the Soviet steamer that was carrying him from Naples to the Crimea. Moura bade him a last farewell, and he sailed on into the Black Sea. He would never return to the West. He had been given three fabulous houses, and had his adoring followers and access to his wealth, but he lost his freedom.

Only a couple of months after his return to Russia, Moura wrote to say she was planning a brief trip to visit him there. She apparently had no doubts about her ability to gain entry and exit visas for a country where this was practically an impossibility. And so it proved. Once Gorky was home, Moura mysteriously acquired the ability to enter and leave the USSR without let or hindrance – as if the two things were somehow connected.

Meanwhile, Lockhart's memoirs had reached completion. He sent the manuscript to Moura for her approval. She thought it was '*very good*' but wanted changes made to the chapters relating to their relationship. She asked him to refer to her as 'Madame Benckendorff'. He didn't comply. But he did give way to her insistence that he remove the passages about 'the spying business' which gave her 'a Mata Hari touch which is quite unnecessary for the book . . . and quite impossible for me'.[47] He also gutted his account of the plot with the Latvian riflemen, detaching himself from the heart of the conspiracy, in line with the version that had been cooked up between him, Moura and Yakov Peters in the Kremlin in 1918.

The book was published in November 1932 as *Memoirs of a British Agent*, and became a bestseller. The following year it was adapted for the cinema by Warner Bros. Starring Leslie Howard as 'Stephen Locke' and Kay Francis as 'Elena Moura', the film was titled *British Agent* and directed by Michael Curtiz (who would later direct *Casablanca*). The film, which was poorly scripted, was less successful than the book. The story of the love affair between 'Locke' and 'Elena Moura' was simple and sensational. Elena is a Cheka agent set to spy on Locke, who is planning to assassinate Lenin. Elena gives Trotsky (the chief villain) information leading the Cheka to Locke's hiding place, and Trotsky orders the building destroyed with Locke inside it. But having fallen in love with the British agent, when the confrontation comes Elena sacrifices herself for him, choosing to die with him. Both are reprieved, however, when Lenin recovers from his wounds and orders an amnesty for all political prisoners.

Moura was unfazed by the film, and seemed to enjoy the notoriety it gave her. One of its most interesting features was the portrayal of her as spying for the Cheka and then sacrificing herself. Neither of these aspects of the story were publicly known at the time; Lockhart had excised both from the book. Given the very short production time, it may be that screenwriter Laird Doyle, who worked in consultation with Lockhart on the script, had access to information not in the book.

If anything in the film really moved or upset Moura, it might have been the ending, in which Elena and Locke leave Moscow together, bound for England. Yet again artistic 'truth' trumped empirical fact.

Lockhart continued battling his vices. He complained in his diary that he must make 'one last strenuous effort to lead an ascetic life. Surely by now I have reached the age when other things than drink, self-indulgence and whoring will satisfy me'.[48] He was never to reach that age.

In an attempt to build on the success of *Memoirs of a British Agent*, he began working diligently on its sequel. When she saw the manuscript, Moura thought it better than its predecessor. But she was rattled by the accounts of his affairs with other women between 1918 and 1930 – seven of them ('You go crescendo!' she told him). And she was mortified to learn that he had been given two offers of postings to Russia in 1919, while she was doing everything in her power to be reunited with him, and had declined both of them. 'Why??' she asked.[49] She had evidently forgotten (and he omitted to mention it in the book) that he was under sentence of death if he ever set foot in Russia again.

20

A Cheat and a Liar

1933–1934

Despite his devotion to Moura, Wells had not lost his philandering urge.

Hilda Matheson (known as 'Stoker'), head of the Talks strand on the BBC, persuaded H. G. to take part. The chance to disburse his wisdom to a rapt nation was irresistible to him. His topics included 'Can Democracy Survive?', 'World Peace' and 'Whither Britain'.[1] He became an overnight radio star and he and Hilda became friends. At this time Hilda was the lover of Vita Sackville-West, but Wells knew nothing of her sexual preferences and, early on in their friendship, made an attempt to seduce her in his flat. Writing to Vita she complained that due to the flat's position at the top of the block, 'No shouts would have been heard anywhere. So I had to do the best I could'. Violent resistance would only serve to excite him, she believed, so she 'took it with the utmost lightness and laughed at him . . . and by the end he had become ruefully avuncular'.[2]

On another occasion, wintering at Grasse, he lunched with his old flame, the novelist Elizabeth von Arnim – known as 'Little e'. He told her afterwards he had enjoyed her latest book but castigated her playfully, 'I could spank you (very lovingly and wanting to kiss the place afterward) for some of your involved sentences.'[3] He might have been devoted to Moura but he could never be satisfied with just one woman.

In late summer 1933 Moura and H. G. planned a holiday at Portmeirion, the faux Italian village that Clough Williams-Ellis had begun building in a little enclave on the North Wales coast. But on 28 July Moura sent him a letter confirming what they had feared and had been joking about for some time. She was pregnant.[4] She was forty-one years old and Wells was sixty-seven.

The news was hardly welcome for either of them and Moura decided to have an abortion. She seemed very blasé about the whole affair, calling it a small and unimportant matter that she would hardly have bothered to write to him about had they not been planning to spend part of the holiday at the home of Wells' friend Christabel Aberconway at Bodnant near Llandudno; Moura would have to miss the first two weeks of the visit as she would be away in Europe undergoing the operation. (Abortion was not only illegal in Britain in 1933; the law had recently been tightened.)

She told H. G. that he could not write to her at the place where she would be staying (which she didn't specify); instead he could write to another address and she would arrange to collect any post.

Was she really pregnant? If this was a ruse, it must have been a cover for something very important – not merely some joy trip with Paul Scheffer or Cony Benckendorff. Portentously, she told H. G. not to be alarmed. She assured him that she was thinking of him and asked him to take care of Kira, Tania and Paul if she should fail to return.[5] Abortion was a risky procedure, and the only European country in which it was legal was Russia, where it had been decriminalised in 1919. If this was her secret destination, she might have been as worried about the visit as she was about the operation. She'd had letters from Gorky complaining that he was now unable to leave the country. Did she think the same thing might happen to her?

It didn't. She either had the operation or completed whatever business the pregnancy was a cover for, and was soon back with H. G., rejoining him in time for the last part of the holiday at Portmeirion and Bodnant.

Now that Gorky was lost to her, she continued in earnest to cement her relationship with Wells, despite turning down his persistent offers of marriage. Paul Scheffer and Cony Benckendorff provided passion, and Lockhart was her true love, but without Gorky in her life, H. G. was her refuge, her source of safety and influence.

Although she was still only a visitor, Moura was becoming settled in London. She acquired a flat at 88 Knightsbridge, which she shared with her old friend Liuba Hicks, now a widow. 'Hickie', who had suffered from tuberculosis for years, had died in 1930. Liuba had been left with nothing and was supporting herself by running a small dress shop.

Despite coming from different backgrounds, Liuba and Moura had their shared experiences in Russia to keep them together, and despite both wanting to be the centres of their own worlds they remained friends.[6]

There was no longer any need to visit Estonia to see the children – they were all here in England. Kira and Hugh Clegg were living in London. Paul had moved to England in 1933 (leaving behind the Russian name 'Pavel'); he studied agriculture and took up farming in Yorkshire. In 1934 Tania came to London, got work in an office and moved into a room in the same building as Moura and Liuba. She found them both difficult. Moura would invite her to parties but never introduced her to anyone, holding forth among the mêlée and leaving Tania alone with nobody to talk to.

Moura had not lost her love of her bed. She conducted her morning's work from it, and liked to stay there until lunchtime, making appointments for the remainder of the day and writing her letters. Often she lunched with friends and would visit H. G. for an hour or two in the afternoon, then in the early evening invited guests would drop in for sherry; after an hour or so she would shoo everyone out, but would expect someone to escort her out for dinner if she was not dining with H. G. At weekends she would usually accompany H. G. to the country homes of his rich, influential and famous acquaintances.

H. G. was still convinced that Moura would marry him. He arranged a huge party at the Soho restaurant Quo Vadis to celebrate their 'marriage'. It was a wedding reception without a wedding. All their friends were invited. The guest list included the cartoonist David Low, Violet Hunt, Max Beerbohm, Maurice Baring, Harold Nicolson, Juliette Huxley, Lady Cunard and Enid Bagnold. When Enid went up to Moura to congratulate her, she smiled and said she had no intention of marrying him. In the middle of the dinner, Moura announced to the guests that the whole event had been a joke. 'We tricked you. We never got married today and have no plans to do so in the future.'[7]

Given that H. G. Wells was unlikely to play such a 'joke' on his friends, he must have been hoping that the prospect of public shame would force her to play along and marry him. In making her announcement, Moura must have achieved some payback for having been railroaded into the party, and at the same time impressed upon him once and for all that her refusals were serious.

After the dinner the guests were invited to Wells' flat in Bickenhall

Mansions, where hired gilt chairs had been laid out in rows in anticipation of a performance by the harpist Maria Korchinska, otherwise known as Countess Benckendorff. Whose unfortunate idea it can have been to ask the wife of Moura's lover to perform at her bogus wedding supper is not known. The Countess did not make her anticipated appearance. Enid Bagnold, surprised, recalled that nobody thought to move the chairs out of the way so the guests sat on them in rows until the end of the evening.[8] The couple borrowed Enid's home in Rottingdean, Sussex, for their 'honeymoon', which went ahead as planned.

Afterwards, H. G. continued living alone with his daughter-in-law Marjorie as his housekeeper and secretary.

Like Gorky before him, Wells was perpetually upset by Moura's constant flitting abroad. She always told him where she was going, and he trusted her, but couldn't shake off a nagging suspicion. Eventually, by a freak accident, the truth about one of her liaisons came out. Their relationship would never be quite the same again.

In 1934 H. G. asked her to accompany him on a trip to the United States, explaining, with a persistent, forlorn hope, that they must marry prior to going; unmarried couples received dreadful hounding from the puritanical press (not much had changed since Gorky and Maria Andreyeva's tour in 1905). She told him that in that case he would have to travel on his own. He also asked her to go with him to Russia later in the year as he wished to meet Stalin.

Wells' ego was a vast entity. He was attempting a one-man crusade to bring about world peace and to influence it according to his vision of a unified world state. To achieve this he wanted to meet up with both President Roosevelt and Stalin and engineer a rapprochement between them. Where legions of diplomats were failing, he saw no reason why Mr H. G. Wells should not succeed. Moura assured him that Russia was out of bounds for her and that if allowed entry, she would, like Gorky, probably not be allowed to leave. She told him that she might even be shot.

He travelled alone, leaving for America aboard the RMS *Olympic* in April. He was not happy. He wanted a lover in his old age who would stay by his side, caring for his every need and providing companionship. He was beginning to accept that it was never going to happen with Moura. During the voyage he wrote to Christabel Aberconway:

I think I am really going to break up with Moura. She's lovely to me
– she's adorable – but I can't stand any more of this semi-detached life.
I'm tired, I'm bored by a Moura whom I can't bring to America & who
rambles round corners & for all I know is a drug trafficker or a spy or
any fantastic thing.[9]

He was closer to the truth than he realised. As soon as he was safely off
on his transatlantic voyage, Moura put in motion a plan to visit Gorky
in the Soviet Union. She had written to him that it would give her joy
to see him in Moscow, but she believed she would find life there too
hard for her now. Instead she intended to visit him during one of his
stays at his dacha on the Crimean coast.[10]

In July, after his return from America, H. G. made another attempt to
persuade her to go to Russia with him, and again she insisted that it
would be impossible. She told him she was going to Estonia. She suggested that he make his homeward journey via Estonia and join her for
a month's break at Kallijärv. He agreed. When the time came, H. G. saw
her off tenderly from Croydon airport, kissing her goodbye and watching
her smiling face as the plane taxied off. It was the last glimpse he would
have of the Moura he thought he knew.[11]

He and Gip set off for Russia a week later.

In Moscow and Leningrad they attended several literary parties at
which they were introduced to those writers – including Aleksei Tolstoy
– who had been able to reconcile themselves with the regime and had
not yet been killed or sent to Siberia. Wells found the restrictions placed
on his movements very tiresome; he became irritable and unwell. He
had a conversation with Stalin, hampered by their inability to speak each
other's languages. Wells was suspicious of Stalin, thinking him a potential despot, but he had to admit that the country was being governed
and becoming successful. Despite Stalin's disagreeableness ('a very
reserved and self-centred fanatic, a jealous monopoliser of power'),
Wells decided that he was good for the country. 'All suspicion of hidden
emotional tensions ceased for ever, after I had talked to him for a few
minutes . . . I have never met a man more candid, fair and honest.'[12] His
assessment was about as accurate as his first summation of Moura in
1920. Once again H. G. Wells had been hoodwinked by his Soviet hosts.

And then he made a dreadful discovery. A couple of days after his talk
with Stalin, Wells was taken to dine with Gorky at his huge dacha near

Moscow.[13] Wells was pushing for freedom of expression in Russia, a sentiment with which the Gorky of 1920 would have been in passionate agreement. However, this was a new Gorky that greeted Wells. Although looking little different despite the passage of years, he had turned into an 'unqualified Stalinite'.[14] An argument ensued, clumsily conducted through an interpreter.

In the awkward atmosphere that followed, the interpreter, making conversation, asked Wells about his itinerary. Wells mentioned that he would be spending time in Estonia with his friend Baroness Budberg. The interpreter was pleasantly surprised; he remarked blithely that the Baroness had been with Gorky just the previous week.

'But I had a letter from her in Estonia,' Wells said, 'three days ago!'[15]

The interpreter, embarrassed and confused, fell silent. 'Surprise' wasn't the word to express what Wells felt. He managed to contain himself and continued his conversation with Gorky, 'with a sort of expectation that suddenly Moura might come suddenly smiling round a corner to greet me'. As the party got ready for dinner, Wells, unable to let the subject lie, brought it up again. Gorky confirmed that Moura had been to visit him three times in the past year. There was a hasty consultation between the interpreter and the official guide, who explained to Wells that 'there had to be a certain secrecy about Moura's visits to Russia, because it might embarrass her in Estonia and with her Russian friends in London'. It would be better, Wells was told, if he didn't mention her visits to anyone.[16]

With those few words, 'my splendid Moura was smashed to atoms'. Wells didn't sleep for the rest of his time in Russia. 'I was wounded as I had never been wounded by any human being before. It was unbelievable. I lay in bed and wept like a disappointed child.' No excuse he could imagine would explain why Moura had not told him she was coming to Russia or waited for him there. He felt betrayed, abandoned, 'a companionless man'.

Before leaving Russia, he cancelled the tickets for his and Moura's journey from Estonia to Britain and made a codicil to his will, cutting her out of it. He was determined to excise her from his life altogether. He intended to skip the trip to Estonia and fly straight from Leningrad to Stockholm, but he couldn't help himself; he had to see her.

Moura met him at Tallinn airport, as self-possessed as ever, and as full of affection, despite his having sent her a postcard hinting at what he now knew. Wells stewed silently and waited for the moment to interrogate her. 'That was a funny story of your being in Moscow,' he said. She asked him how he heard of it, and he fenced with her for a few moments. But he hadn't the patience for it. 'Moura, you are a cheat and a liar,' he said. 'Why did you do this to me?'

She claimed it had been arranged suddenly after she got to Estonia. Gorky had made the arrangements at short notice, and she hadn't been able to resist the chance to see her country again. 'You know what Russia is to me,' she said. But why had she not waited for H. G., knowing that he would soon be in Russia? She claimed she couldn't risk being seen publicly with him in Russia. She denied that she had been there three times, insisting that it must have been the interpreter's mistake. 'You are the man I love,' she told him.

Wells wished he could believe her, but his innocent trust in her, which had remained unsullied for fourteen years, had been utterly ruined.

But, as with Odette, he couldn't make the break he knew he ought to make. They talked, they quarrelled, they made love during their stay at Kallijärv, 'but we had the canker of this trouble between us', Wells recalled. She came to see him off at Tallinn – 'For she loves partings and meetings; she does them superbly.'

H. G. wrote down those impressions a year later, in summer 1935.[17] They still hadn't separated. 'We have got on together because of a real inability to part,' he wrote. 'She held on tenaciously.' He had become suspicious and jealous, and Moura had become defensive. He watched everything she did. Wells went and stayed with Christabel Aberconway at Bodnant. 'We all cheat,' Christabel told him after he had poured out the story. In her view, women cheated on their men for one good reason: 'Not because we don't love you, but because you are such unreasonable things that you would not let us live anything you would call a life if we didn't.' He grumbled, but Christabel knew him better than he knew himself. 'Stick to her, H. G., and shut your eyes,' she told him. 'Of course you love each other. Isn't that good enough?'

Wells didn't think it was; he either wanted her whole – 'skin and bones, nerves and dreams' – or not at all. He no longer trusted her. 'Like a child she believes a thing as she says it,' he wrote, 'and she is indignant, extremely indignant, at disbelief. I do not now believe a single statement she makes without extensive tacit qualifications.'[18]

But he couldn't let her go, and they went on the way they were – sometimes recapturing the spirit of their old happy friendship, at other times they argued, slammed doors, stormed out, but were drawn back to each other. They holidayed at Marseilles, and spent Christmas at Somerset Maugham's villa at Cap Ferrat, where Wells enjoyed a burst of creative inspiration. He worked on a film treatment for his fantastical story 'The Man Who Could Work Miracles'. When Moura travelled back to England without him, H. G. took up with Constance Coolidge, an American widow who reminded him of Moura. The two women met shortly after, and Moura was 'amused and on her mettle' to see H. G. apparently in love with another woman. She teased him about it.

One day H. G. found her in tears, a telegram in her hand. She let him see it. It was from Estonia; Micky was seriously ill. Wells told her she should fly to Estonia immediately. 'You'll be angry again if I go,' said Moura tearfully.

'You'll never forgive yourself if Micky dies,' he told her, and helped her pack.

While she was in Estonia, he sailed for America, where he met Roosevelt and published articles about the New Deal. On his way home, he wrote to Moura an ultimatum: 'Either come into my life completely, or get out of it.' It was hopeless, and Moura knew it. Whenever he issued these declarations and demands, she would say to him in her wounded manner, 'Why do you write such unkind things?' and resume their relationship with 'invincible imperturbability'.

Wells, of course, did not discover exactly what Moura had been doing in Russia.

In May 1934 she had heard the news that Gorky's son, Max had, died, apparently of pneumonia. He was hurriedly buried the following day. He was only thirty-seven and seemingly fit, so it was surprising that he should be struck down by such an illness. Gorky was devastated; he never really recovered.[19] In order to try to stop him grieving for the death of his son, Stalin had sent him on a river trip along the Volga.

'I embrace you very tenderly,' Moura wrote to Gorky from London. 'My dear, my most valuable treasure'.[20] Immediately afterwards, she flew off, ostensibly to Estonia but actually to Moscow, leaving behind the still innocently trusting H. G. And evidently this wasn't the first time she had been allowed in and out of the USSR to visit Gorky.

So much for the danger of being shot if she set foot in Russia. C. P. Snow, who became one of Moura's friends in later life, said that she 'was the only woman Stalin would speak of with respect'. Baron Boothby, the controversial Conservative MP, agreed: 'She was treated in Moscow like a visiting princess.'[21] It was apparently around this time that the French Deuxième Bureau picked up the rumours of Baroness Budberg's travels to the USSR and noted them in her file.

Gorky himself was coming more and more under the control of Stalin. The holiday on the Volga was a special fillip to help restore him to his former Bolshevik self. His commitment to the Party was beginning to slip after the death of Max and the realisation of how restricted his own travels were. Life in Russia was not quite as he had expected it to be.

When Wells arrived in Moscow, Gorky had just returned from the river voyage and Moura had slipped away to Estonia. If it hadn't been for the interpreter's momentary gaffe, H. G. would never have known. Writing from Estonia, probably when Wells was with her and remonstrating with her about her deceit, Moura wrote to Gorky.

> All the trouble is still not over, but it is settling down. In my thoughts I am always with you, especially after the visit to see you. Everything here seems unreal, devoid of meaning. It is harder to live here. My dear friend, how are you? You know how difficult it is for me to write to you. Neither you nor I like certain words. But you truly feel how strong and indestructible this closeness is to you.[22]

She was surely lying to him just as glibly as to Wells. Neither man trusted her now. But neither man could bear to be without her, and each wished that he could have her all to himself, permanently by his side.

If anyone heard anything close to the truth it must have been Lockhart. She met up with him after her return to England. She regaled him with her troubles, and afterwards wrote to apologise for being 'such an egocentric ass' and giving him such a dull evening. 'But it helped me a lot. *Please* tell me *que tu ne m'en veux pas** and that we'll have another, better evening.' She added: 'And you'll never mention to anybody what I told

---

* coll.: you aren't cross with me.

you, will you. You know I never "complain" as a rule, and you're the only person I could make such "revelations" to.'[23]

It is unlikely that she told even Lockhart anything approaching the whole truth. Her involvement in the Gorky affair was deeper than anyone could have imagined. She still had possession of the suitcase of letters she had carried away from Sorrento and the key to the Dresden safe deposit box – both hidden away somewhere known only to her.

21

The Mysterious Death of Maxim Gorky

1934–1936

Even though he wrote down a detailed narrative of his shocking discovery in Moscow, his confrontation with Moura and of the disputes that harried them in the months that followed, H. G. never committed to paper the full account of Moura's claims about her activities in Russia. It might well be that at the time of his writing in 1935 she hadn't yet resorted to her last line of defence. That probably occurred in late 1935 or early 1936.

Wells confided to his son, Anthony West, what Moura had told him when confronted again with the evidence of her visits to Russia. Having reached a point where her nonchalant dismissals and her charms were no longer sufficient to mollify him, she told him an incredible story.[1]

Moura claimed that her life had not been her own since 1916, at the height of the Great War, when the Germans caught her spying for the imperial Russian government. Under sentence of death, she had been turned, and began spying on the Russians for the Germans. Ever since, she confessed, she had been forced by circumstance to do the bidding of whichever government had the greatest hold on her. Hence her trips to Russia at the demand of Stalin, for the purpose of keeping Gorky pacified and happy. What had happened to her, she said, was the consequence of revolution; one must do what one has to do, or die.

H. G. was inclined to believe the story – and Anthony certainly believed it when he heard it later. But Wells was appalled at what he regarded as a mere excuse. In his opinion, he said, there were 'things that could not be done in any circumstances – things so utterly ignoble that it would be preferable to die'. Moura laughed at him, but forgave him his moral glibness. She reminded him that he had 'never known what it was to be absolutely helpless'. As long as survival was possible, as long as one was not so damaged physically that death was inevitable, 'one more day of life was worth whatever it might cost. Anything might happen in the course of another twenty-four hours.'[2]

And that was all she would tell him. Aside from that, the ashes would have to be left unraked, and episodes from her past that she would rather not relive would have to remain untold. If H. G. wanted to continue with their relationship, he would have to take her on her own terms, 'the first of which was that all her skeletons should stay in the dark in the cupboards in which she had put them'.[3]

What Moura told H. G. was a mixture of truth and lies. When Tania read Anthony's account half a century later, she recognised the fundamental falsehood at the heart of it: it was quite impossible for Moura to have been in any position in 1916 where she could have been caught spying by the Germans and sentenced to death. That would require her to have been in German territory, which was impossible.[4] Tania denied the possibility of her mother having been a spy.

And yet there were facts that Tania never knew – that nobody knew at the time. Moura didn't need to go near the front lines to be a spy during the war. Tania knew nothing about 'Madame B' and her salon in Petrograd where Russians sympathetic to Germany gathered and were spied on by their hostess for Kerensky's secret service. The gatherings were run by German agents who were willing to murder anyone seen as a threat to their security.[5] For years afterwards, Moura was rumoured in Petrograd to be a German spy, and only British SIS agents such as George Hill, and probably Lockhart, knew the truth of it – that she had pretended to spy for the Germans while working for Russia.

The rest of the tale Moura told H. G. was a fair representation of the forces that had pushed and pulled her one way or another ever since. She had been to places – physical and emotional – that even the prodigious imagination of H. G. Wells could not encompass. She had suffered dreadful privations; he had not. She had looked death in the face and been beset on all sides by state-enacted mass murder, in a culture in which the people of her class had been officially declared less than human. Only a moral theorist who had never known anything but safety and security could believe that there were things 'so utterly ignoble that it would be preferable to die'. Only those men and women who had been obliged to make that choice were qualified to judge.

And so life went on. By 1936, when H. G. had moved into his new house at 13 Hanover Terrace, Regent's Park, which he planned as his home for his 'concluding years', he had given her a key. 'Maybe there is a limit to estrangement,' he wrote, 'just as there is an aphelion set to the path of a planet. I doubt if we shall ever have quite done with each other. There is an irrational gravitation between us.'[6]

He would undoubtedly have agreed with Arthur Koestler, who, although he liked Moura, described her as 'a man-eating flower, not unlike one of those insect-devouring orchids if not as pretty'.[7]

H. G.'s prediction was correct. In spite of the rupture that had occurred, he would always love her. The one thing he could never reconcile was that she was his equal and an independent person. He knew he needed her but could never quite understand why, because he couldn't entirely value her for herself.

Their close friend Peter Ritchie Calder, the Scottish socialist writer, believed that Moura 'was H. G.'s match, mentally. With her quick wit and unexpectedly wide knowledge of many subjects, she could hold her own with him. More than that, she could handle him in his sometimes querulous moods – with a laugh or a joke or even a regal snub at his expense.' Ritchie Calder saw Moura as 'a Catherine Parr to H. G., a tower of strength to him, a fount of spiritual consolation'.[8]

But she also brought him anxiety and self-reproach. That was Moura's way, and she could do no other.

Their relationship worked as long as they were in London and could go about their lives separately. When they holidayed abroad and were forced to be in each other's company the strain would show, especially during those tense times after 1934. 'It has such a dreadful sapping character about it,' Moura wrote to Lockhart at the end of that year, when she and H. G. were staying with Somerset Maugham at his villa. (She liked Maugham, who had worked for the SIS in Russia during the British intervention in 1918–1919, although sometimes his viciousness exasperated her.) 'I feel imprisoned in a net of considerations which are the most deadly of all – compassion, pride, self-reproach.'[9] Lockhart was on the verge of a nostalgic voyage to the Orient, and hoped to write a book about it.[10] Half-joking, she implored him, 'Darling, take me away with you to the East.'

Meanwhile, Gorky's health was declining, and he was missing Moura. She was a fount of spiritual consolation for him too, and of anxiety. He felt ill and lonely, and he needed her. He wrote asking her to visit him again. It wasn't possible, she told him, blaming it on unspecified 'dark forces' which had become 'unexpectedly stronger' and 'now seem insurmountable'. H. G.'s angry suspicions, perhaps? Or maybe some more powerful force was keeping her out of Russia. 'Don't be angry with me,' she wrote, 'and do not blame me, my dear and only person. This is not at all easy for me, as you might think. But I will come, of course. Maybe a bit later.'[11]

In September 1935 Gorky travelled to the Crimea for his winter sojourn. He had a dacha there in the Tesseli area of the seaside town of Foros.[12] The coast here was rocky and picturesque, a little like Sorrento. His movements had become ever more restricted; he could stay at one of his homes or commute between them; nowhere else. A friend heard him mumbling to himself, 'I'm so very tired. It's as if they'd put up a fence around me and I can't step over. I'm surrounded, trapped. No way forward or back! I'm not used to this.'[13] Moura visited whenever she could, and her visits must have had the full authorisation of the headquarters in the Lubyanka, if not from the Kremlin itself. Genrikh Yagoda, whose security and intelligence department had evolved from the Cheka into the GPU and now the almighty NKVD,[14] must have known and approved of every visit, as must Stalin. Not only was the Soviet Union now the most tightly controlled territory in the world, but Maxim Gorky was one of its most guarded assets. Yagoda, via Pyotr Kriuchkov, was even providing her with cash, without receipts, presumably to cover her considerable travel expenses. And a letter written by Gorky indicates that on one visit she was accompanied by Stalin himself.[15]

The simple truth was that the USSR needed Gorky – the people needed him as a symbol, and the Soviet regime needed to control that symbol. Not only as a figurehead but as a writer of propaganda. (In 1934 he published a notorious book hailing the completion of the White Sea–Baltic Canal as a triumph of Soviet achievement. In fact, it had been achieved with slave labour, under Yagoda's direction, and tens of thousands of workers had died in its building.) And just as his country needed Gorky, Gorky needed Moura. Even though he knew that their days of being master and 'wife' were long gone, she brought him comfort and joy.

That was the simple truth; the more complex truth was wrapped up in the obligations and deceits Moura incurred through her involvement – the lies to Wells, the entanglement of other members of her family, and the risk to her reputation and safety in the West. And that truth only Moura really knew about. There was also the matter of the dangerous archive of letters to Gorky from the anti-Stalinist Russian émigrés which was still in her keeping. Gorky was anxious about it, Yagoda wanted it, and Moura had it, cached away somewhere safe.

Later that year, back in London, Moura received a surprising and unsettling visit.

Timosha Peshkova, widow of Gorky's son, Max, along with her mother-in-law, Yekaterina Peshkova, Gorky's first and only legal wife, had been allowed out of the USSR to clear up the last remaining items of Gorky's property at the Sorrento villa. Both women had had long and intimate working relationships with the Cheka and NKVD; Timosha indeed had had an affair with Yagoda. While she was outside the Soviet Union, Timosha travelled to London, where she called on Moura in the hope of persuading her to relinquish Gorky's archive. She failed, and went back to Moscow empty-handed.[16]

H. G., despite being in his seventieth year, carried on having affairs. He had a fling with Constance Coolidge, a rich American divorcee, and with the journalist Martha Gellhorn. He was lonely, and hated it; he had a child's fear of loneliness, he told Constance. 'But I suppose I want my woman at my beck and call. I don't want to follow her about. I want her to follow me about.' It maddened him that he couldn't have that with Moura. 'She is always flitting off. I scream with rage when I am left alone, like a bad child.'[17] He was still the 'greedy little boy' Enid Bagnold had been smitten by more than twenty years earlier. In H. G.'s eyes (those sparkling sea-blue eyes) it was Moura's fault that he had to go on having affairs. As for whose fault it had been during the decades of affairs before her, he didn't comment.

His relationship with Constance became largely one of letters. The one with Martha Gellhorn came to nothing, but Wells continued his search for the elusive 'shadow lover', that person who would mirror him both sexually and intellectually and look after him into his old age. She remained unobtainable and he would have to settle for the often-absent Moura to fulfil that role from her flat at 81 Cadogan

Square (whither she and Tania had moved after their home in Knightsbridge was pulled down).

While he fumed over Moura's absences and deceptions, Wells managed to continue his work. Among other things, he co-wrote screenplays based on two of his stories. *The Man Who Could Work Miracles* and *Things to Come* (based on *The Shape of Things to Come*) were both released in 1936, both produced by Alexander Korda, the British-Hungarian movie mogul. Moura knew Korda, possibly through the émigré community in London, or perhaps through the film deals she had negotiated on Gorky's behalf during the 1920s. Korda had left Hungary in 1919 to escape the counter-revolutionary White Terror. (Michael Curtiz, director of *British Agent* and *Casablanca*, was also a Hungarian émigré who left in 1919.) It was Moura who introduced Korda to H. G. Wells and initiated their collaboration.

Korda was also acquainted with Lockhart, who dined with him at Sibyl Colefax's house in May 1935, together with the Prince of Wales and Wallis Simpson. The Prince of Wales showed his political colours at the gathering; according to Lockhart the Prince 'came out very strong for friendship with Germany: never heard him talk so definitely about any subject before'.[18]

For the time being H. G. and Moura enjoyed being part of the movie crowd, especially if it included royalty. And Wells would not have to wait much longer for Moura's visits to Russia to end.

At the beginning of 1936, H. G. sailed home from a trip to America. As he walked down the platform at Waterloo station, dodging the inevitable reporters, he saw Moura waiting for him. She jokingly accused him of having another lover while he had been away. Yes, he replied in kind; he had been unfaithful to the very best of his ability. A weight fell away from him. He believed at last that he had lost the obsession with her and that their relationship could now enter a more relaxed phase, free from his obsessive jealousy.[19]

Moura continued to dart in and out as she pleased. They spent weekends away together, had scintillating conversations and made love in a comfortable rather than passionate manner.

At the end of May H. G. noticed that Moura seemed depressed and would begin crying for no reason that he could fathom. She would not tell him the cause of her distress.

In March she had secretly travelled to the Crimea for a short visit to Gorky at Tesseli. In April, back in England, she sent what was to be her last letter to him. 'My dear friend,' she wrote, 'it is now almost a month since I have left you and yet it seems that I will wake up, come to disturb you at your desk, help working in the garden and everything else that makes life pleasant.' She told him it had struck her 'how inseparable and valuable my relationship to you is, my dear'.[20]

Then, not long after receiving Moura's letter, Gorky heard news that both of his beloved grandchildren were ill with influenza. Despite his own poor health, on 26 May he left his nurse and companion, Lipa, to go to Moscow to visit them.

Some said that he became ill on the train as a result of a cold draught from the windows; others that he was ill before he left Tesseli. Still others believed that Gorky did not become ill until several days after visiting the children, and that he caught their infection. Influenza in a person with Gorky's tuberculosis would be very serious. In *Pravda* it was stated that he was stricken with illness on 1 June – after he had returned to his home near Moscow. Seventeen physicians gathered around his bedside.

In Moscow, the first round of Stalin's infamous show trials, by means of which he would eventually purge all his rivals and their allies and supporters, were about to get under way. Ultimately, most of the prominent Bolsheviks still surviving from the era of the Revolution would be arrested, tried and executed. There would be only two notable exceptions – Stalin himself and Trotsky, who was in exile abroad. Proceedings had begun in secret the previous year, with the arrest and interrogation of Lev Kamenev, the former deputy chairman of the Council of People's Commissars, and Grigory Zinoviev, the former head of the Petrograd Soviet and Northern Commune. After Lenin's death, Stalin, Kamenev and Zinoviev had formed a triumvirate which had ruled the Soviet Union for a while. In the struggle for dominance that followed, Stalin was the victor, and from the mid-1920s he had become effective autocrat of the USSR. But they were still alive, still a threat and needed to be purged. They were arrested and interrogated under the direction of Yagoda (who would himself be purged during the third round of trials in 1938).

Kamenev had been Gorky's friend. Zinoviev had been his bitter enemy. Now, facing trial and execution, they both appealed to him for support. Gorky was still worshipped by the masses, and had never been able to ignore a plea for help, even from an old enemy. Stalin, who planned many more such trials and executions, realised that Gorky had become more of a liability than an asset. But to dispose of him through trial and execution would be unthinkable. For Stalin, Gorky's illness, if it should prove fatal, would be a blessed coincidence.

The NKVD had a sophisticated toxicology department in which they developed poisons and biological weapons including pneumococcus bacteria capable of inducing pneumonia. Rather than putting Gorky on trial and upsetting the Russian people, what better than exposing him to a deadly infection?[21] For a man known to suffer from lung disease, such a death would be expected anyway and nothing sinister would be suspected. Several other members of Gorky's household, including the superintendent, his wife and the cook, all became ill with what was diagnosed as angina. They displayed symptoms similar to Gorky's, although none had had direct contact with him. Yet of all those who sat with him throughout his illness not one fell ill.

Within days, Moura arrived at his bedside. Another extraordinary coincidence. How had she been informed of his illness, obtained a visa and organised the journey so quickly? Possibly it was a pre-planned visit that just happened to coincide with Gorky's sudden illness. Or possibly not. According to a close friend, she was collected from her home in Knightsbridge by a black limousine which had been sent by Ivan Maisky, the Soviet Ambassador. She flew to Berlin and then on to Moscow on 5 June; her entry into the USSR was not marked in her passport.[22]

Not for the first or last time, Tania was required to provide a cover for her mother's absence; she wrote to tell H. G. that Moura had become ill while visiting her sister in Paris and had to recuperate in a nursing home. H. G., either suspicious or worried – possibly both – kept pestering Tania for the name of the home so that he could contact her. Tania hated telling him all these lies. She had begged Moura to let her reveal the truth. At first Moura refused, but after a couple of days she relented. Tania was allowed to tell H. G. that Moura had heard news of Gorky's illness and had left the nursing home hurriedly to visit him prior to his likely death. 'Thank goodness no more lies required,' Tania wrote in her diary. 'Still have to pretend I knew nothing of all this till today. Fed up being intermediary every time. Makes me look a complete fool.'[23]

Did Gorky really want Moura there at his deathbed? He was being nursed by Lipa, who hated Moura. Given the speed of her passage from Knightsbridge to Moscow, it was quite possibly on Stalin's direct orders that Moura was invited into Russia so that she could bring with her the remaining archives. But although she brought some papers with her, much still remained unaccounted for.

Gorky's illness became worse, and by 8 June he was not expected to live. His close friends and relatives began to gather to pay their last respects. Yekaterina, Timosha and Moura were among them.

> Gorky opened his eyes and said: 'I am already far away, it is very hard for me to return . . .' After a pause, he added: 'All my life I have thought how I might improve this moment . . .' Kriuchkov entered the room and announced that Stalin was on his way . . . 'Let them come, if they can get here in time,' said Gorky.[24]

He was injected with camphor, which rallied him for a while, and by the time Stalin arrived Gorky seemed so much improved that he was surprised at having been brought to see what he had supposed to be a dying man. He demanded that everyone leave; he wanted time alone to speak with Gorky.

Despite rallying for a while once more on 16 June, Gorky suffered a relapse. On the night of 17 June a raging storm began and hailstones pelted the roof. Gorky was kept alive with oxygen but by morning it was clear that nothing further could be done. He died at eleven o'clock. Moura, overcome by grief, lay beside his dead body for some time.

The funeral was a rushed affair, carried out the next day. Gorky had wished to be buried next to his son, but instead a cremation was hastily arranged and the ashes placed in the Kremlin wall. Despite the rush, a massive crowd, estimated at eight hundred thousand, attended the funeral procession in Red Square. Word of his death had travelled fast. People were hurt in the inevitable crush. Moura attended the funeral as part of his family, sitting between Yekaterina and Maria Andreyeva, his other long-term lovers; in front sat Timosha with his granddaughters Darya and Marfa. André Gide made a speech at the funeral. According to Moura, while Gide was in mid-speech, Stalin turned to the writer Aleksei Tolstoy and asked, 'Who's that?' Tolstoy replied, 'That's Gide. He's our great conquest. He's the leading writer of France and he's ours!'

Stalin grunted and said, 'I never trust these French fellows.'[25] Stalin was right; on his return to France, Gide wrote a long anti-Communist work entitled *Retour de l'URSS*.

Moura's role in the last illness and death of Maxim Gorky was never clear. There was a rumour that she administered a fatal dose of poison during his last days. But even if she could be persuaded to do such a thing (the mortal fear that Stalin inspired might be enough to make her comply) with several NKVD personnel and a nurse at hand it was unlikely that Moura would be chosen for such a task. And her love and admiration for Gorky, while nowhere near as strong as her love for Lockhart, were sincere. But she did not come away from the business with her hands clean. She might well have been brought there on Stalin's or Yagoda's instructions. And part of the plan might have been that she bring the Gorky archive that was in her keeping. But she did not bring it all, and if she hoped to get something in return, she did not get all of that either.

During the course of Gorky's illness, Moura and Pyotr Kriuchkov prepared a will in Gorky's name, assigning Moura the rights to the archive in her possession and to the foreign royalties on his published works, and everything else to Kriuchkov. He refused to sign it. So Moura did what she is alleged to have done on numerous previous occasions – she forged his signature. Moura gave the document to Yekaterina, with the instruction to hand it on to either Stalin or Vyacheslav Molotov, chairman of the Council of People's Commissars. Yekaterina read it, and was appalled that Gorky had left nothing to her. She claimed later that she had given it to Stalin, and that he gave it to 'someone else'. It disappeared and was never seen again.[26] Nonetheless, Moura, who had been receiving Gorky's foreign royalties under power of attorney, continued to receive them for a further three years before the right expired under Soviet law.

Moura's only account of the whereabouts of Gorky's archives – including not just the letters but manuscripts as well – was that she left them in Kallijärv, where they were burned when the Nazis invaded the country in 1941. H. G. Wells believed that Moura had dealt with Gorky's papers in exactly the way she had promised to when she left Sorrento in 1933; despite the pressure on her, she had kept them out of the hands of the NKVD, and thereby preserved dozens, if not hundreds, of lives.

But again Wells was deceived. Shortly after attending the funeral Moura returned briefly to London, but on 26 July she flew abroad again. She let it be known that she was going to Estonia. However, there is evidence that she had returned to Moscow in late September to put Gorky's archive 'in order'. This probably meant that she brought another instalment of archive material back into Russia with her, possibly from a cache hidden in Estonia. The evidence is that in March 1937, Yagoda, via Pyotr Kriuchkov, gave her £400 in payment for this work.[27] Shortly afterwards, Yagoda was arrested on Stalin's order, and charged with corruption and spying. Moura did not visit Russia again until after Stalin's death.

What happened to the rest of Gorky's archive? Did it really burn in Estonia? Or is it true that when the Soviet Union annexed Estonia in 1940, the NKVD searched for and found the Gorky papers that Moura had secreted there? Whatever went on in Estonia, it seems that much of the archive Moura took out of Italy in 1933 remained in her keeping for the rest of her life.[28]

22

A Very Dangerous Woman

1936–1939

Saturday 13 October 1936, London

The lobby and staircase of the Savoy Hotel were a carnival of literary eminence that evening. The Poets, Essayists and Novelists Club (PEN) was giving a banquet to celebrate the seventieth birthday of its former president, Mr H. G. Wells. The guest of honour stood at the top of the stairs; on one side of him was J. B. Priestley, performing the office of master of ceremonies; on the other was Baroness Budberg, performing the role of stand-in wife. Priestley's wife was also there, lending an air of respectability.[1]

H. G.'s dinner was held in the Savoy ballroom; it seated five hundred, and PEN had received eight hundred applications from its members. Almost every notable British writer had come (J. M. Barrie had sent his apologies; he was too old for such things, he felt, although he was only six years older than H. G.).

Leaving the crush at the head of the stairs, Moura entered the ballroom and walked among the tables. The people responsible for the seating plan had worried over where to place Baroness Budberg; should they treat her as his wife or not? She had done much herself for PEN, trying unsuccessfully to persuade the Russian authorities to allow its writers to join. Her place was marked at the head of the main table, next to H. G. Nearby were name cards marked for J. B. Priestley, Lady Diana Cooper, George Bernard Shaw (who was one of the speakers), Julian Huxley, Christabel Aberconway, Vera Brittain, J. M. Keynes, Somerset Maugham, and dozens of others. It might prove awkward at such a large gathering, with such intense attention focused on H. G., so Moura took her card and swapped it with another, further down the table among the humbler names.

On this one occasion, Moura had no desire to be the centre of attention. This was an evening for H. G. and his friends. The menu for the evening was illustrated with a drawing by the *Evening Standard* political cartoonist David Low, showing Wells leaping youthfully over his seventieth milestone. Everyone knew that it was Moura who kept him on his toes.

Elsewhere in London, Moura was receiving attention of a darker, more sinister kind. A week earlier, David 'Archie' Boyle of the Air Ministry's intelligence section had received a long letter from Air Vice Marshal Conrad Collier, Air Attaché at the British Embassy in Moscow. It was marked *Most Secret* and contained some worrying observations.[2]

Collier described a recent conversation with Maurice Dayet, the First Secretary of the French Embassy, in the course of which Moura Budberg's name had been mentioned. Dayet said he thought she was a very dangerous woman. He had heard that she had been in Moscow for Gorky's funeral, where she met with Stalin on at least three occasions and to whom she presented a gift of an accordion (which Stalin was known to be fond of playing). She had no Soviet visa but had obtained a special *laissez-passer* directly from the Soviet Embassy in Berlin.

Dayet had also heard that earlier that year she had been at a social event where Duff Cooper, the British Secretary of State for War, was a guest. He had discussed many issues of political importance in front of Moura, which Dayet considered to be of great concern to British security. A couple of weeks after Duff Cooper's indiscretion, Moura had made one of her trips to Moscow, where again she met with Stalin.

Furthermore, Collier added, Dayet had said that although Moura had not been seen in France for the previous three years, her last visit had coincided with an espionage case involving a naval officer who had been charged with the loss of important ciphers. The woman believed to be at the head of this conspiracy had never been caught, but was known as 'Mary'. In Dayet's opinion, this woman was Moura Budberg. It is true that Moura had told H. G. that she was taking 'the cure' in Brides-les-Bains, a spa town in the French Alps, in October 1934.[3] Possibly this was yet another of her cover stories.

Air Vice Marshal Collier added his own observation that he knew Baroness Budberg slightly, as his son had attended her adopted daughter Kira's wedding.

On 14 October (the day after H. G.'s Savoy dinner) Collier's letter was passed to Major Valentine Vivien, head of SIS's Section V, which handled counter-espionage, with a covering memo referring to some case notes from 1935 and noting that 'I confess that I have always felt very doubtful about Budberg and have never regarded her case as having been satisfactorily cleared up.' The memo recommended that inquiries be made about Kira, to determine whether she was 'entirely reliable'.[4]

The letter and memo prompted a flurry of inquiries in Whitehall's intelligence sections. They wanted to verify the source and it was suggested that the French Deuxième Bureau should be contacted. One SIS informant, identified only as 'L. F.', mentioned that his wife had known Moura for over twenty years, and that he himself had met her for the first time earlier that year. L. F. corroborated much of the detail in Collier's letter, including her friendship with Duff Cooper, and added that she was an intimate friend of Paul Scheffer, the German journalist. L. F.'s wife had warned him, he wrote, prior to his meeting with Moura, that she liked to be considered the best-informed woman in Europe, that she talked a lot, knew an immense number of people, and that he should 'watch his step' when speaking to her. L. F. confirmed that Moura had certainly heard things from members of government that should not have been mentioned in her presence.[5]

'L. F.' was undoubtedly Sir Edward Lionel Fletcher, Liuba Hicks' new husband. Fletcher was rather older than Liuba – a retired maritime engineer, member of a wealthy shipping family and naval reserve officer who had been manager of the White Star Line (it was probably through the late Will Hicks' post with Cunard that Fletcher and Liuba had become acquainted). They had married in April 1936; Moura had been at the wedding, naturally, and at the huge reception given afterwards at 15 Wilton Crescent.[6] Liuba was also incidentally a mutual friend of Air Vice Marshal Collier and Maurice Dayet.

A meeting was arranged between British intelligence and Maurice Dayet, who confirmed that what had been written in Collier's letter was true; he added that Moura had been on the French security blacklist and that he believed her to be a 'letter box' acting for the Russians. Her role was to pass on snippets of information that she thought would interest them. However, Dayet did not believe her to be anti-English.

Despite all the whispers, there wasn't enough hard evidence against Baroness Budberg to warrant an arrest. She remained under surveillance by both British and French security services.

Notes and reports accumulated in Moura's file. A later Special Branch report stated that in 1936 and 1937 she had been observed having regular night-time meetings with an unknown man in the Suffolk seaside resort of Felixstowe.[7] The town was rather fashionable at the time – in the autumn of 1936 Wallis Simpson rented a house there while waiting for the outcome of her divorce. The King frequently visited her by plane. She complained that the house was very small and the out of season town too quiet for her liking. Moura knew Wallis and Edward through Lockhart, so she might well have visited them while she was there. She might even have been gathering and passing on information about the development of Britain's looming constitutional crisis. The town had a regular railway service so she would have found it quite easy to make the trip up from London.

There might have been a more banal reason for her visits. She was still conducting her affair with Constantine Benckendorff, who lived a few miles from Felixstowe, at Lime Kiln, Claydon.

Another fact about Moura came to light during the 1930s, when MI5 obtained a Russian document describing her activities in 1918 as a double agent for the Russian Bolsheviks and the Skoropadskyi regime in the Ukraine. The same source revealed that from 1927 to 1929 she had continued spying on the exiled members of the Hetmanate in Berlin, using her sister Assia's husband as a source.[8]

As war in Europe loomed, MI5 believed they detected another German connection in Baroness Budberg's activities. She had become acquainted with the ex-Nazi defector Ernst Hanfstaengl, an American-educated German businessman who had been foreign press officer for the Nazi Party and a long-time friend of Adolf Hitler. By 1937 his lack of steely commitment to the Nazi cause and his unguarded comments about Nazi leaders caused Hanfstaengl to fall out with Goebbels and lose Hitler's confidence. His post was abolished and, sensing that the end was nigh, Hanfstaengl quickly defected to Britain in March 1937.

On 29 December that year, MI5 intercepted a letter from Louis P. Lochner, the American pacifist journalist, who was one of Moura's many publishing contacts from her Berlin days (he was director of the Berlin bureau of the Associated Press and a colleague of Paul Scheffer).

The letter was addressed to Hanfstaengl and suggested that he should make contact with Moura, describing her as a 'very clever Russian'. He gave Hanfstaengl her London telephone number.[9] A year later, in December 1938, Lochner wrote to Hanfstaengl again, mentioning that Moura had been to Estonia. He asked Hanfstaengl if he knew when 'the grand show' was due to start.

According to the MI5 summary, this letter also made reference to a visit that had been paid by Karl Bodenschatz, a Luftwaffe officer, to Hanfstaengl in London in spring 1937.[10] According to Hanfstaengl's own later account, Bodenschatz had been sent by Goering with a promise that he could resume his former post with his original staff. But with war looming, Hanfstaengl didn't fancy the idea, and declined.[11] The motive for Goering's proposal was reported in the United States, but not apparently in Britain: when Hanfstaengl arrived in London it had been rumoured that he intended to write a memoir entitled 'Why I Joined Hitler and Why I Left Him'. The Nazi leadership were desperate to stop him. He was invited by Bodenschatz to a meeting at the German Embassy in London, but 'on the advice of his lawyer declined to attend,' said one newspaper report. 'Later it was learned that all preparations had been made to seize him and take him into Germany.'[12]

Hanfstaengl's book, had it been published, would have been immensely powerful anti-Nazi propaganda. Paul Scheffer and Louis Lochner would have been keen to help it come about, and Moura would have the contacts to help it happen. But for reasons unknown, it didn't surface.

While suspicions darkened in Whitehall and war approached, Moura's personal life carried on as it had for years.

She was now living semi-permanently in London. She and H. G. had settled into their relationship, having both accepted their respective roles. He accepted (reluctantly) that she would never marry him and never be his permanent companion, and she accepted (quite contentedly) his intermittent sideshows with other women.

In 1937, after a holiday with both Moura and Constance Coolidge, Wells went to the South of France to stay with Somerset Maugham. He was suffering from neuritis in his right arm, possibly caused by his diabetes, which had been giving him a great deal of pain.

The emotional pain that Moura had caused him (or rather that he had inflicted on himself through her) seemed to have subsided at last. H. G. commented that 'Moura remains what she is; rather stouter, rather greyer, sometimes tiresome, oftener charming and close and dear'. By 1938 he was noting that 'Moura is Moura as ever; human, faulty, wise, silly, and I love her'.[13]

She continued to see Lockhart. He was now a single man. In 1937 Jean had finally reached the end of her tolerance; she left him and began divorce proceedings. Her lawyers combed Lockhart's published memoirs, taking note of all the references to his romance with Moura. Lockhart discussed it with her over lunch, though Moura had heard the gossip already. She was more interested in the fact that the writer Aleksei Tolstoy, who had arrived in London for the National Congress of Peace and Friendship with the USSR (an event sponsored by Britain's left-leaning writers and politicians), was in a constant state of terror, accompanied everywhere he went by a 'Cheka man'.[14]

Lockhart's career path had changed again. He had been writing the regular 'Atticus' column in the *Sunday Times*, but had been persuaded to return to the Foreign Office after an absence of more than twelve years. With the start of the war he joined the Political Warfare Executive, and soon became its head. He was responsible for radio broadcasts, leaflet drops, postcards and documents designed to lift the morale of people in German-occupied countries and lower morale of the Germans.

If Moura still harboured hopes that Lockhart, free of his wife, might finally give himself to her completely, she didn't show it. They continued to dine regularly, often consuming too much food and alcohol. Moura passed him titbits of information for use in his gossip column and later in his propaganda work, for Moura still had strong and regular links to the Baltic and to Russia. But by late 1937, when she returned from a trip to Estonia, Lockhart realised that since Gorky's death and the arrest of Yagoda, she had been 'cut off' by the Bolsheviks. She was concerned about the show trials, which were sweeping up people she knew who were still in the country, and feared that Lockhart's old acquaintance Maxim Litvinov might be the next to fall.[15] Everyone was watching their back. Perhaps that was the reason for Aleksei Tolstoy's terror during his visit to London. (If so, he had no need to fear – his star was rising, with appointment to the newly created Supreme Soviet.)

Wells too was concerned about what was going on in Russia. His friends Beatrice and Sidney Webb had written a book, *Soviet Communism*, in which they gave their view that the ultimate result of the Moscow trials would be a better civilisation in Russia. Many left-wing writers in Britain shared this opinion. Wells, who had seen Stalin in the flesh, was not so optimistic. He wrote to Beatrice, saying that although both he and Moura largely agreed with Beatrice's assessment of the situation, they felt she was underestimating the personal power of Stalin. What everyone agreed on at the time was that Stalin's reconstructed Soviet Union was a new and better order, which needed to be preserved at almost any cost.

In 1938 the Moscow trials intensified. Kriuchkov, Gorky's secretary and former member of the Kronverksky commune, was tried for his alleged role in Gorky's death, and was executed by firing squad in March. The file on Kriuchkov included a list of eight people who had been compromised by him.

Moura's name was on the list.

It said that she had been a 'participant in an anti-soviet Rightist organisation'.[16] A reference to her relationship with Scheffer, perhaps, and his alleged anti-Soviet work for the Nazis. Of the eight people on the list, seven were arrested and put to death. Moura was the only survivor. She was also the only one living in London, but that needn't have been sufficient protection. Two years later, the NKVD went all the way to Mexico to assassinate Trotsky. And Moura was a frequent traveller; it would have been quite simple to arrest or kill her in Estonia. And yet nothing was done. There may be many explanations, not least the fact that some of Gorky's archive was still in her keeping. Or perhaps, as in 1918 and 1921, the Soviet regime concluded that her value outweighed her alleged crimes.

On 21 February 1940 *The Times* carried a small notice in its Forthcoming Marriages column:

MR B. G. ALEXANDER AND MISS T. BENCKENDORFF
The engagement is announced between Bernard G. Alexander . . . and Tatiana von Benckendorff, daughter of Baroness Marie Budberg, 11, Ennismore Gardens, London, S.W., and the late Johan von Benckendorff, Jendel, Estonia.[17]

Moura hadn't liked the look of Bernard Alexander when Tania introduced him to her. 'He is intelligent,' Moura admitted, 'but he is not for

you. He has a cold analytical lawyer's mind and a temperament too different from yours.'[18] Bernard was a newly qualified barrister, the son of
a textile tycoon. Smitten by Tania in London, he had pursued her to
Tallinn and holidayed with her at Kallijärv. Tania hadn't liked him at
first; he was politically right-wing, a strict Roman Catholic, reserved,
and, as Moura observed, a cold, dispassionate thinker.[19] Tania's friends
didn't like him either. But he intrigued her at the same time as he infu-
riated her, and he had hidden romantic depths. Showing the same
unwisdom as her mother, Tania fell in love.[20]

H. G. had long since abandoned any hope that Moura would marry
or even consider living with him. Indeed, it had become a private jest
between them. When he went on his one and only trip to Australia in
the English winter of 1938/39, he wrote to her, 'Dear Moura, darling
Moura. Don't forget you belong to me'.[21] He told her that the Australians
were not at all as he had expected – no billy cans, kangaroos or wallabies
were in evidence. The people rose early, around 6.30 am, and went to
bed at half past ten: 'No place for Moura,' he commented. 'Are you
being a good Moura goodasme? And is your weight falling and falling?'[22]
The answer to both his questions was quite likely an emphatic *no*.

Moura spent that last summer of peace at Kallijärv with Paul and
Tania. It had been here, in the bliss of Yendel, that she had spent that
other golden summer twenty-two years earlier, swimming and sporting
with Meriel, Cromie and Garstino and all the rest while Petrograd
boiled and threatened revolution. Everything was different now. The
children were grown up, Tania was being wooed by Bernard, Moura
was deep into middle age. And Micky was no longer with them. Moura's
oldest and dearest friend, her second and best-loved mother, had fallen
ill and died earlier that year. In the last twenty years, Micky had grown
to *be* Yendel in the children's minds – the focus of their visits. But when
she died they were all in London, unable to be with her – 'on the day
she died,' Tania would recall, 'my mother and I hung on to the phone
to Estonia and wept'.[23]

This would be their last ever visit to Yendel. Estonia was enjoying its
last year of independence; it was about to fall under the darkest shadow
in all its troubled history. The Wehrmacht was driving into the west of
Poland, and soon the eastern states would fall to the Soviet Union.

From Estonia Moura flew to Stockholm, where she was due to meet
H. G. at a PEN conference. They were there on 3 September when the

United Kingdom and its allies declared war on Germany. Moura and H. G. had some difficulty finding a plane to take them to Amsterdam, where they were stuck for another week until they managed to get a passage on the last boat to leave for England.

23

'Secretly Working for the Russians'

1939–1946

H. G. was seventy-four, but neither age nor war could curtail his travelling habit. In September 1940, with the Battle of Britain at its height and the Blitz about to start, he sailed from Liverpool aboard the Cunard ship *Scythia*, bound for one of his regular speaking tours of the United States. The North Atlantic was U-boat territory; the *Scythia* was delayed in port, waiting for a place in a convoy, and was caught in an air raid on the docks. Fortunately, she was unharmed, and sailed on without mishap.

Touring the States, from the snows of New York to the heat of Florida, by way of Dallas, Detroit, Birmingham and San Francisco, Wells was periodically asked by acquaintances where Moura was, and he wrote a bitter letter telling her that he had to make the usual excuses for her non-appearance at his side. (She had come to Liverpool to wave him off, but that was the limit of her wish to travel with him.) He met his friend Charlie Chaplin and 'everybody in New York', and probably managed to see some lady friends. He had ongoing friendships with Margaret Sanger, the leader of the birth control movement, and Martha Gellhorn. He also spent a good deal of time with his tour agent, Harold Peat, who organised celebrity lecture tours through his company, Management of Distinguished Personalities (on Wells' recommendation, Winston Churchill had undertaken lucrative speaking tours with Mr Peat). Wells was pleased to note that Peat attracted young women to his side, and he managed to enjoy a 'last flare of cheerful sensuality'.[1]

Back in England Moura often stayed away from London, where the air raids kept her awake. She spent time with Paul on his farm at Crayke in Yorkshire, which he rented from a family friend. She also stayed with Tania, who was living in Oxfordshire. She had married Bernard in spite of Moura's objections, and moved to Great Haseley. By the end of 1940 she was pregnant and Bernard was in the Ox and Bucks Light Infantry. Tania took in evacuees, and by 1943 she had a son and daughter of her own.

Despite the raids, Moura still spent time in London. After Liuba's marriage, Moura had moved from Cadogan Square and began sharing a flat in Ennismore Gardens, Kensington, with another old friend, Molly Cliff, whose son Tony owned the farm in Yorkshire that Paul rented. Molly, who was a part-time air raid warden, had the upper floor of the house, and Moura the ground floor.[2] Ennismore Gardens would be her home for the next two decades — first at number 11, later at number 68. Wherever Moura lived, her domestic environment was always the same; her sitting room resembled a rather down-at-heel salon, where she received her evening guests, and her bedroom, where she did the bulk of her work from her single bed, resembled the back office of a busy publishing house, shelves crammed with books and papers, every sur-face bearing a tower of dog-eared manuscripts.

At the start of the war, Moura's old friend (and H. G.'s nemesis) Hilda Matheson contacted her. Hilda had left the BBC and spent several years compiling a survey of Africa. During Chamberlain's period of appease-ment, it had been realised that it would be helpful if pro-British propaganda could be sent out to friendly nations as well as potential enemies. At the beginning of 1939 Hilda had been approached by Section D of the SIS (or MI6, to give it its new wartime codename) and asked to run a secret propaganda organisation, the Joint Broadcasting Committee. She jumped at the chance to return to broadcasting.

During the lead-up to the war, the JBC spread positive information illustrating Britain's strength and resources. The plan was to display British life, its culture and war activities, depicting a country that didn't necessarily want war but was prepared for it should it come.[3] Time was bought on various European radio stations and the pro-grammes were styled as travelogues, highlighting the wonders of Britain. Hilda built up a roster of foreign émigrés who had a good command of languages and knowledge of Europe. Moura joined the team in September 1939. Hilda neglected to have MI5 vet her employees; had she done so, Moura would undoubtedly have been barred from working with the JBC.

She wasn't the only person of doubtful loyalties taken on by Hilda. Guy Burgess, who had been a member of the BBC Talks department since 1936, was also invited to join. He was already working for the Soviet Union as a Comintern agent. Working inside the British propaganda machine was an ideal opportunity for him.

Ways and means of reaching as large an audience as possible were thought up. As Hilda commented, there were no problems with accessing countries such as Sweden, Spain and Portugal, Turkey was reached by cable, Cairo by diplomatic bags and recordings were sent to both South and North America by ship and plane. By ingenious means most countries were soon being sent regular messages. They included Scandinavia, the Netherlands, Hungary, Romania, Yugoslavia, Greece, Bulgaria, the Middle East, parts of Africa, Ceylon, the West Indies and even Germany itself. About one hundred and fifty discs were recorded each month from which around three and a half thousand pressings were made. Subjects ranged from innocuous frippery to serious military matters – 'Kew Gardens', 'George Eliot', 'London's Dress Collection', 'Girls of the London Blitz' and 'Britain's Allies in the Air'.[4]

At the commencement of hostilities, MI5 grew concerned about Hilda's use of so many unchecked aliens. Some of the names rung alarm bells, and searching questions were soon being asked about Baroness Budberg's employment. At the end of February 1940 MI5 briefed one of its agents, codenamed U35, to investigate her.

U35 was Jona 'Klop' Ustinov, a Russian émigré with German connections. Klop's father had fled Tsarist Russia as a religious refugee, settling in Palestine, where Klop was born in 1892. Being born in the same year was not the only thing he had in common with Moura. He had an intricate connection with Germany, having received most of his schooling there and having served in the German army in the First World War. After returning to Russia, in 1920 he met Nadia Benois, a theatrical set designer and artist. Nadia was involved with the House of Arts in Petrograd, one of the institutions Maxim Gorky had helped set up.[5] Moura was also involved in this work – both through Gorky and Maria Andreyeva, and through her work in Korney Chukovsky's Art Theatre studio in 1919.[6] Almost certainly she and Nadia would have been acquainted, and Moura might even have met Ustinov during their engagement.

The couple married, left Russia the same year and moved first to Berlin; but with the rise of the Nazis, they travelled on to London, where Ustinov worked as a press attaché at the German Embassy and as a journalist for a German news agency. In 1935, upon being required to prove his Aryan descent, Ustinov left the employment of the German Embassy, and soon after was recruited into the private network of foreign informants run by Sir Robin Vansittart at the Foreign Office. He proved invaluable, and through Vansittart's influence he was granted British citizenship and employed by MI5. Klop Ustinov became one of their most prized and effective agents.[7]

How he came to know Moura is unclear, but by the start of the war they were good friends.[8] As her friend and a trusted counter-intelligence agent, Klop was the perfect person to report on her. According to his son, the actor Peter Ustinov, Klop 'seemed to fancy himself as something he was really not, a man of mystery, at least not in the way he understood it'.[9] A neat, precise gentleman who sported a monocle, he seems to have been fundamentally honest and open, despite being a successful undercover agent.

He dined with Moura, attended her parties, met her alone for drinks at her flat, and submitted regular reports on who her friends were, her movements and her activities. In March 1940 he reported that Moura was 'extremely difficult to sum up. She is very intelligent indeed and approaches all political questions from a highbrow standpoint'. He judged her to be pro-Soviet, but knew for a fact that she had been badly shaken by the Russian annexation of Poland and the Baltic states (he had been with her and H. G. when they heard the news about Poland). 'I consider it quite out of the question that Baroness Budberg should be pro-Nazi,' Klop stated. 'As far as I know she is *au fond* anti-German.'[10]

Klop even succeeded in using Moura as a source of intelligence – or rather she succeeded, as was her wont, in making herself valuable as a source. She told him that a man called Yates-Brown, who had a Russian wife, had invited her to dinner. During the meal the entire conversation had been pro-Nazi and Fifth Column; Moura told Klop that she had been horrified by their opinion that Britain needed a Hitler of its own. Klop reported this, and a watch was put on the couple.

Anti-Nazi she might be, but Moura remained a loyal Russian and a suspicious character. In June 1940 she was dismissed from the JBC. The permit entitling her to work for the organisation was revoked, and a 'red refusal' was marked on her police registration certificate – the licence to live which most foreigners staying in Britain had to have.[11] The mark would bar her from doing any work that might be of a sensitive nature. There was even talk of her being interned, but it came to nothing.

Moura probably benefited from her friendly relations with members of the intelligence agencies – including Klop Ustinov himself, who liked her. She also became friendly with a tall, willowy young man called Anthony Blunt, who had been recruited by MI5 in May 1940 and rose rapidly in the service. And there was Commander Ernest Boyce, her old friend and employer from the Petrograd and Helsingfors SIS stations. Following Moura's ejection from the JBC, Boyce wrote a strong letter of support. 'Although she seems to have a flair for getting herself into all sorts of apparently compromising situations,' he wrote, 'I can personally vouch for her as being a staunch upholder of all the British Empire stands for.' He suggested that she be reinstated, but in a position where use could be made of her fluency in English, Russian, French, German, Italian and Polish, but where there was no need for secrecy.[12]

Given the possibility that Boyce might have been a double agent employed by the Soviet Union, he could have had an interest in securing Moura's position. Alternatively, she might have possessed compromising information about him. He had been her boss in 1918; the SIS Petrograd station had been notably lax about security, and Moura had allowed no snippet of inside information to evade her attention. The same applied to Anthony Blunt, who had already been working for the NKVD for several years when he joined MI5.

But the red refusal mark remained on her papers, and Moura was locked out of the JBC. Hilda Matheson wasn't able to help – she fell ill with a thyroid problem and died during an operation in October 1940.

While MI5 watched her every move, Moura went about her life – packing H. G. off on his travels, keeping him company when he was at home, staying with Paul or Tania, making her constant round of social occasions, and going on with the task that would occupy her intermittently through most of her life – collating and translating into English the works of Maxim Gorky.

Almost exactly a year after Moura had been barred from working at the JBC, Germany declared war on the USSR. The BBC, which had taken over the responsibilities of the JBC, was asked to arrange a Russian propaganda service and Moura's name was once again put forward. The Aliens War Service Department, which was in charge of issuing work permits for foreigners, was approached by the BBC, but a heavy black

No was returned. Baroness Budberg should not be allowed to cross the BBC's threshold and should not be employed by the BBC in any capacity. One anonymous MI5 operative was surprised by this brusque dismissal, as he knew that the Baroness was a friend of Duff Cooper, Harold Nicolson, Brendan Bracken and 'probably the Prime Minister'.[13]

The British government had not reckoned with Moura's blasé tenacity. Despite the ban on her working for the BBC, they had been using her as a source of opinion and advice on Russian matters for some time. When this was discovered, a tart note was added to the MI5 minute sheet saying, 'Whatever our view upon the reliability of the Baroness, it is not encouraging to learn that much of the information gathered by the BBC about present conditions in Russia is drawn from her.'[14]

In the end neither Boyce nor Moura's other admirers managed to overturn the decision that had been made. She was still considered too great a security risk to be allowed near the BBC. Nonetheless, they couldn't keep her away. On 24 June 1941, a year after her official dismissal, Moura met Lockhart for dinner. Germany had invaded the USSR two days earlier, inspiring a rush of sympathy in Britain. Moura told Lockhart that the BBC people were 'all very pro-Russian and full of wishful thinking'.[15]

The troubled love affair between Moura and the BBC ran and ran. In 1942 she met the writer and diplomat John Lawrence, who had set up the BBC World Service European section in 1939, and was now being posted to Moscow to set up a Russian section. (He was an adventurous sort – when his ship was torpedoed off the north Russian coast, he swam the rest of the way to Murmansk.) On being given the posting, he immediately sought Moura's guidance. 'I wanted to ask her advice on what to do, what to avoid, whom to see and whom not to see. She gave me good advice.'[16]

Moura persuaded people from 'various high quarters' to write on her behalf to the security services. The result was that in August 1941 the red stamp was removed from her police certificate. But as the person conveying the decision to the Home Office said, 'This was really rather a distinction without a difference and the only practical result is the removal of the formal stigma represented by the endorsement of the red refusal'.[17] The Baroness would still not be allowed to do work connected with the war effort, and MI5 kept a close eye on her.

And yet it was proving impossible for MI5 to stop her meddling in affairs concerning the BBC. They could have arrested and interned her, but shied away from doing so; she was too well connected.

It was still officially believed that she was a potential threat to national security, and as the war progressed, the interest in Moura moved up a gear. The hard men of British intelligence were getting involved. In August 1941 the Deputy Assistant Commissioner of Special Branch, R. Pilkington, reported to MI5: 'The activities of a certain Baroness Budberg are inimical to the best interests of the Allied war effort'. He noted her close friendships with Lockhart, former Minister of Information Duff Cooper and H. G. Wells. He reported that 'Baroness Budberg used to see Mr Duff Cooper at least three times a week'. She had denied knowing Ivan Maisky, the Soviet Ambassador, 'but she is in fact secretly in touch with him', and both she and Maisky gave separate but similar reports to Duff Cooper in such a way as to make it appear that they came from different sources 'in order to influence his decisions'. The Assistant Commissioner concluded: 'It would appear that the Baroness is secretly working for the Russians.'[18]

The recipient of the report was Colonel Edward Hinchley-Cooke, a seasoned MI5 interrogator, spy and bloodhound. He didn't take it lightly. He was particularly bothered by Moura's connection with Maisky and wanted more information about how they had met. Hinchley-Cooke discovered that Moura was close to Madame Maisky and regularly met with her and her husband socially at 'musical parties' and other events.

MI5 had plenty of circumstantial evidence that Moura was spying, but they needed something more concrete before they could expel or intern her. Her high-profile contacts and friends could roast any MI5 officer who made a mistake.

In 1943 word reached Duff Cooper that MI5 were interested in Moura, and probably that his name had been mentioned. No doubt aware that he had said indiscreet things in front of her, in May 1943 he asked MI5 officer Richard Butler what information they held on her. The situation was getting serious; Butler's report on the query went directly to David Petrie, the Director General of MI5.

Duff Cooper distanced himself from Moura and played down her significance, describing her as an 'excessively tiresome old woman' who was 'probably harmless', but pressed Butler for information about her.[19]

He was evidently worried. The year before, he had been appointed by Churchill as head of the Security Executive, the government's supreme domestic security committee. But in September 1943 he was removed from the post and demoted to a role as liaison with the Free French government in Algeria.[20]

In spite of everything, Moura retained his friendship, and that of his wife, Lady Diana Cooper, who called her 'my very dear Moura' and testified that Lord Beaverbrook, Maurice Baring and Raymond Asquith all liked her, as did her husband.[21]

Decades earlier, when Moura was young and trapped in Russia, desperate to be allowed to come to England, she had despaired of the constant rumours about her. Now, older, wiser and happily secure in her deceits, she laughed them off. She told H. G.'s friend Martha Gellhorn about a famous palmist who had given her a reading, on the prompting of Aldous Huxley. Studying her elegant hand (everyone remarked how fine Moura's hands were, even if they were sometimes grubby) the woman had declared, 'Your life is more interesting than you are.'[22] Moura was amused – 'she had a splendid laugh,' Gellhorn recalled – and was intrigued enough to study palmistry herself, with a view to taking it up professionally. She certainly had the bluff and charm to carry it off, but it came to nothing.[23]

While MI5 investigated and the government tried to keep her away from the BBC, Moura pursued other interests.

Lockhart, now working for the Political Warfare Executive, had introduced her to the French exile André Labarthe, who ran a London-based propaganda magazine, *La France Libre*. Intended as the official voice of the Free French movement, it was hugely successful. Labarthe had formerly been a favoured member of General de Gaulle's staff, advising him on all things, including armaments. He was brilliant, a schemer and an adventurer, and his acquaintances found it difficult to distinguish fact from fiction in him.[24] He had a lot in common with Moura.

It soon became apparent that the magazine needed the services of an additional staff member with a good knowledge of the French language and of French politics. Moura's name was suggested, and she joined their team, helping with fund-raising by appealing to the Ministry of Information, a task no doubt made easier by her contact with Lockhart.

She wrote and edited articles and opened *La France Libre* to her literary contacts, including George Bernard Shaw, J. B. Priestley and of course H. G. They all wrote for the magazine.

Although de Gaulle had originally given *La France Libre* his blessing, its failure to lend itself to his cult of personality displeased him. Eventually he fell out with Labarthe over the Muselier affair. Émile Muselier had been commander of the Free French Navy but became concerned about de Gaulle's growing megalomania and suggested the formation of an executive in which he would be the head and de Gaulle the figurehead. Churchill stepped in to mediate and a French National Committee was formed with de Gaulle at the head and Muselier in a subordinate post. Labarthe sided with Muselier, and *La France Libre* took on an anti-Gaullist position.[25]

Moura shared this feeling. She detested de Gaulle's autocratic style, and her anti-Gaullism became a part of her political and social stock in trade. At his house in Hanover Terrace H. G. glued a blown-up portrait of de Gaulle into the bowl of the toilet. Moura thoroughly approved. 'It's the place for him,' she said.[26]

MI5 tolerated her work for the magazine. The head of the Aliens section said it was 'obvious from her entire history that she is interested in political intrigue and I should be very surprised if she is not being used to some extent by the Russians, though probably in a fairly open manner'. Her work with *La France Libre* was to the Allies' advantage, he said, and there was no need to take any further action, other than to give her a watch-it lecture. 'If anyone is to warn her I think it should be the Foreign Office, though I suspect she would make rings round whoever tried to interview her.'[27]

The editorial staff of *La France Libre* became part of Moura's social world, and she would often take them – sometimes with H. G. in tow – down to Oxfordshire to stay at Tania's house and escape from the Blitz for a few days. They would write the magazine during the day and in the evening play bridge. They pooled their rations, supplemented by fresh vegetables from the garden, and ate well. H. G., who had grown fond of Tania during family holidays at Kallijärv, liked being there, and sometimes stayed on after Moura had returned to London.

Despite all these distractions, Moura had not let go of her own publishing work. In 1939, with the expiry of the standard three-year term since Gorky's death, she had lost her power of attorney over his translation rights, and therefore her income from them. In 1940 she published a new translation of his *Fragments from My Diary*, and so brought to an end one of the most important phases of her life. She continued working on translations of Gorky and other Russians throughout her life, but she was no longer in control of his legacy (except for the remaining papers hidden in that elusive suitcase).

She needed all the work she could get, in order to subsidise her life-style: quartered in one of the smartest areas in London, taking trips abroad, throwing parties, eating out; it all added up.

On 6 March 1942 Moura celebrated her fiftieth birthday. H. G. was reminded that it had been over twenty years since their first sexual encounter. She had been 'a tall and slender young woman' in those days, but 'now I told her she was like a Vatican cherub, three times life size but still delightful'. He thought her 'an ample woman; she is very grey but that queer sub-dropsy that attacks so many women of her age, and thickens their ankles, has spared hers altogether'.[28]

That same day, Moura lunched with Lockhart; he passed no comment on her appearance. Rather he remarked that 'She is full of the de Gaulle-Muselier quarrel' and was insisting that it was time to remove the troublesome General from power. Lockhart noted that her opinion corresponded with the private views of Anthony Eden and the Cabinet.[29]

By 1944 H. G.'s health was deteriorating. In August Moura confided to Lockhart that he had cirrhosis of the liver and dementia. He continued to write, but 'his mind is gone' and the writing had become 'mechanical'; also he had grown 'arrogant and intolerant of any contradiction'. In Lockhart's opinion this was no change. 'He has written a new and savage indictment of humanity in general for not following his advice.' (This was indeed no change; back in 1941, in a preface to a new edition of his prophetic 1908 novel *The War in the Air*, Wells had said that his epitaph should be 'I told you so. You *damned* fools.')

Their conversation took place at the Carlton Grill, on the corner of Pall Mall and the Haymarket, where Lockhart treated Moura to lunch. 'Good conversation,' he recorded, 'but she is expensive to feed or, rather, to water. Today she drank only beer with luncheon, but she had an apéritif of three double gins at eight shillings apiece and with her coffee a double brandy at twelve shillings!'[30]

Life in war-damaged London continued. During the 'doodlebug summer' of 1944 H. G.'s house at 13 Hanover Terrace (or 'Hangover

Terrace' as Moura called it) was damaged by a bomb. Moura was staying in Oxfordshire with Tania (who had recently made her a grandmother for the second time). H. G. wrote to her – 'just a love letter to say nothing in particular except that everything is well here and that all your commands have been meticulously obeyed. The carpenters turned up duly & nailed up the back door and most of our lost glass has been swept up.'[31]

The time had come for other broken remnants to be swept up.

As the war came to an end, so did Moura's affair with Constantine Benckendorff. It had continued throughout all these years, without H. G. ever having an inkling of it, despite Cony having holidayed with Moura in Estonia on at least one occasion in the 1930s. Presumably the fact that this was Benckendorff territory and Cony was accompanied by his adolescent daughter Nathalie made the visit seem innocuous. Nathalie herself, who knew perfectly well what was going on, had been disgusted by it.

In the end, Cony's wife, Maria Korchinska, who had tolerated the affair for years, took a stand and after a terrible argument with Constantine she told him to choose between Moura or her. Cony rang Moura to tell her it was finished.[32]

More significantly for Moura, and for the world at large, time was drawing down for H. G. Wells.

On the Thursday after VE Day, Lockhart treated Moura to lunch again at the Carlton. All she wanted to talk about was H. G. She had been visiting him daily. The royal physician, Lord Horder, had diagnosed cancer eighteen months earlier and given him six months to live. Horder was wrong – there was no cancer, and H. G. lingered on. In July Moura took him to vote in the general election; he cast his ballot for Labour. By August she was convinced he had no more than a month to live.[33] She too was wrong. He survived into his eightieth year, but he was becoming weaker and weaker, and employed day and night nurses to help him manage. He wasn't in pain but was wasting away. Moura visited constantly; so did Gip and his wife Marjorie, who had been looking after H. G.'s domestic affairs for years, fulfilling the role he had hoped Moura would take up.

Despite his weakness he continued to write almost to the end, his last two books – *The Happy Turning* and *Mind at the End of Its Tether* – appearing in 1945, and his last article in July 1946.

He had become known for a vision of a future in which war could be prevented by the establishment of a world state with the power to limit the armaments and actions of every country. Man, he said, must adapt or perish like the dinosaurs. In the midst of a global war his ideas had seemed absurd. In 1941 George Orwell had written that 'All sensible men for decades past have been substantially in agreement with what Mr. Wells says; but then sensible men have no power and, in too many cases, no disposition to sacrifice themselves.' Wells had failed to appreciate that mankind did not live by reason, and had therefore misjudged twentieth-century history, including the temper of the early Bolsheviks, who in Orwell's opinion 'may have been angels or demons, according as one chooses to regard them, but at any rate they were not sensible men'. Their rule was 'a military despotism enlivened by witchcraft trials'. Wells had been 'quite incapable of understanding that nationalism, religious bigotry and feudal loyalty are far more powerful forces than what he himself would describe as sanity'. Orwell felt guilt at criticising Wells in this way, likening it to parricide:

> Thinking people who were born about the beginning of this century are in some sense Wells's own creation . . . I doubt whether anyone who was writing books between 1900 and 1920 . . . influenced the young so much. The minds of all of us, and therefore the physical world, would be perceptibly different if Wells had never existed. Only, just the singleness of mind, the one-sided imagination that made him seem like an inspired prophet in the Edwardian age, make him a shallow inadequate thinker now.[34]

H. G. Wells was, in the last analysis, 'too sane to understand the modern world'.

He hadn't long left in which to be bewildered by it all. On the afternoon of 13 August 1946, six weeks short of his eightieth birthday, H. G. Wells died. For the third time in her life Moura was left on her own by a man whom she had loved. For despite everything, he had been dear to her, just not as dear as he had wanted to be. This time there was nobody upon whom she could fall back.

PART 5

Moura's Salon: 1946–1974

I find the photographs that insist that she was a plain woman who dressed dowdily so many inexplicable mysteries, and cannot forget my first breath-taking sight of her as she sat talking to my father in the garden at Easton Glebe one day in 1931. Her fatalism enabled her to radiate an immensely reassuring serenity, and her good humour made her a comfortable rather than a disturbing presence: I always looked forward eagerly to my next meeting with her, and remember my last with pleasure.

Anthony West, *H. G. Wells: Aspects of a Life*

24

The Movie Mogul

1946–1948

After the train pulled away from the darkened Moscow station on that October night in 1918, taking Lockhart with it, Moura's life became a sequence of endings. Doors closing, curtains falling, clasps snapping shut on travel trunks full of memories and secrets. Some of the doors she kept knocking on even though they were bolted against her.

Lockhart's departure had been the end of the great adventure of her life. She had persuaded herself at the time that it was just the prelude, but really it was the close of a first act which had begun that day in January when he arrived at the British Embassy on the snowbound Palace Quay. When had its final end come? Perhaps in that damp woodland in Terijoki, when she threw herself on the wet ground and sobbed her heart out for her lost love. Or with the news that Lockhart had a son, and that the dream of little Peter was over.

Moura's life as a 'Russian of the Russians' ended when she crossed the border into Estonia two days later. After that day, she would never have a home on Russian soil again, and even her visits would be fleeting. With the death of Maxim Gorky, her existence as a Russian effectively ceased; the last meaningful tie was cut, the door closed.

H. G.'s death meant the end of her time as a mistress, a lover, a paramour. Another door clicked shut, another of life's avenues closed off.

And so it would go on, doors closing, curtains falling, cases snapping shut. Moura's life was growing smaller and narrower. But still there was life in her, still choices to be made and paths to tread.

The evening of H. G.'s death, Moura went ahead with a small drinks party with two friends, writer Denis Freeman and his partner, actor

Neville Phillips. She had helped Freeman with his war memoir, and knew Phillips through her new job as head of Alexander Korda's script department. All she wanted to do all evening was drink vodka and talk about H. G. While Neville went home at the end of the evening, Denis, who had known Wells, listened through the night.[1]

On the morning after, Moura was as alone as she had been in 1919. Lockhart was slipping ever further away from her. After his divorce, he had set up home with 'Tommy' Rosslyn in Surrey, and they met only occasionally when he travelled up to London. There were no longer any of the night-long soirées they had enjoyed before the end of the war.

At the age of fifty-four, Moura began another metamorphosis. All her adult life she had been accustomed to being part of a vast social world, full of interesting people. Being attached to figures like Maxim Gorky, H. G. Wells or even Lockhart provided access to the kind of acquaintances and influence that she craved. Now H. G. was gone, she found herself in a near-vacuum, which she quickly set out to fill.

She began to cultivate a new persona for herself as a matriarchal hostess. She had for years been a giver of drinks parties, luncheons and dinners, and an organiser of outings and gatherings. Now she made it the centre of her existence. She became known for her salon. Trading on her air of mystery and intrigue, and exerting the magnetic charm that almost everyone was susceptible to but almost nobody could explain, she turned her modest and rather untidy little Kensington flat into one of the hubs of the postwar social world. Actors, writers, film directors, politicians, spies – they all came. It wasn't just her charm and intrigue that drew them; it was her contacts. She seemed to know everybody, and her salon enhanced her ability to make matches between writers, directors, producers and publishers.

It also brought her work. Besides the crisis in her social life, she needed additional earnings to boost her income. H. G. had left her several legacies in his will, but they didn't add up to very much. There was £3,000, free 'of all duty in her lifetime', to put into an annuity, another £1,000 in cash, plus two-eighteenths of his total estate, which worked out at £6,240.[2] Had she given in and married him, she would have inherited most of it, and been a wealthy woman now. Moura liked money, but she valued her liberty more.

The annuity would yield a small income, but not nearly enough to live on even modestly; for a woman with Moura's tastes and habits, it wouldn't cover her drinks bill, let alone the rent on a Kensington flat or any of her other expenses. The total amount wouldn't last long at her rate of spending.

Moura had foreseen this, and was already shifting sideways from editing and translating books to working on film scripts as well. Her acquaintance with Sir Alexander Korda went back to the 1930s. They were a similar age, both émigrés from the revolutions of eastern Europe. Korda had been born Sándor László Kellner in Hungary in 1893. He had built a career for himself in film-making and developed an interest in left-wing politics before fleeing to Austria in 1919 when White forces overthrew the socialist government. He was ambitious and talented. He adapted his name, taking his surname from his first wife, the actress Maria Corda, and lived the life of a rich man even when he was poor. His clothes were the best; his belief was that if one looked the part then one became the part. Through the 1920s he and Maria developed their careers, first in Austria and Germany and then in Hollywood. In 1932 Korda came to Britain and started building up his own empire. By the outbreak of war he was Britain's first and greatest movie mogul.

How he became acquainted with Moura isn't known. Possibly their paths crossed socially, perhaps in Germany in the early 1920s when she was negotiating film deals for Gorky; or perhaps it was a political connection. Before the fall of the Communists in Hungary, he had been involved with plans to make films adapted from works by Gorky and Tolstoy. Certainly Korda and Moura had become friends by 1935, when she introduced him to H. G. Wells and helped bring about the films *Things to Come* and *The Man Who Could Work Miracles*.[3]

Korda's practices often stretched the boundaries of professional ethics. According to Frank Wells (H. G.'s son, who worked for Korda), if he believed that a finished film might not make enough money, rather than release it he would store it as a phantom asset which he would then use to lever finance from the banks.[4] Lockhart also knew Korda, and had heard many stories about his methods of obtaining financial backing. In 1938 he met an accountant who had represented the creditors when Korda's production company London Films was in trouble; he told Lockhart that Britain's cinema industry had lost the banks and insurance companies about £4 million. Most of it had been lost by Korda and his fellow Hungarian Max Schach. In the accountant's opinion, Korda was by far the worse man of the two – an evil crook.[5]

While Korda lived like a lord – still looking the part and becoming the part – his creditors often lost everything. It didn't seem to worry him. Along with his old name and his marriage to Maria Corda, the man who had got his start making Communist propaganda films had abandoned left-wing politics long ago. He became a thoroughgoing Conservative, and in 1942 his friend Winston Churchill arranged a knighthood for him. Some people in Britain considered it distasteful to give a knighthood to a divorced Hungarian Jew who made films for a living.[6]

The award was ostensibly for services to the British film industry; in fact, it was for his war services. He had produced and directed a number of propaganda-driven films, including the popular *That Hamilton Woman* (also released as *Lady Hamilton*), starring Vivien Leigh in the title role and Laurence Olivier as Lord Nelson. Churchill had greatly admired the film. The parallels between Napoleon and Hitler were obvious and one line in the film was allegedly suggested by Churchill himself: 'Napoleon can never be master of the world until he has smashed us up – and believe me, gentlemen, he means to be master of the world. You cannot make peace with dictators, you have to destroy them.'[7]

Making timely films wasn't Korda's only contribution to the war. Churchill had persuaded him to engage in covert activities while in America. In 1940, on Churchill's instructions, MI6 had set up a secret section in New York, called British Security Coordination; part of its job was to sway opinion in the United States away from isolationism and towards joining the war. Korda's role was to act as a secret courier between British and American intelligence, and to allow his New York office to be used as a clearing-house for intelligence information.[8]

A bad odour seemed to emanate from Korda's empire. Those who sensed it were deeply wary of him. Lockhart was among them. In October 1947 – possibly through Moura's influence – Lockhart was invited to a meeting at Korda's penthouse suite at Claridge's.[9] He had been offered a job as an adviser. His former employer Lord Beaverbrook told him to demand a salary of £5,000, since Korda was so rich. But by November, although Lockhart had resigned from his column with *The Times*, he was having qualms about taking the job. His friend Brendan Bracken (former Minister of Information, friend of Churchill and vehement opponent of the Attlee government's nationalisation programme) warned Lockhart not to take the work, and advised him to back out of the contract he had signed. In Bracken's opinion films were unclean. Or at least Alex Korda was. Lockhart concurred; he withdrew, saying goodbye to a salary of £12,000.[10]

If Moura detected the bad aroma, it didn't faze her. A woman who had been intimate with Yakov Peters and done the bidding of Stalin was hardly likely to be deterred by a faint whiff of off-colour business practices. And she wasn't alone. Accountants and members of the ruling class might hold their noses in his presence, but Sir Alexander Korda was at the centre of Britain's postwar film industry, and most of the great names of the era worked with or for him. Among others, Carol Reed and David Lean directed, Terence Rattigan had written screenplays, and the roster of actors included Ralph Richardson, David Niven, Orson Welles, Charles Laughton, Robert Donat and Jack Hawkins. Many who knew of his shady dealings loved him all the same. Richard Burton, from whom he made $500,000 by selling him to 20th Century Fox, called him 'the loveable larcenous Sir Alex'. Korda bought a Canaletto with the proceeds and showed it smugly to the young actor. 'Enjoy it my boy, you paid for it.'[11]

Another of Moura's friends who worked for Korda – quite possibly through her influence – was Cecil Beaton. He had avoided working in films, regarding film-makers as vulgar (although he adored movie stars). Korda's initial approach to him confirmed this impression: 'I want to buy you,' he said. 'But I don't want to be bought,' Cecil objected, 'and I'm terribly expensive.' But bought he was, for a high price (just as well, since he needed the money badly), and produced exquisite designs for the 1948 film *Anna Karenina*, starring Vivien Leigh (Moura was an adviser on the film). Cecil eventually grew to like the man who had purchased him.[12]

Korda liked Moura and enjoyed hearing her gossip. He gave her a job as his resident literary agent and script editor. She also did translations, but most importantly she was employed to keep Sir Alex happy.[13] It was a little like her relationship with Gorky all over again, but without the requirement to manage his household and be his mistress. And also, of course, without the sense of being in the presence of a towering, mercurial literary genius and national hero. Although Korda gave her a desperately needed income and enabled her to enlarge her social world, it was a step down for Moura.

But she made the best of it, as only she could. Korda's nephew Michael was present at a drinks party at the Claridge's suite in 1947, when he was thirteen. It was a typical affair, with film directors, actors and politicians – including Brendan Bracken, here despite the uncleanness of the host. (Moura spread a rumour that Bracken was Churchill's illegitimate son.) Carol Reed was in attendance, and Vivien Leigh was expected to turn up (although her fragile emotional temperament made her unpredictable). Even in this company, when Moura arrived she managed to make herself the star. When the butler opened the door, she exploded into the room with a theatrical flourish and swept over to embrace Alex and his brother Vincent, engulfing each of them in one of the hungry bear hugs that were becoming her trademark. She wore what appeared, in the eyes of thirteen-year-old Michael, to be a floor-length black tent with a panel of gauze, and carried a beaded bag and a gold lorgnette. Her accent, which she had cultivated all her adult life, dripped with the flavour of Russia. 'D-aaaah-ling,' she said to the astonished Michael, dropping onto the chair next to him, 'give me just a little v-oooh-dkah and a bite of caviar, just to restore an old lady who has had a terrible long taxi ride all the way from Kensington.'[14] He complied, and watched as the 'old lady' drained the glass in one gulp and asked for another.

All evening she made herself the focus of attention by feeding Korda's addiction for gossip. Everybody else was drawn to her as well. Her gravelly accent, voluminous size and deep throaty laughter, gained through years of heavy smoking, made her an object of fascination rather than ridicule, and her acute intellect allowed her to hold the attention of the guests at every gathering.

After dinner the company moved into the drawing room, where Moura joined the men, lit a big cigar for herself and listened to the conversation. After all, a dispenser of gossip must collect it too. Everything was of interest, but most of all politics, and she had a talent for teasing out indiscretions (as Duff Cooper had discovered). She never missed or forgot what was said, no matter how much vodka she had consumed.

Michael Korda, who came to know her well after he grew up, recognised that Moura had never lost her love of Russia, but believed that her loyalty to Britain was strong. She had not changed with the passage of the decades. Michael was fascinated by her ability to hold people's attention, especially if the guests were men of fame, power and influence. She regaled them with incredible stories laden with embellishment and garnished with lies. Michael felt that she was less interested in women than men, and was something of a *saloniste* or courtesan. 'She was a kind, fascinating, brilliant woman on the outside but inside she had a core of stainless steel.'[15]

Moura was a *saloniste* in the fullest sense, although she had shed her role as a courtesan. And her salon, whose regular home was at Ennismore Gardens, she took with her wherever she went.

Moura's loyalty to Britain came under scrutiny in 1947. All three of the children had become British years ago – Tania and Kira through marriage, and Paul through naturalisation. Moura, apparently realising only now, after more than a decade, that London would always be her home, finally decided to apply.

She was interviewed by Special Branch as part of the process.[16] She took the meeting only slightly more seriously than she took her social conversations. Unable to produce either a birth or a marriage certificate, she gave an account of her life in which facts were spiced up with lies. On this occasion, the untruths were slight. She had gone to stay with her sister in Berlin at the age of sixteen, where she had met her first husband, which was true. At the outbreak of the Russian Revolution, she had been arrested and remained in prison for ten months because of her association with Lockhart, which was a mixture of truth and outrageous fiction. She described her life with Gorky, and her move to Estonia in 1921, where she claimed to have worked for 'a Dutchman' selling diamonds and gold. This was the only time in Moura's life she admitted to the role she had been tasked with by Maria Andreyeva and the *valiuta* programme.

At the time of her application, Moura was still working for *La France Libre*. She received £400 a year for this, and made a further £300 from her literary agency. Her bank account was overdrawn by £600. She omitted to mention her earnings from Korda. MI5's investigation eventually uncovered information from a 'reputable person' that Baroness Budberg was being paid a good salary of over £2,000 per annum by him. As the recording agent noted, it would more than 'cover the flow of gin'.[17] Socially Moura kept her financial situation secret, giving the impression of genteel poverty. Even Tania was under the impression that she received only a small weekly wage from Korda, despite the fact that she had her own office and a secretary.[18]

On politics, Moura told Special Branch that she had no interest in subversive politics and that she was not a member of the Communist Party, although she did not deny that many of her friends were left-wing, or that the Soviet Ambassador Ivan Maisky and his wife were friends of hers. No, she said when prompted, she did *not* despise the Soviet regime.

MI5 and Special Branch had continued to monitor the Baroness throughout the war, and in 1944 had stated, 'There is not the slightest doubt that this clever woman is working in an underground capacity for the Russians.'[19] And yet not only was she never arrested, interned or deported, she was never even formally interrogated by MI5, other than the naturalisation interview. Her application was investigated, and a five-page document produced, mostly consisting of reasons not to approve the application. Nonetheless, in June her Certificate of Naturalisation was approved.[20] Moura had achieved the status she had been hoping for ever since 1919. She was a British subject.

But still MI5 kept an eye on her.

Towards the end of 1947, with her new passport in hand, Moura made her first trip to the United States. *La France Libre* had just been wound up and Moura needed something to fill the gap in her life and her income.

The fact that she was issued a US visa must suggest that either MI5 had not informed the FBI, the CIA or the State Department that she was suspected of being a Soviet spy, or that they were informed but decided that it was worth letting her into the country and watching what she did.

Her prime contact in America was Henry Regnery, a well-known publisher of conservative books by authors such as Wyndham Lewis, William F. Buckley, Russell Kirk and Frank Meyer. Regnery was a controversial figure who published provocative essays and until 1941 had been a member of the isolationist America First Committee. He had just set up Regnery Publishing when Moura visited; he was interested in publishing European books with European ideas, especially those with a German slant.

On Regnery's staff was Paul Scheffer, Moura's old lover from Berlin. Following his resignation from *Berliner Tageblatt* due to Nazi interference he had left Germany and ended up in America, where he was interned as a suspected Nazi spy. The allegations against him in the 1938 Moscow trials in connection with the alleged Goebbels/Chernov conspiracy to cause famine in the Ukraine had pursued him. The US government changed its mind about Scheffer and took him into its intelligence and special operations division, the Office of Strategic Services, the forerunner of the CIA. At the end of the war he became a prosecution adviser at the Nuremberg trials. He'd begun working for Regnery on an informal basis, reading manuscripts and suggesting projects. It was almost certainly at his suggestion that Moura visited the embryonic company. She became Regnery's British agent and made suggestions about what she believed he ought to publish.

Soon after her return to England, Regnery wrote with the good news that at her suggestion a translation of Max Picard's *Hitler in uns selbst* (*Hitler In Our Selves*) had been published. He also told her that Scheffer would soon be contacting her about finding European publishers for a number of books Regnery was bringing out the next year.[21] They included *The German Resistance to Hitler* by Hans Rothfels, *The Treaty of Versailles and the Present* by Leonard von Muralt and *The Peace* by Ernst Junger. In return, Moura told him that she would also look out for a European 'masterpiece' for him. She also brought Regnery together with Victor Gollancz, the British publisher.[22] Politically, the socialist Gollancz was the antithesis of Regnery, but his strong sympathy with the plight of Germany gave him an affinity with Regnery Publishing's list.

If MI5 or the CIA were keeping watch, they would have taken note of Moura's contact with Scheffer, his Soviet connections, and the connection with the socialist Gollancz.[23]

While her publishing business regained the vitality it had achieved before the war, Moura went on working for Korda. Although she liked the social mêlée, she often complained that the work wasn't always much fun.

One evening in August 1948 Lockhart took her out for dinner at the Ivy restaurant in the West End. (It was popular with Moura's film and theatre crowd.) She was in a subdued mood and, unusually, drank very little. She told him she found working for Korda difficult – a friend of Lockhart's had said, 'Korda is an interesting man to know but impossible to work for', and Moura couldn't disagree.[24] She worked hard for her £2,000 a year – or at least she found it hard to fit the work in between her escalating publishing interests.

That evening, Moura, in a black mood, complained about everyone – the small size of the legacy H. G. had left her, the mean-spiritedness and vanity of George Bernard Shaw (still hanging on in his nineties), and above all the egotistical meanness of Somerset Maugham. He was a friend of hers but she thought him the 'king of snobs' who was a 'good but vicious writer'. What irked her most was his abominable treatment of his female lovers; one poor woman he had kept dangling 'because she was very smart', only to cut her off publicly with cruel abruptness. Moura and Lockhart discussed the various 'practising homosexualists' they knew, including Maugham and their old Russian friend Hugh Walpole (whom Maugham despised and never spoke about 'without venom, hate and jealousy'). Lockhart was entertained by Moura's sour commentaries – 'She certainly made a sad mess of our famous writers,' he recorded. 'It is a great mistake for the reader ever to get to know his favourite authors. Every writer must be in some sort an exhibitionist, and exhibitionists are not attractive types.'[25]

But even in her darkest mood she was loyal to H. G.'s memory, which touched and impressed Lockhart. Moura's loves were precious to her, even when they had been troubled.

A Russian Patriot

1948–1956

Suspicions about Moura extended into her salons. MI5, continuing their watch on her after her naturalisation, kept a particularly close eye on this side of her life.

People looked forward to receiving invitations to Baroness Budberg's parties. At her quieter soirées she played hostess to twelve to fifteen guests, but whenever her finances permitted she would throw dinner or drinks parties for as many as fifty. Part of the attraction was Moura herself; part was the eclectic mix of fellow guests who congregated in the incongruously shabby flat with its heavy old furniture, religious icons and drab paintings of Russia and Italy on the walls.

In those days, there were four distinct groups of acquaintances, summed up in October 1950 by MI5 Section B2a.[1] First there were her friends from the Foreign Office. Then there was the 'circle of pansy young men' (B2a believed them all to be 'interior decorators', but most were writers and actors). Of greatest interest to MI5 was her circle of foreign friends, including 'many Russians and known Soviet supporters'. Finally there were her 'grand friends', including people such as Lady Diana Cooper and her husband Duff Cooper, Laurence Olivier and Lady Ottoline Morrell, together with many of her old friends from H. G.'s day.

Moura was a strong social draw. In a conversation at Harold Nicolson's house between George Weidenfeld and his publishing partner Nigel Nicolson (Harold's son) on the subject of the ideal dinner guest, Moura came out top of their list.[2] Indeed, Harold, who had known her since Berlin in the 1920s, considered her 'the cleverest woman of her day in London'.[3] He ought to know – over the years he had seen her in action at parties holding her own with some of the brightest and most arrogant intellects of their day – H. G. Wells, George Bernard Shaw, Somerset Maugham, Arthur Koestler and dozens of others.

Her soirées were divided among the different sets, and few people crossed between them. George Weidenfeld, who was grouped with the boisterous literary and artistic set, once mistook his dates and arrived to find her drawing room filled with 'greying men of military bearing, many of them with moustaches and monocles'. Moura was embarrassed. 'Darling,' she said, 'you have come a day early.' And he was graciously shepherded out, to return the next evening, when the familiar set of writers, publishers and artists were gathered.[4]

One of the most frequent guests at her salon was civil servant Guy Burgess. Moura had known him during her time at the Joint Broadcasting Committee at the start of the war. He probably came into her social circle through mutual friends such as Harold Nicolson and Isaiah Berlin.[5] Section B2a probably classed him with the Foreign Office group rather than the 'pansy young men', and regarded him as less interesting than the 'known Soviet supporters'. George Weidenfeld, who as an Austrian Jewish émigré was one of the 'foreign' contingent at Moura's parties, didn't like Burgess. He thought him a vain attention-seeker who had a habit of breaking into conversations and 'bursting into a soliloquy without regard to the people present'.[6] At one of Moura's evenings, Burgess accused Weidenfeld of supporting a pro-European policy. In his view, the only powers that counted were the United States and the Soviet Union, and one must choose between those two.

Moura liked Burgess a great deal and he was often at her parties. She seemed to see a kindred spirit in him. Anthony Blunt described Burgess as 'not only one of the most intellectually stimulating people I have ever known but also had great charm and tremendous vivacity', and although Burgess was 'perverse in many ways, there was no subject which one could discuss with him without his expressing some interesting and worthwhile views'.[7] Also, Moura and Burgess both enjoyed drinking more than was good for them.

Most of the regular *salonistes* had opinions on whether Moura was a spy. The rumours about her had been gossiped over many times. George Weidenfeld considered her a Russian patriot; 'but those among her social circle who were politically tolerant and benevolently inclined towards her might have conceded that she could have been a double agent, leaving to individual guesswork the question as to which side Moura was more likely to have favoured'.[8]

In July 1950 a new development occurred which heightened MI5's concerns about Baroness Budberg. Moura threw a very small party to which she had invited her old friend Scottish publisher James MacGibbon (co-founder of MacGibbon & Kee); he had a background in wartime intelligence, was a known Communist and was also being watched by MI5. Guy Burgess was a guest that evening too, along with four others. After several hours, a surveillance team watched them leaving. 'Each of the six was somewhat the worse for drink,' the agent reported, with the Baroness leading by example, 'as no doubt a hostess should'.[9] Burgess was still considered a trustworthy Foreign Office employee, if not entirely respectable. In B2a's opinion, Baroness Budberg was 'not a desirable acquaintance' for a man with Burgess's doubtful character and in his position. She might prove a bad influence.[10]

Rather than scrutinising Burgess, who had secretly been working for the Soviet Union since the 1930s, MI5 focused on MacGibbon. During the war he had worked for MI3, which was responsible for the intelligence side of the plans for D-Day. Concerned by how much better the Western Allies' military intelligence was than that of the Soviets, MacGibbon had passed information about German forces to the NKVD. In doing so, he believed he was helping the Soviet war effort, and therefore also the war effort as a whole. At the end of the war, he was offered £2,000 by the Soviet Embassy in gratitude, and several anonymous Russians had tried to persuade him to continue as their informant, but he declined. The war was won, his job was over, and he had no intention of making a career of spying.[11] But MI5 had been told about his activities, and watched him closely.

It is possible that Moura was one of the Russians who tried to steer him towards Soviet service. On one occasion in 1950 she asked him to come and see her on an urgent and personal matter. MacGibbon, expecting a private meeting, was not happy to find a party in full swing rather than his expected solitary tête-à-tête. The guests included the 'curious chap from the FO' called Burgess, whom MacGibbon didn't like. Later that night the MI5 operatives who were bugging his house heard him complain to his wife that 'Moura was an absolute devil' for deceiving him.[12] MacGibbon's telephone was also tapped, and his watchers recorded Moura telling his wife that the Russians would 'rather

James did it than somebody else'.[13] Exactly what 'it' was couldn't be discerned.

MacGibbon was taken in and questioned by Jim Skardon, MI5's star interrogator. Skardon had become legendary for his soft-spoken, gentle-mannered but inexhaustible and irresistible probes into suspects' minds. It was Skardon who had broken Klaus Fuchs, the 'atomic spy' who had passed inside information from the Manhattan Project to the Soviet Union. Those who were subjected to Skardon's interrogations were simultaneously seduced by his warm, flattering manner and terrified by his reputation. His technique was to exhaust the subject with his patient persistence, disorient them with rapid changes of subject, and lay subtle traps.

Eventually Skardon cleared MacGibbon, and he was taken off the list of suspected Soviet agents. He wasn't the only man to survive Skardon's probing. MI6 operative Kim Philby, who had also come under suspicion, sweated through a long series of interrogations at his hands; he too was taken off the list. Skardon failed to break him, and concluded that he was probably innocent, but MI5 disagreed and kept Philby under surveillance.[14] James MacGibbon was luckier; off the hook for the time being, he continued his career in publishing and his friendship with Moura.

One of Jim Skardon's contacts suggested that Moura could be useful to MI5 as an informant. With her access to Soviet diplomats, she could be a valuable source. Section B2a, running the investigation, added the opinion that Moura was an extremely intelligent woman who was very self-centred and had little integrity and no loyalty other than to herself. Also, as a result of a recent breast cancer diagnosis she had become frightened of falling ill and losing her income. It was noted by B2a that she was a brilliant literary critic and a very good conversationalist; men found her entrancing to listen to.[15]

MI5 could not decide what to do – recruit her for their use or keep going after her as a spy? One report ended by saying, 'As to Moura – I am no further than before – somewhere between doubt and benefit of the doubt.'[16]

Shortly after this report, fresh testimony about Baroness Budberg arrived on the desk of an MI5 official. The novelist Rebecca West, H. G. Wells' former lover, had recently seen Moura at a party given by their mutual friend, the American journalist Dorothy Thompson. Like

Moura she had an interest in publishing foreign literature and had worked in Berlin in the 1930s. Other guests at the party, according to Rebecca, included 'a most unsavoury crowd of Communist sympathisers judging by their adulation of Baroness Budberg'.[17] She added that H. G. Wells' family had always considered Budberg to be a Soviet agent.

Retrospective jealousy or patriotic concern? It could have been a little of both. H. G. had confided to his and Rebecca's son Anthony that Moura had confessed to being a Soviet spy, and Anthony had believed the claim, and presumably passed it on to his mother. Rebecca had cause to be jealous on that count too, as Anthony was almost as smitten by Moura as his father had been.[18]

Evidence like Rebecca West's had trickled into MI5's files regularly over the thirty-year course of their inquiries. Sometimes it would prompt another Home Office warrant and Moura's phone would be tapped, her house bugged, her mail opened and her whereabouts checked. Moura knew she was the subject of an investigation and mentioned it to Klop Ustinov, saying that she was being followed. She might even have been aware that he was one of the agents watching her.

In February 1951, two weeks after their interview with Rebecca West, MI5 reviewed Moura's status once more, and came to a critical decision. Commenting that it was a shame that she had not been thoroughly interrogated at the time of her application for naturalisation, they decided to make good the omission now, partly to justify the huge cost of keeping her under surveillance. 'As she is in contact with so many of our major suspects,' her minute sheet noted, 'there seems no other choice for us but to interrogate her in the hope of getting further information.'[19]

Rather than bringing her in for a formal interrogation it was decided to make use of Klop Ustinov again. His wartime service as a secret agent had made him even more highly valued by the intelligence services. The rationale was the same as in 1940 – as Moura knew both him and his wife it would be easy for him to investigate her without her becoming suspicious (or so they assumed). Klop was briefed to gain access to Moura's inner circle of friends, obtain her trust, and discover once and for all exactly where her loyalties lay. On top of this, if it should prove viable, he was authorised to recruit her as a double agent. He arranged meetings and meals, ensuring that he was regularly invited to her parties, at which he would often come face to face with Burgess and her other crypto-Communist friends. Some of them were coming close to exposure.

Suddenly, in May 1951, a crisis occurred which took everyone by surprise and pushed Moura's case to a turning point.

Donald Maclean was under investigation by MI5, and the KGB believed that if he were put under heavy interrogation he would crack and reveal his fellow spies. The KGB, guessing what was about to happen, decided to yank the iron out of the fire, and recalled Maclean to Moscow; at the last minute it was decided that Burgess should leave with him. On 25 May 1951, three days before the date MI5 had set to begin Maclean's interrogation, Burgess collected him from his home and drove him to Southampton. They took a ferry to Saint-Malo in Brittany, then travelled on false passports to Moscow. Their 'disappearance' sparked an international panic. No one in the West knew where they had gone, and the media speculated wildly.

Moura was immediately put back on a Home Office warrant. The bugs in her flat picked up conversations among her guests speculating about where the missing men could have gone. In June Moura gave a party to which she invited Klop. The other guests included a couple of publishers, a woman from the British Council and Vera Traill, a Russian who was also under MI5 investigation. The conversation turned to the subject of Guy Burgess. Everyone there had known and loved him despite his alcohol problem and self-centredness. One of the publishers believed that he must have defected. Moura suggested that he might have been kidnapped or had an accident while on the Continent. Whatever the case, everyone was convinced he must have been a spy of some sort rather than merely a Foreign Office functionary.

Moura was aware that she was being watched and probably guessed that the situation was about to get extremely uncomfortable for Soviet agents and sympathisers in England. And with her long experience of detecting changes in the wind and bending with them, she had an ulterior purpose in throwing that party.

When the other guests left, Moura asked Klop to stay behind. She explained that she had invited the others especially for his benefit – she thought it would interest him to hear what people who were friends of Burgess thought about the affair. One of the publishers, she said, had a Communist sister who had been in touch with MacGibbon; he had told her that he had only met Burgess at Moura's parties. The lady did not believe him.

In his report on the evening, Klop expressed his surprise at how helpful Moura had been, and thought it was now up to MI5 to exploit the situation.[20]

He fixed another appointment with her. Her next soirée was on 28 June. The guests included George Weidenfeld, who speculated that Burgess and Maclean might be in Germany. He had known Burgess for seven years, he said, and didn't think he was in any position to be able to obtain secrets from the Foreign Office that the Russians would find of interest.[21]

A few days later Klop and Moura dined at the Sherry Bar in Pelham Street. When it closed at nine they went back to his flat, where they talked until the early hours. They discussed James MacGibbon, Burgess and Maclean and another of Moura's visitors – Alexander Halpern and his wife Salomea. Halpern was an associate from the old days – a lawyer who had served as private secretary to Kerensky in 1917. Migrating to Britain, he had joined the SIS and during the Second World War had worked for British Security Coordination in New York – the same organisation with which Alexander Korda had liaised.[22] Salomea, a former *Vogue* model, had openly expressed Communist sympathies.

During their conversation Moura said that as she had so many left-wing friends she was surprised that she had never been interrogated. Klop suggested that the reason was probably her friendship with him. 'Ever since the war started,' he told her, 'there has been a lively interest in your activities. Every time I've been asked about you my answer was: This woman is much too intelligent to do anything foolish.'

Moura played innocent. 'Even if I'd wanted to divulge information to the Soviets,' she said, 'what information do I have that would be of interest to them?'

'In this field there are tasks that you would be admirably suited to perform,' he told her. 'Talent-spotting, for one.'

It had come to the moment of truth – the moment Klop's superiors had authorised him to take advantage of. But it had to be handled correctly – it wasn't done to put ideas in a potential agent's head.

Moura told him that she liked left-wingers because they seemed more intelligent than other people. Anyway, in her opinion the whole world would eventually be Communist – even though it would not happen for a long time.

It was as if she were giving her flag one last loyal wave before submitting.

MacGibbon, she told Klop, had not so far confessed anything of interest to her, other than crying on her shoulder about his business partner Kee's attempted suicides, but if she heard anything of interest she would certainly let Klop know.

It was two o'clock in the morning when Moura said goodnight. In parting, she invited Klop to help her mix the drinks for two large parties she had coming up. She was planning to invite fifty guests to each. With this invitation hanging in the air, she set out through the London night towards Ennismore Gardens.[23]

Over the following weeks and months, while the newspapers continued to speculate over the 'missing diplomatists' Burgess and Maclean (traitors? kidnap victims?), Moura edged her way out of the searchlight and closer to Klop. She told him that she was out of favour with the Soviets – none of her letters to Gorky's family were being delivered, and none sent back to her. Klop came to her parties, at which she offered up her guests as a buffet of suspects – 'Here are people who may be of interest to you, help yourself,' as Klop expressed it in his report.[24]

Most of Moura's offerings were British. There were few Russian émigrés in her circle. Many of them had never trusted her, and shunned her. One who did come to her parties was Kyril Zinovieff, a writer and translator who went by the pen-name FitzLyon (taken from his wife, the author April FitzLyon). He had known Moura since the 1920s in Berlin, when he was a teenage student; as an acquaintance of the former Hetman Skoropadskyi, he knew about her spying in the Ukraine in 1918. He remained in her circle because he was fascinated by her, but felt that he 'could never respect or trust her'; he believed that her covert activities had 'led to the deaths of several people'.[25] If some of the more outlandish rumours had any truth in them, Moura was implicated in the deaths of considerably more than 'several'.

Moura went on meeting regularly with Klop Ustinov. She passed on the latest gossip about Burgess and Maclean. Some people were saying that they were lovers and had gone to the Mediterranean on a yachting trip together. No 'iron curtain' was involved, she said.

If Moura was mistaken about Burgess and Maclean (or deliberately feeding Klop misinformation), her next revelation was the real thing. Anthony Blunt, she said, to whom Guy Burgess had been 'most devoted' and who had been an occasional guest at her soirées, was a member of the Communist Party.

Klop was astonished. 'All I know about him is that he looks after the King's pictures,' he said.

Moura said sourly, 'Such things happen only in England.'[26]

Klop probably knew more about Blunt than he admitted; they had both served in the counter-intelligence section of MI5 during the war. At the end of the war Blunt had returned to his first love – art history. By 1947 he held a professorship at the University of London, was Director of the Courtauld Institute, and had been appointed Surveyor of the King's Pictures. When Moura spoke to Klop, Blunt was already under suspicion because of his closeness to Burgess. Between 1951 and 1952 he was interrogated eleven times by Jim Skardon, but like Philby, he couldn't be broken. Baroness Budberg's information was deemed 'insufficiently reliable' and was never added to his file. Although he was never entirely free from MI5's suspicions, Blunt went on with his life, and a few years later was knighted for his services to the Crown.

By October 1951, when Moura dined with Klop again at his flat, she was pledging herself to report every person moving in her sphere whom she suspected of being a traitor to Britain – 'actual or potential'. In return, Klop offered the possibility of being put on the MI5 payroll. Moura mentioned a couple of names which caught his interest. Singling out one of them – 'an important member of the Soviet Embassy' – he told her, 'If you can bring this man and his wife on our side, it might have a wholesome effect on your finances.'

Moura had told him over dinner that her financial situation was precarious and needed 'straightening out'. Klop added, 'Smaller fry will also do if you can manage to establish contacts in time.'

Money was always welcome, but for Moura the real incentive was the same as it had always been – safety, security and survival. And the thrill of it all.

Klop Ustinov, under his codename U35, submitted his report on this conversation on Monday 25 October 1951.[27] It was processed and placed in Moura's file, which now ran to three copious volumes. The file was closed, deactivated and placed in an archive. It would never be reopened.

Baroness Moura Budberg had been successfully recruited as a British spy. Again.

To a woman who had served several dangerous masters during the revolutions of 1917 and the Red Terror, who had crossed borders in secret as a roving agent, liaised directly with Stalin, and seen the inside of several Cheka prisons, this was nothing very remarkable. In a sense, Moura had come full circle, back to the beginning of her career in espionage, when 'Madame B' had kept her salon in Petrograd for pro-German Russians and spied on them for Kerensky and her friend George Hill of the SIS.

Her soirées at Ennismore Gardens continued as they had before. The range of guests was the same eclectic mix of 'pansy young men', film and literary stars, Foreign Office types and 'grand friends'. But now there was a new and invisible underlying purpose. But if Moura ever passed information on any of her guests – and she must have done – it remains hidden by secrecy. Her own file had been closed, and her presence continued only in other people's files, where she would exist only as a number, a yet-unidentified agent codename.

Meanwhile, up on the surface, in the daylight, life went on.

Moura loved her bed. She had grown to love it with a special fondness in that first week at Kallijärv in 1921, after her release by the police in Tallinn.

Having a job tended to interfere with her love of bed. Moura's working life – in its ideal state – resembled her social life: travelling, negotiating, meeting new and fascinating people, and making herself the indispensable nexus between them. She found working for Korda arduous because it required her to rise each day, go to the offices of London Films at 146 Piccadilly and do a day's toil in the Korda script-mill. That didn't suit her at all – especially now that age was slowly eroding her ability to shake off the effects of the previous night's over-indulgence – so she came to an arrangement with her secretary. If the phone rang and it was anyone of importance – particularly Sir Alex himself – the secretary would explain that Baroness Budberg had just popped out for a moment. Then she would ring Moura, who would haul herself out of bed, throw on her clothes (she had lost the habit of dressing with any care decades ago) and hail a taxi.

In all likelihood Korda knew what she was doing, but saw no harm in it. Moura had lost none of her ability to charm and inveigle. Twenty years earlier she would certainly have made Korda her lover, as she had Wells, Gorky, and many better and greater men. But that side of her had died with H. G. and the onset of age. Instead she did the deed by proxy, setting herself the task of finding him a woman to sustain him in his autumnal years.

He had been keeping a mistress for a while. Christine Norden was a flighty, aspiring young actress who had suddenly flown off with an American air force sergeant. Sir Alex had begged her to stay and marry him, but to no avail.[28] There was a vacancy to be filled, and Moura decided to find a candidate.

Korda had been married twice before, to the actress Maria Corda, and then in 1939 to British film star Merle Oberon, who was eighteen years his junior. Their marriage had lasted six years. As he aged, his brides grew younger. The woman Moura found for him in 1953 was just twenty-four, whereas Korda was sixty. Her name was Alexandra Boycun; she was a Canadian of Ukrainian parentage, a budding singer, and exquisitely beautiful. She had no ambition to be an actress, and neither did she seem to be a fortune-seeker. Korda had confided in Moura that he was through with actresses; he wanted a stay-at-home wife who could minister to his every whim in his old age.

In other words, he wanted exactly what H. G. had hoped for from Moura. And like Wells, his chances of gaining it were fairly slim. Alexa might not be a fortune hunter, but she was a free spirit.

To everyone's surprise, in June 1953, after a short courtship, the mismatched couple married. Moura was a witness. Alexa's father sent a telegram saying, 'Sir Alexander is too old for my daughter.'[29] The whole thing was a mistake; not necessarily for Korda or Alexa, but for Moura. Once Alexa became the woman in the Korda household and no longer needed to be Moura's protégée, she began asserting herself, and elbowed Moura away. Moura's attempts to steer or advise her began to be seen as pushiness. She was still on the guest list for Korda's dinner parties, but not as frequently or as warmly welcomed as she had been.[30]

Korda paid the regular price for involving himself with a much younger woman – the same price that Gorky had paid with Moura. Alexa sometimes grew tired of her old and by now unwell husband, and flitted off on escapades of her own. She grew close to his young nephew Michael. The thirteen-year-old boy who had been so stunned by Moura in 1947 was now in his early twenties, close in age to Alexa, and they became attached to each other, despite Michael's father warning him against it. There was no sexual relationship between them; they were intimate friends, and Michael covered for Alexa's absences. Korda was jealous, and the two were forbidden to see each other.

The marriage survived for as long as it needed to, which turned out to be three years. In late January 1956 Sir Alexander Korda died, finished off by a heart problem that been troubling him for years.

26

. . . The End of Everything

1956–1974

May 1963, London

Moura parted the heavy curtain and looked out into the evening dark, moving close to the glass to see through the lamplit reflection of her own glittering eyes. The bloom of early summer lay over Kensington, turning the late evening deep blue and hazing the smoke that hovered above the rooftops. Below her window, taxis flitted by and the night buses heaved their way down the arrow-straight gorge of the Cromwell Road, whining down through the gears as they slowed for the Earls Court junction.

Countryside was all very well, but Moura needed the city as she needed breath. There was life here. It was a good night for a party; a good night to live and be one with the world.

She hummed happily to herself. The reflection in the glass smiled back. Such a changed face. The lines were deep, the features thickened, and the hair grey, pinned and lacquered in a coronet of silver waves flowing back from her forehead. But the eyes were still the same shining, feline jewels that had looked out on the snows of Yendel under the moonlight of a different age.

Her breath hazed the cool glass. A good night for a party indeed.

Behind her, the clink of glasses and babble of voices suddenly erupted in gales of laughter, and Moura came out of her dream. She let the curtain fall back into place and turned back to the room. The laughter had been caused by Peter Ustinov – he was on his knees, acting the part of Queen Victoria praying for victory in the Boer War; it was part of a charade based on the Nazi film *Ohm Krüger*; an amazing mimic, he switched effortlessly into the ranting title part and back again.[1] Snapping up another gin and setting light to another cigar, Moura waded in among the throng; it parted for her, and she resumed her place at its heart.

They were all here – all her best friends. Klop Ustinov's darling boy Peter, becoming quite the film star these days, and one of Moura's dearest friends. Hamish Hamilton and his wife Yvonne were regular guests, as was George Weidenfeld. Baron Bob Boothby, the scandalous Tory peer, was another. A tower of flesh surmounted by two glowering eyes, Boothby had a prodigious sexual appetite. He swung both ways and had eclectic tastes; his lovers including Dorothy Macmillan, wife of the Prime Minister, and more recently (if gossip was to be believed) Ronnie Kray, the gangster.[2] Boothby considered Moura 'one of the most remarkable and discerning women I have ever known, as well as the best friend'.[3]

Writers, actors, directors, diplomats had all come to the party. Old friends and new, but none from the old days of Yendel. They were all dead – Meriel had died a few years ago, having published a memoir in which she relived those holidays, quoting Garstino's poem – '. . . oh to be / In Yendel for eternity . . .' All dead and gone. This was a new world now, with other worlds of memory stretching from that day to this.

The guests talked loudly, laughed uproariously, and drank oceans. They were welcome; after all, they'd paid for it. They hadn't actually *intended* to pay, but nonetheless it was their money that was being drunk.

Times had become hard for Moura. After Alex Korda's death in 1956, she no longer had regular work to boost the income from her publishing ventures.

She had some help from the theatrical impresario Hugh 'Binkie' Beaumont, the king of London theatreland. He had often done deals with Alexander Korda; actors under contract but not being used by Sir Alex would be lent out to Binkie for his plays. Binkie was renowned for both his financial cunning and for his extreme generosity, and after Korda died he helped subsidise Moura's income.[4]

There were other valuable contacts too, and Moura carried on working in films with other producers and directors, taking whatever odd jobs and tasks she could. In 1959 she was a technical adviser on *The Journey* (starring Deborah Kerr and Yul Brynner), a drama set in Communist Hungary. In 1961 Peter Ustinov gave her a bit part in his comedy *Romanoff and Juliet*, as Kiva the cook. Producer Sam Spiegel and director David Lean, who had taken a great liking to Moura, employed her as a researcher for *Lawrence of Arabia*. She was often a go-between – her vast, carefully spun network of friends and acquaintances brought her many tasks. When Lean first had an urge to turn E. M. Forster's *A Passage to India* into a film, he asked Moura to approach Forster, who was among her friends, to ask him to sell the film rights. He turned her down, as he did everybody. Forster was 'simply terrified of the cinema', Lean believed.[5]

Moura's translation work provided a modest regular income. She had acquired considerable stature as a translator of Gorky and Chekhov, and earned glowing reviews for both. L. P. Hartley called her one of the most felicitous translator's of Gorky's work, and she was praised for her beautiful translation of his *Fragments*.[6] Her work wasn't always good; in need of money, Moura would take any commissions she could get, and her heart sometimes wasn't in it; some of her translations of lesser works were skimped (occasionally missing out whole sentences and paragraphs if they were too challenging), and her professional reputation suffered. But the work still came in, because publishers couldn't resist her persuasions.[7]

Although Moura had always worked hard, she had never acquired the ability to be careful – or even basically responsible – with money. Without regular support from a figure like Gorky, Wells or Korda, she was perpetually short of cash and perennially unable to use it wisely when she did get it.

In 1963 the rent on her flat at 68 Ennismore Gardens went up. She simply couldn't afford it any longer. Moura felt not the slightest embarrassment about this; she had become one of that upper-class breed who turn being destitute into a profession. (Lockhart was another.) She had plenty of rich friends, and never had any compunction about letting others pay for things. Roger Machell, publisher and deputy to Hamish Hamilton, once arrived at Ennismore Gardens for one of Moura's soirées to find her just getting out of a taxi. She enveloped him in one of her bear hugs and then kept him chatting by the roadside for some minutes, while the cab's meter went on ticking. Then she turned and went indoors, leaving him alone with the idling taxi and its expectant driver. Machell did what any gentleman would do – he paid the fare himself.[8] Many of Moura's cab fares were handed off with this technique. Despite the shortage of money, Moura always had the charm, the gall and the resourcefulness to live her life without having her wings too severely clipped. She never took buses, and never ventured into the Underground.

Rent was a different matter. After looking around for new accommodation, she found a cheaper flat on the second floor of a genteel Edwardian block at 211 Cromwell Road, and in May 1963 she left the home she had first moved into in 1939. The move was such an event, it was reported in the *Observer*'s Pendennis column: 'The sound of steel on wood echoed through the empty, bare-floored room ... Moura Ignatievna, in a blue-spotted dressing-gown, was sorting papers from an old ottoman that had not been opened, she said, for at least 20 years.' Moura's move, said Pendennis, meant the disappearance of 'another of London's landmarks'. The names of those who had been entertained here over the years were listed like an epitaph: Wells, Maugham, Koestler, Hemingway, André Gide, William Walton, Harold Nicolson, Graham Greene, Robert Graves, Bertrand Russell . . . All had come 'not for the exquisiteness of her surroundings but for the stimulation of her company and the warm bear-hug of her Russian personality'.[9] A few men of her age group fancied more than that. Bertrand Russell, who'd met her first in the Kronverksky apartment in 1920, had said after H. G.'s death, 'She's welcome to a place in my bed.'[10]

She was photographed for the *Observer* in the new flat, weary but cheerful among her half-unpacked possessions.

Her closest friends were worried about her. Moura had just turned seventy-one. She had always been known to be short of money, but the enforced move shook them. Her situation must be serious. Peter Ustinov led the way; putting in a generous £1,000 himself, he invited all Moura's friends to contribute. They all gave, some of them quite large amounts, and the total raised came to around £6,000.[11] Ustinov organised a gathering at which the cheque was ceremoniously handed over.

Moura was grateful; she was touched and overcome with love for all her good friends. So overcome, she immediately threw a series of enormous parties. On three consecutive nights, all her closest friends, as well as her less close friends, her casual acquaintances and all their hangers-on crowded into her new flat and celebrated with her. By the time they were through, she had blown the whole lot, and was as broke as ever.[12]

When Moura started shoplifting, her friends grew even more concerned. In December 1964 she was caught stealing from Harrods. She took an umbrella, a spectacle case and other items (which she concealed inside the brolly) worth a total of £9. 7s. She asked the magistrates to take into consideration a previous theft of 'a toilet bag and other goods' from a shop in Sloane Square. The police estimated her income at a well-to-do £2,000 a year; accordingly she was given a hefty fine of £25, plus 9 guineas costs.[13]

The items she stole were intended as gifts for her friends, Moura claimed, and she hadn't the cash to pay for them. This noble intent was undermined somewhat when on another occasion she said plaintively to Bob Boothby that the umbrella 'contained only junk'. Boothby asked her why she would choose to steal junk. She wasn't amused. To Hamish Hamilton she confided that it was all about the challenge – 'pitting my wits against theirs'.[14] Once upon a time there had been the Cheka, then MI5, the KGB and the combined wits of Europe's intelligence services; now all that was left was the Metropolitan Police and the staff of Knightsbridge's department stores. Eventually she was threatened with prison, and promised to give up the habit; from then on her friends received fewer gifts.

It was an addiction. When Hamish's wife Yvonne noticed that one of her objets d'art had gone missing, she mentioned it to her butler, who said, 'I should speak to the Baroness Budberg, madam, if I were you.'[15]

Moura's old enemy Rebecca West, who had earlier tried to blacken her with MI5, eccentrically thought her innocent of the shoplifting charge, on the grounds that she didn't think Moura was really that short of money. 'I thought she was very tiresome in her perpetual protestations of poverty,' she wrote, 'but this is a vice which affects many people who are suffering from other forms of insecurity and cannot face them.' Rebecca didn't specify what form of insecurity she thought Moura suffered from.[16] Perhaps she was right to think that there was a deeper unrest in Moura's unconscious mind; if so, she was more accurate than Moura's friends, who thought her merely eccentric.

Everyone who knew Moura liked to think that he or she possessed the key to her mysterious personality, but only a select few – including Lockhart and H. G. – knew her well enough to judge her, and even they struggled to understand. Many seemed to agree with the palmist that her life was more interesting than she was. During the 1950s it had begun to occur to people in Moura's publishing circles that her life would make an excellent memoir.

Long ago, during the transitional period between Maxim Gorky and H. G. Wells, Moura had made a start on a book of her own, which appears to have been a memoir. At the beginning of the 1930s, while Lockhart was working on *Memoirs of a British Agent*, Moura was writing something she referred to variously as '*À côté de la mêlée*' and '*Au milieu de la mêlée*'.[17] It never came to anything – either due to distractions or the inability to put down on paper any version of her life that she would be able to live comfortably with. There were too many secrets, too many contradictory tales told to different people. The '*Mêlée*', if it was ever written, never saw the light of day.

In 1951 Blanche Knopf, wife and business partner of the New York publisher Alfred A. Knopf, wrote Moura a flattering letter, asking her to consider writing an autobiography, and offering to raise an advance from European and American publishers and sell serialisation rights to an American magazine.[18] Moura agreed, and presumably the advance was paid. She and Blanche met in the Ritz bar in Paris to discuss the book, and at the end of the year Blanche wrote again, asking how the synopsis was progressing. A whole year went by before she received a letter back from Moura. She had had to abandon the project because it interfered with her other work. 'Never mind,' she wrote, 'I'll do it once upon a time and you *will* have it!'[19] She didn't. Years went by and there was still no synopsis and no book, and the advance had long ago been burned up in taxi fares and parties. In 1956 Hamish Hamilton told Blanche that Moura was ready to begin her autobiography at last. There was jubilation for a short while, but again not a word was written, and the project came to nothing.

In the 1960s the idea was floated once more. Moura had been invited by Kenneth Tynan to contribute an interview on Gorky for his ITV arts programme *Tempo*. She asked the programme's researcher, Joan Rodker, if she would act as an amanuensis to help her write an autobiography. Joan was in some ways a fellow spirit – a left-wing activist with a penchant for holding court, described as the closest thing London had to a Communist salon. She spent many mornings sitting on Moura's bed, listening to her talk about her life and about Gorky. But again no book grew out of those sessions.[20]

During Moura's lifetime and afterwards, Hamilton made several attempts to get either a memoir or a biography off the ground, but there was too much resistance from the family and too little information.

Robin Bruce Lockhart – the boy whose birth so broke her heart in 1921 – was approached many times by authors wanting his help with their projected biographies of Moura Budberg. He knew about her espionage work from his father, but for most periods of her life there was too little information to work with. Moura had seen to that.[21]

Moura liked being mysterious; she liked keeping people guessing. And she must have realised that those things which she most wanted to keep secret were precisely the things that her friends and acquaintances most wanted to read about. She was so interesting because she was such a mystery.

Although no memoir was ever written, Moura's other work continued. Her efforts as a translator and writer had expanded from books to the theatre and cinema. In 1962 she created a new translation of Gorky's seminal play *The Lower Depths* for a staging by the playwright Derek Marlowe. The production starred Fulton Mackay and featured the young Prunella Scales.[22] As well as Gorky she translated Chekhov, and in 1967 she was commissioned by Laurence Olivier to translate *Three Sisters* for a National Theatre production starring Joan Plowright, Anthony Hopkins and Derek Jacobi; it was well received, and Moura's translation was compared favourably with other recent versions.[23]

That same year Moura wrote the screenplay for Sidney Lumet's film *The Sea Gull*, based on her own translation of Chekhov's play. It starred Vanessa Redgrave, James Mason and Simone Signoret. During the filming, Signoret – another magnetically attractive woman whose appearance had deteriorated with age – developed an intense dislike for Moura: 'The old hag claims to be a baroness but we all suspect her of being an old Russian phony.'[24] It was a comment that perhaps said more about the middle-aged French actress than about the elderly Russian screenwriter.

In 1972 Moura made her last contribution to film, when she was employed as a 'Russian adviser' on the BBC adaptation of *War and Peace*, starring Anthony Hopkins as Pierre Bezukhov. Her work had brought her full circle, back to the beginning. Everything connected up, through her bond with Gorky, for whom Leo Tolstoy had been both mentor and admirer; and through the worlds of imperial St Petersburg and rural Russia in the days before the Revolution swept it all away. Moura had been born into that other world, which had changed little between the days of Bonaparte and Alexander I to those of Rasputin and Nicholas II.

All gone now, beyond reach. Soon it would be time to follow it into the darkness.

Moura had been back to Russia. It was all different now, but a few of the old people were still there.

It came about after Stalin had gone to his grave and Nikita Krushchev had begun to relax some of the dictator's more repressive instruments of power. Moura's first visit was in 1959 – after a gap of twenty-three years. She was accompanied by George Weidenfeld, who was hoping to make contact with Soviet authors and publishers.[25] While he stayed at a hotel in Moscow, Moura was welcomed back into the Gorky household. It was still there, the place she had last visited in 1936, when he lay dying. The house was filled now with his family and presided over by the elderly Yekaterina Peshkova, Gorky's legal widow. It remained a crowded little commune. Korney Chukovsky was still around; his remaining hair was white, and the bushy moustache had gone, but he still had the same warm smile as on that cold December day when he first took Moura to meet Gorky and watched in amusement as the great man displayed his intellect like a peacock for the spellbinding young woman.

The house had become the Soviet state's official Gorky museum, and the downstairs rooms were open to the public at certain times of the day while the family retired to the upper quarters. In the evenings, as in days past, they entertained lavishly. The table was overflowing with food and wine. Guests arrived from eight in the evening until after the theatres closed and they played the piano, danced, sang and discussed world affairs. 'It was all very Russian and very elitist,' the bewildered Weidenfeld recalled.

Yekaterina welcomed Moura, but she was still wary of her, even after all these years. When Moura asked to visit again in 1962, Yekaterina confided to Chukovsky her anxieties about the Gorky papers, which were still in Moura's possession. She had heard that the papers unaccounted for included many dangerous items, including jottings by Gorky in which he put down his true thoughts about Stalin. Yekaterina had heard also (wrongly, in fact) that Moura had sold some of these writings to the British press. And the business of Gorky's vanished will still bothered her; she didn't know that Moura had forged the signature, but she knew that there had been something not right about that episode.[26] But the visit went ahead, and Moura, Yekaterina and Timosha went on a Volga river trip together.

On one occasion Moura was accompanied to Russia by Peter Ustinov, who was on a journey into his parents' past. In Moscow, he watched in amazement as she gestured to a policeman and demanded that he hail her a taxi. He declined to be treated as a servant: 'I am a militiaman,' he said, 'and I control traffic.'

'Don't give me that nonsense,' Moura replied. 'Find me a taxi. I'm an old comrade, and where are your manners?'

The policeman 'was reduced to tears', Ustinov recalled, 'and he found her a cab'.[27]

Nobody ever knew whether she saw anything of her old friend Guy Burgess in Moscow. But another of her friends, Graham Greene, did meet Burgess there, and recalled their peculiar conversation. 'I don't know why he particularly wished to see me,' Greene wrote, 'as I didn't like him . . . However, curiosity won and I asked him for a drink.' Burgess sent Greene's government escort away, saying that he wished to talk to him alone, 'but the only thing that he asked of me was to thank Harold Nicolson for a letter and on my return to give Baroness Budberg a bottle of gin!'[28]

Maxim Gorky's life was history now, his former home a museum, and in 1968 there was a ceremony to celebrate his centenary. Moura was there, his most beloved and only surviving lover and confidante (Yekaterina had died in 1965, while Maria Andreyeva had been in her grave since 1953).

In England the same strange process had happened to H. G. Wells, but with rather less pomp; in 1966 a blue plaque was put up at 13 Hanover Terrace, and the house opened to the public for the day. A huge crowd turned up. The new owner, slightly alarmed, spotted an elderly lady looking around on her own, and decided to 'have a courteous word'. The old lady was Moura, revisiting the past. 'This place I know,' she said. 'Mr Wells once pinched my bottom.'[29]

He had pinched rather more than that. However unsettled their relationship had seemed, there had been a bond. H. G.'s son Anthony West remembered the impact Moura had on him, and upon his father.

I . . . cannot forget my first breath-taking sight of her as she sat talking to my father in the garden at Easton Glebe one day in 1931. Her fatalism enabled her to radiate an immensely reassuring serenity, and her good humour made her a comfortable rather than a disturbing presence: I always looked forward eagerly to my next meeting with her, and remember my last with pleasure. I believed unquestioningly in her *bona fides*, and had never a doubt but that without her warmth, affection, and calm stoicism behind him, my father would have been a gloomier and more pessimistic man in the years that lay between his seventieth birthday and his death. Whenever I saw them together I felt sure that they were truly happy.[30]

Gorky's life, Wells' life and her own life – they were all history now, the stuff of museums. Doors closing, curtains coming down . . . nothing left but memories and secrets.

One set of memories, one avenue of life, the one that outshone and outlived the rest, reached its end in 1970.

In 1948, after living briefly with 'Tommy' Rosslyn, Lockhart had married his wartime secretary, Mollie Beck. She was a sensible woman who set about trying to sort out his finances. She took him out of London and they lived for many years in Edinburgh and then Falmouth in Cornwall. But he still couldn't stay away from Moura. Whenever he was in London he would meet up with her, and he would often make the long journey to the capital for that sole purpose.

They were growing old – sometimes together, more often apart. In March 1953 she wrote to remind him that she would soon become 'The Great Sixty' and they arranged to meet up for a celebratory meal.[31] She was still his darling Moura, and he was still her Baby. As they aged, they grew ill and infirm. As in every other aspect of their lives, it was Moura who proved the more resilient. She survived breast cancer, while during the 1960s Lockhart's health, which had been shaky ever since his return from Russia in 1918, and worsened by his habits throughout his life, began to break down badly. By the late 1960s he had begun to suffer from dementia. His brilliant mind and his compelling, quixotic personality were crumbling. His son and daughter-in-law nursed him at home in Hove, until he was admitted to a local nursing home.

Moura visited him there, and was with him in his final hours.[32]

Sir Robert Hamilton Bruce Lockhart died in his sleep on 27 February 1970. He was eighty-two years old.

His obituary in *The Times* made a sketch of his life's adventures and noted that 'he was twice married',[33] but made no mention anywhere of the woman who had meant most to him, the woman who had shared his darkest dangers, who had sold herself to save his life, and who had loved him with a fierce passion that was stronger than death.

Two days after his funeral in Hove, Moura held a memorial service for him at the Russian Orthodox church in Ennismore Gardens, Kensington, close to her former home.[34]

The service began at noon, and as she had stipulated, there was a choir, and incense, and all the ceremonial of an Orthodox requiem under the hallowed gilt dome of the church. The only thing missing was the congregation. Moura had placed an announcement in *The Times*, but she was the only participant. His relatives disapproved strongly, and his friends stayed away out of respect for them. It suited Moura well enough – this service was not for them; it was for herself and her Baby-Boy, for the memory of their love, for the memory of little Peter who never was, for the man Moura had loved as she believed no other woman had ever loved a man. At last, in death, she had him to herself.

Moura made her last trip to Moscow in 1973. Her health was failing. Arthritis had been dogging her for years, and she had had two hip-replacement operations. She could scarcely function without a drink to stimulate her.

Her time was coming; all the doors had closed, there was little now to live for. Her children she loved, and her grandchildren; but they were the future. Moura was of an age where all that really mattered was the past.

In 1974 Moura left London for Italy. She was going to visit Paul; now in his early sixties, he had retired from farming in the Isle of Wight, and he and his wife had settled in Tuscany. Hamish Hamilton believed that Moura had quite deliberately 'decided to go away to die'.[35] She booked a room in a small country hotel close to Paul's home, and set off.

Another of her close friends, the poet Michael Burn, wrote a poem for her entitled 'Moura Budberg: on her proposed departure from England'.[36] He loved Moura. He had been introduced into her circle by Guy Burgess, who had been his boyfriend; later he married an old friend of Moura's, and he was moved by Moura's kindness to her in her last illness, when Moura herself was unwell. She had the 'power to solace', he recalled.[37] Of all Moura's friends in her last years, Michael

Burn was possibly the one who loved her most keenly and sincerely.

In his poem he gently satirised the myths that Moura and everyone she knew had built up around her.

> Isn't it a fact
> That Talleyrand adored you,
> And that for your want of tact
> In the Commune of eighteen-seventy
> Marx praised and Eugenie deplored you?
>
> Brilliant balloons
> Of fantasy and gossip
> Inflate to legends,
> . . . How well *did* you know Solomon?
> And was he wise? In Berlin, certainly,
> The Kaiser took you for the Queen of Sheba.
>
> That you were born
> Is also sure, and bred
> In deepish purple
> You preferred red.
> Grey's not your wear,
> London not yours to nest in,
> Not now, not any more.
> Too many rats. Where to then, citizen
> Baroness, what fresh fields to rest in?[38]

There were no fresh fields for Moura – she had been everywhere, done everything, seen it all. Italy had been the land of Gorky for a while. They had both loved it. It would do as a final place to rest, if not nest in.

A story was told that when she left London in 1974, she took with her a certain suitcase. Somewhere between the Italian border and Paul's home, the trailer in which her belongings were being transported caught fire. The cause was a mystery. Equally mystifying was the elderly Baroness's refusal to allow the flames to be extinguished.[39]

Gorky's papers, the letters, the diary jottings, the photographs, everything she had withheld from Stalin and Yagoda – all went up in a column of smoke over the Italian countryside. Everything else went with it – all the papery minutiae of her life. Lockhart's letters, H. G.'s, Gorky's, the manuscript of her '*Mêlée*' probably, if it still existed. Nobody, if Moura had anything to do with it, would ever penetrate the mysteries of her life. She had given instructions to her children that they were to destroy all that they had of hers. All that would remain would be the traces she had left in the possession of others – in letters, in their memories and in their hearts.

On 31 October 1974 Baroness Moura Budberg died in Italy. Paul and Tania were with her in her last days. She was eighty-two years old.

Moura had called in a priest when she realised that the end was close. She asked for a personal requiem mass to be given for herself on the theme of contrition.[40]

Her body was taken back to England, the country she had come to with such hope and ambition on that distant day in the late summer of 1929. Her funeral was held at the Russian Orthodox church in Kensington. The building was packed. Her children and grandchildren – all grown up now and most married. Kira and her son Nicholas were also there. The list of friends was long – the French Ambassador, Baron Bob Boothby, Lady Diana Cooper, Hamish Hamilton, Alan Pryce-Jones, Tom Driberg, Kenneth Tynan, Alan Moorehead, Carol Reed . . . She was buried in Chiswick New Cemetery. Her gravestone was inscribed:

MARIE BUDBERG

née ZAKREVSKY

(1892 – 1974)

СПАСИ И СОХРАНИ*

The person who had meant more to her than any other wasn't there. He had gone before her. He had brought her to life in the frosts of Russia, loved her and abandoned her, but she had loved him and gone on living for him. In the cruel winter in early 1919, when firewood could hardly be bought and the people of Petrograd struggled to eat, Moura wrote a letter to him.

---

* Save and preserve.

My dearest Babykins

Do you remember how you used to say: 'Our love must stand a 6 months' test.' Well – do you think yours is going to stand it? As to mine – it needs no test, it is there – linked with me until death – and perhaps – Beyond.

It would seem strange to me to hear you say 'Do you still love me?' just as if you were to ask me: 'Are you still alive?' And these months of waiting – how beautiful they could be . . . for there is beauty in parting, rapture in the thought that the day shall come, when one shall be able to offer a soul, purified by suffering and longing and by the ardent desire of perfection . . . Oh Baby-Boy – what I would give to have you here, near me, with your arms round me, and have you comfort me and cuddle me and make me forget all the nightmare . . .

. . . Sleep well, my Baby – may God protect you.

I kiss your dear lips.

Goodnight.

Your Moura.[41]

Notes

Preface

1 Wells, *H. G. Wells in Love*, p. 162.
2 Lord Ritchie Calder, letter to Andrew Boyle, Jun./Jul. 1980, CUL Add 9429/2B/85.
3 Andrew Boyle, 'Budberg Outline', CUL Add 9429/2B/127 (i).
4 Moura Budberg, Preface to Gorky, *Fragments from My Diary*, p. ix.

Chapter 1: The Eve of Revolution

1 Moura's exact birthdate is a matter of doubt. Her official documents give the date as 3 March, although she celebrated her birthday on 6 March. The change from the Julian to the Gregorian calendar does not account for the discrepancy. Furthermore, Moura's daughter Tania stated that her mother's year of birth was 1893 (Alexander, *An Estonian Childhood*); in all other sources, including her passport applications, it is given as 1892.
2 Now spelled Berezova Rudka, the house has survived, but in a sad state of repair. The bright paint has faded and peeled, the gardens are desolate and the fountain is corroded and dried up.
3 Russian surnames have male and female forms. Zakrevskaya is the female form of Zakrevsky.
4 Alexander, *Estonian Childhood*, p. 37.
5 Alexander, *Estonian Childhood*, p. 27.
6 Figes, *A People's Tragedy*, p. 158.
7 The First World War was known by various names in Russia. It was occasionally called the Second Fatherland War (the first being the war against Napoleon in 1812), but more commonly the Patriotic War or Great Patriotic War. These latter terms had also been used in 1812, and were revived again in 1941, and are nowadays mostly associated with the Second World War.
8 Sir Michael Postan, interview with Andrew Boyle, CUL Add 9429/2B/123.
9 Keane, *Séan MacBride*, p. 3.
10 White & Jeffares, *The Gonne–Yeats Letters*, p. 9.

11 Maud narrated this story in her own memoir, wherein she referred to Margaret by the pseudonym 'Eleanor Robbins' (Ward, *Maud Gonne*, p. 13). Maud herself was unmarried at this time, having turned down many proposals from her lover W. B. Yeats. In 1894 Maud gave birth to an illegitimate daughter of her own, named Iseult. She managed to bring up both girls. Eventually in 1904 Maud married an army officer called MacBride, who was subsequently discovered to have had an affair with the teenage Eileen Wilson (Toomey, *Oxford Dictionary of National Biography*).

12 Alexander, *Estonian Childhood*, pp. 16–17.

13 It is not impossible that Micky *was* Moura's mother. She had previously had an affair with a married older man and borne a child. And it is suggestive that Moura was born so soon after Micky's arrival. But there is no evidence to support this conjecture.

14 Berberova, *Moura*, pp. 165–6.

15 Berberova, *Moura*, p. 359. The matter is also referred to in her MI5 file (visa application and related letter from E. T. Boyce). Some of the claims about Moura's sexual conduct in this period come from H. G. Wells, and could be the products of mere gossip filtered through his own jealous imagination. He alleged that she had in fact been briefly married to Engelhardt (Wells, *H. G. Wells in Love*, p. 164; Wells, suppressed pages from *H. G. Wells in Love*).

16 Quoted in Alexander, *An Estonian Childhood*, p. 31.

17 Alexander, *Estonian Childhood*, p. 33.

18 Buchanan, *Recollections of Imperial Russia*, p. 46.

19 This recollection was told to the young Michael Korda, nephew of film-maker Alexander Korda, at one of his uncle's functions (Korda, *Charmed Lives*, p. 214).

20 Alexander, *Estonian Childhood*, p. 17.

21 Yakov Peters, who was head of the Cheka, the Bolshevik secret police, with whom Moura became involved in 1918, claimed in a memoir that 'according to the confession of [a] detainee and to documents found with Prince P., [Moura] had been a German spy during the Imperialist war' (Peters, 'Memoirs of Cheka Work During the First Year of the Revolution', in the journal *Proletarian Revolution*, 1925, quoted in Berberova, *Moura*, p. 128).

Chapter 2: Choosing Sides

1 Buchanan describes this visit in some detail in his memoir *My Mission to Russia*, pp. 42–52. He gives the date as 12 January 1917 (NS).

2 Lockhart, *Memoirs of a British Agent*, p. 117.

3 Buchanan, *My Mission to Russia*, p. 41.

4 Buchanan, *Ambassador's Daughter*, p. 143.

5 Buchanan, *My Mission to Russia*, p. 20; Benckendorff, *Last Days at Tsarskoe*, translator's introduction, gives Paul's title as Grand Marshal of the Court. Counts Paul and Alexander were distant cousins of Djon.

6 Sir George Buchanan's attempt to warn the Tsar about the danger to Rasputin, which he said was based on 'idle gossip' (*My Mission to Russia*, p. 48), has

contributed to a theory that the assassination was actually orchestrated by Britain's Secret Intelligence Service. An English friend of Prince Felix Yusupov (the principal conspirator, in whose palace Rasputin was killed), Oswald Rayner, was implicated in the murder, and may have supplied the revolver that was used. Sir George made inquiries about this allegation, but was assured by the head of the Petrograd division of the SIS that it was 'incredible to the point of childishness' (Milton, *Russian Roulette*, pp. 25–6). However, a case has been made that SIS agents were deeply involved if not wholly responsible (Cullen, *Rasputin*). One does wonder why Buchanan would try to warn the Tsar if his worry really was based on nothing more than 'idle gossip'. Also, the Tsar himself became convinced that a British conspiracy had been responsible.

7 Buchanan, *My Mission to Russia*, p. 49.

8 Buchanan, *My Mission to Russia*, p. 51.

9 Sir Michael Postan, interview with Andrew Boyle, CUL Add 9429/2B/123. Sir Michael Postan was born in Bessarabia, but left Russia after the Revolution. One wonders about the credibility of the claim. If there was reason to believe that she was both a German spy and a woman of such easy virtue, it seems unlikely that a man such as Sir George Buchanan, who was a very long way from being a fool, would have let his daughter be so friendly with her, or tolerated the Embassy's military attachés having such an extensive social involvement with her.

10 Meriel Buchanan (*Petrograd*, p. 93) writes that the night was 'moonless', but on 26 February 1917 (OS) there was a full moon which would have been low in the sky at the time of the departure from Yendel (www.timeanddate.com/calendar/moon phases.html?year=1917&n=242; wwp.greenwichmeantime.co.uk/time-gadgets/moonrise/index.htm).

11 Buchanan, *Petrograd*, p. 94.

12 The Baltic station was sometimes known as Tsarskoye Selo station, as that was originally the main destination of trains travelling from it. It was (and still is) the main station for routes to the Baltic states. It is now called Vitebsky station.

13 An ambassador's chasseur was a combination of aide, manservant, butler and shield-on-shoulder. The job had a ceremonial element, and William was often required to wear a uniform, carry a sword and don a feathered hat (Buchanan, *The Dissolution of an Empire*, p. 5; Cross, 'Corner of a Foreign Field', p. 348).

14 Buchanan, *Ambassador's Daughter*, p. 145. Knox had only recently been promoted from colonel to brigadier general (*Burke's Peerage* vol. 3, p. 3271). Captain Francis Cromie, commander of the Royal Navy's Baltic submarine flotilla, stationed at Reval, was also present at this encounter, having travelled to Petrograd on the same train to begin a week's leave (Cromie, letter to Adm. Phillimore, Mar. 1917, in Jones, 'Documents on British Relations' II, p. 357). Cromie was a friend of Meriel and Moura, but despite writing that he 'arrived with Miss Buchanan', he must have been merely on the same train rather than travelling with them, as he is not mentioned in any other sources.

15 Knox, *With the Russian Army*, p. 553.

16 Buchanan, *Petrograd*, pp. 94–5. Capt. Cromie, who was present at the arrival, wrote that Knox 'considered the disorders as quite minor affairs' (letter to Adm. Phillimore, Mar. 1917, in Jones, 'Documents on British Relations' II, p. 357). Since Knox

considered them no such thing, this confirms that he was talking down the situation so as not to alarm the ladies.

17　Buchanan, *Ambassador's Daughter*, pp 146–7; *Recollections*, pp. 267–8.

18　Buchanan, *Recollections*, pp. 267–8.

19　Buchanan, *Petrograd*, pp. 94–7.

20　Figes, *A People's Tragedy*, pp. 312–13. Znamenskaya Square was renamed Vosstaniya Square ('Uprising Square') after the Revolution.

21　Some foreign observers, including Meriel Buchanan and her father, seem to have misunderstood the calls for a republic headed by a 'Tsar'; they thought the simple workers had failed to grasp the concept of democracy (e.g. Buchanan, *Petrograd*, p. 107).

22　Lockhart, *British Agent*, pp.178–80.

23　Abraham, *Alexander Kerensky*, p. 301.

24　Prince Alexis Scherbatow, letters to Serge Troubetskoy and Andrew Boyle, via Robert Keyserlingk, 27 & 29 Sep. 1980, CUL Add 9429/2B/55–60. Prince Alexis (1910 2003) was a child at the time of the Revolution, and knew both Kerensky and Moura in later life.

25　Hill gives an account of Madame B's work in his memoir (*Go Spy the Land*, pp. 87–8). He certainly knew Moura well, and was not the only one who referred to her discreetly as 'Madame B'. Gen. Knox did the same in his published diary.

26　Walpole, 'Denis Garstin and the Russian Revolution', p. 587.

27　Garstin, letter, Jul. 1917, reproduced in Walpole, 'Denis Garstin and the Russian Revolution', p. 594.

28　Buchanan, *Petrograd*, pp. 125–6.

29　Quoted in Buchanan, *Ambassador's Daughter*, pp. 170–71.

30　Abraham, *Alexander Kerensky*, p. 343. Among those who suffered reprisals in the period that followed were Boris Flekkel (former administrative secretary to Kerensky), who was captured and shot by the Cheka, and Kerensky's brother Fyodor, shot in Tashkent by the Red Army in 1919. The deputy head of the Cheka said of Flekkel, 'He admitted that he had been Kerensky's secretary – that's enough to be shot for' (quoted in Abraham, p. 343).

Chapter 3: Red Winter

1　Denis Garstin, letter, 27 Nov. 1917 (NS), reproduced in Walpole, 'Denis Garstin', p. 595.

2　Figes, *People's Tragedy*, pp. 540–44.

3　The precise date of this incident is uncertain. Buchanan (*Ambassador's Daughter*, p. 181) implies that it was before Christmas 1917, citing it as the reason Christmas couldn't be spent at Yendel, whereas Moura's daughter Tania (Alexander, *Estonian Childhood*, p. 7) seems to place it in late 1918, during a second outbreak of anarchy after the German withdrawal. However, Tania does state that there were many such incidents at various times; also, she was too young to remember the incidents directly.

4 Smith, *Former People*, p. 131.

5 Garstin, letter, 8 Dec. 1917 (NS), reproduced in Walpole, 'Denis Garstin', p. 596.

6 Russia, one of Britain's most important diplomatic missions, was Buchanan's first ambassadorial posting, which he took up in 1910 (Buchanan, *Ambassador's Daughter*, pp. 87–8).

7 Garstin, letter, 6 Jan. 1918 (NS), reproduced in Walpole, 'Denis Garstin', p. 598.

8 Sir George Buchanan, *My Mission to Russia*, pp. 239, 243; Cabinet minute quoted in Kettle, *The Allies and the Russian Collapse*, p. 181.

9 Buchanan, *Ambassador's Daughter*, pp. 190–91; *Petrograd*, p. 249.

10 Buchanan, *Dissolution*, pp. 273–4.

11 Buchanan, *Petrograd*, p. 249.

12 Buchanan, *Ambassador's Daughter*, p. 191.

13 Meriel Buchanan (*Ambassador's Daughter*, pp. 194–5; *Petrograd*, pp. 233–4); Sir George Buchanan (*My Mission to Russia*, pp. 249–50). Gen. Knox noted the presence of 'Madame B—' and remarked that 'more [Russians] would have come if they had dared' (*With the Russian Army*, p. 740).

14 Lockhart (*British Agent*, p. 191) refers to her as a 'Russian Jewess', but Kenneth Young, editor of his published diaries, identifies her as French and names her (in Lockhart, *The Diaries of Sir Robert Bruce Lockhart, vol. 1*, p. 30).

15 Smith, *Former People*, pp. 133–7.

Chapter 4: The British Agent

1 Lockhart, *British Agent*, p. 220; *Diaries vol. 1*, p. 33.

2 Lockhart, *British Agent*, p. 3.

3 Lockhart, *British Agent*, pp. 25–8.

4 Lockhart, *Diaries vol. 1*, pp. 22–8; Hughes, *Inside the Enigma*, p. 66.

5 Lockhart, *British Agent*, pp. 191–2.

6 Lockhart, *British Agent*, pp. 198–200.

7 Kettle, *The Allies and the Russian Collapse*, p. 164. Col. John Buchan (the novelist) was at this time an assistant director in the Ministry of Information.

8 Lockhart, *British Agent*, pp. 198–200. Colonel Byrne had recommended that Lockhart be sent to Kiev, and that Gen. Frederick C. Poole (who had previously been responsible for British supplies to the Russian Army) be put in charge in Petrograd (Kettle, *The Allies and the Russian Collapse*, p. 166). Lloyd George disagreed. Poole was instead tasked with an ongoing scheme to buy up Russian banks and use them as a means of channelling funds to anti-Bolshevik movements (Kettle, pp. 204ff.).

9 Maxim Litvinov (born Meir Wallach-Finkelstein) was a socialist who came from a Russian Jewish banking family. His appointment as Bolshevik Ambassador was said by some to be Trotsky's joke – an insult to Britain (Garstin, letter, 8 Dec. 1917, in Walpole, 'Denis Garstin', p. 596). However, Litvinov took it entirely seriously, and went on to have a distinguished diplomatic career, serving as Soviet Ambassador to the United States and as People's Commissar for Foreign Affairs.

10 Lyons' Corner Houses were a chain of large, popular restaurants founded by the food conglomerate J. Lyons & Co in 1909. The Lockhart–Litvinov meeting most likely occurred in the one at the corner of Coventry St and Rupert St (near Piccadilly Circus) or Strand/Craven St (off Trafalgar Square).

11 Lockhart, *British Agent*, pp. 201–3. Reginald 'Rex' Leeper worked for the Ministry of Information during the First World War, and headed the Political Intelligence Dept in the Second World War. Rothstein was a Russian émigré journalist who wrote for the *Manchester Guardian*; he later returned to Russia, joined the Party and became a diplomat.

12 Lockhart, *British Agent*, p. 204.

13 Lockhart, *British Agent*, pp. 76–8; editor's note in Lockhart, *Diaries vol. 1*, p. 22.

14 Kettle, *The Allies and the Russian Collapse*, p. 190.

15 Lockhart, *British Agent*, pp. 204–5.

16 Lockhart, *British Agent*, pp. 211–12; Buchanan, *Ambassador's Daughter*, pp. 195–200.

17 Lockhart, *British Agent*, p. 115.

18 Lockhart, memoranda to Sir George Buchanan, 12 Aug. 1915, quoted in Hughes, *Inside the Enigma*, p. 66. Lockhart's diary entries from late 1915 (*Diaries vol. 1*, pp. 25–6) also indicate his awareness of the growing popular unrest and how dangerous it could be.

19 Lockhart, *British Agent*, pp. 221–2.

20 Lockhart, *British Agent*, p. 224. In his unpublished diaries, Lockhart gives the address as 10 Dvortsovoy Naberezhnoy (Russian for Palace Quay), and the moving-in date as 10 February (NS).

21 Lockhart, unpublished essay, 'Baroness Budberg', p. 3. Their first recorded encounter took place on Sunday 17 February, whereas in his *Memoirs of a British Agent* (pp. 243–4) he implies that he first met Moura in March. Interestingly, he is more discreet about her in his private diary than in his published memoir, referring to her always as 'Mme Benckendorff' and giving no hint that there was any personal involvement between them. Possibly he was wary of his diary falling into Bolshevik hands; when he wrote his memoir in the early 1930s, his relationship with Moura was too well known for him to gloss over it.

22 Lockhart, unpublished diary entry for 17 Feb. 1918.

23 Rabinowitch, *Bolsheviks in Power*, pp. 157–60.

24 Lockhart, diary entry for 15 Feb. 1918, reproduced in *British Agent*, pp. 226–7.

25 Lockhart, *British Agent*, p. 227.

26 Hughes, *Inside the Enigma*, pp. 122–3; Kettle, *The Allies and the Russian Collapse*, pp. 122–3.

27 Hughes, *Inside the Enigma*, p. 123.

28 Rabinowitch, *The Bolsheviks in Power*, pp. 160–61.

29 Lockhart, diary entry for 18 Feb. 1918, *Diaries vol. 1*, p. 33; *British Agent*, p. 228.

30 Figes, *People's Tragedy*, p. 545.

31 Lockhart, unpublished essay, 'Baroness Budberg', pp. 3–4.

32 Lockhart, *British Agent*, pp. 243–4.

Chapter 5: 'What Children We Were'

1 Moura, letters to Lockhart, 31 Oct. and 16 Dec. 1918, LL.
2 Lockhart, *British Agent*, p. 242.
3 Lockhart, *British Agent*, p. 76.
4 Moura, letter to Lockhart, 31 Oct. 1918, LL.
5 Wells, *H. G. Wells in Love*, p. 168; Hughes, *Inside the Enigma*, p. 130.
6 Wells, *H. G. Wells in Love*, pp. 165–6.
7 Moura, letter to Lockhart, 31 Oct. 1918, LL.
8 Figes, *People's Tragedy*, pp. 741–2. Alexandra Kollontai advocated (and practised) free 'marriage' throughout her adult life, in speeches and in pamphlets such as 'The Social Basis of the Woman Question' (1909) and 'Sexual Relations and the Class Struggle' (1921) – see Kollontai, *Selected Writings of Alexandra Kollonta*. Her ideas were badly misunderstood at the time, sometimes with tragic results for women. When a call for the 'socialisation of women' was given out in early 1918, in some districts it resulted in mass rapes, with women being forcibly turned into unpaid prostitutes for soldiers (Smith, *Former People*, p. 133). As a radical socialist Kollontai initially rose high in the Bolshevik movement, and campaigned for women's education and working conditions. Placing her socialist principles and the interests of the workers above the political interests of the Party, she was later sidelined by Lenin.
9 The measured pace of Moura's relationship with Lockhart (evidenced by her letters of the time) tends to contradict the lurid, lascivious reputation that was retrospectively attached to her by people who didn't actually know her personally at this time (e.g. Sir Michael Postan, interview by Andrew Boyle).
10 Moura, letter to Lockhart, 31 Oct. 1918, LL.
11 Lockhart, *British Agent*, pp. 229–32.
12 Michael Kettle (*The Allies and the Russian Collapse*, pp. 220–22) traces the origin of these papers to the summer of 1917. The documents were intended to discredit the Bolsheviks and prevent them overthrowing the Kerensky government. They were commissioned by Russian Military Intelligence and created by a Pole called Anton Ossendowski, a professional propagandist, and a Russian newspaper editor called Semenov. The 'Sisson papers' (named after an American agent who bought copies and disseminated them) were part of a larger campaign of disinformation, and were promoted by British interests, including the head of the Secret Intelligence Service office in Petrograd, Cdr E. T. Boyce. The US government continued to believe in the documents, and was still publicising them as late as September 1918.
13 Lockhart, *British Agent*, p. 231.
14 Cabinet minutes quoted in Kettle, *The Allies and the Russian Collapse*, pp. 226–30.
15 Hughes, *Inside the Enigma*, p. 130.
16 Lockhart, *British Agent*, p. 236.
17 Kettle, *The Allies and the Russian Collapse*, pp. 220–21, 262–3; Hughes, *Inside the Enigma*, pp. 130–31.
18 Lockhart, *British Agent*, pp. 236–8.
19 Lockhart, *British Agent*, p. 238.

20 Bainton, *Honoured by Strangers*, pp. 198–9.

21 Bainton, *Honoured by Strangers*, pp. 201 and *passim*. Her real forename was Sonia, but friends knew her as Sophie.

22 Cross, 'A Corner of a Foreign Field', p. 353.

23 Some of Moura's personal letters during this period (LL and HIA) were written on Leech & Firebrace headed notepaper, indicating the close connection between the branches of Leech's business and propaganda enterprises.

24 The name actually used at this time was 'Secret Service Bureau', under the cover name 'MI1c'. But the name Secret (or Special) Intelligence Service came into use around the end of the First World War, and both terms were used concurrently for a while. The cover name 'MI1c' was replaced by 'MI6' during the Second World War. (See Jeffery, *MI6*, pp. 50, 162–3, 209.) The abbreviation SIS is generally used by non-specialist historians, and is accordingly adopted here.

25 Kettle, *The Allies and the Russian Collapse*, pp. 136–7, 152, 256–7.

26 The fact that Moura was employed in this way (not to mention her long-standing closeness to the embassy people) seems to confirm that the popular reputation she supposedly had at this time for being a German spy must be a later addition to the Moura mythology. It doesn't rule out the (unlikely) possibility that she might have been a spy for the Germans, but it argues against the idea that she was widely *believed* to be a spy (which is the claim made).

27 Kettle, *The Allies and the Russian Collapse*, pp. 260–61.

28 Lockhart (*British Agent*, p. 244) describes this event as a birthday party for Cromie, which is repeated by Cromie's biographer (Bainton, *Honoured by Strangers*, p. 139). In fact Cromie's birthday was on 30 January (17 January OS). Maslenitsa, which is held seven weeks before Easter, ran from 11 to 17 March 1918 (NS), and the party was held on Monday the 11th (Lockhart, unpublished diary entry for 11 Mar. 1918). It's possible that it was in fact a belated birthday for Moura herself (usually 6 March). Equally likely, the 'birthday' might have been misunderstanding or faulty memory on Lockhart's part. It isn't clear from his account whether there were any Russian guests, but it appears not.

29 Cromie, letter to Cdre S. S. Hall, 1/19 Feb. 1918, in Jones, 'Documents on British Relations' IV, p. 550. In 1918 £2 was equivalent to about £100 now.

30 Gen. Finlayson, quoted in De Ruvigny, 'Garstin, Denys Norman', p. 66.

31 Garstin, letter, 14 Feb. 1918, reproduced in Walpole, 'Denis Garstin', pp. 600–01.

32 Lockhart, *British Agent*, p. 244.

33 Lockhart, *British Agent*, pp. 245–6.

34 Tania describes this journey sketchily (Alexander, *Estonian Childhood*, p. 5). The date isn't given, but it was said to be early spring, and there was snow still on the ground. Tania also doesn't specify where Micky's passport was obtained. Possibly Moura used her secret service connections; alternatively Lockhart might have used his influence with Trotsky. Tania implies that the journey was done in a day, which in a horse-drawn vehicle over a distance of more than 200 miles is highly unlikely.

Chapter 6: Passion and Intrigue

1 Lockhart, *British Agent*, pp. 258–9. Lockhart identifies the house as belonging to someone called Gracheva, but gives no further information. It is possible that the owner was Maria Gracheva, an art collector who was among the wealthy émigrés who fled Russia after the Revolution. Her collection (or the part which survived) was seized by the state and ended up in the Rumantsyev Museum (Senenko, 'Late 19th Century Private Collections', pp. 19–21).

2 Moura, letter, 16 Apr. 1918, LL. This is one of her occasional letters written on the headed notepaper of Hugh Leech's firms, this one headed 'Farran Farranovich Leech' in Cyrillic. The 'red sweater' is probably a garment he had left with her; there are occasional references in Moura's letters in which she has been asked by him to bring him some article he has left behind in one of his various moves.

3 The Elite Hotel (named at various times the Rossiya and the Aurora) is now the Hotel Budapest, in Ulitsa Petrovskiye Linii, off Petrovka Street.

4 Lockhart, *British Agent*, pp. 262–3.

5 Lockhart, *British Agent*, pp. 256–7. Lockhart refers to the Metropol as the 'First House of Soviets'; in fact it was the Second, the First being the former National Hotel.

6 Lockhart, *British Agent*, p. 257.

7 Often mistranslated as 'man of steel', the name Stalin has no literal English translation; it would be more akin to 'Steelman' or 'Steelson', made up of the Russian for 'steel', *stal*, with the standard surname suffix *-in*.

8 Avrich, *The Russian Anarchists*, p. 184.

9 Lockhart (*British Agent*, p. 258) gives the number killed as 'over a hundred', but Avrich (*The Russian Anarchists*, p. 184) states 40 killed or wounded. Possibly some of the bodies seen by Lockhart were Chekists.

10 Werth, 'A State Against Its People', p. 64.

11 Deacon, *A History of the Russian Secret Service*, p. 168; Leggett, *The Cheka*, pp. 118–19. In an interview with a Moscow paper in November 1918, Peters insisted, 'I am not as bloodthirsty as they say' (quoted in Werth, 'A State Against Its People', p. 75). Peters' surname is sometimes rendered as Peterss, and his forename variously as Yakov, Iacob or Jan.

12 Lockhart, *British Agent*, pp. 258–9.

13 Lockhart seems to imply that it was the former, but since prostitutes did good business inside the Cheka headquarters in both Petrograd and Moscow (Figes, *People's Tragedy*, pp. 683–4), it seems unlikely that Peters took this view.

14 Moura, letter to Lockhart, HIA. Undated: probably Jun. 1918. (Most of the 28 letters Moura wrote to Lockhart prior to October 1918 are undated, and their chronology has had to be pieced together from content and context. She makes frequent reference to current events, which is helpful in dating.)

15 Cromie, letter to Cdre S. S. Hall, Apr. 1918, in Jones, 'Documents on British Relations' IV, pp. 550–51. Cromie didn't specify whether the 'five million' was pounds, roubles or marks; however, as it follows just after his mention of '£50,000',

one can infer that it was pounds. In 1918 £5 million would be equivalent to about £300 million today – a bargain price for a flotilla of submarines.

16 Downie report, quoted in Bainton, *Honoured by Strangers*, pp. 214–15.

17 Bainton, *Honoured by Strangers*, pp. 220–23.

18 Cromie, letter to Adm. W. R. Hall, Apr. 1918, in Jones, 'Documents on British Relations' IV, pp. 551–2.

19 Cromie, letter to Cdre S. S. Hall, Apr. 1918, in Jones, 'Documents on British Relations' IV, pp. 550–51.

20 Moura's fascination with gossip, intelligence and politics comes through in many of her letters between 1918 and the early 1920s.

21 A. E. Lessing, addendum to telegram to Col. Keyes, 17 Mar. 1918, quoted in Kettle, *The Road to Intervention*, p. 3.

22 Lockhart, *British Agent*, pp. 251–2.

23 Lockhart, entry for 19 Mar. 1918, *Diaries*, pp. 34–5. Balfour (born 1848) was actually 69 at this time.

24 Lockhart, unpublished diary entry, 21 Apr. 1918; *British Agent*, p. 269.

25 Kettle, *The Road to Intervention*, pp. 16–17.

26 Cabinet minute, 18 Apr., quoted in Kettle, *The Road to Intervention*, pp. 68–9.

27 Lockhart, unpublished diary entry, 21 Apr. 1918.

28 In *British Agent* (p. 263) Lockhart has nothing but praise for Maj. McAlpine ('a man of first-class intellect') and implies that the two were in agreement in their opposition to Allied military intervention in Russia. He does, however, mention him in connection with officers who didn't understand his policy and 'intrigued against me'. In fact, McAlpine's view on intervention seems to have been as muddled and indecisive as everyone else's (e.g. see Kettle, *The Road to Intervention*, pp. 99–100).

29 Moura, letter to Lockhart, HIA. Undated: probably between 16 and 20 Apr. 1918. (Most of the 28 letters Moura wrote to Lockhart prior to October 1918 are undated, and their chronology has had to be pieced together from content and context.)

30 Lockhart, *British Agent*, p. 269.

31 Lockhart, unpublished diary entry, 21 Apr. 1918.

32 Lockhart, *British Agent*, p. 260.

33 Lockhart, *British Agent*, pp. 261–2. Fittingly, Okhotny Ryad became the site of a Moscow Metro station in 1935, and later still an underground shopping mall. Alexander Vertinsky was a major star in early 20th-century Russia (Stites, *Russian Popular Culture*, pp. 14–15). He was later alleged to be a Soviet spy.

34 Lockhart, *British Agent*, pp. 260–61.

35 Lockhart's recollection that Moura 'was never to leave' after their reunion in Moscow was figurative rather than literal, referring to the fact that it was at that encounter that their relationship entered a new, unbreakable phase.

36 In 1918 in Russia Easter began on 5 May.

37 Moura, letter to Lockhart, HIA. Undated: probably between 28 and 30 Apr. 1918.

38 Lockhart, *British Agent*, pp. 267–8. Lockhart gives credit for this victory to Evgenia Shelepina, Trotsky's secretary, who later married Lockhart's friend Arthur Ransome. He repaid the favour by using his position to provide her with an under-the-counter British passport which enabled her to leave Russia with Ransome.

39 Lockhart, *British Agent*, p. 268.

40 Kettle, *The Road to Intervention*, pp. 71–2.

41 Swain, *The Origins of the Russian Civil War*, pp. 139–41; Kettle, *The Road to Intervention*, pp. 66–7.

42 Lockhart, telegram to Balfour, 21 Apr. 1918, cited in Long, 'Searching for Sidney Reilly', p. 1227. In his memoirs, Lockhart makes no mention of having had contacts with anti-Bolshevik elements this early in 1918. The date of his telegram to Balfour coincides with the arrival of Moura and Le Page in Moscow.

43 Kettle, *The Road to Intervention*, p. 83; see also Leggett, *The Cheka*, p. 280.

44 Moura, letter to Lockhart, HIA. Undated: probably between 28 and 30 Apr. 1918. It isn't absolutely clear whether she feared a German invasion or was anticipating a British one, but her tone in the letter is anxious, so it was probably the former.

45 Advice by Adm. Reginald Hall and annotations thereon, Foreign Office document FO 371/3332, file 91788, 155–158, cited by Lynn, *Shadow Lovers*, pp. 192–3. Oddly, Lynn interprets this as evidence that Moura was not trusted by the British. The annotation on the document says 'I did not know there were other ladies besides Mme Benckendorff. I think all our missions should be warned against employing them.' The sense of this is clearly that 'them' refers to the 'other ladies'.

46 Kettle, *The Road to Intervention*, p. 83.

Chapter 7: Old Enemies, Strange Alliances

1 Moura, letter to Lockhart, HIA. Undated: probably between 7 May, the day Lockhart summoned Boyce to Moscow, and 9 May, the day appointed to travel.

2 Lockhart, *British Agent*, p. 276.

3 Lockhart, *British Agent*, pp. 276–7; Robin Lockhart, *Ace of Spies*, pp. 67–8.

4 Hill, *Go Spy the Land*, p. 201.

5 Opinions differ on Reilly's origins. Robin Lockhart (*Ace of Spies*, p. 22) describes him as a Russian-Ukrainian Catholic called Georgi, whereas Jeffery (*MI6*, p. 136) identifies him as Shlomo Rosenblum, a Ukrainian Jew. Kettle (*The Road to Intervention*, pp. 85–6) gives his name as Sigmund Georgievich Rosenblum, the son of a Polish-Jewish landowner.

6 Lockhart, *British Agent*, p. 277.

7 Robin Lockhart, *Ace of Spies*, p. 68; Hill, *Go Spy the Land*, p. 239; according to Long ('Searching for Sidney Reilly', p. 1229) Reilly's Cheka post has been taken as evidence for suspecting him of being a double agent. However, there was a surprising degree of covert cooperation between the SIS and the Cheka at this time; also a very wide variety of ethnicities served in the Cheka. Russia had been a cosmopolitan empire and was less sensitive to 'foreignness' than most Western European countries.

8 Dorril, *MI6*, p. 193. Tamplin later worked as a banker in Riga, and in the Second World War was a colonel in the Special Operations Executive. He died of a heart attack in 1943 while on active service in Egypt – see 'War Office: Roll of Honour, Second World War'. Database. Army Roll of Honour 1939–45. Soldiers Died in World War Two. (WO304). CD-ROM. Naval & Military Press. Available online at ancestry.com (retrieved 23 Apr. 2014).

9 Not to be confused with Grand Duchess Maria Nikolaevna, daughter of the Tsar.

10 Lockhart, *British Agent*, pp. 279–80. Lockhart gives the date of this event as the night of 24/25 May, but according to his unpublished diary Moura went back to Petrograd on 20 May. Other dating evidence in the diary (published and unpublished) suggests that the true date was 19/20 May. It's unusual for him to be so inexact, as he wrote *British Agent* by reference to his diaries. We do know that Moura insisted that he alter the original text of his memoir in several places where the story concerned her (letter 18 Jun. 1932, LL). This could be one of them.

11 Lockhart, *British Agent*, pp. 277–8.

12 *Manchester Guardian*, 27 Jun. 1918, p. 4.

13 Leggett, *The Cheka*, p. 62.

14 Lockhart, *British Agent*, p. 280.

15 Lockhart, *British Agent*, p. 280.

16 Moura, letter to Lockhart, HIA. Undated: probably 21 or 22 May 1918.

17 Moura, letter to Lockhart, HIA. Undated: probably 21 or 22 May 1918.

18 Moura, letter to Lockhart, LL. Undated: probably 22 May 1918.

19 Moura, letter to Lockhart, LL. Undated: probably 22 May 1918. According to Cook (*Ace of Spies*, pp. 187–8), General Poole was having affairs with two women; it's possible that Moura was alluding to this as well.

20 Kettle, *The Road to Intervention*, p. 83; *Churchill and the Archangel Fiasco*, pp. 428–9.

21 Moura, letter to Lockhart, HIA. Undated: late May 1918.

22 Moura, letter to Lockhart, HIA. Undated: probably 22 or 23 May 1918.

23 Moura, letter to Lockhart, HIA. Undated: probably 22 or 23 May 1918; and letter to Lockhart, LL. Undated: probably 22 May 1918.

24 Jeffery, *MI6*, p. 102. Even his obituary (*The Times*, 16 Aug. 1952, p. 6) noted that Cudbert Thornhill's attitude 'was sometimes mistaken . . . for lack of judgment' and implied that his later service with the Special Operations Executive in the Second World War was marred (unfairly) in the same way. No evidence has survived to indicate the specific cause of dislike between him and Moura.

25 Subtelny, *Ukraine*, ch. 19.

26 Subtelny, *Ukraine*, ch. 19.

27 Hill, *Go Spy the Land*, pp. 182, 202–3; see also Swain, *Origins of the Russian Civil War*, pp. 149–50.

28 Lockhart, diary entry for 15 May 1918, *Diaries vol. 1*, p. 36.

29 Lockhart, *British Agent*, p. 271.

30 Hill, *Go Spy the Land*, pp. 88–9, 202–4; see also Kettle, *The Road to Intervention*, pp. 81–2. The Irish-Canadian Joseph W. Boyle was an adventurer and privateer who travelled in Europe and Russia during the First World War. For Hill, Trotsky and the GRU, see Deacon, *A History of the Russian Secret Service*, pp. 160–61.

31 Lockhart makes no mention of Moura being involved in any kind of espionage in his memoirs. However, it appears that he did put it in his original draft (which has apparently not been preserved). We don't know what he wrote, but we do know that Moura, who had a veto on the text, insisted that he remove 'the bit about the spying business', which she claimed gave the book a 'Mata Hari touch' that would be 'quite impossible for me' (Moura, letter to Lockhart, 18 Jun. 1932, LL).

32 Leggett, *The Cheka*, p. 293.

33 Lockhart, *British Agent*, p. 278. When he arranged for Kerensky's exit from Russia in mid-May, he didn't dare telegraph London about it until he was certain that the fugitive was safely out of the country, because he suspected that his encrypted messages were being decoded by the Bolsheviks.

34 For example, Berberova, *Moura*, pp. 44–7; Lynn, *Shadow Lovers*, pp. 193–4. It is far from clear whether this allegation has any truth. Neither author had any notion of Moura's involvement in espionage in the Ukraine (or the Cheka/SIS cooperation), and both seem to have overlooked the fact that Lockhart would not be the only British diplomat who used the same cipher.

Diplomatic ciphers at this time were usually of the code-book or 'dictionary' type, in which words had predetermined four- or five-digit number substitutes, listed in a 'dictionary'. The numbers were not sequential, so a coded message could not be read without a copy of the dictionary (which depending on the system could be pocket-size or a very substantial volume containing tens of thousands of words and their number equivalents). Some systems used an additional step which further encrypted the encoded message by altering the numbers mathematically according to a further, separate cipher (see Gannon, *Inside Room 40*, ch. 4; Beesly, *Room 40*, ch. 3). A code + cipher system is much more secure. Properly speaking, a code involves disguising words according to predetermined word/letter/number equivalents; a cipher disguises words on the fly, using an alphabetical or numerical algorithm where the substitutions are unpredictable. Ciphers are thus much more efficient and capable of being more secure (because the cipher key is easier to hide and easier to change), but can be vulnerable to mathematical deciphering.

Cryptography in most diplomatic services in 1918 was very lax, both in coding/ciphering procedures and security (e.g. see Andrew, *Secret Service*; Plotke, *Imperial Spies Invade Russia*). If the Bolsheviks had the British diplomatic code dictionary by May 1918 (and/or the cipher, if one was used), it could have come from a wide variety of sources in Petrograd, Moscow, Vologda or Murmansk.

35 Moura's movements throughout most of 1918 are accounted for, either in her letters or the diaries and memoirs of others. The only blank is in June. Throughout most of that month she did not write to Lockhart, and was not with him. This is the most likely time for her to have made her trips between Russia and Kiev. Coincidentally, there are two week-long gaps in Lockhart's diary during the second half of June. It is possible (though less likely) that she made short trips to the Ukraine in July and August.

36 Moura, letter to Lockhart, HIA. Undated: probably 31 May 1918. Lockhart was in Vologda from 29 to 31 May (*British Agent*, pp. 281–4).

37 Katchanovski et al., *Historical Dictionary of Ukraine*, pp. 347–8.

38 Moura Budberg MI5 file, document 16.Y, 1932, translation of original Russian document.

39 Kyril Zinovieff, interview with Andrew Boyle, CUL Add 9429/2B/125. As a young man in 1929, Zinovieff dined with Pavlo Skoropadskyi in Berlin, and asked the former Hetman if he knew Moura Budberg. After a moment's thought, Skoropadskyi recalled her: 'He had known her in the Ukraine after the revolution and had taken her to be an agent working for him. Later he came to realise that all the time she had been spying for the Bolsheviks.'

Chapter 8: A Hair's Breadth from War

1 Lockhart, *British Agent*, pp. 285–6.
2 Lockhart, message to Foreign Office, 6 June 1918, cited in Hughes, *Inside the Enigma*, p. 132.
3 Swain, *Origins of the Russian Civil War*, p. 151.
4 Subtelny, *Ukraine*, ch. 19.
5 Moura, letter to Lockhart, LL. Undated: probably 5 Jul. 1918.
6 Moura, letter to Lockhart, LL. Undated: probably 5 Jul. 1918.
7 Moura, letter to Lockhart, HIA. Undated: probably mid-Jul. 1918.
8 Moura, letter to Lockhart, LL. Undated: probably 6 or 7 Jul. 1918.
9 Moura, letter to Lockhart, LL. Undated: probably 21 May 1918.
10 Cromie, letter to Adm. W. R. Hall, 26 Jul. 1918, in Jones, 'Documents on British Relations' IV, p. 560.
11 Moura, letter to Lockhart, LL. Undated: probably 8 Jul. 1918; see also Ullman, *Intervention*, p. 230; Kettle, *The Road to Intervention*, p. 256.
12 The official name 'Russian Soviet Republic' was adopted at the Third Congress of Soviets on 8 January 1918. Almost nobody outside the governing parties used the name.
13 Hill, *Go Spy the Land*, pp. 206–9; Lockhart, *British Agent*, pp. 295–300. Hill's and Lockhart's accounts of the Congress differ slightly in some details (such as the order of the speakers and assignment of boxes) but agree on the atmosphere and main events.
14 Quoted in Lockhart, *British Agent*, pp. 297–8.
15 Hill, *Go Spy the Land*, p. 209.
16 Quoted in Lockhart, *British Agent*, p. 299.
17 Leggett, *The Cheka*, pp. 71–4.
18 Accounts of the incident differ in details. Lockhart (*British Agent*, p. 301) was told that Mirbach had been killed by Blyumkin's revolver fire, whereas Figes (*People's Tragedy*, p. 633) states that the bullets missed, and it was the bomb that killed the Count. Leggett (*The Cheka*, p. 74) adds the detail of the broken leg. Lockhart says that Blyumkin's pretext to gain entry was to discuss an alleged assassination plot uncovered by the Cheka, whereas Leggett (who provides the details about the warrant) states that the ostensible business was to discuss the arrest of Mirbach's nephew.
19 Swain (*Origins of the Russian Civil War*, pp. 172–5) suggests that Lockhart was complicit in Savinkov's coup. Lockhart himself always denied it. He had been ordered by Balfour to have nothing to do with Savinkov, but on 6 July he telegraphed the Foreign Secretary to urge Allied military intervention as quickly as possible to make good the strategic position Savinkov was trying to secure; in the weeks that followed, he channelled funds to Savinkov without authorisation (Ullman, *Intervention*, p. 231).
20 Quoted in Leggett, *The Cheka*, p. 82.
21 Moura, letter to Lockhart, LL. Undated: probably 8 Jul. 1918.

22 Rabinowitch, *Bolsheviks in Power*, pp. 184, 299.

23 A later investigation by the Cheka showed that the Left SRs in Petrograd, most of whom were not dedicated militants who were not aware of the Moscow uprising, had not intended to rise against the Bolsheviks. The Red Army's assault on the Pazhesky Korpus was a deliberate provocation designed to destroy the Left SR power base in Petrograd (Rabinowitch, *Bolsheviks in Power*, pp. 300–301).

24 Moura, letter to Lockhart, LL. Undated: probably 8 Jul. 1918.

25 Cromie, letter to Adm. W. R. Hall, 26 Jul. 1918, in Jones, 'Documents on British Relations' IV, pp. 559–60.

26 Moura, letter to Lockhart, LL. Undated: probably 8 Jul. 1918.

27 Moura, letter to Lockhart, HIA. Undated: probably 8–10 Jul. 1918.

28 Moura, letter to Lockhart, HIA. Undated: probably 8–10 Jul. 1918.

29 Lockhart later claimed that he had laughingly refused the guard offered by the Bolsheviks (*British Agent*, p. 303), but Moura seems to have been under the impression that he had accepted it.

30 Moura, letter to Lockhart, LL. Undated: probably 6–7 Jul. 1918.

31 Moura, letter to Lockhart, HIA. Undated: probably 10-15 Jul. 1918.

Chapter 9: Across the Border

1 Moura, letter to Lockhart, HIA. Written at Narva, undated: probably 15 Jul. 1918. Moura makes no mention of permits for entry to Estonia, but as the wife of an Estonian native, she would have been entitled to a 'protection certificate' which would allow her to cross the border. The date of the journey is inferred from Lockhart's statement (*British Agent*, p. 307) that by 25 July it was ten days since Moura had 'left Moscow' for Yendel; comparison with other evidence (e.g. his diary and historical events mentioned in her letters) indicates that he meant Petrograd rather than Moscow.

2 Swain, *Origins of the Russian Civil War*, pp. 172–5. In his memoir, Lockhart flatly denies that he supported Savinkov or the Yaroslavl uprising (*British Agent*, p. 303). In fact, he knew of it, and attempted to help Savinkov with money after the uprising had started (Ullman, *Intervention*, p. 231).

3 Lockhart, *British Agent*, p. 304.

4 Moura, letter to Lockhart, HIA. Written at Yendel, dated 'Saturday': probably 20 Jul. 1918.

5 Raun, *Estonia and the Estonians*, pp. 105–7.

6 Moura, letter to Meriel Buchanan, 13 Oct. 1918, LL.

7 Moura, letter to Lockhart, HIA. Written at Yendel, dated 'Saturday': probably 20 Jul. 1918.

8 Swain, *Origins of the Russian Civil War*, pp. 172–6.

9 Kettle, *The Road to Intervention*, p. 298; Ullman, *Intervention*, p. 234.

10 Lockhart, entry for 25 Jul. 1918, *Diaries vol. 1*, p. 39.

11 Lockhart, *British Agent*, pp. 306–7.

12 Hill, *Go Spy the Land*, p. 212.

13 In *British Agent* (p. 307) Lockhart writes that it was ten days since she had left Moscow; the evidence of letters and diary suggests that this was an error, and he meant Petrograd. It is possible that his error was due to the fact that in this part of his memoir, he was glossing over and covering up aspects of Moura's movements and activities.

14 Moura, letter to Lockhart, LL. Undated: probably 6–7 Jul. 1918.

15 Lockhart, *British Agent*, p. 307.

16 Liuba Malinina was the niece of the former Moscow mayor, Mikhail Chelnokov, who had been a good friend of Lockhart during his earlier days at the Moscow Consulate.

17 Lockhart, *British Agent*, p. 307.

18 Moura, letter to Lockhart, 28 Oct. 1918, LL.

19 Lockhart, unpublished diary entry for 29 Jul. 1918.

20 Moura, letter to Lockhart, HIA. Written at Narva, undated: probably 15 Jul. 1918.

21 According to her daughter Tania (Alexander, *Estonian Childhood*, p. 152), who was deeply sceptical about the claim.

22 In *British Agent*, which Moura had oversight of, and which she insisted he alter to remove 'the spying business' (Moura, letter to Lockhart, 18 Jun. 1932, LL).

23 Official press release cited in *The Times*, 1 Aug. 1918, p. 6.

24 Lockhart, diary entry for 31 Jul. 1918, *Diaries vol. 1*, p. 39; Lockhart, *British Agent*, p. 308.

25 *The Times*, 13 Aug. 1918, p. 6.

26 *The Times*, 15 Aug. 1918, p. 5; Kettle, *The Road to Intervention*, p. 298.

27 Hill, *Go Spy the Land*, pp. 213–14.

28 Cromie, letter to Adm. W. R. Hall, 26 Jul. 1918, in Jones, 'Documents on British Relations' IV, p. 559. Knowing the people Cromie had available to him, together with the recorded movements of known SIS agents, it is difficult to guess who this 'trusted agent' would be if not Moura.

29 *Neue Freie Presse*, quoted in *The Times*, 15 Aug. 1918, p. 5.

30 Moura, letter to Lockhart, LL. Undated: probably 5 Jul. 1918. The Soviet report was exaggerated. Having arrived secretly in London he met with Lloyd George, whom he persuaded that the Russians were ready to expel the Germans. The British government tried to keep him quiet, for fear of upsetting the Bolsheviks (Ullman, *Intervention*, p. 209). On 26 June he made a surprise appearance at the Labour Party Conference; most delegates gave him an ovation, but a vocal minority barracked him severely. There was mystification at how he had managed to come 'straight from Moscow' as he claimed (*Manchester Guardian*, 27 Jun. 1918, p. 5; 28 Jun. 1918, p. 4).

Chapter 10: The Lockhart Plot

1 According to Kettle (*The Road to Intervention*, pp. 313–14), Helfferich was recalled because of his intemperate anti-Bolshevik suggestions. Lockhart (*British Agent*, pp. 309–10) was told it was because of his fears about the coming invasion.

2 Moura's movements during most of August 1918 are unrecorded. However, there are no letters from her, so she was probably with Lockhart. The few glimpses of her in other sources (e.g. Lockhart) indicate her presence in Moscow. It's not impossible that she journeyed to Kiev again in her role as spy, but there is no evidence for it.

3 Figes, *People's Tragedy*, pp. 516–17. The full text of the Declaration can be found online (in Russian) at www.hist.msu.ru/ER/Etext/DEKRET/declarat.htm and (in English) at www.marxists.org/archive/lenin/works/1918/jan/03.htm (retrieved 8 Apr. 2014).

4 Lenin, telegram to Penza Soviet, 9 Aug. 1918, quoted in Werth, 'A State Against Its People', p. 73.

5 Smith, *Former People*, pp. 133–7.

6 Moura, letter to Lockhart, HIA. Undated: probably May 1918. By this time, 10,000 roubles was not a great deal of money. As a rough guide, 1 *pood* (approx. 16 kg) of flour could change hands for over 350 roubles; a cab ride could cost 100 roubles; Russia was in the grip of hyperinflation, and by early 1919 black bread cost 20 roubles per pound, a suit of second-hand clothing could be 2,000 and a pair of boots 800 roubles (various reports in Foreign Office, *White Paper on Russia*, pp. 16, 22, 24).

7 Food was so short and so expensive, Francis Cromie warned in April that any British officials being sent out to Russia should bring six months' supply of provisions with them (letter to Adm. W. R. Hall, 16 Apr. 1918, in Jones, 'Documents on British Relations' IV, p. 552).

8 Moura, letter to Lockhart, LL. Undated: probably 6/7 Jul. 1918.

9 Moura, letter to Lockhart, LL. Undated: probably 8 Jul. 1918. She did hint later that some costly bargaining had been involved, and that she had had to '*se mettre en quatre*' (bend over backwards) to 'find some way out of it' (Moura, letter to Lockhart, 18 Feb. 1919, LL).

10 Martin Latsis, article in the Cheka periodical *Red Terror*, Nov. 1918, quoted in Leggett, *The Cheka*, p. 114.

11 Lenin, speech on 7 Nov. 1918, quoted in Leggett, *The Cheka*, p. 119.

12 Lockhart, unpublished diary entry, 3 Aug. 1918; *British Agent*, p. 308. The exact address is given in Malkov, *Reminiscences of a Kremlin Commandant*, ch. 20; and in Latsis, *Two Years of Struggle on the Home Front*, p. 19.

13 In *British Agent* (p. 314) Lockhart claims that visit took place at his flat on 15 August. However, other sources indicate that it was at his mission office in Bolshaya Lubyanka and must therefore have occurred prior to 5 August, when all Allied mission premises were closed down (based on an account given by one of the Latvians, cited in Long, 'Searching for Sidney Reilly', pp. 1230, 1238–9 n. 46).

14 Decades later, when the story began to be pieced together by Soviet and Western historians, Lockhart and Cromie were judged to be grossly naive and gullible to believe that the Latvian regiments could be subverted (e.g. Long, 'Plot and Counter-Plot in Revolutionary Russia'), but as Swain points out ('An Interesting and Plausible Proposal', pp. 91–100), the situation at the time and the shaky morale of the Latvian regiments made it a plausible idea. On the repatriation of the Latvians see Kettle, *The Road to Intervention*, p. 259.

15 Lockhart, *British Agent*, p. 315.

16 Cromie, letter to Adm. W. R. Hall, 26 Jul. 1918, in Jones, 'Documents on British Relations' IV, p. 559.

17 Doubt is cast on the misspelt note by Long ('Searching for Sidney Reilly', pp. 1238–9 n. 46), who points out that Lockhart used the same story in an entirely different context in a report on his mission in Russia (Lockhart to Balfour, 5 Nov. 1918, FO 371/3348/190442). Long suggests that the Latvians may have been vouched for by Reilly, but there is no reason to think that Lockhart would cover that up.

18 Wardrop, telegram to Foreign Office, 24 Mar. 1918, cited in Hughes, *Inside the Enigma*, pp. 135–6.

19 Wardrop, despatches from Moscow, 5–8 Aug. 1918, in Foreign Office, *White Paper on Russia*, pp. 1–2.

20 Lockhart, diary entry for 5 Aug. 1918, *Diaries vol. 1*, pp. 39–40. Lockhart states that George Hill was among those arrested. This must be a mistake, because the SIS agent's own memoir (*Go Spy the Land*, p. 228) indicates that he had gone into hiding by this time; furthermore, he is not listed among those arrested in any contemporary despatches or memoirs (e.g. Wardrop, despatches from Moscow, 5–8 Aug. 1918, in Foreign Office, *White Paper on Russia*, pp. 1–2; Lingner, 'In Moscow, 1918'; report in *The Times*, 10 Aug. 1918, p. 6; report from the *Times* Petrograd correspondent, 14 Aug. 1918, printed in *The Times*, 25 Sep. 1918, p. 9; report from Reuters' Moscow correspondent, *Manchester Guardian*, 27 Aug. 1918, p. 5).

21 Cromie, telegram to Gen. Poole, 9 Aug. 1918, in Foreign Office, *White Paper on Russia*, p. 1.

22 Wardrop, despatch 5 Aug. 1918, in Foreign Office, *White Paper on Russia*, p. 1.

23 Cromie, telegram to Gen. Poole, 9 Aug. 1918, in Foreign Office, *White Paper on Russia*, p. 1.

24 Lingner, 'In Moscow'.

25 Lockhart, *British Agent*, pp. 310–11. In justice to Gen. Poole, he had waited for reinforcements, and had hurried his landing because of the anti-Bolshevik uprisings that were taking place. The force landed included one battalion of French soldiers, a detachment of British Royal Marines and about 50 American sailors (Ullman, *Intervention*, p. 235). Furthermore, Poole was relying primarily on the Czechs (Kettle, *The Road to Intervention*, p. 306).

26 Cromie, letter to Adm. W. R. Hall, 14 Aug. 1918, in Jones, 'Documents on British Relations' IV, p. 561.

27 Lockhart, *British Agent*, p. 310.

28 Lockhart (*British Agent*, pp. 314–15) claims that this was his first meeting with any Latvian officers, and states that the date was 15 August. In fact, the date was 14 August (e.g. see Long, 'Searching for Sidney Reilly', p. 1231 and other sources) and it was his second meeting with Smidkhen and his first with Berzin.

29 Long, 'Searching for Sidney Reilly', p. 1232; Peters, 'The Lockhart Case', pp. 489, 491.

30 Lockhart, *British Agent*, p. 316.

31 Hill describes Reilly's plan (*Go Spy the Land*, pp. 236–8), which was to capture the leading Bolsheviks alive and 'march them through the streets of Moscow bereft of

their lower garments in order to kill them by ridicule'. Hill claimed that Lockhart played no part in the plot. However, he is contradicted by his own report ('Report of Work Done in Russia', FO 371/3350/79980, quoted in Cook, *Ace of Spies*, p. 171), in which he described keeping Lockhart abreast of developments via messages in SIS cipher. Also, the Latvian officer known as Smidkhen later stated that Lockhart approved the plan for a Kremlin coup and even alleged that he was insistent that Lenin be killed (multiple Russian sources cited in Long, 'Plot and Counter-Plot', pp. 132, 140 n. 38).

32 Lockhart, *British Agent*, pp. 316–17.

33 The true complexity of the Cheka double-cross took a long time to emerge. The details were gradually released over the course of decades, and it was the release of Cheka documents that revealed their involvement (see Long, 'Plot and Counter-Plot' for a history).

34 Rabinowitch, *Bolsheviks in Power*, pp. 326–8; Leggett, *The Cheka*, pp. 105–6. Uritsky's reputation for cruelty was unfair; he had tried fruitlessly to block a number of executions, but as head of the local Cheka it was his name that was given publicly as having ordered them. It later emerged that a friend of Kannegisser had been among those executed.

35 Witness testimony quoted in Mitrokhin, *Chekisms*, pp. 65–7; Lyandres, '1918 Attempt on the Life of Lenin', pp. 432–3.

36 Mitrokhin, *Chekisms*, pp. 65–6. Kaplan (whose real surname was Roitman) has been known variously as 'Fanny' and 'Dora'.

37 *Krasnaya Gazeta* (*Red Gazette*), 1 Sept. 1918, quoted in Figes, *A People's Tragedy*, p. 630.

Chapter 11: *The Knock on the Door in the Night*

1 The events that day have been described in multiple accounts, often conflicting, and further distorted by the many inaccurate press reports, British and Russian. Francis Cromie's biographer has collated the various witness statements and extracted a semi-coherent account from them (Bainton, *Honoured by Strangers*, pp. 250–57; see also Britnieva, *One Woman's Story*, pp. 76–81). The narrative given here is primarily based on that account, with the main contradictions resolved.

2 Cromie, letter to Adm. W. R. Hall, 14 Aug. 1918, in Jones, 'Documents on British Relations' IV, p. 561. Cromie's biographer is puzzled by his failure to be armed. It is possible that SIS colleagues such as Reilly advised him not to carry a gun. George Hill wrote that 'nine times out of ten a revolver is of no earthly use and will seldom get a man out of a tight corner', and was more likely to get its carrier into trouble (Hill, *Go Spy the Land*, p. 214). In classic Victorian adventurer style, Hill favoured a sword-stick for self-defence.

3 Report by W. J. Oudendijk (Netherlands Minister in Petrograd), 6 Sept. 1918, in Foreign Office, *White Paper on Russia*, pp. 3–4.

4 Cromie's death was reported in the British press as murder. There were claims that Cromie's body was mutilated and burial was refused, and that he was shot in the

back while at his desk, or killed while defending women and children from attack. It became so established in the public mind that it caused a heated argument in a House of Commons committee between Teddy Lessing (who had been present at the scene and denied that Cromie was murdered) and Commander Oliver Locker-Lampson and various other members (*Hansard*, Foreign Office HC Deb, 7 Jul. 1924, vol. 175, cc1847–9).

5 Malkov recounts this conversation in his memoir, *Reminiscences*, pp. 303–4.

6 Malkov, *Reminiscences*, pp. 307–9.

7 Malkov (*Reminiscences*, p. 310) definitely states that '*Poproboval potyanut dver na sebya . . .*', which Berberova (*Moura*, p. 65) also translates as 'I tried to pull the door toward me'. Possibly it was an outer protective door.

8 The British always called Malkov 'Mankoff' (Malkov, *Reminiscences*, p. 311; Lockhart, *British Agent*, p. 317). It seems to have irritated him.

9 Malkov, *Reminiscences*, pp. 311–3; Lockhart, *British Agent*, p. 317. Malkov had read *British Agent* when he wrote his own memoir, and is scathing about Lockhart's version, claiming that he did not draw his pistol during the arrest. Regarding Lockhart's claim that there were ten armed men in the room, Malkov suggests that fear often gives people double vision, and that in Lockhart's case it was tripled. However, it seems unlikely, given the obstructiveness of Moura and Hicks, and the fact that he was dealing with a case of attempted assassination, plus the fact that two Petrograd Chekists had been killed that day while attempting to arrest British subjects, that Malkov would not draw his weapon as a precaution. He seems to have thoroughly disliked Lockhart, and in this episode seems intent on portraying him in as abject a manner as possible. It's possible that Malkov's dislike stemmed from an incident at the Smolny Institute in February when he tried to detain Lockhart and prevent him seeing Trotsky; this earned him a sharp rebuke from Trotsky and a patronising put-down from Lockhart (Malkov, *Reminiscences*, pp. 306–9). Malkov seems to have been conscious of his peasant origins, and although he idolised Lenin he was not overly fond of Trotsky.

10 Lockhart, *British Agent*, pp. 318–19.

11 Lockhart, *British Agent*, pp. 317–20.

12 Malkov, *Reminiscences*, pp. 315–20. The document is reproduced in a report by Yakov Peters ('The Lockhart Case', p. 495). According to Peters, Maria Fride was arrested at a nearby flat in Sheremetievskiy pereulok (now Romanov pereulok) that was being used by Sidney Reilly. This has been cited in several biographies of Reilly. However, aside from being contradicted by Malkov, who was present at the interrogation and gives a vividly detailed account, Peters' report contains several other discrepancies which cast doubt on the reliability of several statements relating to Lockhart. See Chapter 12.

13 Malkov, *Reminiscences*, pp. 317–18.

14 Peters, 'The Lockhart Case', pp. 502–3. Aleksandr Fride was later sentenced to death and shot (Rabinowitch, *Bolsheviks in Power*, p. 338).

15 Mitrokhin, *Chekisms*, pp. 65–6.

16 Mitrokhin, *Chekisms*, p. 70.

17 Lockhart, *British Agent*, p. 320.

18 Lockhart, diary entry for 1 Sept. 1918, in *Diaries vol. 1*, p. 40. In *British Agent* (p. 320) he says he was released at 9 a.m., whereas according to Malkov it was a few hours later. In his diary, Lockhart confusingly states that he was in custody *from* 9 a.m. (*Diaries vol. 1*, p. 40).

19 Malkov, *Reminiscences*, p. 319; Peters, 'The Lockhart Case', p. 514. Lockhart himself is the source for Chicherin's intervention (*British Agent*, p. 320).

Chapter 12: Sacrificial Offering

1 Berberova (*Moura*, p. 79) claims she was told by Moura that when she was first interrogated she denied the affair. The Chekist interrogator then showed her a collection of compromising photos of herself with Lockhart, whereupon Moura fainted. Aside from the dubious melodrama of this scene, there is the anachronism of covert long-lens surveillance photography in 1918, plus the fact that the relationship was well known at the time (even Moura's mother in Petrograd knew about it). This appears to be one of the flourishes with which Moura liked to embellish her life story.

2 Leggett, *The Cheka*, pp. 193–4.

3 Reports by ministers of neutral nations, 3–9 Sept. 1918, in Foreign Office, *White Paper on Russia*, pp. 2–5.

4 Lockhart, *British Agent*, pp. 320–21.

5 Lockhart, *British Agent*, p. 321. Wardwell had replaced Lockhart's friend Raymond Robins, who had doubled as Red Cross chief and unofficial diplomatic agent.

6 Lockhart, diary entry for 3 Sept. 1918, *Diaries vol. 1*, pp. 40–41.

7 Lockhart, *British Agent*, p. 324.

8 Lockhart, *British Agent*, p. 324; Peters, 'The Lockhart Case', p. 514. In his report, Peters states that he only agreed to a secret meeting on condition that Lockhart didn't say anything slanderous about Soviet Russia – presumably an addition to cover his own back.

9 Lockhart, *British Agent*, pp. 340–41.

10 Lockhart, *British Agent*, pp. 326–7; *Diaries vol. 1*, pp. 41–2.

11 Report by W. J. Oudendijk, 6 Sept. 1918, in Foreign Office, *White Paper on Russia*, p. 5; also Ullman, *Intervention*, p. 293.

12 Report by W. J. Oudendijk, 6 Sept. 1918, in Foreign Office, *White Paper on Russia*, p. 6.

13 Letter from Petrograd prisoners, 5 Sept. 1918, in Foreign Office, *White Paper on Russia*, pp. 6–7.

14 Report by W. J. Oudendijk, 6 Sept. 1918, in Foreign Office, *White Paper on Russia*, p. 5.

15 Malkov, *Reminiscences*, p. 327. According to Lockhart (*Diaries vol. 1*, p. 42; *British Agent*, p. 329), his rooms were in the Kavaliersky Korpus. But Malkov, as Kremlin Commandant, probably knew the geography of the place better than Lockhart. Also, Lockhart's remark that the rooms had been a lady-in-waiting's apartment is consistent with Malkov's account.

16 Lockhart, *British Agent*, pp. 329–30. Lockhart's fears are reflected in his diary entry for 8 September (*Diaries vol. 1*, p. 42), in which, presumably fearing that it would be read, he implied that he hadn't the faintest idea who Smidkhen was ('I have been put in with a Russian(?) called Smidchen who is said to be my agent!').

17 Moura, letter to Lockhart, LL. Undated: probably 9 Sept. 1918. Note: British diplomatic etiquette at the time accorded Russian officials the French-style honorific 'M.' – hence 'M. Peters'.

18 Moura, letter to Lockhart, LL. Undated: probably 10 Sept. 1918.

19 Lockhart, *British Agent*, pp. 331–2.

20 Some 20 letters sent by Moura to Lockhart during his time in the Kremlin have survived; of these, 6 are in English, and the rest in Russian. The latter are mostly very brief notes. Some of the longer, more significant, Russian letters have translations interpolated in a different (?Lockhart's) hand.

21 The claim that Moura became Peters' lover comes from a summary report on Moura by SIS officer Ernest Boyce (11 Jul. 1940, Moura Budberg MI5 file). Kyril Zinovieff (interview, 1980, Andrew Boyle archive) believed that her favoured treatment indicated that she had become a Soviet agent.

22 Berberova, *Moura*, p. 63.

23 In the first part of his memoir, *British Agent*, Lockhart narrated the events of September 1918 more or less in the order in which they occurred, and didn't try to explain Moura's release. But in *Retreat from Glory* (p. 5) he claimed falsely that 'I had secured her release at the cost of my own re-arrest'. Moura had more editorial control over this volume than over its predecessor and was concerned to strike out anything that made her look mercenary (letters to Lockhart, 1933–4, LL).

24 Moura, letter to Lockhart, LL. Undated: probably about 12–15 Sept. 1918.

25 The sequence of these events given by Lockhart in his memoir appears to differ from that in his diary, which in turn is slightly different from the sequence of Moura's letters. The version given here resolves the contradictions, taking the letters and diary as the more reliable evidence.

26 Moura, letter to Lockhart, LL. Undated: probably 18 Sept. 1918.

27 Lockhart, *British Agent*, p. 337.

28 Moura, letter to Lockhart, LL. Undated: probably 18 Sept. 1918.

29 Lockhart, diary entry for 23 Sept. 1918, *Diaries vol. 1*, p. 44.

30 Moura, letter in Russian to Lockhart, HIA. Undated: probably 23 Sept. 1918.

31 Moura, two letters to Lockhart, LL. Both undated: probably 23–30 Sept. 1918; one Russian, one English.

32 Lockhart, diary entry for 28 Sept. 1918, *Diaries vol. 1*, p. 45.

33 Moura, letter to Lockhart, 29 Nov. 1918, LL.

34 Peters, 'The Lockhart Case', p. 489. This version was promoted by the Soviet authorities until the 1960s, when the publication of an account written in 1918 by the political commissar of the Latvian Rifle Division revealed that the plot had been an *agent provocateur* operation, orchestrated from the beginning by Dzerzhinsky and Peters (see Long, 'Plot and Counter-Plot', pp. 130ff). Peters also compressed the timescale of his investigation to give the impression that the Cheka had acted more promptly than it had. The publication of Pavel Malkov's *Reminiscences of a Kremlin Commandant*, first in 1961, then in a more detailed 1967 edition, also

exposed some of the falsehoods in Peters' report, such as the location of the arrest of Maria Fride.

35 Peters' account was the official version, and went unchallenged until the publication of Malkov's account of the interrogation of Maria Fride, and continued to be accepted even afterwards.

36 The breach was realised immediately, and *Izvestia* was told (and promptly reported) that Lockhart had been arrested mistakenly and released as soon as he was identified (*Izvestia*, 3 Sept. 1918, quoted by Berberova, *Moura*, p. 71), a lie contradicted by both Lockhart's and Malkov's accounts.

37 Ullman, *Intervention*, pp. 290–91.

38 Peters, 'The Lockhart Case', p. 516.

39 Peters, 'The Lockhart Case', p. 516.

40 Peters, 'The Lockhart Case', p. 516.

41 Moura remarked twice in her letters that she expected to be able to get money from the Ukraine (letters to Lockhart, 26 Jan., 14 Feb. 1919, LL and HIA), and it is presumed that this must have been from her father's estate. Some doubt is cast on this by the fact that although at the time the plans were first made the Hetmanate government was still in place, by the time of the letters it had fallen and the Red Army was recapturing the Ukraine, so there would certainly have been no property to inherit.

42 Lockhart, diary entry for 1 Oct. 1918, *Diaries vol. 1*, p. 46.

43 Lockhart, *British Agent*, pp. 344–5.

44 Moura, letter to Lockhart, LL. Marked 'Thursday': certainly 3 Oct. 1918.

45 Moura, letter to Lockhart, LL. Marked 'Thursday': certainly 3 Oct. 1918.

Chapter 13: *The End of Everything*

1 Gen. Finlayson, quoted in De Ruvigny, 'Garstin, Denys Norman', p. 66.

2 Garstin, letter, 6 Jun. 1918, reproduced in Walpole, 'Denis Garstin', p. 605.

3 Hugh Walpole, preface, in Denis Garstin, *The Shilling Soldiers*, p. xi.

4 Garstin, letter, 6 Jun. 1918, reproduced in Walpole, 'Denis Garstin', p. 605.

5 Moura, letter to Meriel Buchanan, 13 Oct. 1918, LL.

6 Moura, letter to Lockhart, LL. Undated: probably 10 Oct. 1918.

7 Moura, letter to Meriel Buchanan, 13 Oct. 1918, LL. Moura must presumably have left Garry with her mother while she was away with Lockhart in Moscow.

8 Moura, letters to Lockhart, 14 Nov. and 2 Dec. 1918, LL.

9 Cross, 'A Corner of a Foreign Field', pp. 352–4; Buchanan, *Victorian Gallery*, pp. 103–45.

10 Moura, letter to Lockhart, LL. Undated: probably 10 Oct. 1918.

11 R. L. Stevenson, *Virginibus Puerisque*, I.

12 R. L. Stevenson, *Virginibus Puerisque*, 'Crabbed Age and Youth'.

13 R. L. Stevenson, *Virginibus Puerisque*, III: 'Falling in Love'.

14 Moura, letter to Lockhart, LL. Undated: probably 10 Oct. 1918.

15 Moura, letter to Lockhart, 2 Dec. 1918, LL.

16 Moura, letter to Lockhart, 28 Oct. 1918, LL.

17 Moura, letter to Lockhart, HIA. Undated, written on American Red Cross paper; probably 10–15 Oct. 1918.

18 Moura, letter to Lockhart, 24 Jan. 1919, LL.

19 Lockhart, *Retreat from Glory*, p. 11. It is not impossible that Moura's illness was also Spanish flu, and that she passed it to Lockart, but this is unlikely given the time lapse between their contact and Lockhart succumbing. More likely he picked up the infection during his travels. Moura's illness was possibly an infection connected with her miscarriage.

20 Lockhart, *Retreat from Glory*, p. 6.

21 Lockhart, *Retreat from Glory*, pp. 5–6.

22 Lockhart, *Retreat from Glory*, p. 43.

23 Lockhart, diary entry for 14 Nov. 1918, *Diaries vol. 1*, p. 48.

24 Lockhart, diary entry for 16 Nov. 1918, *Diaries vol. 1*, p. 48.

25 Lockhart, diary entry for 23 Nov. 1918, *Diaries vol. 1*, p. 51.

26 The Tribunal and sentences were reported in *Izvestia* on 25 Nov. and 10 Dec. 1918 (cited in Long, 'Searching for Sidney Reilly', p. 1234). Col. Aleksandr Fride was sentenced to death by the same court, and was shot.

27 Moura, letter to Lockhart, HIA. Undated: probably 13 Oct. 1918.

28 Moura, letter to Lockhart, LL. Undated: probably 4 Oct. 1918.

29 Moura, letter to Lockhart, 24 Jan. 1919, LL.

30 Moura, letter to Lockhart, 31 Oct. 1918, LL.

31 Moura, letter to Lockhart, 16 Dec. 1918, LL.

Chapter 14: *Se Mettre en Quatre*

1 Moura, letter to Lockhart, 26–28 Dec. 1918, LL.

2 Moura, letters to Lockhart, Feb. 1919, HIA and LL. See also reports on conditions in Russia in 1919 in Foreign Office, *White Paper on Russia*, pp. 30ff. Wages had been set by decree in July 1918; inflation had raised them to ten times their pre-war rates, but prices outstripped them, especially for rare commodities like tea, butter and firewood.

3 Moura, letters to Lockhart, 26–28 Dec. 1918 and 18 Feb. 1919, LL.

4 Moura, letter to Lockhart, 26–28 Dec. 1918, LL.

5 Moura, letter to Lockhart, LL. Undated: probably 13 Oct. 1918.

6 Moura, letter to Lockhart, 14 Feb. 1919, HIA.

7 According to a letter from Moura to Lockhart (LL, undated: probably 1933), Chukovsky had been an interpreter for Thornhill on the Archangel front. If so, he presumably set no store by the negative opinions of Moura she believed Thornhill propagated. Chukovsky later achieved fame in Russia as a children's author.

8 Moura, letter to Lockhart, 26–28 Dec. 1918, LL.

9 Moura, letter to Lockhart, 18 Feb. 1919, LL. The reference is to Gabriele D'Annunzio, the Italian writer and political idealist.

10 Moura, letter to Lockhart, 26–28 Dec. 1918, LL.

11 Moura, letter to Lockhart, 1 Jan. 1919, LL. John Gibson Lockhart (1794–1854) wrote his *Life of Walter Scott* in 1837–8 and was married to Scott's daughter; he was not related to Robert Bruce Lockhart, though Moura might well have believed he was. A rough calculation indicates that to earn the same as a skilled workman (between 500 and 1,000 roubles per month), Moura must have had to translate about eight to twenty pages a day.

12 Moura, letter to Lockhart, 4 Jan. 1919, LL.

13 Moura, letter to Lockhart, 4 Jan. 1919, LL.

14 Moura, letter to Lockhart, 5 Jan. 1919, LL.

15 Moura, letter to Lockhart, 24 Jan. 1919, LL.

16 Moura, letter to Lockhart, 18 Feb. 1919, LL.

17 Moura, letter to Lockhart, 25 Jan. 1919, HIA.

18 Moura, letter to Lockhart, 26 Jan. 1919, LL.

19 Lockhart, unpublished diary entry, 23 Feb. 1919; Moura, letters to Lockhart, 2 Nov. 1918, 14 Feb. 1919, HIA.

20 Moura, letter to Lockhart, 14 Feb. 1919, HIA.

21 Moura, letter to Lockhart, 14 Feb. 1919, HIA.

22 Moura, letters to Lockhart, 12–13 Feb. 1919, LL.

23 Moura, letter to Lockhart, 5 Mar. 1919, HIA.

24 Moura, letter to Lockhart, 6 Mar. 1919, LL.

25 Whitman, 'Song of Myself', *Leaves of Grass*.

26 Moura, letter to Lockhart, 12 Apr. 1919, LL.

27 Moura, letters to Lockhart, 12–20 Apr. 1919, LL and HIA. The account that follows is based on this series of letters. There are pages missing from the letters – possibly removed by Lockhart in order to suppress Moura's statements about her movements at this period.

28 Maurice Magre, '*Avilir*', *L'Oeuvre amoureuse et sentimentale* (Paris: Bibliothèque des curieux, 1922), p. 174 (translation Jeremy Dronfield); Moura, letter to Lockhart, 12 Feb. 1919, LL.

29 Alexander, *Estonian Childhood*, pp. 1–3, 8.

30 Moura, letters to Lockhart, 18 Apr. and Easter Day [20 Apr.], 1919, LL and HIA.

31 Moura, letter to Lockhart, 9 May 1919, HIA. In Tania's account (*Estonian Childhood*, pp. 1–3) the murder took place on the 18th. Note: 'Esthonia' was the contemporary English spelling.

32 In her letter to Lockhart on 9 May 1919, Moura writes that her mother was to undergo an operation the next day. According to Tania (*Estonian Childhood*, p. 12), Madame Zakrevskaya died 'in April, only a week or two after my father'. Presumably Tania was mistaken about the exact date, and her grandmother actually died from the operation on or after 10 May.

33 Moura, letter to Lockhart, 18 Apr. 1919, LL.

34 Moura, letter to Lockhart, 24 Jan. 1919, LL.

35 Moura, letter to Lockhart, 12 Apr. 1919, LL.

36 Lockhart, diary entry for 24 Oct. 1919, *Diaries vol. 1*, p. 54.

37 Lockhart, *Retreat from Glory*, p. 43.

Chapter 15: 'We're All Iron Now'

1 Wells, *Russia in the Shadows*, pp. 14–15.

2 Wells, *H. G. Wells in Love*, pp. 161–4.

3 Berberova, *Moura*, pp. 98–100; Alexander, *Estonian Childhood*, pp. 56–9. Berberova produced a garbled account, apparently based on a misunderstanding of Moura's own oral tale. She states that in early 1919 Moura was homeless and given accommodation by the elderly Gen. Aleksandr Mosolov. This is contradicted by Moura's letters, which show her living with her mother. Both Berberova and Tania state that she approached Chukovsky in the spring or summer of 1919 begging for work as a translator; he gave her none, and instead he took her to meet (for the first time) Maxim Gorky. Thus she became his live-in secretary. We know from Moura's letters that she was approached first by Chukovsky and by the beginning of January 1919 was already translating books for him (see Chapter 14). The account given here is arrived at by resolving the contradictions and errors in previous versions.

4 Moura, letter to Lockhart, 9 May 1919, HIA; Alexander, *Estonian Childhood*, p. 12.

5 Chukovsky, diary entry for 4 Sep. 1919, *Diary*, p. 53.

6 Berberova's and Tania's accounts both have Moura asking for translation work in mid-1919 and meeting Gorky for the first time then. Both women seem to have misunderstood Moura's story and conflated two events into one. Berberova isn't precise about the time when Moura entered Gorky's household, but Tania states that it was September 1919.

7 Khodasevich, 'Gorky', p. 228.

8 Berberova, *Moura*, p. 100.

9 Moura, letter to Lockhart, LL. Undated: probably 1933. Moura does nothing to clarify the chronology in this letter, in which she refers to events several years apart (e.g. the Kerensky period and her time in the Gorky commune) as if they were virtually contemporaneous. All she specifies is that the 'peacock' reaction occurred at her very first meeting with Gorky.

10 Quoted in Figes, *A People's Tragedy*, p. 208.

11 Gorky, *Novaya Zhizn*, 7 Nov. 1917 and 9 Jan. 1918, quoted in Leggett, *The Cheka*, pp. 45, 304.

12 Moura, letter to Lockhart, 18 Feb. 1919, LL.

13 Leggett, *The Cheka*, p. 65.

14 Moura, letter to Lockhart, 24 Jan. 1919, LL.

15 Recollections of Valentina Khodasevich (niece of Vladislav) quoted in Alexander, *Estonian Childhood*, p. 61.

16 Khodasevich, 'Gorky', pp. 227–8.; Valentina Khodasevich, quoted by Alexander; Vaksberg, *The Murder of Maxim Gorky*, p. 67.

17 Troyat, *Gorky*, pp. 62–3.

18 Troyat, *Gorky*, p. 87.

19 Troyat, *Gorky*, pp. 104–5.

20 Gorky, letter to Yekaterina, 5 May 1911, quoted in Vaksberg, *The Murder of Maxim Gorky*, p. 40.

21 Fitzpatrick, *The Commissariat of Enlightenment*, pp. 149, 293.

22 Berberova, *Moura*, p.105.

23 Various sources are in conflict over the date and location of this escape bid. The narrative given here is, again, achieved by resolving the conflicts between the sources.

24 Moura, letter to Lockhart, LL. Undated: probably 1933; also Anna Kotschoubey (Assia), letter to H. G. Wells, 27 Dec. 1920, RBML, and Wells, *Russia in the Shadows*, p. 10. These three accounts contradict that given by Tania (Alexander, *Estonian Childhood*, pp. 65–6), which states that her mother's escape attempt took place in December 1920 and was across the frozen river Narva into Estonia. Tania's date is contradicted by contemporary evidence proving that it was late February or early March. Furthermore, by February 1920 crossing the frozen Narva would not be necessary to gain entry to Estonia, as it was no longer the frontier line – under the Russo-Estonian peace treaty of February 1920, the agreed frontier was several miles east of the river (Article III, Peace Treaty of Tartu, in *League of Nations Treaty Series* vol. XI, 1922, pp. 51–71).

25 Leggett, *The Cheka*, p. 251.

26 Quoted in Vaksberg, *The Murder of Maxim Gorky*, p. 105.

27 McMeekin, *History's Greatest Heist*, pp. 57–61 and *passim*. By the end of 1919, 36 million gold roubles' worth of materials had been collected in Petrograd alone. By spring 1921 Andreyeva was carrying out the role of saleswoman openly and from 1922 was working for the Commissariat for External Trade (Fitzpatrick, *Commissariat of Enlightenment*, p. 293).

28 The evidence (most of it circumstantial) for Moura's involvement is summarised in an unpublished paper by G. L. Owen, 'Budberg, the Soviets, and Reilly', acquired by H. G. Wells' biographer Andrea Lynn and passed to Deborah McDonald.

29 Berberova, *Moura*, p. 115. The 'Bronze Venus' was Alexander Pushkin's nickname for a woman with whom he had an affair in 1828 and on whom he based two of his fictional characters; she is believed to have been Countess Agrafena Zakrevsky. According to Berberova, Gorky believed mistakenly that Countess Zakrevsky was Moura's ancestor.

30 Vaksberg, *The Murder of Maxim Gorky*, p. 99.

31 Russell, *The ractice and Theory of Bolshevism*, p. 22.

32 Russell, *The ractice and Theory of Bolshevism*, pp. 43–4.

33 Wells, *Russia in the Shadows*, p. 31.

34 Alexander, *Estonian Childhood*, p. 33.

35 Wells, *H. G. Wells in Love*, p. 163. The hat was made for Moura from beaver felt, a common hat-making fabric at the time, by Valentina Khodasevich (Berberova, *Moura*, p. 127; Berberova's translator has rendered the term incorrectly as beaver *fur*).

36 Wells, *H. G. Wells in Love*, p. 164.

37 Wells, *Russia in the Shadows*, pp. 9–10. In fairness to Moura, some of the untruths she appears to have told Wells could be his misunderstandings or mistaken memories; for instance, a distant cousin of her late husband *had* been Russian Ambassador in London, and she *had* been in a Bolshevik prison three times. But knowing her

proven tendency to fabricate and embellish, it is quite probable that she told exactly the lies that Wells naively quoted.

38 Wells, *Russia in the Shadows*, pp. 16, 26.
39 Wells, *Russia in the Shadows*, pp. 15–16.
40 Wells, *Russia in the Shadows*, pp. 19–20.
41 Wells, *Russia in the Shadows*, pp. 69–70.
42 Wells, *Russia in the Shadows*, p. 22.
43 Khodasevich, 'Gorky', pp. 226–8.
44 Wells, *Russia in the Shadows*, pp. 51–2.
45 Wells, *H. G. Wells in Love*, p. 164. According to Berberova (*Moura*, p. 123), the gossip in the commune was that Wells went to Moura's room uninvited, and there were several versions of what happened, ranging from her giving him a 'swift kick' to him spending the night chatting to her. Berberova did not believe Moura had slept with him.
46 Wells, *Russia in the Shadows*, p. 96.
47 Khodasevich, 'Gorky', p. 229.
48 Wells told this to sculptor Clare Sheridan, who was in Moscow awaiting a chance to make a bust of Lenin (Sheridan, *Mayfair to Moscow*, pp. 109 –110).
49 Vaksberg (*The Murder of Maxim Gorky*, pp. 105–6) is completely perplexed by this, and suggests a complicated conspiracy of Gorky's other women (including Maria Andreyeva and Yekaterina) using their influence to separate her from Gorky. It's possible, but if they'd wanted that, they could simply have left her to rot in the Cheka jail.
50 McMeekin, *History's Greatest Heist*, pp. 61, 143–6; Owen, 'Budberg, the Soviets, and Reilly', p. 3.
51 Moura, letter to Lockhart, 24 Jun. 1921, HIA. Lockhart's son Robin was born in 1920; he grew up to become an author, and wrote a book about Sidney Reilly. The letter gives no indication of how the news reached Moura, but her wording suggests that it was not from Lockhart himself. It could have been a communication from H. G. Wells, or from Liuba and Will Hicks.

Chapter 16: Baroness Budberg

1 Berberova, *Moura*, pp. 127–8. Berberova's account is based on the story told to her by Moura. However, she wrongly places it in January; in fact it was May. According to a letter left for Gorky, she departed Petrograd on 18 May (Moura, letter to Gorky, 18 May 1921, via Scherr). In this letter, she told him that she loved him, observed that she believed in God while he didn't, and informed him that she was going to Estonia to see her children.
2 Moura Budberg MI5 file, report on Moura by Ernest Boyce, 11 Jul. 1940.
3 There are occasional references to Jews in her letters, and while there is no hostility, there is a degree of casual contempt. The same is true of the writings of Lockhart, Meriel Buchanan, Denis Garstin and nearly all non-Jews during this period. Unlike some of their contemporaries, none of Moura's circle regarded Jews as a threat or set much store by the fact that so many Bolsheviks were Jews.

4 Alexander, *Estonian Childhood*, p. 69; Moura Budberg MI5 file, report on Moura by Ernest Boyce, 11 Jul. 1940.

5 Alexander, *Estonian Childhood*, p. 68.

6 Berberova (*Moura*, p. 130) describes the reunion happening in Tallinn, but Alexander (who of course was there) says it occurred at Kallijärv on the Yendel estate.

7 Alexander, *Estonian Childhood*, pp. 67–70.

8 Alexander, *Estonian Childhood*, p. 67.

9 Alexander, *Estonian Childhood*, p. 70.

10 Alexander, *Estonian Childhood*, pp. 70–71.

11 Moura Budberg MI5 file, Metropolitan Police Special Branch note, 31 Mar. 1947. This note was a record of an interview with Moura in connection with her application for British naturalisation.

12 McMeekin, *History's Greatest Heist*, pp. 143–6, 158–61.

13 Moura, letters to Gorky, 18 Aug.–1 Oct. 1921, GA. Some have suspected that Moura managed to make a covert, illegal visit to England at this time, but she almost certainly didn't; in October 1921 H. G. Wells suggested to his friend Maurice Baring (who was an old Russia hand) that they visit 'Countess Benckendorff' in Cromer, Norfolk (Wells, letter 1335 to Baring in *Correspondence of H. G. Wells vol. 3*). Most likely this would be Countess Sophie Benckendorff, widow of the late Ambassador to the UK, who was then living in Suffolk.

14 The first entry in the first section (KV2 1971) is dated 9 Dec. 1921, and is an extract from an intercepted letter to Prince Pierre Volkonsky mentioning Moura's recent marriage to Budberg.

15 Berberova, *Moura*, p. 130.

16 Moura, letter to Gorky, 16 Dec. 1921, GA. There is a note in Moura's MI5 file indicating that a Russian source identified Budberg as having worked for the secret police in St Petersburg, but doesn't specify whether this was the imperial Okhrana or the Bolshevik Cheka.

17 There is a note to this effect in Moura's MI5 file, and the French Deuxième Bureau also noted it (Deuxième Bureau Documents Rapatriés, dossier on 'Russian Personalities of Emigration Suspected of Informing the Soviets: Countess Benckendorff, Baron Budberg, Trilby Espenberg, 1921–1936', Carton 608, Dossier 3529. Quoted in Lynn, *Shadow Lovers*, pp. 195–6).

18 Alexander, *Estonian Childhood*, pp. 71–2.

19 Moura, letter to Lockhart, 6 Jan. 1923, HIA. When Lockhart was writing his memoirs in the 1930s, she made him remove all reference to Budberg, protesting that she could never have 'married a man *in order to* get some facility' (Moura, letter to Lockhart, LL. Undated: probably 1933). When he wrote an essay in which he again referred to her marriage of convenience, she crossed it out, put angry exclamation marks in the margin, and emended the passage to say that 'after her return to Estonia she married Baron Budberg, an old friend of the family' (Lockhart, 'Baroness Budberg', unpublished draft, HIA).

20 Moura, letter to Lockhart, 24 Jun. 1921, HIA.

21 Moura, letter to Gorky, May 1921, quoted in Vaksberg, *The Murder of Maxim Gorky*, p. 104. 'Kobelyak' was a contemporary spelling; it is now 'Kobeliaky'.

22 Moura, letters to Gorky, Jun.–Aug. 1921, GA.

23 Gorky, letter quoted in Alexander, *Estonian Childhood*, p. 72.

24 Alexander, *Estonian Childhood*, pp. 72–3.

25 Gorky, letter to Lenin, 22 Nov. 1921, quoted in Vaksberg, *The Murder of Maxim Gorky*, p. 141.

26 Moura, letter to Gorky, 1921, quoted in Vaksberg, *The Murder of Maxim Gorky*, p. 148.

27 Gorky, letter to Lenin, 25 Dec. 1921, quoted in Vaksberg, *The Murder of Maxim Gorky*, p. 144.

28 Vaksberg, *The Murder of Maxim Gorky*, p. 150.

29 Berberova, *Moura*, p. 166.

30 Moura Budberg MI5 file, note added 15 May 1922. Meiklejohn is identified as the Tallinn station chief in Jeffery, *MI6*, p. 184.

31 Moura, letter to Wells, 28 Jul. 1922, RBML.

32 Now 15 Karl-Marx-Damm.

33 Khodasevich, 'Gorky', pp. 231–2.

34 Khodasevich, 'Gorky', pp. 231–2.

35 Khodasevich, 'Gorky', pp. 231–2.

36 Moura, Preface to Gorky, *Fragments*, p. vii.

37 Moura, Preface to Gorky, *Fragments*, p. ix.

38 Moura, Preface to Gorky, *Fragments*, pp. ix–x.

39 Berberova, *The Italics are Mine*, pp. 178–9.

40 Moura, letter to Wells, 11 Oct. 1923, RBML.

41 Moura, letters to Wells, 1923, RBML.

42 Moura, letter to Wells, 26 Jan. 1923, RBML.

43 Moura, letter to Wells, 11 Oct. 1923, RBML. The Hôtel Hermitage on the Côte d'Azur was occasionally used by Wells.

44 Lockhart, diary entry for 22 May 1919, *Diaries vol. 1*, p. 53.

45 Wells, *H. G. Wells in Love*, p. 104.

Chapter 17: One Perfect Thing

1   Moura, letter to Lockhart, 6 Jan. 1923, HIA.

2   Moura, letter to Lockhart, 6 Jan. 1923, HIA.

3   Moura, letter to Lockhart, 6 Jan. 1923, HIA.

4   Moura Budberg MI5 file, 31 Jul. 1923, SIS Section 1B.

5   Moura, letter to Gorky, 7 Aug. 1923, GA.

6   Moura, letters to Gorky, 4–29 Aug. 1923, GA.

7   Moura, letter to Wells, 10 Feb. 1924.

8   Khodasevich, 'Gorky', pp. 234–5.

9   Vaksberg, *The Murder of Maxim Gorky*, p. 173.

10 Khodasevich, 'Gorky', pp. 236–7.

11 Kathleen Tynan, interview with Moura Budberg, *Vogue* (US), 1 Oct. 1970, p. 210. This tale might be one of the many Moura invented or elaborated. But it was certainly true that Gorky and Moura were subjected to surveillance.

12 Editor's note in Lockhart, *Diaries vol. 1*, p. 55.

13 Lockhart, diary entry, 30 Jul. 1923, *Diaries vol. 1*, pp. 56–7.

14 Lockhart, *Retreat from Glory*, pp. 232–3.

15 Lockhart, *Retreat from Glory*, p. 233.

16 Lockhart, *Retreat from Glory*, p. 233; unpublished diary entry for 29 Jul. 1918. Oddly, Lockhart (who wrote his memoirs from his diaries) gives the date of Moura's call from Vienna and recalls the earlier incident, but doesn't comment on the coincidence of the dates.

17 Lockhart, *Retreat from Glory*, p. 234.

18 Lockhart, *Retreat from Glory*, p. 234. Lockhart compresses the timescale, saying that he went 'the next night', but this is contradicted by his diary for 2–4 Aug. 1924 (*Diaries vol. 1*, pp. 58–9).

19 Lockhart, *Retreat from Glory*, p. 235.

20 Lockhart, diary entry, 2–4 Aug. 1924, *Diaries vol. 1*, p. 58.

21 Lockhart, *Retreat from Glory*, p. 237.

22 Lockhart, *Retreat from Glory*, p. 237.

Chapter 18: Love and Anger

1 Wells, *H. G. Wells in Love*, pp. 167–8.

2 Lockhart, *Retreat from Glory*, p. 238.

3 Lockhart, *Retreat from Glory*, p. 240.

4 Lockhart, diary entry, 2–4 Aug. 1924, *Diaries vol. 1*, p. 58.

5 This proposition isn't mentioned in Lockhart's memoir and is only alluded to in contemporary letters, but it is referred to by Moura in a letter written to Lockhart some years later (30 May 1933, LL).

6 Moura, letter to Lockhart, HIA. Undated (labelled 'Thursday'): probably 7 Aug. 1924.

7 Moura, letters to Gorky, 4–14 Aug. 1924, GA.

8 Moura, letter to Gorky, 20 Aug. 1924, GA.

9 Gorky, letter to Romain Rolland, 15 Jan. 1924, quoted in Vaksberg, *The Murder of Maxim Gorky*, p. 167.

10 Gorky, letter to Romain Rolland, 3 Mar. 1924, quoted in Vaksberg, *The Murder of Maxim Gorky*, p. 167.

11 Gorky, 'A Person', quoted in Vaksberg, *The Murder of Maxim Gorky*, p. 167.

12 Khodasevich, 'Gorky', p. 238.

13 Gorky, letter to Yekaterina Peshkova, Jun. 1924, quoted in Vaksberg, *The Murder of Maxim Gorky*, p. 175.

14 Moura, letter to Gorky, 29 Jul. 1925, GA.

15 Gorky, letter to Moura, 2 Aug. 1925, GA.

16 Moura, letter to Gorky, 5 Aug. 1925, GA.

17 Gorky, letter to Moura, 8 Aug. 1925, GA.

18 Moura, letter to Gorky, 29 Sep. 1925, GA.

19 Researchers who have studied the Budberg/Gorky correspondence (including

Vaksberg, *The Murder of Maxim Gorky*, p. 186n, and Barry P. Scherr, unpublished notes) presume that 'R' (who is referred to directly just once in a letter from Moura to Gorky, 19 Apr. 1926) was Robert Bruce Lockhart. However, Moura never referred to Lockhart as 'Robert' or 'R'. Intimately, he was always 'Baby' (or variations thereof). Early in their relationship he was briefly 'Locky' and 'Bertie', but never 'Robert'. Therefore the identity of 'R' is a mystery. The only clue is in her alleged confession to H. G. Wells that she had had an (unnamed) Italian lover in Sorrento (Wells, *H. G. Wells in Love*, p. 168). This is the most likely explanation.

20 Moura, Preface to Gorky, *Fragments*, p. ix.

21 Moura, letter to Gorky, 23 Oct. 1925, quoted in Vaksberg, *The Murder of Maxim Gorky*, pp. 184–5.

22 Gorky, letter to Moura, 21 Dec. 1925, quoted in Vaksberg, *The Murder of Maxim Gorky*, p. 185.

23 Moura, letters to Gorky, 23 Dec. 1925, GA; and 29 Dec. 1925, quoted in Vaksberg, *The Murder of Maxim Gorky*, p. 185.

24 Gorky, letter to Moura, 30 Dec. 1925, GA; extract quoted in Vaksberg, *The Murder of Maxim Gorky*, pp. 185–6.

25 Moura, letter to Gorky, 8 Jan. 1926, GA.

26 Sergei Yesenin, 'Goodbye, My Friend, Goodbye', Dec. 1925.

27 Gorky, letter (probably never sent) to Moura, 3 Feb. 1926, GA.

28 Moura, letter to Gorky, 19 Apr. 1926, quoted in Vaksberg, *The Murder of Maxim Gorky*, p. 186.

29 Alexander, *Estonian Childhood*, p. 84.

30 Quoted in Troyat, *Gorky*, p. 160.

31 Moura, letter to Gorky, 20 Aug. 1926, GA.

32 Alexander, *Estonian Childhood*, p. 93.

33 Gorky, in debate with Russian writers, 12 Jun. 1931, quoted in Troyat, *Gorky*, p. 162.

34 Moura, letter to Wells, 12 Feb. 1926, RBML.

35 Moura, letter to Wells, 4 Oct. 1926, RBML.

36 Personal communication from Barry P. Scherr.

37 Deuxième Bureau Documents Rapatriés, dossier on 'Russian Personalities of Emigration Suspected of Informing the Soviets: Countess Benckendorff, Baron Budberg, Trilby Espenberg, 1921–1936', Carton 608, Dossier 3529. Quoted in Lynn, *Shadow Lovers*, pp. 195–6. The reliability of this source is questionable. It specifies no dates (it's a general summary of 15 years of observation) and appears to conflate several individuals, including one Trilby Espenberg and at one point confuses Moura with Countess Sophie Benckendorff, widow of the late Russian Ambassador to the UK, who settled in England after the Revolution.

38 Moura Budberg MI5 file, document 16.Y, 1932, translation of original Russian document.

39 Kyril Zinovieff, interview with Andrew Boyle, CUL Add 9429/2B/125.

40 Vaksberg, *The Murder of Maxim Gorky*, p. 200.

41 Vaksberg, *The Murder of Maxim Gorky*, pp. 200–201; Troyat, *Gorky*, p. 165.

42 Quoted in Vaksberg, *The Murder of Maxim Gorky*, p. 200.

43 Troyat, *Gorky*, pp. 165–8.

44 Wells, *H. G. Wells in Love*, p. 165.
45 Moura, letter to Wells, 2 May 1928, RBML.
46 Moura, letter to Wells, 10 Feb. 1924, RBML.
47 Moura, letter to Lockhart, 4 Jul. 1928, HIA.
48 Moura, letter to Lockhart, 28 Jul. 1928, HIA.
49 Moura, letter to Lockhart, 1 Nov. 1928, LL.
50 Spence, *Trust No One*, p. 483; Cook, *Ace of Spies*, pp. 259–63.
51 Moura, letter to Gorky, 21 Aug. 1928, quoted in Vaksberg, *The Murder of Maxim Gorky*, p. 211.
52 Scherr, notes on letter from Moura to Gorky, 24 Mar. 1929, GA.
53 Alexander, *Estonian Childhood*, p. 119.
54 Wells, *H. G. Wells in Love*, p. 140.
55 Nicolson, letter to Vita, 12 Apr. 1929, in *The Harold Nicolson Diaries and Letters*, p. 69.
56 Wells, *H. G. Wells in Love*, p. 141.
57 Lockhart, diary entry for 9 Apr. 1929, *Diaries vol. 1*, p. 81.
58 Moura, letter to Lockhart, HIA. Undated: written immediately after reunion in Berlin, 1929.
59 Moura Budberg MI5 file: Boyce, letter to Maj. Spencer, Passport Control Office, London, 10 Jun. 1929. Boyce's retirement, Jeffery, *MI6*, p. 191.

Chapter 19: Not Such a Fool

1 When she made her visa application, Moura claimed that she had visited Britain before, in 1911, and had stayed at Claridge's (Moura Budberg MI5 file, notes by British Passport Control, Paris, 13 Jun. 1928). Nothing is known of the details of this visit, including whether or not it really happened.
2 Lockhart, diary entry for 5 Sep. 1918, *Diaries vol. 1*, p. 41.
3 Moura, letter to Wells, RBML. Undated: postmarked 1929, probably late Sept.
4 Moura, letter to Wells, 29 Sept. 1929, RBML.
5 Alexander, *Estonian Childhood*, p. 148.
6 Wells, *H. G. Wells in Love*, p. 143.
7 Moura, letters to Gorky, Mar.–Jul. 1930, GA.
8 Anthony West, 'My Father's Unpaid Debts of Love', *Observer Review*, 11 Jan. 1976, p. 17.
9 Rupert Hart-Davis, interview with Andrew Boyle, CUL Add 9429/2B/119.
10 Rupert Hart-Davis, interview with Andrew Boyle, CUL Add 9429/2B/119.
11 Lockhart, diary entry for 4 Oct. 1930, *Diaries vol. 1*, p. 127.
12 Nathalie Brooke (née Benckendorff, daughter of Constantine), interview with Andrew Boyle, CUL Add. 9429/2B/114 (i). The relationship between Constantine and Djon is uncertain, but they appear to have been fourth cousins, their common ancestor being a Johann Michael Ivanovich von Benckendorff (1720–1775).
13 Benckendorff, *Half a Life*, p. 150.
14 Nathalie Brooke (née Benckendorff, daughter of Constantine), interview with Andrew Boyle, CUL Add. 9429/2B/114 (i).

15 Kyril Zinovieff, interview with Andrew Boyle, CUL Add 9429/2B/125.

16 Nathalie Brooke, interview with Deborah McDonald.

17 Quoted by Michael Burn, interview with Andrew Boyle, CUL Add 9429/2B/115 (ii).

18 She found her 'plump, big boned, forceful, not attractive . . . she repelled me' (Nathalie Brooke, interview with Andrew Boyle, CUL Add. 9429/2B/114 (i)).

19 Nathalie Brooke, interview with Andrew Boyle, CUL Add. 9429/2B/114 (i).

20 Nathalie Brooke, interview with Andrew Boyle, CUL Add. 9429/2B/114 (i).

21 Nathalie Brooke, interview with Deborah McDonald.

22 Wells, *H. G. Wells in Love*, p. 168.

23 Lockhart, diary entry for 6 Jan. 1931, *Diaries vol. 1*, p. 145.

24 Lockhart, diary entry for 2–4 Aug. 1924, *Diaries vol. 1*, p. 59.

25 Moura, letter to Lockhart, 29 Dec. 1931, HIA.

26 Moura, letter to Lockhart, HIA. Undated: probably 1931.

27 Moura, letter to Gorky, 4 Apr. 1931, GA.

28 Kira and Hugh Clegg produced a son, Nicholas. In due course he grew up and married and produced a son, also called Nicholas; he grew up to become a politician, leader of the Liberal Democrats and Deputy Prime Minister.

29 Moura, letter to Lockhart, 17 Mar. 1932, HIA.

30 Robin Bruce Lockhart, *Reilly: The First Man*, pp. 12, 115.

31 Reilly, letter to Lockhart, 24 Nov. 1918, quoted in Robin Bruce Lockhart, *Reilly: The First Man*, p. 115.

32 Wells, *H. G. Wells in Love*, p. 159.

33 Wells, *H. G. Wells in Love*, p. 162.

34 Wells, *H. G. Wells in Love*, p. 163.

35 Vaksberg, *The Murder of Maxim Gorky*, pp. 287–9.

36 Scheffer, 'Hungersnot in Russland', *Berliner Tageblatt*, 1 Apr. 1933; Gareth Jones, 'Balance Sheet of the Five-Year Plan', *Financial Times*, 13 Apr. 1933. Both available online at www.garethjones.org (retrieved 20 Jun. 2014).

37 Sayers & Kahn, *Sabotage*, pp. 17–21.

38 Moura, letter to Paul Scheffer, included in Moura Budberg MI5 file, translation by MI5. Undated but probably written in June 1932.

39 Moura, letter to Paul Scheffer, included in Moura Budberg MI5 file, translated by Caroline Schmitz.

40 Moura, letter to Paul Scheffer, included in Moura Budberg MI5 file. Postmarked Österreich, date unclear but copy dated 11 Jun. 1933. Translated by Caroline Schmitz.

41 Lord Willis, letter to Andrew Boyle, 11 Jul. 1980, CUL Add 9429/2B/109.

42 Moura, letter to Lockhart, LL. Undated: probably 1933.

43 Wells, *H. G Wells in Love*, p. 170.

44 Lockhart, diary entry for 3 Oct. 1931, *Diaries vol. 1*, p. 189.

45 Berberova, *Moura*, p. 257.

46 Bagnold, *Autobiography*, pp. 130–34.

47 Moura, letter to Lockhart, LL. Undated: probably 18 Jun. 1932.

48 Lockhart, diary entry for 5 Feb. 1932, *Diaries vol. 1*, p. 202.

49 Moura, letter to Lockhart, LL. Undated: probably 1933.

Chapter 20: A Cheat and a Liar

1   Smith, *H. G. Wells*, pp. 316–22.
2   Matheson, letter to Vita Sackville-West, quoted in Carney, *Stoker*, p. 45.
3   Wells, letter to von Arnim, no. 1,971, 22 Jan. 1934, in *The Correspondence of H. G. Wells vol. 3*, pp. 513–14.
4   This letter, dated 28 July but with no year, has been inserted into Wells' published letters as 1930 but this does not fit with the facts. In letter no. 1,941 dated 2 August 1933 Wells comments to a friend about a proposed holiday to Portmeirion. Moura did not specify where she wrote her letter from but did say that she had had the pregnancy confirmed by a doctor whom she had known in Russia. In 1930 Gorky did not go to Russia, Moura was in Berlin in August and wrote to H. G. saying she was missing him and her trips to Britain were very infrequent.
5   The original of this letter is in the RBML archive. On this original it is clear that it is the three children she is referring to: Kira, Tania and Paul. In the published letters, no. 1,735, it is 'Victor, Tania and Paul', obviously a mistranscription. From this time on Pavel, her son, was known as Paul.
6   In 1936 Liuba married Sir Lionel Fletcher, a retired engineer and shipping magnate, with whom she moved to Tanzania.
7   Berberova, *Moura*, p. 257.
8   Bagnold, *Autobiography*, p. 134.
9   Wells, letter to Christabel Aberconway, 20 May 1934, quoted in Lynn, *Shadow Lovers*, pp. 199–200.
10 Moura, letters to Gorky, Jan.–Dec. 1934, GA.
11 Wells, *H. G. Wells in Love*, p. 174.
12 Quoted in Robin Bruce Lockhart, *Reilly: The First Man*, pp. 57–8.
13 The dacha was in the small town of Gorki, not to be confused with the town of Gorki where Lenin spent his final months, or Gorky's birthplace, which was renamed Gorki in honour of him. 'Gorki' is a common name for towns in Russia; the one where Gorky had his dacha was known as Gorki-10 and the other was renamed Gorki-Leninskie. Possibly the location was chosen for him because of the coincidence of names.
14 Wells, *Experiment in Autobiography vol. II*, p. 809.
15 Wells, *H. G. Wells in Love*, p. 175.
16 Wells, *H. G. Wells in Love*, pp. 175–6.
17 The essay on Moura in *Shadow Lovers* (pp. 161–200) was written in June and August 1935, amended slightly in 1936, but not published until decades after his death.
18 Wells, *H. G. Wells in Love*, p. 164.
19 During the show trials of 1938 Yagoda and Kriuchkov were accused of Max's murder. The quick funeral was given as proof of their guilt. Yagoda was having an affair with Max's wife, Timosha.
20 Moura, letter to Gorky, 1934, quoted in Vaksberg, *The Murder of Maxim Gorky*, p. 316.
21 Baron Robert Boothby, interview with Andrew Boyle, CUL Add 9429/2B/113.

22 Moura, second letter to Gorky, 1934, quoted in Vaksberg, *The Murder of Maxim Gorky*, p. 316.

23 Moura, letter to Lockhart, HIA. Undated: probably mid-1934.

Chapter 21: *The Mysterious Death of Maxim Gorky*

1 West, *H. G. Wells*, pp. 140–41. West is vague about when this conversation took place; he implies that it occurred immediately she was confronted with the evidence in Estonia. More likely it was some time after summer 1935 (based on the nature of Wells' own account written at that time).

2 West, *H. G. Wells*, p. 141.

3 West, *H. G. Wells*, p. 141.

4 Alexander, *Estonian Childhood*, p. 154. West's book was published in 1984, and Tania's in 1987.

5 See Chapter 2 in this book and Hill, *Go Spy the Land*, pp. 87–8.

6 Wells, *H. G. Wells in Love*, p. 196.

7 Quoted by Lord Vaizey in letter to Andrew Boyle, 15 Oct. 1980, CUL Add 9429/2B/100.

8 Lord Ritchie Calder, interview with Andrew Boyle, CUL Add 9429/2B/124 (i).

9 Moura, letter to Lockhart, 26 Dec. 1934, LL.

10 The book, entitled *Return to Malaya*, was published in 1936.

11 Moura, letter to Gorky, Aug. 1934, quoted in Vaksberg, *The Murder of Maxim Gorky*, p. 352.

12 Foros was a popular resort for senior Soviet politicians, and many had dachas there. Mikhail Gorbachev was held under house arrest at his Foros dacha during the 1991 coup.

13 Shkapa, quoted in Shentalinsky, *The KGB's Literary Archive*, p. 267.

14 The NKVD, or People's Commissariat for Internal Affairs, had existed since the Revolution, and competed with the Cheka. Successive reorganisations produced the GPU, the OGPU and eventually the newly reformed NKVD in 1934, which took full responsibility for intelligence and security. In 1954 the NKVD was split and reformed again, and espionage and political policing became the responsibility of the newly formed KGB, while criminal policing was handled by a separate organisation.

15 Vaksberg, *The Murder of Maxim Gorky*, p. 354.

16 Vaksberg, *The Murder of Maxim Gorky*, pp. 342–3.

17 Wells, letter to Constance Coolidge, no, 2073, 14 Mar. 1935, in Wells, *Correspondence of H. G. Wells vol. 4*, p. 15.

18 Lockhart, diary entry for 27 May 1935, *Diaries vol. 1*, p. 321.

19 Wells, *H. G. Wells in Love*, p. 208.

20 Moura, letter to Gorky, Apr. 1936, quoted in Vaksberg, *The Murder of Maxim Gorky*, pp. 364–5.

21 This theory was developed and published by Arkady Vaksberg in his book *The Murder of Maxim Gorky*.

22 Weidenfeld, *George Weidenfeld*, pp. 132–3. Weidenfeld knew Moura much later, and heard this story apparently from a third party.

23 Diary entries quoted in Alexander, *Estonian Childhood*, pp. 127–8.

24 Witness accounts compiled by Shentalinsky, *The KGB's Literary Archive*, p. 272.

25 Told by Moura to Lockhart, Lockhart diary entry for 28 Nov.1936, *Diaries vol. 1*, p. 358.

26 Vaksberg, *The Murder of Maxim Gorky*, p. 386. Vaksberg claims the existence of several documents in the Russian state archives proving this, but does not identify them. Due to his failure to make proper citations, Vaksberg's theory about the circumstances of Gorky's death is controversial. However, the existence of the will is confirmed by Korney Chukovsky, who was told the story by Yekaterina herself (Chukovsky, diary entry for 30 Apr. 1962, *Diary*, p. 464).

27 Vaksberg, *The Murder of Maxim Gorky*, pp. 402–3.

28 Vaksberg, *The Murder of Maxim Gorky*, pp. 397–8.

Chapter 22: *A Very Dangerous Woman*

1 Hundreds of writers were present at this dinner, and many of them left behind accounts of it in their memoirs. The general details given here are drawn variously from a selection of these. The details of Moura's involvement come from Berberova, *Moura*, p. 256.

2 Moura Budberg MI5 file, letter from Collier to Boyle, 6 Oct. 1936.

3 Wells, letter to Keeble, no. 2,016, 13 Oct. 1934, in Wells, *Correspondence of H. G. Wells vol. 3*, p. 541.

4 Moura Budberg MI5 file, note to Maj. V. Vivien, 14 Oct. 1936.

5 Moura Budberg MI5 file, note by 'L.F.', 15 Nov. 1936.

6 *The Times*, 4 Apr. 1936, p. 17.

7 Moura Budberg MI5 file, Special Branch report, 24 Apr. 1944.

8 Moura Budberg MI5 file, document 16.Y, 1932, translation of original Russian document; Kyril Zinovieff, interview with Andrew Boyle, CUL Add 9429/2B/125.

9 Moura Budberg MI5 file, note on Lochner letter to Hanfstaengl, 29 Dec. 1937, cross ref from Hanfstaengl file, 25 Sep. 1939. (Lochner, despite being a pacifist, took a keen interest in the war when it started. He got himself embedded with the Germany army in 1939 and reported on the invasion of Poland.)

10 Moura Budberg MI5 file, note on Lochner, letter to Hanfstaengl, 6 Dec. 1938, cross ref with Hanfstaengl file, 25 Sep. 1939.

11 Hanfstaengl, *The Unknown Hitler*, p. 312.

12 *Altoona Tribune*, 27 Jul. 1937, p. 4. Hanfstaengl did eventually publish a memoir in 1957, *Hitler: The Missing Years*.

13 Wells, *H. G. Wells in Love*, pp. 217, 219.

14 Lockhart, diary entry for 12 Mar. 1937, *Diaries vol. 1*, pp. 368–9.

15 Lockhart, diary entry for 22 Nov. 1937, *Diaries vol. 1*, p. 382.

16 Quoted in Shentalinsky, *The KGB's Literary Archive*, p. 254.

17 *The Times*, 21 Feb. 1940, p. 11.

18 Alexander, *Estonian Childhood*, p. 105.

19 Tania Alexander obituary, *The Times*, 9 Dec. 2004, p. 74.

20 Alexander, *Estonian Childhood*, p. 105.

21 Wells, letter to Moura, no. 2,360, 22 Dec. 1938, *Correspondence of H. G. Wells vol. 4*, p. 213.

22 Wells, letter to Moura, no. 2,366, 18 Jan. 1939, *Correspondence of H. G. Wells vol. 4*, p. 219.

23 Alexander, *Estonian Childhood*, p. 161.

Chapter 23: 'Secretly for the Russians'

1 Wells, *H. G. Wells in Love*, p. 224.

2 Alexander, *Estonian Childhood*, p. 129; Moura Budberg MI5 file, report on inhabitants of 11 Ennismore Gardens, 21 Jun. 1940; report by Cassandra Coke, a cousin of Mrs Cliff, 5 Mar. 1942.

3 Carney, *Stoker*, p. 117.

4 Carney, *Stoker*, p. 119.

5 Ustinov, *Klop and the Ustinov Family*, p.

6 Chukovsky, diary entry for 4 Sep. 1919, *Diary*, p. 53.

7 Dorril, *MI6*, pp. 407–8; Liddell, *Diaries*.

8 Kathleen Tynan, in an interview with Moura Budberg (*Vogue*, 1 Oct. 1970), mentioned that the actor Peter Ustinov, who was Klop's son and a close friend of Moura, had known her since childhood (he was born in 1921). If Moura and Klop didn't know each other in Petrograd, perhaps Moura's connections to Paul Scheffer and later Ernst Hanfstaengl had caused them to cross paths in the 1930s.

9 Quoted in Dorril, *MI6*, p. 408.

10 Moura Budberg MI5 file, report by agent U35, 8 Mar. 1940.

11 Moura Budberg MI5 file, note 106, minute sheet, 26 Jun. 1940. A police registration certificate is still required by foreign nationals from certain countries residing in Britain. Russia is still on the list of countries.

12 Moura Budberg MI5 file, letter from Ernest Boyce, 28 Jun. 1940.

13 Moura Budberg MI5 file, note 12 Aug. 1941.

14 Moura Budberg MI5 file, minute sheet note, 17 Jul. 1941.

15 Lockhart, diary entry for 24 Jun. 1941, *Diaries vol. 2*, p. 107.

16 Sir John Lawrence, interview with Andrew Boyle, CUL Add 9429/2B/120. The Murmansk story is given in his obituary in the *Guardian*, 2 Feb. 2000.

17 Moura Budberg MI5 file, F. P. Osborne, letter to Capt. Strong, 11 Aug. 1941.

18 Moura Budberg MI5 file, Special Branch, Metropolitan Police, letter to Col. E. Hinchley-Cooke, 13 Aug. 1941.

19 Moura Budberg MI5 file, Richard Butler, note to D.G., 26 May 1943.

20 Lewis, *Prisms of British Appeasement*, p. 140. Lewis gives the date of Cooper's secret appointment as January 1943, but this appears to be a misprint for 1942. The diaries of Guy Liddell, MI5's Director of Counter-Intelligence, indicate that he was already settling into that role by July 1942 (Liddell, *Diaries vol. 1*, p. 280). Liddell

himself was MI5's expert on Russia; he later came under suspicion and was blocked from succeeding to the director generalship of MI5. Following the defection of Guy Burgess (to whom he had been very close), Liddell was eased out of the service altogether. He promoted Anthony Blunt and was very close to Duff Cooper during his period with the Security Executive.

21 Lady Diana Cooper, interview with Andrew Boyle, CUL Add 9429/2B/30.
22 Martha Gellhorn, letter to Andrew Boyle, 30 Jun. 1980, CUL Add 9429/2B/40. Moura told TV producer Joan Rodker that it was Aldous Huxley's suggestion that she should see the palmist (Rodker, letter to the editor, *Observer*, 29 Dec. 1974, p. 8).
23 Lord Vaizey, letter to Andrew Boyle, 15 Oct. 1980, CUL Add 9429/2B/100.
24 Flood, 'Andre Labarthe and Raymond Aron'.
25 Flood, 'Andre Labarthe and Raymond Aron'.
26 Lord Ritchie Calder, interview with Andrew Boyle, CUL Add 9429/2B/124 (i).
27 Moura Budberg MI5 file, note on minute sheet by K. G. Younger, 8 Apr. 1942.
28 Wells, *H. G. Wells in Love*, p. 227.
29 Lockhart, diary entry for 6 Mar. 1942, *Diaries vol. 2*, p. 149.
30 Lockhart, diary entry for Aug. 1944, *Diaries vol. 2*, p. 348. The Carlton Grill was all that survived of the Carlton Hotel, which had been wrecked by a bomb in 1940. In the 1950s it was demolished and New Zealand House was built on the site.
31 Wells, letter to Moura, no. 2,747, summer 1944, *Correspondence of H. G. Wells vol. 4*, p. 500.
32 Nathalie Brooke (née Benckendorff), interview with Andrew Boyle, CUL Add. 9429/2B/114 (i).
33 Lockhart, diary entries for 10 May and 3 Aug. 1945, *Diaries vol. 2*, pp. 431, 480.
34 Orwell, 'Wells, Hitler, and the World State', *Horizon*, August 1941, pp. 133–8.

Chapter 24: The Movie Mogul

1 Phillips, *The Stage Struck Me*, pp. 130–31.
2 Will of H. G. Wells. The total amount of £10,240 in 1946 would be equivalent to about £374,000 now.
3 Korda, *Charmed Lives*, p. 120. Michael Korda believed that his uncle had first met Moura in Britain in the early 1930s.
4 Frank Wells, cited in Kulik, *Alexander Korda*, pp. 126–7.
5 Lockhart, diary entry for 23 Aug. 1938, *Diaries vol. 1*, p. 392. £4 million in 1938 is equivalent to about a quarter of a billion now.
6 Korda, *Charmed Lives*, p. 156.
7 Korda, *Charmed Lives*, p. 154 n.
8 Kulik, *Alexander Korda*, pp. 256–7.
9 Lockhart, diary entry for 21 Sep. 1947, *Diaries vol. 2*, p. 630.
10 Lockhart, diary entry for 8 Jan. 1948, *Diaries vol. 2*, pp. 630–35. £12,000 in 1947 would be equivalent to over £400,000 now.
11 Burton, *The Richard Burton Diaries*, pp. 575–6.

12 Vickers, *Cecil Beaton*, p. 307. Beaton's diaries indicate that his friendship with Moura dated back to at least the early war years (Beaton, *The Years Between*, p. 69: 'Moura Budberg dined and we found that with the help of a good bottle of claret the evening went easily. Wars, we agreed, knocked one from one level of age down to another.').

13 Moura Budberg MI5 file, Metropolitan Police report, 14 Jul. 1948, written upon her entry to Britain from Warsaw via Prague; Michael Korda, interview with Deborah McDonald, 12 Jan. 2012.

14 Korda, *Charmed Lives*, p. 214.

15 Michael Korda, interview with Deborah McDonald, 12 Jan. 2012.

16 Moura Budberg MI5 file, Metropolitan Police Special Branch note, 31 Mar. 1947.

17 Moura Budberg MI5 file, note, 30 Mar. 1950.

18 Alexander, *Estonian Childhood*, p. 143.

19 Moura Budberg MI5 file, Metropolitan Police Special Branch note, 24 Apr. 1944.

20 Moura Budberg MI5 file, note recording Home Office Certificate of Naturalisation No. B 319, MI5 No. PFR 3736, 19 Jun. 1947. The note states: 'MI5: A certificate of naturalisation has been granted to Marie Budberg of 68 Ennismore Gardens, London, S W 7 and the Oath of Allegiance has been duly taken.' It is not known why this surprising decision was reached. The appraisal mentions Professor J. B. S. Haldane, a 'prominent member of the Communist Party', which one would expect to count against her. The document then speculates about how truthful her interview had been, noting that what she had said was broadly consistent with the facts as they knew them. Moura's nocturnal meetings in Felixstowe in 1935 are mentioned. The document notes Wells' wish to take Moura to Russia with him and his opinion that she ought to be naturalised. Duff Cooper is mentioned as saying that he had refused to allow her to work in Auxiliary War Services. The appraisal also lays out her relationship with Ambassador Maisky and his wife. But it was noted that Moura had apparently passed on some information regarding the Russian Embassy to Duff Cooper, which must have counted in her favour. But on the whole one can only conjecture that Moura used a great deal of her natural charm, or possibly that the approval was a bureaucratic blunder which could not be undone. After the decision was made and she was naturalised, several papers in the MI5 file comment on the mistake that had been made.

21 Regnery, letter to Moura, 10 Dec. 1947, HIA.

22 Regnery, letter to Moura, 11 Jul. 1948, HIA.

23 There is no information on how close the renewed relationship between Moura and Scheffer became; probably not close. He carried on working with Regnery until 1951, living in very modest circumstances and suffering continual pain from the injuries he had sustained during the war. He died in 1965.

24 Lockhart, diary entry for 26 Aug. 1948, *Diaries vol. 2*, pp. 672–4.

25 Lockhart, diary entry for 26 Aug. 1948, *Diaries vol. 2*, pp. 672–4. Despite her opinion of him ('the vainest man in the world') Moura retained Maugham as a friend. Later that year, she had him and Lockhart to dine at Ennismore Gardens. Maugham would soon be seventy-five, but had a physique that Lockhart thought 'wonderful'. Over dinner, Maugham explained that an attack he had made on Hugh Walpole in *Cakes and Ale* was due to Walpole having attempted to style

himself the 'father of English letters'; Maugham claimed that he had now achieved that position himself despite having 'never tried to push myself' (quoted by Lockhart, diary entry for 16 Nov. 1948, *Diaries vol. 2*, pp. 684–5).

Chapter 25: A Russian Patriot

1 Moura Budberg MI5 file, report by B2a, 9 Oct. 1950.
2 Weidenfeld, *George Weidenfeld*, p. 131.
3 Quoted by Robin Bruce Lockhart, *Reilly*, p. 84.
4 Weidenfeld, *George Weidenfeld*, p. 132.
5 Lord Weidenfeld, personal communication to Deborah McDonald, 6 Jan. 2012.
6 Weidenfeld, *George Weidenfeld*, p. 158.
7 Quoted in Carter, *Anthony Blunt*, p. 79.
8 Weidenfeld, *George Weidenfeld*, p. 134.
9 Moura Budberg MI5 file, note on Budberg/MacGibbon, 26 Jul. 1950.
10 Moura Budberg MI5 file, note from agent B2a to Mr B. A. Hill, 15 Aug. 1950.
11 MacGibbon related this story in a 12-page affidavit signed on his deathbed in 2000 (see articles by Michael Evans and Magnus Linklater in *The Times*, 30 Oct. 2004, pp. 1–3; also H. MacGibbon, 'Diary: My Father the Spy', *London Review of Books*, 16 Jun. 2011, pp. 40–41).
12 Moura Budberg MI5 file, note, 26 Jul. 1950.
13 Moura Budberg MI5 file, extract from note by B2a on 'Developments in the MacGibbon Case', 18 Aug. 1950.
14 Macintyre, *A Spy Among Friends*, pp. 169–70. Skardon's reputation was probably overinflated by his success with Fuchs. He failed to break both Kim Philby and Anthony Blunt, despite interrogating them both multiple times.
15 Moura Budberg MI5 file, note from B2a, 28 Aug. 1950.
16 Moura Budberg MI5 file, note marked Top Secret, 2 Oct. 1950.
17 Moura Budberg MI5 file, interview with Rebecca West, 30 Jan. 1951.
18 West, *H. G. Wells*, pp. 139–40. West recalls his mother's jealousy in 'My Father's Unpaid Debts of Love', *Observer Review*, 11 Jan. 1976, p. 17.
19 Moura Budberg MI5 file, minute sheet, no. 239, 12 Feb. 1951.
20 Moura Budberg MI5 file, report by U35, 19 Jun. 1951.
21 Moura Budberg MI5 file, report by U35, 28 Jun. 1951.
22 West & Tsarev, *The Crown Jewels*, p. 180; Carter, *Anthony Blunt*, pp. 321, 331.
23 Moura Budberg MI5 file, report by U35, 2 Jul. 1951. Klop gave a detailed account of this vital meeting in his report.
24 Moura Budberg MI5 file, report by U35, 10 Aug. 1951.
25 Kyril Zinovieff, interview with Andrew Boyle, CUL Add 9429/2B/125.
26 Moura Budberg MI5 file, report by U35, 28 Aug. 1951.
27 Moura Budberg MI5 file, report by U35, 25 Oct. 1951.
28 Drazin, *Korda*, pp. 346–7.
29 Korda, *Charmed Lives*, p. 323.
30 Korda, *Charmed Lives*, p. 403.

Chapter 26: The End of Everything

1   Weidenfeld, *George Weidenfeld*, p. 132.
2   Boothby began a relationship with Kray in 1963 and later campaigned for the brothers' release from prison. In 1964 the *Sunday Mirror* ran a story suggesting a sexual relationship between the two. Boothby sued and won. Decades later, letters came to light confirming that there was a close relationship (see *Sunday Telegraph*, 26 Jul. 2009).
3   Boothby, *Boothby*, p. 199. Moura's discernment, in Boothby's opinion, was confirmed by her sharing his love of Turgenev.
4   Michael Burn, interview with Andrew Boyle, CUL Add 9429/2B/115 (i).
5   David Lean, interview in *The Times*, 9 Dec. 1981, p. 8.
6   L. P. Hartley, 'The Sheep and the Goats', *Observer*, 25 Jun. 1939, p. 6; Edward Crankshaw, 'Russian vignettes', *Observer*, 18 Jun. 1972, p. 33.
7   Some who knew Moura's work claimed that she was generally not a good translator. For instance, Nina Berberova makes derogatory remarks about her translations into Russian. Likewise, Moura's friend Hamish Hamilton, from whom she obtained a lot of work, said that her translations were not always good. In Hamilton's case, it may be that he conflated the translations she did in old age (when, according to George Weidenfeld, she lost her ability to work so diligently and began farming out to her relatives) with her earlier work. Archived reviews of her translations between the 1930s and 1960s are generally excellent. When she felt that the source material warranted it, she exerted herself and produced fine work; in other cases, it was alleged, she would fail to pin down the true meanings of idioms, and even passages if they were difficult.
8   Roger Machell, interview with Andrew Boyle, CUL Add 9429/2B/118(i).
9   Pendennis, *The Observer*, 5 May 1963, p. 13.
10 Quoted by Michael Burn, interview with Andrew Boyle, CUL Add 9429/2B/115(ii).
11 Equivalent to about £110,000 now.
12 Hamish and Yvonne Hamilton, Roger Machell, Baron Robert Boothby, interviews with Andrew Boyle, CUL Add 9429/2B/113 & 118(i).
13 *The Times*, 11 Dec. 1964, p. 5.
14 Baron Robert Boothby, Hamish Hamilton, interviews with Andrew Boyle, CUL Add 9429/2B/113 and 118.
15 Hamish and Yvonne Hamilton, interview with Andrew Boyle, CUL Add 9429/2B/118(i).
16 Rebecca West, letter to Andrew Boyle, 9 Sep. 1980, CUL Add 9429/2B/106(i).
17 Moura, letters to Lockhart, 29 Dec. 1931, 17 Jan. 1932, HIA.
18 Mrs A. Knopf, letter to Baroness Budberg, 14 Sep. 1951, AAK.
19 Moura Budberg, letter to Blanche Knopf, 27 Dec. 1952, AAK.
20 Joan M. Rodker, letter to the editor, *Observer*, 29 Dec. 1974; obituary of Joan Rodker, *Daily Telegraph*, 23 Jan. 2011.
21 Hamish Hamilton, interview with Andrew Boyle, CUL Add 9429/2B/118; Robin Bruce Lockhart, *Reilly*, p. 83.

22 *The Times*, 24 Apr. 1962, p. 14.

23 *The Times*, 8 Apr. 1967, p. 9; reviewed in the *Guardian*, 5 Jul. 1967.

24 Quoted in Robin Bruce Lockhart, *Reilly*, p. 84.

25 Weidenfeld, *George Weidenfeld*, pp. 133–4.

26 Chukovsky, diary entry for 30 Apr. 1962, *Diaries*, p. 464.

27 Ustinov, *Dear Me*, p. 345.

28 Graham Greene, letter to Robert Cecil, 14 Feb. 1989, papers of Robert Cecil in possession of his daughter, via Andrew Lownie.

29 Lord Ritchie Calder, interview with Andrew Boyle, CUL Add 9429/2B/124 (ii).

30 West, *H. G. Wells*, p. 142.

31 Moura, letter to Lockhart, LL. Undated: probably Mar. 1953.

32 Marina Majdalany, interview with Andrew Boyle, CUL Add 9429/2B/121(ii).

33 Obituary, Sir Robert Bruce Lockhart, *The Times*, 28 Feb. 1970, p. 8.

34 *The Times*, 4 Mar. 1970, p. 20; Robin Bruce Lockhart, *Reilly*, p. 84.

35 Hamish Hamilton, interview with Andrew Boyle, CUL Add 9429/2B/118(ii).

36 Included in his anthology *Out on a Limb*.

37 Michael Burn, letter to Andrew Boyle, 20 Jun. 1980, CUL Add 9429/2B/14(i).

38 Michael Burn, extract from 'For Moura Budberg: On her proposed departure from Britain', *Out on a Limb*, pp. 40–41.

39 Vaksberg, *The Murder of Maxim Gorky*, p. 396.

40 Michael Burn, interview with Andrew Boyle, CUL Add 9429/2B/115(ii).

41 Moura, letter to Lockhart, 13 Feb. 1919, LL.

Bibliography

AAK   Alfred A. Knopf Records
CUL   Cambridge University Library
GA   Gorky Archive
HIA   Hoover Institution Archives, Stanford, California.
LL   Lilly Library, Indiana University Bloomington, Indiana
RBML   Rare Book & Manuscript Library of the University of Illinois at
             Urbana-Champaign, Illinois

Archives and unpublished materials

Budberg, Moura (aka Benckendorff, Zakrevskaya), letters to R. H. Bruce Lockhart. R B Lockhart mss, Boxes 2 and 5: Correspondence of Moura Budberg and R. H. Bruce Lockhart, LL.

Budberg, Moura (aka Benckendorff, Zakrevskaya), letters to R. H. Bruce Lockhart. Robert H. B. Lockhart papers, Box 1: Correspondence of Moura Budberg, HIA.

Budberg, Moura (aka Benckendorff, Zakrevskaya) and others, letters to H. G. Wells. Correspondence of H. G. Wells, RBML.

Gorky Archive: Letters between Moura Budberg and Maxim Gorky. Russian state archives, translations and notes via Professor Barry P. Scherr.

Knopf, Mrs A., letters to Baroness Moura Budberg, Alfred A. Knopf Records, Harry Ransom Center, University of Texas at Austin.

Lockhart, R. H. Bruce, unpublished diaries and papers. Beaverbrook Papers, House of Lords Record Office.

Lockhart, R. H. Bruce, 'Baroness Budberg' (with emendations by Moura Budberg), unpublished essay, *ca* 1956. Robert H. B. Lockhart papers, Box 6, Folder 14, HIA.

Regnery, Henry, letters to Baroness Moura Budberg, Henry Regnery archive, HIA.

MI5 file on Moura Budberg, 1922–1952. KV2/979, KV2/980, KV2/981, National Archives, Kew.

Interviews and correspondence

Conducted by Deborah McDonald, 2010–2012

Nathalie Brooke (née Benckendorff), 16 May 2012
Miranda Carter, 13 January 2012
Philip Day, 13 January 2012
Michael Korda, 12 January 2012
Jamie Bruce Lockhart, 1 February 2012
Andrea Lynn, December 2010
Professor Barry P. Scherr, Dartmouth College, New Hampshire, January 2012
Teresa Topolski, 1 April 2012
Karen Vaughan, Royal Academy of Music (pupil of Maria Korchinska, wife of Count Constantine Benckendorff), 13 May 2012
Lord George Weidenfeld, 6 January 2012
Nigel West, December 2010

Conducted/collated by Andrew Boyle, 1979–1980 (CUL Add 9429/2B/1-178)

Correspondence. Paul Benckendorff, Isiah Berlin, Nathalie Brooke (neé Benckendorff), Michael Burn, Kira Clegg, Tony Cliff, Lady Diana Cooper, Alastair Forbes, Martha Gellhorn, Martin Gilbert, Harman Grisewood, Robert Keyserlingk, Marina Majdalany, Nigel Nicolson, Sir Michael Postan, Lord Ritchie Calder, Alexis Scherbatow, Count Nikolai Tolstoy, Feliks Topolski, Lord Vaizey, Alan Walker, Rebecca West, Ted Willis.
Interviews. Enid Bagnold, Baron Robert Boothby, Nathalie Brooke (neé Benckendorff), Michael Burn, Tony Cliff, Lady Diana Cooper, Hamish and Yvonne Hamilton, Sir Rupert Hart-Davis, Sir John Lawrence, Marina Majdalany, Malcolm Muggeridge, Sir Michael and Lady Postan, Lord Ritchie Calder, Kyril Zinovieff.

Books & articles

Abraham, Richard, *Alexander Kerensky: The First Love of the Revolution* (London: Sidgwick & Jackson, 1987).

Alexander, Tania, *An Estonian Childhood: A Memoir* (London: Heinemann, 1987).

Andrew, Christopher, *Secret Service: The Making of the British Intelligence Community* (London: Heinemann, 1985).

Avrich, Paul, *The Russian Anarchists* (Oakland CA: AK Press, 2005; orig. pub. 1967, Princeton University Press).

Bagnold, Enid, *Autobiography (from 1889)* (London: Heinemann, 1969).

Bainton, Roy, *Honoured by Strangers: The Life of Captain Francis Cromie CB, DSO, RN, 1882–1918* (Shrewsbury: Airlife, 2002).

Beaton, Cecil, *The Years Between: Diaries, 1939–1944* (London: Weidenfeld & Nicolson, 1965).

Beesly, Patrick, *Room 40: British Naval Intelligence 1914–1918* (London: Hamish Hamilton, 1982).

Benckendorff, Count Constantine, *Half a Life: The Reminiscences of a Russian Gentleman* (London: Richards, 1954).

Benckendorff, Count Paul, *Last Days at Tsarskoe Selo: Being the Personal Notes and Memories of Count Paul Benckendorff*, transl. Maurice Baring (London: Heinemann, 1927), available online www.alexanderpalace.org/lastdays/intro.html (retrieved 17 Mar. 2014).

Berberova, Nina, *The Italics Are Mine*, transl. Philippe Radley (London: Longmans, 1969).

Berberova, Nina, *Moura: The Dangerous Life of the Baroness Budberg*, transl. Marian Schwartz & Richard D. Sylvester (New York: New York Review of Books, 1981, 2005).

Boothby, Baron Robert, *Boothby: Recollections of a Rebel* (London: Hutchinson, 1978).

Britnieva, Mary, *One Woman's Story* (London: Arthur Barker, 1934).

Buchanan, Sir George, *My Mission to Russia vol. II* (London: Cassell, 1923).

Buchanan, Meriel, *Petrograd: The City of Trouble, 1914–1918* (London: Collins, 1918).

Buchanan, Meriel, *Recollections of Imperial Russia* (London: Hutchinson, 1923).

Buchanan, Meriel, *The Dissolution of an Empire* (London: John Murray, 1932).

Buchanan, Meriel, *Victorian Gallery* (London: Cassell, 1956).

Buchanan, Meriel, *Ambassador's Daughter* (London: Cassell, 1958).

Burke's Peerage, Baronetage and Knightage 107th edn, (Cambridge: Burke's Peerage, 2003).

Burn, Michael, *Out on a Limb* (London: Chatto & Windus, 1973).

Burton, Richard, *The Richard Burton Diaries*, ed. Chris Williams (Yale University Press, 2012).

Carney, Michael, *Stoker: The Life of Hilda Matheson* (Michael Carney, 1999).

Carter, Miranda, *Anthony Blunt: His Lives* (London: Macmillan, 2001).

Chukovsky, Kornei, *Diary, 1901–1969*, ed. Victor Ehrlich, transl. Michael Henry Heim (New Haven CT: Yale University Press, 2005).

Cook, Andrew, *Ace of Spies: The True Story of Sidney Reilly* (Stroud: History Press, 2004).

Cross, Anthony, 'A Corner of a Foreign Field: The British Embassy in St Petersburg, 1863–1918', *The Slavonic and East European Review* 88/1&2 (Jan/ Apr 2010), 328–58.

Cullen, Richard, *Rasputin: The Role of Britain's Secret Service in His Torture and Murder* (London: Dialogue, 2010).

Day, Peter, *Klop: Britain's Most Ingenious Spy* (London: Biteback, 2014).

Deacon, Richard, *A History of the Russian Secret Service*, rev. edn (London: Grafton, 1987).

Debo, Richard K. 'Lockhart Plot or Dzerhinskii Plot?', *The Journal of Modern History* 43/3 (Sept. 1971), 413–39.

De Ruvigny (publisher), 'Garstin, Denys Norman' in *De Ruvigny's Roll of Honour 1914–1924*, CD-ROM, Navy & Military Press, available online at www.ancestry.com (retrieved 6 Apr. 2014).

Dorril, Stephen, *MI6: Inside the Covert World of Her Majesty's Secret Intelligence Service* (London: Simon & Schuster, 2002).

Drazin, Charles, *Korda: Britain's Movie Mogul* (London: I. B. Taurus, 2011).

Figes, Orlando, *A People's Tragedy: The Russian Revolution 1891–1924* (London: Pimlico, 1997).

Fitzpatrick, Sheila, *The Commissariat of Enlightenment: Soviet Organization of Education and the Arts under Lunacharsky* (Cambridge: Cambridge University Press, 1970, 2002).

Flood, Christopher, 'Andre Labarthe and Raymond Aron: Political Myth and Ideology in "La France Libre"', *Journal of European Studies* 1/23, 139–58.

Foot, Michael, *H. G.: The History of Mr Wells* (London: Doubleday, 1995).

Foreign Office (UK), *White Paper on Russia No. 1 (1919): A Collection of Reports on Bolshevism in Russia* (London: HM Stationery Office, 1919).

Fuhrmann, Joseph T., *Rasputin: The Untold Story* (New Jersey: Wiley, 2013).

Gannon, Paul, *Inside Room 40: The Codebreakers of World War 1* (Hersham: Ian Allen, 2010).

Garstin, Denis, *The Shilling Soldiers* (London: Hodder & Stoughton, 1918).

Gorky, Maxim, *Fragments from My Diary*, rev. edn transl. Moura Budberg (London: Allen Lane, 1940, 1972).

Hanfstaengl, Ernst, *The Unknown Hitler* (London: Gibson Square, 2005).

Hill, Captain George A. *Go Spy the Land: Being the Adventures of I.K.8 of the British Secret Service* (London: Cassell, 1932).

Hughes, Michael, *Inside the Enigma: British Officials in Russia, 1900–39* (London: Hambledon Press, 1997).

Jeffery, Keith, *MI6: The History of the Secret Intelligence Service 1909–1949* (London: Bloomsbury, 2010).

Jones, David R. (comp. & ed.), 'Documents on British Relations with Russia,

1917–1918, II-IV: F. N. A. Cromie's Letters', *Canadian-American Slavic Studies* 7 (1973), 350–75, 498–510; 8 (1974), 544–62.

Katchanovski, Ivan, Zenon E. Kohut, Bohdan Y. Nebesio & Myroslav Yurkevich, *Historical Dictionary of Ukraine* (Plymouth: Scarecrow Press, 2013).

Keane, Elizabeth, *Séan MacBride: A Life* (Dublin: Gill & Macmillan, 2007).

Kettle, Michael, *The Allies and the Russian Collapse: March 1917–March 1918* (London: André Deutsch, 1981).

Kettle, Michael, *The Road to Intervention: March–November 1918* (London: Routledge, 1988).

Kettle, Michael, *Churchill and the Archangel Fiasco: November 1918–July 1919* (London: Routledge, 1992).

Khodasevich, Vladislav, 'Gorky' in *Gorky's Tolstoy & Other Reminiscences: Key Writings by and about Maxim Gorky*, transl. & ed. Donald Fanger (Yale University Press, 2008).

Knox, Alfred William Fortescue, *With the Russian Army, 1914–17*, vol. II (London: Hutchinson, 1921).

Kollontai, Alexandra, *Selected Writings of Alexandra Kollontai*, ed. Alix Holt (London: Allison and Busby, 1977).

Korda, Michael, *Charmed Lives: A Family Romance* (New York: Random House, 1979).

Kulik, Karol, *Alexander Korda: The Man Who Could Work Miracles* (London: W. H. Allen, 1975).

Latsis, Martin, Два года борьбы на внутреннем фронте (*Two Years of Struggle on the Home Front*) (Moscow, 1920).

Leggett, George, *The Cheka: Lenin's Political Police* (Oxford: Clarendon, 1981).

Lewis, Terrance L., *Prisms of British Appeasement: Revisionist Reputations of John Simon, Samuel Hoare, Anthony Eden, Lord Halifax and Alfred Duff Cooper* (Brighton: Sussex Academic Press, 2010).

Liddell, Guy, *The Guy Liddell Diaries*, 2 vols (1939–1942; 1942–1945), ed. Nigel West (Abingdon: Routledge, 2005).

Lingner, George, 'In Moscow, 1918: A Briton's Experiences', *King Country Chronicle* (New Zealand), 12/1175 (18 Feb. 1919), 2.

Lockhart, R. H. Bruce, *Memoirs of a British Agent* (London: Putnam, 1932).

Lockhart, R. H. Bruce, *Retreat from Glory* (London: Putnam, 1934).

Lockhart, R. H. Bruce, *The Diaries of Sir Robert Bruce Lockhart, vol. 1: 1915–1938*, ed. Kenneth Young (London: Macmillan, 1973).

Lockhart, R. H. Bruce, *The Diaries of Sir Robert Bruce Lockhart, vol. 2: 1939–1965*, ed. Kenneth Young (London: Macmillan, 1980).

Lockhart, Robin Bruce, *Ace of Spies* (London: Hodder & Stoughton, 1967).

Lockhart, Robin Bruce, *Reilly: The First Man* (Harmondsworth: Penguin, 1987).

Long, John W., 'Plot and Counter-Plot in Revolutionary Russia: Chronicling the Bruce Lockhart Conspiracy', *Intelligence and National Security* 10/1 (1995), 122–43.

Long, John W., 'Searching for Sidney Reilly: The Lockhart Plot in Revolutionary Russia, 1918', *Europe-Asia Studies* 47/7 (1995), 1225–41.

Lowe, C. J. & M. L. Dockerill, *The Mirage of Power, vol. 2: British Foreign Policy, 1914–22* (London: Routledge, 1972).

Lowe, C. J. & M. L. Dockerill, *The Mirage of Power, vol. 3: The Documents* (London: Routledge, 1972).

Lyandres, Semion, 'The 1918 Attempt on the Life of Lenin: A New Look at the Evidence', *Slavic Review* 48/3 (1989), 432–48.

Lynn, Andrea, *Shadow Lovers: The Last Affairs of H. G. Wells* (Colorado: Westview Press, 2001).

Macintyre, Ben, *A Spy Among Friends: Kim Philby and the Great Betrayal* (London: Bloomsbury, 2014).

McMeekin, Sean, *History's Greatest Heist: The Looting of Russia by the Bolsheviks* (New Haven CT: Yale University Press, 2009).

Malkov, Pavel, Записки коменданта Кремля *(Reminiscences of a Kremlin Commandant)* (Moscow: Chernovol, 1967).

Milton, Giles, *Russian Roulette* (London: Sceptre, 2013).

Mitrokhin, Vasiliy, *Chekisms: Tales of the Cheka, a KGB Anthology*, transl. Harry Spinnaker (London: Yurasov Press, 2008).

Nicolson, Harold, *The Harold Nicolson Diaries and Letters: 1907–1964*, ed. Nigel Nicolson (London: Phoenix, 2005).

Norman, Bruce, *Secret Warfare: The Battle of Codes and Ciphers* (Newton Abbot: David & Charles, 1973).

Orwell, George, 'Wells, Hitler, and the World State', *Horizon* August 1941, 133–9.

Owen, G. L., 'Budberg, the Soviets, and Reilly', unpublished paper, 1988 (via Andrea Lynn).

Peters, Yakov, 'Дело Локкарта. Работа тов. Петерса о деле Локкарта 1918 г' ('The Lockhart Case: Report by Comrade Peters on the Lockhart Case, 1918') in Архив ВЧК: Сборник документов *(Cheka Archives: A Collection of Documents)*, eds V. Vinogradov, A. Litvin, V. Hristoforov; comps: V. Vinogradov, N. Peremyshlennikova (Moscow: Kuchkovo Pole, 2007). (English transl. courtesy John Puckett.)

Phillips, Neville, *The Stage Struck Me* (Leicester: Matador, 2008).

Plotke, A. J., *Imperial Spies Invade Russia: The British Intelligence Interventions, 1918* (Westport CT: Greenwood Press, 1993).

Rabinowitch, Alexander, *The Bolsheviks in Power: The First Year of Soviet Rule in Petrograd* (Bloomington IN: Indiana University Press, 2007).

Raun, Toivo U., *Estonia and the Estonians* (Stanford CA: Hoover Institution, 2001).

Reilly, Sidney, *Britain's Master Spy: The Adventures of Sidney Reilly: An Autobiography* (New York: Carroll & Graf, 1986; first pub. London: E. Mathews & Marrot, 1931).

Russell, Bertrand, *The Practice and Theory of Bolshevism* (London: George Allen & Unwin, 1920).

Sayers, Michael & Albert Eugene Kahn, *Sabotage! The Secret War Against America, vol. 2* (New York: Harper & Bros, 1942).

Senenko, Marina, 'Late 19th-century private collections in Moscow and their fate between 1918 and 1924' in *Dutch and Flemish Art in Russia*, eds L. Gortner, G. Schwartz & B. Vermet (Amsterdam: CODART & Foundation for Cultural Inventory, 2005), available online at www.codart.nl/downloads/Dutch_and_Flemish_art_in_Russia_part_1.pdf (retrieved 12 Apr. 2014).

Shentalinsky, Vitaly, *The KGB's Literary Archive*, transl. John Crowfoot (London: Harvill Press, 1997).

Sheridan, Clare, *Mayfair to Moscow: Clare Sheridan's Diary* (New York: Boni and Liveright, 1921).

Smith, David C., *H. G. Wells: Desperately Mortal* (New Haven CT: Yale University Press, 1986).

Smith, Douglas, *Former People: The Last Days of the Russian Aristocracy* (London: Macmillan, 2012).

Spence, Richard B., *Trust No One: The Secret World of Sidney Reilly* (Port Townsend WA: Feral House, 2003).

Stevenson, Robert Louis, *Virginibus Puerisque* (first publ. in series 1876–1881), available online at https://archive.org/details/virginibuspueris05stev (retrieved 9 January 2015).

Stites, Richard, *Russian Popular Culture: Entertainment and Society Since 1900* (Cambridge: Cambridge University Press, 1992).

Subtelny, Orest, *Ukraine: A History*, 4th edn, ebook (Toronto: University of Toronto Press, 2009).

Swain, Geoffrey, *The Origins of the Russian Civil War* (Harlow: Longman, 1996).

Swain, Geoffrey, '"An Interesting and Plausible Proposal": Bruce Lockhart, Sidney Reilly and the Latvian Riflemen, Russia 1918', *Intelligence and National Security* 14/3 (1999), 81–102.

Toomey, Deirdre, 'Gonne, (Edith) Maud (1866–1953)', *Oxford Dictionary of National Biography* (Oxford: Oxford University Press, 2004).

Troyat, Henri, *Gorky: A Biography* (London: Crown, 1989).

Ullman, Richard H., *Anglo-Soviet Relations, 1917–1921, vol. 1: Intervention and the War* (Princeton NJ: Princeton University Press, 1961).

US Dept of State, *Papers Relating to the Foreign Relations of the United States, 1918. Russia, Vol. I* (Washington DC: US Government Printing Office, 1918). Available online at http://digital.library.wisc.edu/1711.dl/FRUS.

FRUS1918VI (retrieved 14 May 2014).

Ustinov, Nadia Benois, *Klop and the Ustinov Family* (London: Sidgwick & Jackson, 1973).

Ustinov, Peter, *Dear Me* (London: Arrow, 1998).

Vaksberg, Arkady, *The Murder of Maxim Gorky: A Secret Execution*, transl. Todd Bludeau (New York: Enigma Books, 2007).

Vickers, Hugo, *Cecil Beaton: The Authorized Biography* (London: Weidenfeld & Nicolson, 1985).

Walpole, Hugh (ed.), 'Denis Garstin and the Russian Revolution: A Brief Word in Memory', *Slavonic and East European Review* 17/51 (April 1939), 587–605.

Ward, Margaret, *Maud Gonne: A Life* (London: HarperCollins, 1993).

Weidenfeld, George, *George Weidenfeld: Remembering My Good Friends* (London: HarperCollins, 1995).

Wells, H. G., *Russia in the Shadows* (London: Hodder & Stoughton, 1920).

Wells, H. G., *Experiment in Autobiography vol. II* (London: Victor Gollancz/ Cresset Press, 1934).

Wells, H. G., *H. G. Wells in Love: Postscript to an Experiment in Autobiography*, ed. G. P. Wells (London: Faber & Faber, 1984).

Wells, H. G. *The Correspondence of H. G. Wells,* 4 vols, ed. David C. Smith (London: Pickering & Chatto, 1998).

Wells, H. G., Suppressed pages from *H. G. Wells in Love*, H. G. Wells Collection, University of Illinois, reproduced in appendix to Andrea Lynn, *Shadow Lovers: The Last Affairs of H. G. Wells* (Boulder CO: Westview Press, 2001).

Werth, Nicholas, 'A State Against Its People: Violence, Repression, and Terror in the Soviet Union' in *The Black Book of Communism*, eds S. Courtois & M. Kramer (Cambridge MA: Harvard University Press, 1999).

West, Anthony, *H. G. Wells: Aspects of a Life* (Harmondsworth: Penguin, 1985).

West, Nigel & Oleg Tsarev, *The Crown Jewels: The British Secrets at the Heart of the KGB Archives* (London: HarperCollins, 1998).

White, Anna MacBride & A. Norman Jeffares (eds), *The Gonne–Yeats Letters, 1893–1938* (New York: W. W. Norton, 1994).

Whitman, Walt, Song of Myself (editions publ. 1855–1892), available online at https://archive.org/details/cu31924022222057 (retrieved 9 January 2015).

Index